THE *139* FAILURE OF PRESIDENTIAL DEMOCRACY

Volume 2

The Case of Latin America

THE
FAILURE OF
PRESIDENTIAL
DEMOCRACY

The Case of
Latin America

Edited by
Juan J. Linz and Arturo Valenzuela

The Johns Hopkins University Press

Baltimore and London

©1994 The Johns Hopkins University Press
All rights reserved
Printed in the United States of America
on acid-free paper

The Failure of Presidential Democracy is published in a hardcover edition
and in two paperback volumes:
The Failure of Presidential Democracy, vol. 1,
Comparative Perspectives and The Failure of Presidential Democracy, vol. 2,
The Case of Latin America.

The Johns Hopkins University Press
2715 North Charles Street
Baltimore, Maryland 21218-4319
The Johns Hopkins Press Ltd., London

Library of Congress Cataloging-in-Publication Data
will be found at the end of this book.

A catalog record for this book is available
from the British Library.

To the memory of

Charles Guy Gillespie

and Carlos Nino

Contents

Preface

IN THE LAST DECADE of the twentieth century, the eyes of the world have focused on the former Soviet Union and Eastern Europe, where a succession of events have had profound implications for the course of human history. In a largely peaceful process, centrally planned, socialist regimes have succumbed to economic and political stagnation, and the way has been opened for elections and democratic reform.

With less drama, democracy has also begun to make headway in other areas of the world, such as Africa, where, after independence, the promise of self-government led to despotic rule. In 1989, when Brazil and Chile elected presidents openly and competitively for the first time since their independence, all of the Ibero-American nations except Cuba had elected heads of state.

There may be grounds for cautious optimism about the future of democracy, particularly in countries where the challenges of economic and political reform are less daunting and experience with democratic institutions longer standing. The growing consensus favoring free-market economic policies has helped reduce polarization and conflict about the fundamental organization of economic life. Except where it is being overwhelmed by nationalist, religious, or ethnic challenges, democracy is no longer challenged as a form of government by alternative ways of organizing the political community.

And yet the long-term viability of democratic governments in several countries remains questionable. Much of the recent scholarship dealing with democratic "governability" has focused on these challenges and on state efforts to implement critical policies designed to correct economic imbalances, address deep social problems, and promote growth. Less attention has been given to the design and performance of democratic institutions per se. There is an implicit assumption among reformers that all democratic rules and procedures are similar in design, that the institutional dimensions of representative government are constants. It is also assumed that democratic institutions affect different societies in similar ways, depending only on the particular social and economic conditions.

These assumptions are not fully tenable. There is substantial variation in the formal and informal political architecture of democratic regimes and the contexts in which they operate. Democratic governments can be organized along unitary or federal lines, with wide variations in the degree of administrative decentralization and local autonomy. Leaders can be elected through winner-take-all or proportional representation systems. Political competition can be organized in two-party or multiparty configurations, which can in turn be either moderately differentiated or polarized.

The most important difference among democratic regimes concerns the generation and accountability of executive authority. In presidential regimes based on the U.S. doctrine of separation of powers, executive authority is generated by direct or indirect elections and is not accountable politically to the legislature. In parliamentary regimes, which evolved gradually in Western Europe, the executive is generated by the legislature and is accountable to legislative majorities for its political survival.

Nor is it the case that all democratic rules and procedures have similar impact. Federal schemes may be more relevant in societies with strong regional or local traditions, while electoral systems based on proportional representation may be more responsive to the realities of highly divided societies.

It is significant that with the notable exception of Latin American countries, few democracies have opted for the U.S. model of presidentialism. In the immediate aftermath of World War II, Karl Loewenstein observed that "the economic and technological prestige of the United States is not equaled by the popularity of its form of government. In this period of hectic political reconstruction remarkably few among the nations seem inclined to follow the constitutional pattern commonly spoken of as presidentialism under the separation of powers. . . . This is not surprising in view of the fact that in the past the transplantation of the American model was likewise the exception and that, in its primary area of adoption, Latin America, it rarely if ever produced lasting political stability."[1]

It is curious that some countries in Eastern Europe, notably Russia and Poland, are toying with the option of establishing presidential regimes when many Latin Americans are having serious doubts about the impact of presidentialism on their continent. The vast majority of the contemporary world's stable democracies have had parliamentary forms of government. Only in Latin America, the continent of presidentialism, have a few presidential regimes had long periods of democratic continuity.

In this day of democratic crafting, the academic literature provides little insight and guidance for reformers concerned with the impact of differing forms of constitutional structure and governmental arrangements for alternative national realities. That is, political scientists are uncertain about the degree to which different formal rules, practices, and governmental structures of democracy encourage or hinder regime efficacy and stability in particular societies. In particular, little is known about the implications for governmental efficacy and stability of the two principal forms of democratic government, presidential and parliamentary, and their contemporary variations.[2] Does it make a difference whether societies seek to strengthen democratic institutions according to the U.S. constitutional principal of separation of powers or to some form of European parliamentarism?

Such questions were of central importance to classical political theorists and constitutional scholars, but they have been neglected by contemporary social scientists. This neglect resulted in part from the postwar revolution that shifted scholarly attention away from public law and formal organizations to such themes as political behavior, political culture and socialization, parties and interest groups, public policy formulation, and the relationship between politics and markets. This behavioral approach took hold in countries in which institutional and constitutional dimensions were taken for granted.

The Eurocentric focus of much of the literature in comparative politics reinforced the neglect of institutional dimensions. Work contrasting democratic institutions and policy outcomes in various national contexts was valuable, but it did not systematically address the relative merits of presidential and parliamentary governments simply because it considered only one example of presidentialism—the United States—which thus became a peculiar "deviant case" with no common referents elsewhere.[3]

Despite the vast body of literature on the U.S. presidency, there is very little serious work on comparative presidentialism, and no studies systematically compare presidential regimes with parliamentary ones. A review of 94,000 articles abstracted in the *International Political Science Abstracts* from 1975 to 1991 reveals that only 141 dealt with the presidency or presidential systems outside of the United States, and of these only 22 dealt with presidentialism in Latin America, the continent of presidentialism.[4]

The lack of consideration of Latin American presidential democracies, some of which have had longer periods of democratic rule than many European countries, has impoverished our understanding of the relationship between regime type and democratic stability in varying political contexts. For example, Latin America has several presidential regimes that have functioned with multiparty systems, leading to a pattern of coalition politics very dissimilar to that of the United States and more comparable to that of European countries. This variation in presidential regimes casts a different light not only on coalition behavior but on the broader literature dealing with political parties.

While institutional factors were taken for granted in the European literature, in Latin America they were dismissed as irrelevant. Influenced by neo-Marxist and structuralist perspectives, scholars focused on social classes and movements and on political actors such as the church and the military. Politics was analyzed from the point of view of broad social forces, and democracy or its promise was viewed as nonexistent. Studies of Latin American authoritarianism were principally concerned with explaining the underlying causes of military regimes and the political economy of authoritarian regimes. Governmental institutions, constitutions, and the rules of the game were viewed as irrelevant or epiphenomenal. The question of the fit of certain institutional forms with the social and political realities of a given country was not posed.

The concern for institutional dimensions of democratic stability expressed in this book had its origins in the research project on the breakdown of democracy begun in the early 1970s by Juan Linz. In developing his theoretical writings on the subject, Linz drew primarily from the European experience. The Latin American cases, however, could not be ignored when the breakdown of democratic regimes was addressed. The insights derived from the Chilean and Brazilian case studies by Arturo Valenzuela and Alfred Stepan, respectively, and the work of Guillermo O'Donnell on the Argentine conundrum entered into his thinking. The 1978 volume on democratic breakdowns edited by Juan Linz and Alfred Stepan departed from the general orthodoxy of the time by highlighting the importance of political variables, leadership, and choice and stressing the importance of the institutional context and the formal rules of the game in explaining democratic failures.[5]

Although the relationship between regime type and democratic breakdown was not made fully explicit in the "breakdown" project, Linz concluded that the nature of presidential regimes had to be considered an important variable in accounting for regime crisis. In his own contribution to the volume, he added an excursus noting that the rigidities of presidentialism played a significant role in defining the "impossible" political game in Argentina, one that precluded the consolidation of a viable democracy.[6]

That work stressed the importance of the need to account for the broader institutional and political context that framed the process leading to the collapse of democracy.[7] From this perspective politics and institutions are viewed as independent variables in their own right, not simply as epiphenomena reflecting underlying economic and social forces. Complex organizations are more than aggregates of individual behavior; they are social structures with their own autonomy and logic, affecting and constraining individual behavior and human choice. Political options and decisions are mediated by the rules and structures of the game, rules with closely related formal and informal dimensions.

This perspective should not be viewed as a kind of primitive institutionalism that reifies formal rules and procedures as the fundamental determinants of politics. We would be the first to argue that institutional forms are not magic formulas capable of solving all problems. Indeed this work is primarily behavioral, in that it focuses on the interplay between institutions and political roles, on how the latter are affected by the former and vice versa. Nor is much attention placed on constitutional texts as such. Indeed, they are cited infrequently. We are as concerned with public opinion, political roles, rhetoric, the image and self-assessment of leaders, among other phenomena, as with formal rules. Our premise, however, is that formal rules cannot be ignored in examining political behavior. There is a complex dialectic between rules and behavior.

Invited to present a paper at a 1984 symposium on "Political Parties and Democratic Transition" organized by the Woodrow Wilson International Center for Scholars, Linz turned his attention to a more systematic examination of the implications for democratic stability of presidential versus parliamentary democracy. Arturo Valenzuela, at the same workshop, drew on his own earlier work on the Chilean breakdown to suggest that the crisis of Chilean politics was exacerbated by a lack of congruence between a polarized multiparty system and a presidential regime.

Subsequent to the Wilson Center meeting, Linz and Valenzuela organized a broader research effort, including the commissioning of a range of country case studies and analytical pieces, to examine the questions posed in Linz's 1984 paper. That effort resulted in a research symposium entitled "Presidential or Parliamentary Democracy: Does It Make a Difference?" held at Georgetown University in May 1989 as part of the university's bicentennial celebration. The symposium provided an opportunity to discuss the first drafts of individual papers and to debate the relative merits of presidential and parliamentary forms of government.

In addition to the scholars represented in this volume, we wish to acknowledge the valuable contributions to the symposium made by Ergun Ozbudun and Oyeleye Oyeridan, who shared their perspectives on the cases of Turkey and Nigeria, respectively, and by Fred Riggs, who made an outstanding contribution bringing the U.S case into the comparison. We regret that space limitations made it impossible to include their papers in the final volume. The symposium was enriched by the attendance of Seymour Martin Lipset, Matthew Shugart, Scott Mainwaring, Douglas Chalmers, John Bailey, Carol Lancaster, Colin Campbell, Michael Hudson, and Oscar Godoy as discussants and panel chairs.

The Georgetown symposium aroused considerable attention in Chile, where, in the aftermath of General Augusto Pinochet's defeat in a plebiscite, the issue of constitutional reform had moved to the forefront of public debate. The Institute of Political Science of the Catholic University of Chile, directed by Oscar Godoy, and the Center for Latin American Studies at Georgetown organized a conference in Santiago, Chile, in September 1990 with the participation of Linz, Valenzuela, Arend Lijphart, Giovanni Sartori, and a group of distinguished Chilean political scientists and leaders. Draft versions of the papers by Linz, Lijphart, and Valenzuela were published by the Institute of Political Science at the Catholic University.[8]

In Argentina, a change from a presidential to a semipresidential system was proposed by President Raúl Alfonsín, drawing on the impressive work done by the Comisión para la Consolidación de la Democracia. Although both major parties were close to an agreement on constitutional reforms, fear that Alfonsín was making use of the issue for personal political advantage, combined with Argentina's mounting economic crisis, led to failure of the reform effort.

The country for which the question of the relative merits of presidential and parliamentary government became most salient was Brazil, as Bolivar Lamounier describes in chapter 8 of this volume. In a national referendum held in April 1993, Brazilians chose to retain a presidential regime, rejecting parliamentary and monarchical options. The first drafts of the papers by Linz, Lijphart, Lamounier, and Valenzuela were published in Portuguese in a volume edited by Lamounier; they contributed to the debate on regime change in Brazil.[9] Linz and Valenzuela participated in two international symposia on the issue organized by Lamounier in Brasília.

Together with Bolivar Lamounier and Carlos Nino of the Centro de Estudios Constitucionales of Buenos Aires, Argentina, Linz and Valenzuela participated in a two-year-long project advising the Fundación Milenio in La Paz, Bolivia, on constitutional reform issues. Working with a distinguished panel of Bolivian constitutional scholars, they helped draft a constitutional proposal for Bolivia that responds to some of the issues raised in this volume.[10] We wish to thank Gonzalo Sánchez de Lozada and Jorge Balcazar for their extraordinary hospitality during our time in Bolivia.

The debate on regime type has also been prominent in Italy, where many critics of the Italian political system have urged a move away from parliamentary government to some form of semipresidential system. Giovanni Sartori has played an important role in this debate. Earlier versions of his essay, and those of Linz and Valenzuela, were published in Rome in a special issue of *Arel,* the journal of the Agenzia di Ricerche e Legislazione.[11]

In October 1992 the Council of Europe, European Commission for Democracy through Law, organized in cooperation with the government of Turkey and the Turkish Democracy Foundation a conference on "Constitution Making as an Instrument of Democratic Transition" with the participation of representatives from most of the Commonwealth of Independent States and political scientists from Europe and Turkey in which Linz presented the chapter included in this volume.

In the United States, the *Journal of Democracy* published a short summary of Juan Linz's chapter with critiques by Donald Horowitz and Seymour Martin Lipset and a reply by Juan Linz. The article has been translated into several languages. The *Journal of Democracy* also published a summary by Arturo Valenzuela of the findings of this research project with respect to the "crisis" of Latin American democracy.[12]

We have referred to the long history of this project and our activities since 1985 in order to highlight the interest generated in academic and political circles even before the publication of the present complete and revised text.

We want to thank Louis Goodman, then Secretary of the Latin American Program at the Woodrow Wilson International Center for Scholars, for convening the original conference that began this project and Richard Bloomfield of the World Peace Foundation for his support of a very important effort to bring academics and prominent political leaders from Latin America together in the difficult days before the "democratic transitions" took place. We also want to acknowledge our gratitude to Shepard Forman and the Ford Foundation for the foundation's generous support of the research effort and to the Georgetown symposium that made this project possible. We are particularly honored that the symposium was included as part of Georgetown University's official bicentennial celebrations and are grateful to Charles L. Currie, S.J., and Kathleen Lesko for the magnificent support of the Bicentennial Office.

The National Endowment for Democracy supported research efforts and conferences in Chile, Brazil, and Bolivia directly related to the central debate of this volume. Jeanne O'Neil, Administrative Director of the Center for Latin American Studies at Georgetown, deserves special thanks for her magnificent contributions to the project from start to finish, including the management of several grants. We are also grateful to Henry Tom of the Johns Hopkins University Press who, once again, has patiently waited for a manuscript that seemed to go through endless revisions. Terry Schutz worked patiently and with skill in copy editing a difficult and unwieldy manuscript.

Finally, Juan Linz acknowledges support from the Wissenschaftskolleg zu Berlin for a fellowship in 1990–91 that enabled him to complete the final draft of his contribution. Arturo Valenzuela acknowledges support from the Heinz Foundation and the Fulbright Fellowship Program, which permitted him to update his contribution to this volume.

Notes

1. Karl Loewenstein, "The Presidency Outside the United States: A Study in Comparative Political Institutions," *Journal of Politics* 11, no. 3 (1949): 462.

2. Richard Gunther and Anthony Mughan, "Political Institutions and Cleavage Management," in R. Kent Weaver and Bert A. Rockman, eds., *Do Institutions Matter? Government Capabilities in the United States and Abroad.* (Washington, D.C.: Brookings Institution, 1993), pp. 272–301.

3. The splendid comparative work on democracy by Arend Lijphart and G. Bingham Powell, Jr., is not fully exempt from this criticism. See Arend Lijphart, *Democracies: Patterns of Majoritarian and Consensus Government in Twenty-one Countries* (New Haven: Yale UP, 1984) and G. Bingham Powell, Jr., *Contemporary Democracies: Participation, Stability and Violence* (Cambridge, Mass.: Harvard UP, 1982).

4. *Presidential Studies Quarterly* focuses exclusively on the United States; since 1977 only three articles have had comparative themes. *Legislative Studies Quarterly* has had no articles dealing with the presidency outside of the United States since its founding in 1976.

5. See Juan J. Linz and Alfred Stepan, eds., *The Breakdown of Democratic Regimes* (Baltimore: Johns Hopkins UP, 1978). This work was published in one hardback volume and four paperback versions: Juan J. Linz, *The Breakdown of Democratic Regimes: Crisis, Breakdown and Reequilibration;* Juan J. Linz and Alfred Stepan, eds., *The Breakdown of Democratic Regimes: Europe;* Juan J. Linz and Alfred Stepan, eds., *The Breakdown of Democratic Regimes: Latin America;* and Arturo Valenzuela, *The Breakdown of Democratic Regimes: Chile.*

6. See Linz, *Breakdown of Democratic Regimes: Crisis,* pp. 72–74.

7. For a criticism of the "breakdown of democracy" project for its emphasis on democratic procedures and institutions in their own right and its normative ("extremist") bias in favor of procedural democracy as opposed to "substantive democracy" see Phillippe C. Schmitter's review of *The Breakdown of Democratic Regimes* in *American Political Science Review* 74, no. 3 (Sept. 1980): 849–52.

8. See Juan Linz, Arend Lijphart, and Arturo Valenzuela, *Hacia una democracia estable: La opción parlamentaria* (Santiago: Editorial Universidad Católica de Chile, 1991), prologue by Oscar Godoy. Drafts of essays presented at the Georgetown conference by Juan Linz, Arend Lijphart, and Fred Riggs were published in Consejo para la Consolidación de la Democracia, eds., *Presidencialismo vs. parlamentarismo: Materiales para el estudio de la Reforma Constitucional* (Buenos Aires: Eudeba, 1988).

9. Bolivar Lamounier, *A opçào parlamentarista* (Sao Paolo: IDESP-Editora Sumaré, 1991).

10. Fundación Milenio, *Una constitución para Bolivia* (La Paz: Fundación Milenio, 1993).

11. See *Arel* Quaderni Istituzionali 6 (Rome, May 1991). Sartori has expanded his views of the subject with respect to the Italian experience in his *Seconda Repubblica? Sì, Ma Bene* (Milan: Rizzoli, 1992.)

12. Juan Linz, "The Perils of Presidentialism," *Journal of Democracy* 1 (1990): 51–69. Arturo Valenzuela, "Latin America: Presidentialism in Crisis," *Journal of Democracy* 4 (1993): 3–16.

Part I
Introduction

JUAN J. LINZ

Presidential or Parliamentary Democracy: Does It Make a Difference?

IN RECENT DECADES renewed efforts have been made to study and understand the variety of political democracies, but most of those analyses have focused on the patterns of political conflict and more specifically on party systems and coalition formation, in contrast to the attention of many classical writers to institutional arrangements.[1] With the exception of the large literature on the impact of electoral systems on the shaping of party systems generated by the early writings of Ferdinand Hermens and the classic work by Maurice Duverger followed by the writings of Douglas Rae and Giovanni Sartori, Rein Taagepera, and Matthew Shugart among others,[2] political scientists have paid little attention to the role of political institutions, except in the study of particular countries. Debates about monarchy and republic, parliamentary and presidential regimes, the unitary state and federalism have receded into oblivion and not entered the current debates about the functioning of democratic institutions and practices, including their effect on party systems. When a number of countries initiate the process of writing or rewriting constitutions, some of those issues should regain saliency and become part of what Sartori has called political engineering, in an effort to set the basis of democratic consolidation and stability.

Undoubtedly, the constitutional innovations of the postwar period, the German constructive nonconfidence vote, and the constitution of the French Fifth Republic, whose semipresidential regime reinforces the executive to counter the weaknesses of assembly parliamentarism, have attracted imitators and scholarly attention. But we lack a more systematic and behavioral study of the implications for the political process of different institutions on which to base some of the ongoing debates about institutional and constitutional reform. With the notable exception of the book by Kaltefleiter, in which the cases of a bipolar executive like the Weimar

3

Republic and the French Fifth Republic are analyzed; the paper by Stefano Bartolini,[3] on cases of direct election of the head of state in Europe; the writings of
Maurice Duverger and the new book by Matthew Soberg Shugart and John M.
Carey,[4] the differences between parliamentary, presidential, and semipresidential
regimes have not attracted much attention from political scientists. These differences receive only limited attention in the two most recent works comparing contemporary democracies, those of Bingham Powell and Arend Lijphart,[5] who has,
however, written an excellent chapter on the implications of presidential regimes
for this volume.

The neglect is largely due to the fact that with the outstanding exception of the
United States, most of the stable democracies of Europe and the Commonwealth
have been parliamentary regimes and a few semipresidential and semiparliamentary, while most of the countries with presidential constitutions have been unstable
democracies or authoritarian regimes and therefore have not been included in
comparative studies of democracy.[6] Since many social, economic, cultural, and
political factors appeared central in the analysis of the crisis and breakdown of
democracy in those countries, we find practically no mention of the role of institutional factors in those crises. Only in the case of Chile has there been some reference to the conflict between President Allende and the congress in the analysis of
the breakdown of democracy.[7] It might or might not be an accident that so many
countries with presidential regimes have encountered great difficulties in establishing stable democracies, but certainly the relationship between the two main types
of democratic political institutions and the political process seems to deserve more
attention than it has received. It would have been interesting to turn back to earlier
debates of constitutionalists and intellectuals, particularly in Latin America, about
presidentialism and parliamentarism.[8] But we suspect they would not be particularly helpful for our present concerns because they would reflect, on the one side,
admiration for the great American democratic republic and its presidential government, ignoring to some extent what Woodrow Wilson described as congressional government, and on the other, probably bitter criticism of French parliamentarism from the Latin American legal literature.

In my own work on the breakdown of democratic regimes, at the stage of cor-
recting proofs I was struck in rereading O'Donnell's analysis of the impossible
game in post-Peronist Argentina by the extraordinary difficulty of integrating or
isolating the Peronists in contrast to the Italian communists, which in spite of all
the strains in Italian democracy never led to comparable consequences. As a result
I wrote a brief excursus on the political implications of presidentialism and parliamentarism that I expanded and that constitutes the basic theme of this essay.[9] The
ideas I intend to develop require further research using empirical evidence from
different countries, particularly in Latin America but also the Philippines, South
Korea, Nigeria, and perhaps Lebanon. The essays in this volume represent an important contribution in this direction. Further work on the problem would require

research on the perceptions of both political elites and the public of presidents and legislatures in those regimes.

It is striking that most of the discussion of presidential government in classic works on democratic politics is limited to the United States and comparison between that country and the United Kingdom. There is practically no reference to long experience with presidential regimes in Latin America.[10] This gap in the literature inevitably weakens my analysis in this essay. It should be taken as a stimulus for further and more systematic thinking and research.

Presidentialism: Principles and Realities

It has been argued that the terms *presidentialism* and *parliamentarism* each cover a wide range of political institutional formulas, and that the variety among those formulas is such that it is misleading to generalize about either term. Even two "pure" presidential systems like that of the United States and Argentina, despite the influence of the U.S. Constitution on the constitution Argentina adopted in 1853, are legally quite different—and even more so in practice—so that Carlos Nino contrasts the hyperpresidentialism of his country with a more balanced division of powers in the United States.[11] The same is probably even truer of parliamentary systems when we compare the *gouvernement d'assemblée* of the Third and Fourth Republics in France with the *Kanzlerdemokratie* of the Bundesrepublik.[12] There is the temptation in a debate about the two systems to turn to the extreme—and therefore most questionable—cases for or against the merits of each. As I will show, there are in modern democracies (even leaving aside the so-called semipresidential or semiparliamentary hybrids) some convergencies between the practices of presidentialism in conflictual multiparty systems (like Bolivia's) and parliamentary systems with a personalization of power or leadership similar to presidentialism when one party has an absolute majority or as in Germany with the "rationalized parliamentarism" of the Basic Law (the Bonn Constitution).

However, this should not obscure the fundamental differences between the two systems. All presidential and all parliamentary systems have a common core that allows their differentiation and some systematic comparisons. In addition, most presidential democracies are probably more similar to each other than the larger number of parliamentary democracies are alike, partly because all presidential democracies were inspired by the U.S. model and partly because the societies with such systems (with the outstanding exception of the United States) have some common characteristics. In parliamentary systems the only democratically legitimated institution is the parliament and the government deriving its authority from the confidence of the parliament, either from parliamentary majorities or parliamentary tolerance of minority governments and only for the time that the legislature is willing to support it between elections and, exceptionally, as long as the parliament is not able to produce an alternative government.

Presidential systems are based on the opposite principle. An executive with considerable powers in the constitution and generally with full control of the composition of his cabinet and the administration is elected by the people (directly or by an electoral college elected for that purpose) for a fixed period of time and is not dependent on a formal vote of confidence by the democratically elected representatives in a parliament; the president is not only the holder of executive power but the symbolic head of state and cannot be dismissed, except in rare cases of impeachment, between elections.

Two features stand out in presidential systems:

1. Both the president, who controls the executive and is elected by the people (or an electoral college elected by the people for that sole purpose), and an elected legislature (unicameral or bicameral) enjoy democratic legitimacy. It is a system of "dual democratic legitimacy."

2. Both the president and the congress are elected for a fixed term, the president's tenure in office is independent of the legislature, and the survival of the legislature is independent of the president. This leads to what we characterize as the "rigidity" of the presidential system.

Most of the characteristics and problems of presidential systems flow from these two essential features. Some other nondefining features of presidentialism are often associated with it and are discussed below, such as term limits or no reelection, automatic succession by a vice president, freedom in appointing and (even more) in dismissing a cabinet, sameness of head of state and head of government. One characteristic so normal that it is often included in the definition is that the presidency is a unipersonal office. There have been only two cases of directly elected pluripersonal "presidencies": the two-person Cypriot administration (1960–63) and the Uruguayan Colegiado (which governed twice—1918–33 and 1952–67).[13]

Dual Democratic Legitimacy

The basic characteristic of presidentialism is the full claim of the president, to democratic legitimacy. Very often the claim has strong plebiscitary components although sometimes it is based on fewer popular votes than are received by many prime ministers in parliamentary systems heading minority cabinets that are perceived by contrast as weakly legitimated by the electorate. To mention just one example: Allende with a 36.2 percent plurality obtained by a heterogeneous coalition (1973) was certainly in a very different position from Adolfo Suárez with 35.1 percent of the vote (1979), as were the opponents Alessandri with 34.9 percent and Felipe González with 30.5 percent, and the less successful contenders Tomic with 27.8 percent and Fraga and Carrillo with respectively 6.1 and 10.8 percent. A presidential system gives the incumbent, who combines the qualities of head of state representing the nation and the powers of the executive, a very different aura and self-image and creates very different popular expectations than those redounding to a prime minister with whatever popularity he might enjoy after receiving the same number of votes.[14]

The most striking fact is that in a presidential system, the legislators, particularly when they represent well-organized, disciplined parties that constitute real ideological and political choices for the voters, also enjoy a democratic legitimacy, and it is possible that the majority of such a legislature might represent a different political choice from that of the voters supporting a president. Under such circumstances, who, on the basis of democratic principles, is better legitimated to speak in the name of the people: the president, or the congressional majority that opposes his policies? Since both derive their power from the vote of the people in a free competition among well-defined alternatives, a conflict is always latent and sometimes likely to erupt dramatically; there is no democratic principle to resolve it, and the mechanisms that might exist in the constitution are generally complex, highly technical, legalistic, and, therefore, of doubtful democratic legitimacy for the electorate. It is therefore no accident that in some of those situations the military intervenes as "poder moderador."

It could be argued that such conflicts are normal in the United States and have not led to serious crisis.[15] It would exceed the limits of this essay to explain the uniqueness of American political institutions and practices that have limited the impact of such conflicts, including the unique characteristics of the American political parties that lead many American political scientists to ask for a more responsible, disciplined ideological party system.[16] In my view, the development of modern political parties, in contrast to the American type of parties, particularly in socially or ideologically polarized societies, is likely to make those conflicts especially complex and threatening. *suggest America could be an exception.*

Without going into the complexities of the relationship between the executive and the legislature in different presidential regimes,[17] the relative dangers of predominance of one or the other, and the capacity to veto or stalemate decisions on legislation, there can be no doubt that presidential regimes are based on a dual democratic legitimacy and that no democratic principle can decide who represents the will of the people in principle. In practice, and particularly in developing countries with great regional inequalities in modernization, it is likely that the political and social composition and outlook of the legislature differs from that of the supporters of the president. The territorial principle of representation, sometimes reinforced by inequalities in the districting or the existence of a senate in federal republics, tends to give stronger weight in the legislature to representatives of rural areas and small towns of the provinces than to the metropolises. And it is easy to claim that the democratic credentials of representatives of backward areas are dubious and that these representatives are local oligarchs elected thanks to their clientelistic influences, their social and economic power. Independently of the truth of this claim and of the degree to which a democracy would disqualify voters who, rather than being influenced by trade unions, neighborhood associations, and party machines, are loyal to local notables, tribal leaders, priests, and even bosses, urban progressive elites are tempted to question the representativeness of those elected by them. In such a context, it becomes easy for a president encountering resistance to his program in the legislature to mobilize the people against the oligarchs, to claim true democratic legitimacy, deny it to his opponents, and confront his opponents with his capacity to mobilize his supporters in mass demonstrations.[8]

It is also conceivable that in some societies the president might represent the more traditional or provincial electorates and might use that support to question the right of the more urban and modern segments in a minority to oppose his policies. In the absence of any logical principle to define who really has democratic legitimacy, it is tempting to use ideological formulations to legitimize the presidential component of the system and delegitimize those opposing him, transforming what is an institutional conflict into serious social and political conflicts.

The different "legitimacies" of a popularly elected president and a congress are already well described in this text of 1852:

> While the votes of France are split up among the seven hundred and fifty members of the National Assembly, they are here, on the contrary, concentrated on a single individual. While each separate representative of the people represents only this or that party, this or that town, this or that bridgehead, or even only the mere necessity of electing some one of the seven hundred and fifty, in which neither the cause nor the man is closely examined, he is the elect of the nation and the act of his election is the trump that the sovereign people plays once every four years. The elected National Assembly stands in a metaphysical relation, but the elected President in a personal relation, to the nation. The National Assembly, indeed, exhibits in its individual representatives the manifold aspects of the national spirit, but in the President this national spirit finds its incarnation. As against the Assembly, he possesses a sort of divine right; he is President by the grace of the people.

Incidentially this is not the analysis of an institutionalist (or political psychologist) but of the "sociologist" Karl Marx in his "Eighteenth Brumaire of Louis Bonaparte."[19]

Election for a Fixed Term: The "Rigidity" of Presidentialism

The second main institutional characteristic of presidential systems is the fact that presidents are elected for a period of time that, under normal circumstances cannot be modified: not shortened and sometimes, due to provisions preventing reelection, not prolonged. The political process therefore becomes broken into discontinuous, rigidly determined periods without the possibility of continuous readjustments as political, social, and economic events might require. The duration of the mandate of a president becomes an essential political factor to which all actors in the political process have to adjust, and this has many important consequences.

If I had to summarize the basic differences between presidential and parliamentary systems, I might point to the rigidity that presidentialism introduces into the political process and the much greater flexibility of that process in parliamentary systems. This rigidity might appear to the proponents of presidentialism as an advantage because it reduces some of the incertitudes and unpredictability inherent to parliamentarism, in which a larger number of actors, parties, their leaders, even the rank-and-file legislators, including those changing loyalties, can at any time between elections make basic changes, see to realignments, and above all, change the head of the executive, the prime minister. The search for strong power and predictability would seem to favor presidentialism, but paradoxically, unexpected events from the death of the incumbent to serious errors in judgment, particularly when faced with changing situations, make presidential rule less predictable and often weaker than that of a prime minister, who can always reinforce his authority and democratic legitimacy by asking for a vote of confidence.

The uncertainties of a period of regime transition and consolidation no doubt make the rigidities of a presidential constitution more problematic than a parliamentary system, which permits flexible responses to a changing situation.

One of the presumed advantages of a presidential regime is that it assures the stability of the executive. This has been contrasted with the instability of many parliamentary governments, which undergo frequent crises and changes in the prime ministership, particularly in multiparty European democracies. It would seem that the image of governmental instability in the French Third and Fourth Republics, in Italy today, and more recently in Portugal has contributed to the negative image of parliamentarism held by many scholars, particularly in Latin America, and their preference for presidentialism. In such a comparison it is often forgotten that parliamentary democracies have been able to produce stable governments. Under their apparent instability, the continuity of parties in power, the reshuffling of cabinet members, the continuation of a coalition under the same premier, and the frequent continuity of ministers in key ministries in spite of cabinet crises tend to be forgotten.[20] It is also overlooked that the parliamentary system allows for removal of the prime minister who has lost control of his party or is involved in a scandal, whose continuation in office might create a serious political crisis. He might be replaced by his party, by the formation of a new coalition, or by the withdrawal of support of parties tolerating the minority government, without a major constitutional crisis. Unless parliamentary alignments make the formation of a democratically based government impossible, parliament with more or less difficulty and with more or less delay should be able to produce a new prime minister. In some cases of more serious crisis, there is always the alternative of calling for new elections, although they often do not resolve the problem but, as in Germany in the early 1930s, compound it.

In contrast, presidents are elected for a fixed term in office. The kind of changes that produce government crises and the substitution of one executive by another are excluded for that time. But this entails a rigidity in the political process that makes adjustment to changing situations extremely difficult; a leader who has lost the confidence of his own party or the parties that acquiesced to his election cannot be re-placed) He cannot be substituted with someone abler to compromise with the oppo-sition when polarization has reached an intensity that threatens violence and an ille-gal overthrow. (The extreme measure of impeachment, which is in the constitutional texts, is difficult to use compared to a vote of no confidence) An embattled president is tempted to, and can, use his powers in such a way that his opponents might not be willing to wait until the end of his term to oust him. But there are no mechanisms to remove him without violating the constitution, unless he is willing to resign.[21]

Voluntary resignation under the pressure of party leaders and public opinion would be one way of avoiding the implications of the rigidity of the presidential mandate without the rumbling of tanks or violence in the streets. However, it is an unlikely outcome given the psychology of politicians. Moreover, in a presidential system, particularly one without the possibility of reelection, the incumbent can-not vindicate himself before the electorate. It is difficult for his former supporters to encourage him to such a step, particularly when some consider a vice president, who would automatically succeed him, even less desirable than the incumbent (as in the Fernando Collor crisis in Brazil in mid-1992). After two years and ten months and the complete failure of his administration, President Siles Suazo resigned, pre-venting another breakdown of civilian rule. Pressure from the opposition parties, the MNR (Movimiento Nacional Revolucionario) and the ADN (Alianza Demo-crática Nacional), which had the majority in the congress, the hostility of the major business organizations, and rumors of a possible coup had reduced his mandate in a little more than a year. It was exceptional in Bolivian politics because instead of a coup, the crisis led to an election in July 1985 in which ADN gained 28.57 percent of the votes and MNR 26.42 percent (an election in which the trade union movement and the radical left advocated abstention or void voting). Paz Estenssoro of MNR was elected president, and a period of democratic stability was initiated. Suazo's resignation is today widely recognized as a patriotic act.

Even "voluntary" resignation under pressure is likely to generate a serious polit-ical crisis because the segment of the electorate that brought the president to power might feel cheated of its choice and rally publicly to the incumbent's support) It is difficult to imagine political leaders resolving the issue without bringing the peo-ple into the debate and without using the threat of nondemocratic institutions, like the courts, and, more frequently, of political intervention by the armed forces. The intense conflict underlying such crises cannot be contained within the corridors and smoke-filled rooms of the legislature, as the nonconfidence vote (or more often the threat of it) against a prime minister or a party leader can be.

Identifiability and Accountability

One of the positive characteristics attributed to presidentialism is accountabil-ity and identifiability. The voter in casting his ballot knows whom he or she is vot-ing for and who will govern should this candidate win) The person voting for representatives of a party in a parliamentary system presumably does not know who the party will support to be prime minister, and if it is a multiparty system in which the party cannot expect to gain an absolute majority, the voter does not know what parties will form a governing coalition.

In reality neither of these statements is true or all the truth the voter would need to know in order to make a "reasonable" choice.

In presidential elections the voter may know much less about who will govern than the voters of a party in most parliamentary systems. The presidential candidates do not need and often do not have any prior record as political leaders. They may not be identified with a party with an ideology or program and record, and there may be little information about the persons likely to serve in a cabinet. The choice is often based on an opinion about *one* individual, a personality, promises, and—let's be honest—an image a candidate projects, which may be an image chosen by advisers (who are not necessarily politicians). This is even more the case in our age of "videopolitics."[22]

It may be argued that the voters of PASOK (Panhellenic Socialist Movement) voted for Papandreou, the British Conservatives voted for Mrs. Thatcher, the PSOE (Partido Socialista Obrero Español) voted for Felipe González, and so forth, although some might have voted for those parties in spite of their leaders or the other way around. Personalization of leadership is not exclusive to presidential politics. There is, however, a difference: leaders in parliamentary systems are not likely to have proposed themselves to the voters without having gained, and sometimes retained over many years, the leadership of their parties, either in power or in the opposition (something far from easy in the competitive world of politics). These leaders represent their parties. In addition, the voter knows that those who will form a cabinet will come from the party and, more often than not, are well-known leaders of the party with an accumulated experience in politics. A prime minister today is quite free in selecting his cabinet but certainly not as free as most presidents.

The argument that in a parliamentary system the voter does not know who will govern is not true in most cases because parties are identified with highly visible leaders. Those leaders appeal directly to the voters, and the campaigns increasingly are focused on the leader who aspires to be prime minister or chancellor. No Conservative voter could ignore that he was voting for Mrs. Thatcher, no PSOE voter that he was casting his ballot for Felipe González, no CDU (Christlich Demokratische Union) voter that Helmut Kohl would form the government. It could be argued that the party's parliamentary group or the notables of the party could remove the chosen leaders, that those who voted for Mrs. Thatcher, for example, had for the remainder of the legislature to accept Major as prime minister. But why would a party change leaders after the investment made in building them up, unless there is a feeling that they have proved inadequate? After all, the parliamentarians and party leaders have much to lose if the voters disapprove; they can be held accountable.

As to the indeterminacy of who will govern when coalitions are necessary in multiparty systems, with some exceptions, this again is not true. Parties commit themselves to an alliance, such as the CDU-CSU-FDP (CSU, Christlich Soziale Union; FDP, Frei Demokratische Partei) before the elections, and the voter for any of those parties knows that a particular person will be chancellor and also that unless one party wins an absolute majority (and even then) the government will include representatives of all the parties in the coalition. This is particularly interesting to those wanting a minor coalition party, such as the FDP, to have an influence. Voters do not know the exact composition of the coalition cabinet—which cabinet posts will go to which parties and leaders—but they know much more than voters for a president in the United States or Brazil know. Parties in parliamentary systems often have a well-known shadow cabinet, while a president-elect starts naming a cabinet only after the election. The identifiability in presidentialism is of *one* person; in parliamentary government most of the time it is of a pool of people and often a number of well-known subleaders.

Let us assume a multiparty system, no absolute majority, no previous coalition agreement. The voter still knows that the prime ministership will go to the leader (or one of the top leaders) of the largest party and knows which are the likely coalition partners of that party. The voter may not like one or the other of the parties, their leaders, or their positions but is likely to know more about the possible cabinets than voters for most presidents know. The voter for a major party hopes that it might govern alone. The voter for a minor party (eligible to enter coalitions) knows it and its leader will not govern alone but hopes that the vote will give it a greater share of power. After all only a limited number of coalitions are possible, and noncontiguous coalitions are exceptional. A Catalan nationalist voter for CiU (Convergéncia i Unió) in a Spanish parliamentary election knows that this party will not form a government but also that if no party has an absolute majority CiU representatives can influence the formation of a government and might even enter it. The voter certainly knows more about who and what to vote for than if he only had the choice between two presidential candidates. Should his CiU representative enter a coalition he disapproves the party is more accountable than the party of a president who would disappoint Catalanist sentiments to which he might have appealed.

Accountability to the voters for performance is presumably enhanced by the fact that a president is directly and personally responsible for policies—not the cabinet, not a coalition, and not the leaders of the party that might have occupied the prime minister's office in a succession. Only *one* person is clearly identified as governing for the entire period of a mandate. There are no confused or shared responsibilities. So the argument goes.

Let us analyze this argument. First of all there is no way to hold accountable a president who cannot be presented for reelection. Such a president can neither be punished by the voters by defeat nor rewarded for success by reelection with the same or a larger vote than in the previous election. A president who cannot be reelected is "unaccountable."

This is the case in thirteen presidential systems (counting those that provide for one or two interim terms) compared to six systems that have no limit on reelection or a two-term limit. We could add to these the semipresidential (or premier-presidential systems) of France and Finland, which do not limit reelection, and Portugal, which has a two-term limit.[23]

It could be argued that in the case of no reelection the party that supported the election of the president would be held accountable, but in fact that party's new presidential candidate is the person accountable. He would try to identify with his successful predecessor or to disidentify from him in case of failure. In a personalized election this might be easier than when the voter has to support a party that has not changed its leadership or has done so belatedly. Besides, it is partly unfair to punish a party for the actions of a president who, after the election, could govern independently of its confidence.   → *plausible deviability*

When reelection is possible, the incumbent president who is perceived negatively paradoxically can try, more or less successfully, to escape blame by shifting it to the congress, particularly if it was dominated by the opposition but even if his own party was in the majority. Just before the election he can propose legislation that the congress rejects and can claim that if his policies had been approved he would have been successful. A prime minister with a majority cannot play such a game. The division of powers can therefore provide an alibi for failure. The congress, even the president's party in the congress, can play a similar game by blaming the executive for not implementing policies it has approved or not submitting the measures necessary to deal with problems.

In conclusion, accountability with separation of powers is not easy to enforce. In a parliamentary system the party with a majority, or even a stable coalition of parties, can easily be made accountable to the voters, as long as the voters do not exclude in principle a vote for parties in the opposition.

The objection that in a parliament, parties, their leaders, and the prime ministers they support cannot be made accountable is valid only under certain conditions: when there are many unstable governments or shifting (and even contradictory) coalitions, and when no party has played a central role in the coalition-making process.

This might have been the case in the Third French Republic and in the "third force" governments of the Fourth Republic. Even in such a fractionalized parliamentary system as the Italian, I surmise that the voters had not much doubt until recently that the Democrazia Cristiana was responsible for governing and could have been made accountable if a sufficient number of voters had considered potential alternative coalitions (which probably were impossible without the participation of the Communists). In addition, in the case of coalitions the minor parties can be and have been held accountable for entering or not entering them, and the major parties for including or not including the minor ones.

However, in many parliamentary systems parties can be made fully accountable.

This is true in Westminster-type majoritarian democracies, particularly when a two-party system has emerged, and also in multiparty systems with coalition or minority governments. Voters in such situations often have voted for parties committed to form a particular coalition. The parties campaign with such a commitment although the voters may give more or less weight in the process of policy formation to one or another member of the coalition (checking perhaps the threat of hegemonic rule by one party). This has been the case in the Federal Republic of Germany. Moreover, the coalition parties can be and have been made accountable in the next election. Obviously one party might break out of the coalition, even change sides for the next election, but voters can reward or punish it for its behavior.

Another problem in presidential systems is not to be ignored: even in the case of possible reelection, the voters have to wait for the end of the presidential term to demand accountability. A prime minister can be made accountable to the parliament and his own party by a vote of no confidence at any time; the party becomes accountable to the voters at the end of the period or even earlier should the leadership crisis in parliament or the governing party lead to anticipated elections.

Winner Take All

In a presidential election whatever the plurality gained the victorious candidate takes over the whole executive branch, while a leader aspiring to be prime minister whose party gains less than 51 percent of the seats might be forced to share power with another party or to constitute a minority government. With some 30 percent of the seats he could not form a noncoalition government, while a president with the same vote could (although he might have a hard time getting the congress to support his policies). The control of the executive in presidential systems is in principle "winner take all."

In addition it is "loser loses all" for defeated presidential candidates, who might end without any public office after the election and, unless they have strong positions as leaders of their party, might have gambled away all their political resources. Where is Michael Dukakis or Vargas Llosa today? The loser often loses all.

Adam Przeworski commenting on this point has written:

> Linz (1984) has developed a number of arguments in favor of parliamentary, as opposed to presidential, systems. I am particularly persuaded by his observation that presidential systems generate a zero-sum game, whereas parliamentary systems increase total payoffs. The reasons are the following. In presidential systems, the winner takes all: He or she can form a government without including any losers in the coalition. In fact, the defeated candidate has no political status, as in parliamentary systems, where he or she becomes the leader of the opposition. Hence, in terms of the model developed above, under *ceteris paribus* conditions (under which $W + L = T$ is the same in both systems), the value of victory, W, is greater

and the value of defeat, L, is smaller under presidential than under parliamentary systems. Now, assume that political actors discount the future at the rate of r per annum. Under the presidential system, the term is fixed for some period ($t = $ PRES), and the expected value of the next round is $r^{\mathrm{PRES}} (pW + (1 - p)L)$. Under the parliamentary system, the winner governs only as long as he or she can maintain sufficient support in the parliament, say for the period $t = $ PARL, so that the expected value of the next round is $r^{\mathrm{PARL}} (pW + (1 - p)L)$.

Elementary algebra will then show that unless the tenure expected under parliamentarism is notably longer than under presidentialism, the loser has a greater incentive to stay in the democratic game under parliamentarism.[24]

My critics, however, are right that with the division of powers a successful presidential candidate might not "take all" because his party might be in the minority in the congress. They are also totally right that when in a parliamentary system a disciplined party gains a majority or more of the seats, it is truly a "winner-take-all" situation. This is likely in a Westminster-type parliamentary system where single-member districts might assure a party a disproportionate number of seats in a culturally homogeneous country. As Mainwaring and Shugart put it, the purest examples of what Lijphart calls majoritarian democracy, in which the winner takes all, are parliamentary rather than presidential democracies.[25] However, this is true only when a party is able to gain an absolute majority of seats, something that does not happen often.

Even when a party in a parliamentary democracy gains an absolute majority of seats—a "winner-take-all" situation, which is likely to happen in a Westminster-type democracy—the party leader or premier may not be in the same position as a president. To stay in office the prime minister has to pay attention to his supporters in the parliamentary party; rebellion of backbenchers or of the barons of the party can terminate his tenure. The fate of a powerful, once popular leader, such as Mrs. Thatcher, is paradigmatic. Mrs. Thatcher's party under the new leadership of John Major could win a subsequent election. Nothing similar could have happened when the failure of Alán García of Peru became apparent, and APRA (Alianza Popular Revolucionaria Americana) had to pay the price in the elections.

One of the possible outcomes of a presidential election is that the defeated candidate loses all. This is likely, and probably desirable, for the "amateur" challenger without party support. But it also is likely in a two-party contest. The defeated candidate, regardless of the number of votes obtained, is not likely to be considered a desirable candidate for the next presidential election and therefore probably will have lost his leadership position in the party. In fact, sometimes the defeated party is left leaderless until a candidate is nominated for the next election. Only in highly ideological and structured parties, or in some multiparty situations, do defeated presidential candidates retain a leadership position. Leaders of parties in parliamentary systems, however, are practically always assigned seats in the legislature and sometimes have the status of "leader of the loyal opposition" (although growing personalization in the campaigns might also lead to their resignation from leadership of the party).

No Reelection and Its Implications

The principle of no reelection or of no immediate reelection is not a defining characteristic of presidentialism, but it is clearly the predominant pattern. Shugart and Carey list eight countries (several of dubious democratic credentials) that allow no reelection, four with no immediate reelection, and one—Venezuela—with two interim terms. Among those allowing immediate reelection, five limit the presidency to two terms and six have no limit (including two semipresidential or, in their terminology, premier-presidential systems).[26]

The importance assigned to the no-reelection principle is reflected in the fact that the General Treaty of Peace and Amity signed by all Central American governments at Washington on February 7, 1927, provided that: "The Contracting Parties obligate themselves to maintain in their respective Constitutions the principle of non-reelection to the office of President and Vice President of the Republic, and those of the Contracting Parties whose Constitutions present such reelection, obligate themselves to introduce a constitutional reform to this effect in their next legislative session after the notification of the present Treaty."[27]

The principle of no reelection in many countries has acquired a strong symbolic importance. The memory of lifelong rule by nondemocratic rulers, caudillos and dictators, led to demands of no reelection, like that of Madero against the Porfiriato in Mexico. Attempts to change constitutional provisions barring reelection, efforts to assure what the Latin Americans call *continuismo,* have mobilized public opinion and led to riots and coups not only in Latin America but South Korea.[28] The prospect of reelection of an incumbent in the winner-take-all game often has united presidential hopefuls of quite opposite ideological positions, as some powerful Brazilian governors were united against Goulart.

The continuous support of the electorate for a particular party election after election, which we find in quite a few parliamentary democracies (Scandinavia, the United Kingdom, Italy, India, and Japan) sometimes has assured permanence in the office of prime minister. But it has not led to a demand to limit the term in office and never to violent protest and regime crises comparable to those provoked by efforts of *continuismo.* This tells us something about the different political culture generated by presidentialism and parliamentarism. The stakes in theory are different although in practice parliamentarism might lead to greater continuity in office of highly respected party leaders.

Democracy is by definition a government pro tempore, a government in which the electorate at regular intervals can make those governing accountable and impose a change.[29] The maximum time limit for any government between elections is probably the greatest guarantee against omnipotence and abuse of power, the last hope for those in the minority position. The requirement of periodic elections, however, in principle does not exclude the possibility that those in power might again obtain the confidence of the electorate. A turnover in power can also have dysfunctional consequences, because no government can be assured the time to implement promises, to carry through between the two elections major programs of social change, to achieve irreversible changes in the society. This is even more true when there is term limitation, as in many presidential systems. And all governments, democratic and nondemocratic, would like to assure themselves continuity over a long period of time.   ⟋ *not in Şqjl'q.*

The concentration of power in a president has led in most presidential regimes to attempts to limit the presidency to one or at most two terms. Those provisions have been frustrating for ambitious leaders, who have been tempted to assure *continuismo* legally. Even in the absence of such ambitions, the consciousness that time to carry out a program associated with one's name is limited must have an impact on political style in presidential regimes. The fear of discontinuity in policies and distrust of a potential successor encourage a sense of urgency, of what Albert Hirschman has called "the wish of *vouloir conclure*,"[30] that might lead to ill-designed policies, rapid implementation, impatience with the opposition, and expenditures that otherwise would be distributed over a longer period of time or policies that might contribute to political tension and sometimes inefficacy. A president wants to be sure that he can inaugurate his Brasilia before leaving office, implement his program of nationalizations, and so forth. A prime minister who can expect his party or the coalition supporting him to win the next election is not likely to be under the same pressure; we have seen prime ministers staying in office over the course of several legislatures without any fear of dictatorship arising because removal could take place anytime without recourse to unconstitutional means. Term limits and the principle of no reelection, whose value cannot be questioned, mean that the political system has to produce a capable and popular leader periodically and that the political capital accumulated by a successful leader cannot be used beyond the leader's term of office.   *(lame-Duck) → B/own*

All political leadership is threatened by the ambitions of second-rank leaders, by their positioning themselves for succession, and sometimes by their intrigues. But inevitably the prospect of a succession at the end of a president's term is likely to foster those tendencies and suspicions of them on the part of the incumbent. The desire for continuity, on the other hand, leads a president to look for a successor who will not challenge him while he is in office. Such a person is not necessarily the most capable and attractive leader. The inevitable succession also creates a distinctive tension between the ex-president and his successor, who will be tempted to assert his independence and his differences with his predecessor, even when both belong to the same party—a process that might become quite threatening to the unity of the party. The person who has been president, with all the power, prestige, and adulation accompanying that office, will always find it difficult to relinquish power and to be excluded from the prospect of regaining it in the case of failure of the successor. That frustration might have important political consequences, such as an attempt to exercise power behind the scenes, to influence the next presidential succession by supporting a candidate different from the one supported by the incumbent, and so forth.

When a president is barred from immediate reelection but can run again after an interim period, as in Venezuela, conflict is likely to develop between the incumbent and his predecessor of the same party. The case of Carlos Andrés Pérez and President Lusinchi, discussed by Michael Coppedge (chapter 12) comes readily to mind.

Certainly similar problems emerge in parliamentary systems when a prominent leader leaves the premiership but finds himself capable of and willing to return to power. But probably the need to maintain party unity, the deference with which such a leader is likely to be treated by other leaders of his party and by the successor, and the successor's awareness of needing the cooperation of a powerful leader outside of government might facilitate an alternative positioning of the two leaders of the same party. The departing leader knows that he might be called back into office at any time, and his successor also knows that such a possibility exists. The awareness of both leaders that a confrontation between them might be costly to both creates a situation that very often leads to a sharing of power.

Political Style in Presidential and Parliamentary Democracies

The preceeding discussion has focused on the institutional dimensions of our problem. Some of the legal provisions in presidential constitutions and some of the unwritten rules that differentiate the types of democracies have been referred to. Other aspects that need to be addressed are the way in which political competition is structured in a system in which the people directly elect the president, the style in which authority and power are exercised, the relations among a president, the political class, and the society, and the way in which power is likely to be exercised and conflicts to be resolved. Our assumption is that the institutional characteristics to which we have referred directly or indirectly shape the whole political process and the way of ruling.

Perhaps the most important implication of presidentialism is that it introduces a strong element of zero-sum game into democratic politics with rules that tend toward a "winner-take-all" outcome. A parliamentary election might produce an absolute majority for a particular party, but more normally it gives representation to a number of parties. One perhaps wins a larger plurality than others, and some negotiations and sharing of power become necessary for obtaining majority support for a prime minister or tolerance of a minority government. This means that the prime minister will be much more aware of the demands of different groups and much more concerned about retaining their support. Correspondingly different parties do not lose the expectation of exercising a share of power, an ability to control, and the opportunity to gain benefits for their supporters.

The feeling of having independent power, a mandate from the people, of independence for the period in office from others who might withdraw support, including the members of the coalition that elected him, is likely to give a president a sense of power and mission that might be out of proportion to the limited plurality that elected him. This in turn might make resistances he encounters in the political system and the society more frustrating, demoralizing, or irritating than resistances usually are for a prime minister, who knows from the beginning how dependent he is on the support of his party, other parties, other leaders, and the parliament. Unless the prime minister has an absolute majority, the system inevitably includes some of the elements that become institutionalized in what has been called consensus and sometimes consociational democracy.

Certainly there have been and are multiparty coalition governments in presidential systems, based on the need for "national unity," but they are exceptional and often unsatisfactory for the participants. The costs to a party of joining others to save a president in trouble are high. If the endeavor succeeds, the president gets the credit; if it fails, the party is blamed; and the president always has power to dismiss the ministers without being formally accountable for his decision. Those considerations entered into the decision of Fernando Henrique Cardoso not to serve in the cabinet of President Collor in 1992.

In this context it is important to notice that when democracy was reestablished in two Latin American countries with presidential constitutions in difficult circumstances, the political leaders of the major parties turned to consociational types of agreements to obviate some of the implications of giving one party the entire authority associated with the presidency and the zero-sum implications for those not gaining that office. However the difficulty in forming true coalition governments in presidential regimes has led to more formalized and rigid arrangements. The Colombian *Concordancia*, a form of consociationalism, although democratically legitimized after being agreed to by the politicians, established a system that preempted the rights of the voters to choose which party should govern. To prevent the zero-sum implications of presidentialism, which were feared by the politicians, a system of dubious democratic legitimacy was chosen. The Venezuelan *pacto de punto fijo* had the same purpose but not the rigid constitutionalization of the Colombian solution.[31]

The zero-sum character of the political game in presidential regimes is reinforced by the fact that winners and losers are defined for the period of the presidential mandate, a number of years in which there is no hope for shifts in alliances, broadening of the base of support by national unity or emergency grand coalitions, crisis situations that might lead to dissolution and new elections, and so forth.[32] The losers have to wait four or five years without access to executive power and thereby to a share in the formation of cabinets and without access to patronage. The zero-sum game raises the stakes in a presidential election for winners and losers, and inevitably increases the tension and the polarization.

Presidential elections have the advantage of allowing the people to choose directly who will govern them for a period of time. Many multiparty systems with parliamentary institutions leave that decision to the politicians. Presumably, the president has a direct mandate from the people. If a minimal plurality is not required and a number of candidates compete in a single round, the person elected might have only a small plurality; the difference between the successful candidate and the runner-up might be too small to justify the sense of plebiscitary popular support that the victor and his supporters might sincerely feel. To eliminate this element of chance the electoral laws sometimes require a minimal plurality for the victor and some procedure for choosing when no one reaches that minimum.[33] Those requirements might frustrate the supporters of the most successful candidate. More frequent is the pattern in which the election turns into a confrontation between two leading candidates, either in a first or a second round. Such a bipolar choice under certain conditions is likely to produce considerable polarization. One of the consequences in multiparty systems of the confrontation of two viable candidates is that before the elections, broad coalitions are likely to be formed in which extremist parties with some strength cannot be ignored because success might depend on even the small number of votes they might be able to provide. A party system in which significant numbers of voters identify strongly with such parties gives these voters disproportionate presence among the supporters of the candidates. It is easy for the opponent to point to the dangerous influence of the extremists, and the extremists have a possible blackmail power over a moderate candidate. Unless a strong candidate of the center rallies wide support against those who engage in an alliance with extreme segments of the political spectrum and finds widespread support in the center that cuts into the more clearly defined alternatives, a presidential election can encourage centrifugal and polarizing tendencies in such an electorate.

Where there is great fear of polarization, the politicians may agree on a compromise candidate whom they respect and who does not generate antagonism. Such a candidate may be chosen more for his personal qualities than for the policies he advocates, and he is more likely to be a leader of a small than a large party. Such an option can serve the purpose of making a smooth transition to democracy, with its competition among parties and policies, or of reequilibrating a system in crisis. However, it is very doubtful that such an ad hoc coalition of politicians would want to or could give the president it helped to elect full support to govern, to make difficult decisions that alienate many erstwhile supporters and run counter to their ideological commitments. This problem would be particularly serious in the late years of the mandate. Such a compromise president might therefore provide weak leadership and be left without support in the congress. Many of his former supporters may dissociate themselves from him (without paying the price of a government crisis, as in a parliamentary system) to prepare themselves for legislative elections and the next presidential election.

It can be argued that in a society where the bulk of the electorate places itself at the center of the political spectrum, shares basically moderate positions, agrees on the exclusion of the extremists, and differs only moderately between left of center and right of center, the potentially negative consequences of presidential competition are excluded. With an electorate of overwhelmingly moderate centrist leanings, anyone making an alliance or taking a position that seems to lean toward an extreme is unlikely to win an election, as Goldwater and McGovern discovered on election night. However, most societies facing serious social and economic problems probably do not fit the model of U.S. presidential elections. They are likely instead to be divided in their opinions about an authoritarian regime that had significant support at some point and to have parties that are perceived as extremist with strong organizations and considerable appeal.

In a single-round election, none of the leading candidates in a somewhat polarized society with a volatile electorate can ignore those forces with whom he would otherwise not be ready to collaborate without the very great risk of finding himself short of a plurality. Let us retain for our analysis the potential for polarization and the difficulty of isolating politically extremist alternatives disliked intensely by significant elites or segments of the electorate.

A two-round election with a runoff between leading candidates reduces the uncertainty and thereby might help to produce a more rationally calculated outcome, on the part of both the candidate and the voters. The candidates can point to their own strengths and calculate how much their alliances can contribute to a winning coalition, and those tending more toward the extremes are aware of the limits of their strength. This in some ways would come closer to the process of coalition formation in a parliament in search of a prime minister.

The runoff election would seem, in principle, to be the solution in the case of multiparty presidential systems in which candidates might gain only small pluralities and in which, contrary to "rational" expectations, no broader coalitions are formed to obtain a majority. In a runoff in which only the two leading candidates are allowed to compete, one of them inevitably receives an absolute majority.

However, a number of dysfunctional consequences derive from this method of election:

1. In a highly fragmented system the two leading candidates might enjoy only small pluralities with respect to other candidates and might represent positions on the same segment of the political spectrum.

2. One of the candidates might be an outsider to the party system with no congressional party base.

3. The "majority" generated might not represent a politically more or less homogeneous electorate or a real coalition of parties.

4. The winner, although initially the choice of a small proportion of the electorate, is likely to feel that he represents a "true and plebiscitary" majority.

5. The expectation of a runoff increases the incentive to compete in the first run, either in the hope of placing among the two most favored or of gaining bargaining power for support in the runoff of one of the two leading contenders. Therefore, rather than favoring a coalescence of parties behind a candidate, the system reinforces the existing fragmentation. *may change minor in 2nd ballot*

EXCURSUS: WHAT DIFFERENCE WOULD PRESIDENTIALISM HAVE MADE IN THE SPANISH TRANSITION TO DEMOCRACY?

To illustrate this argument, let us assume that, in 1977 in Spain, the first free election after Franco had been presidential rather than parliamentary. In fact, of course, a referendum on political reform had called for a parliamentary monarchy, and the election was for a constituent parliament.[34] But what would the implications of a presidential election at that juncture have been?

First, in the absence of a record of the distribution of preferences of the electorate, despite all the information provided by public opinion surveys, which politicians would have tended to disregard, the prevailing incertitude would have made it difficult to form coalitions. And certainly the potential front-runners would have been forced to form more than winning coalitions. Assuming that the democratic opposition to Franco would have united behind a single candidate, Felipe González, something that would not have been assured at the time, González would not have been able to run independently in the way he did in the parliamentary election, given the expectations that prevailed about the Communist strength and the more or less 10 percent of the electorate that Communists actually represented. A Popular Front image would have dominated the campaign and probably obliterated the identities of the different political forces from the extreme left to the Christian Democratic center and the moderate regional parties. As it was, these forces could maintain their identities in most districts, except for some senatorial elections.

The problem would have been even more acute for the Center Right, those who had supported the *reforma* and particularly the *reforma pactada* exit from the authoritarian regime. It is not sure that, in spite of the great popularity gained by the prime minister of the transition, Adolfo Suárez, he could have united and would have wished to unite all those to the right of the Socialists. At that point, many Christian Democrats, including those who in 1979 ran on the Unión de Centro Democrático ticket, would have been unwilling to abandon their political friends from the years of opposition to Franco. On the other hand, it would have been difficult for Suárez to present himself with the support of Alianza Popular, which appeared to be a continuist alternative to Franco led by former Franco cabinet members; nor does it seem logical that the AP would have supported a leader ready to legalize the Communist party.

Excluding the possibility that the candidate of the Right would have been

Manuel Fraga, later the accepted leader of the opposition, it would have been very difficult for Suárez to sustain in a presidential campaign his distinctive position as an alternative to any thought of continuity with the Franco regime. In fact, the campaign in 1977 of the UCD was directed as much against the AP as against the Socialists and given the incertitudes about the strength of the AP and the fears and hostility it generated on the Left, much of the campaign was centered on the AP's leader, Fraga. This focus reduced the potential polarization between the longtime democrats *"de toda la vida"* and the neophytes of democracy who constituted an important part of the UCD. Inevitably, in a presidential election, the candidate of the Center Right and Right would have concentrated his attack on the dangerous supporters of the democratic left candidate, the role of the Communists and the peripheral nationalists among his supporters, and the compromises he would have made with them. The candidate of the Center Left and democratic left inevitably would have had to bring up his opponent's continuity with the Franco regime, the importance among his supporters of unreconstructed Francoists, and the absence among his coalition partners of democrats of even the moderate center, those who after the election in 1977 and in the years of constitution making and the first constitutional government after the 1979 election would play a prominent role in supporting the Suárez governments, such as the moderate Catalanists.

There can be no question that a presidential election in 1977 would have been much more polarized than the parliamentary elections that took place on June 15. Should Prime Minister Suárez have rejected an understanding with the AP, or Fraga have rejected an alliance with the Suaristas based on his bloated expectations and his vision of a natural majority of the Right and a two-party system, the outcome would have been either highly uncertain or, more likely, a plurality for the leftist candidate. A leftist president with popular backing, even with a different outcome of congressional elections, would have felt legitimated to undertake the making of a more partisan constitution and radical changes in the polity and the society. He probably would have made more changes than the Socialist prime minister Felipe González would undertake in 1982. González had been a member of parliament for five years, and his party had governed municipalities. The more utopian left wing of his party had been defeated in a party congress, and the main goal of the 1982 campaign was to win votes in the center of the spectrum, where previous elections had shown the bulk of the electorate placed itself. In my view there can be no doubt that the process of transition and consolidation of democracy in Spain would have been very different and probably more difficult with a Socialist victory in 1977. Comments by Felipe González about what a victory of his party even in 1979 would have meant confirm this.[35]

Let me caution that some of the negative consequences of polarization implicit in a presidential competition are not inherent to such a system and are not inevitable. They may be avoided when a massive consensus of the population favors moderate positions to the right and left of center and when the limited weight of the extremes is quite apparent so that no one is particularly interested in alliances with them. This situation is likely when there is a consensus to isolate the extremes, or when they themselves opt for running alone in order to make their propaganda and their presence conspicuous. But I doubt that these conditions would be found in many societies in the process of democratization and consolidation of democracy.

The Ambiguities of the Presidential Office

I have been discussing some of the implications of presidentialism for the electoral process. Some might feel that the election is one thing and what the incumbent does after being elected with all the powers granted to him by the constitution is another. Why should he or she not be ready to overcome the polarization of the campaign, heal the wounds generated, offer the defeated an opportunity to collaborate, ignore and isolate the allies on the extremes of the spectrum, and become the president of all the people? Such a policy and style of governing cannot be excluded, but whether such a policy and style are chosen depends on the personalities of the leader and the opponents. Before an election no one can be assured that this will be the choice of the new incumbent, and certainly the process of political mobilization in a plebiscitary context is not likely to facilitate such a turn of events. Moreover, such a stance might weaken rather than strengthen the new president because it risks alienating the more extremist components of his coalition, who are still in competition with the dominant, more moderate party of the alliance in the congress and other arenas for the support of the electorate. The possibility that extremists might claim betrayal makes it difficult to ignore their demands. In addition, if such a stance is not reciprocated by the defeated candidates, the incumbent's position is likely to be weakened. If a public offer has been made, a refusal may lead him to a more intransigent stand identifying even moderate opponents with the least legitimate members of the coalition that supported his opponent and thus reinforcing the rhetoric generated during the campaign.

Some of the most important consequences of a presidential system for political style result from the nature of the office itself: the powers associated with it and the limits imposed on it, particularly those derived from the need for cooperation with the congress, which might be of a different partisan composition than the winning presidential coalition, and above all the sense of time that an election for a limited number of years with no right of succession often imposes on presidents.

The presidential office is by nature two-dimensional and in a sense ambiguous because a president is the representative of a clear political option, a partisan option, and of his constituency, sometimes in addition representing his party within the coalition that brought him to power. But the president is also the head of state.

The symbolic and deferential dimension of power—those aspects of authority that Bagehot[36] saw represented in the monarchy and sometimes successfully incarnated by presidents in parliamentary regimes (as recently by Sandro Pertini in Italy, or by Theodor Heuss in the early years of the Federal Republic of Germany)—is difficult to combine with the role of the partisan politician fighting to implement his program. It is not always easy to be at the same time the president of all Chileans and the president of the workers, to be the elegant and well-mannered president in La Moneda and the demagogic orator at the mass rallies in a stadium. Many voters and key elites are likely to see the second role as a betrayal of the role of head of state, who is somewhat above party and a symbol of the continuity of the state and the nation that is associated with the presidency. A presidential system, by comparison with a parliamentary monarchy or republic with a prime minister and a head of state, does not allow a differentiation of these roles.

Perhaps the most important consequence of the direct relationship between a president and the electorate, of the absence of any dependency on politicians (to renew his power once elected by the threat of motions of no confidence and the need for confirmation of confidence), is the sense of being the elected representative of the whole people and thus the propensity to identify the people with one's constituency and to ignore those voting for one's opponents. The implicit plebiscitary component of presidential authority is likely to make the opposition and the constraints a president faces immediately in exercising his authority particularly frustrating. In this context, the president is likely to define his policies as reflecting the popular will and those of his opponents as representing narrow interests rejected by the people. This sense of identity between leader and people that encourages or reinforces a certain populism can be a source of strength and power, but it also can lead to ignoring the limited mandate that even a majority, not to say a plurality, can give to implementation of any program. It encourages certain neglect of, sometimes disrespect toward, and even hostile relations with the opposition. Unlike a president, a prime minister is normally a member of a parliament who, although sitting on the government benches, is still a member of a larger body where he is forced to interact to some extent as an equal with other politicians and leaders of other parties, particularly if he depends on their support as head of a coalition government or of a minority government. A president, given his special position as head of state, is not forced into such interactions; he is free to receive his opponents or not, and always in the context of his ceremonial status in the presidential palace.

One has only to observe the exchanges between the prime minister and the leaders of the opposition in the House of Commons, on one hand, and a president's speech before the congress, on the other. Anyone who saw the memorable session in which Mrs. Thatcher presented her resignation will recognize the difference. Even a president facing a critical or hostile congress would not face a similar situation.

In addition, in a presidential system the defeated opponent and the leaders of the opposition occupy ambiguous positions. Although publicly leaders, because they do not hold an office and are not even parliamentarians, they cannot act with respect to the president in the same way as the leader of the parliamentary opposition in Westminster.)

(The absence in a presidential system of a king or a president of the republic who can act symbolically as a moderating power deprives the system of a degree of flexibility and of mechanisms to restrain the exercise of power. A king or other symbolic leader can sometimes exercise a moderating influence in a crisis situation and can even, as a neutral power, facilitate a parliamentary rebellion against the prime minister and maintain contact with forces, particularly armed forces, that are ready to question the leadership of the prime minister. Even the presidents of legislative bodies who in a parliamentary confrontation between parties can exercise some restraints do not have such power over presidents; unlike a president, a prime minister sits on the government bench while the president of a legislative body presides over the chamber or the senate.

(Given the inevitable institutional and structural position of a president, the people, that is, the people who support and identify with the president, are likely to feel that he has more power than he actually has or should have and to center excessive expectations on him) Moreover, they may express those sentiments if the president manipulates or mobilizes them against an opposition. The interaction between a popular president and the crowd acclaiming him can generate a political climate of tension and fear on the part of his opponents. The same can be said about the direct relationship a conservative president or a president with a military background can establish with the armed forces in his capacity as commander in chief. A president has many opportunities to interact with army leaders unencumbered by a prime minister or a minister of defense, one of whom would normally be present in a parliamentary monarchy or republic.

The Election of an "Outsider"

The personalized character of a presidential election makes possible, especially in the absence of a strong party system, the access to power of "outsiders." We mean by this candidates not identified with or supported by any political party, sometimes without any governmental or even political experience, on the basis of a populist appeal often based on hostility to parties and "politicians." The candidacy of such leaders might appear suddenly and capitalize on the frustrations of voters and their hopes for a "savior." Such candidates have no support in the congress and no permanent institutionalized continuity (due to the principle of no reelection) and therefore find it difficult to create a party organization. Only in a presidential system can candidates like Fujimori or Collor de Mello aspire to power. The same is true for military leaders like Hindenburg, Mannerheim, Eisenhower, and Eanes, although the success of these men depended upon the support of political parties. Scott Mainwaring[37] observes that in each of the four presidential elections between 1945 and 1960 in Brazil, one or both of the two top vote-getters were career officers who had no prior involvement with parties.

The "outsider," a presidential candidate running without party support, even against parties, be it Fujimori, Tyminski (who won 23.2 percent of votes against the 40.0 percent of Walesa), Aristide, Perot, or Chung Ju Yung (the founder of Hyundai) in South Korea, is not just the result of a particular crisis situation or of the ambition of particular individuals. There are structural reasons for such a candidacy.

If the purpose of a presidential election is to elect the "best" woman or man to the office and the individual voter has to make the choice, why should he or she think of parties? If voters can get sufficient information, or think they have gotten it, to make up their minds about the "personal" qualifications and positions of the candidates, they are presumably right in voting for a *candidate* irrespective of his links with a party. Voters feel that they do not need a party to tell them how to vote.

In the past this was difficult because no candidate, even one who did a lot of "whistle-stop" campaigning, could reach every voter. Today, perhaps in most countries, people can be reached through television. The "mediation" of parties, through presenting, endorsing, and supporting a candidate and organizing and financing a campaign, seem to be meddling and interfering in the relationship between the candidate and the voter. In some countries institutional changes recognize that fact: open primaries, registration of candidates rather than parties, funding of candidates by public means rather than parties, equal access to the media (either by law or by agreement of media managers) make parties less relevant in a presidential election. If in addition people are free to spend their own money to promote a candidacy—and why should citizens be deprived of this right if the money does not come from a criminal activity?—anyone may try to convince the citizenry of his or her personal qualifications for the office. After all we are supposed to vote for one person and for that person's program or positions. Why should we submit ourselves to the decisions of politicians controlling a party if we, the "sovereign" people, can vote for our candidate directly?

In a world where, for reasons we cannot discuss here, politicians and parties are the objects of relentless criticism, just and unjust, and rank very low in people's confidence, amateur outsiders are favored. In fact, it is tempting to run "against" the parties, which as continuous organizations controlling legislatures and government can easily be made responsible for the problems of a society, both solvable and unsolvable.

In addition, the crisis—not the end—of ideological certitudes and identifications, the loss of traditional party identifications mediated by class and religious identities, in a fluid, socially and culturally increasingly homogenized society, makes for volatility in party loyalties and for weaker links between interest groups—even organized groups like trade unions—and parties. The development of "outsider" candidacies should not surprise us.

It could be thought that the candidacy of an outsider with no party support, no previous experience in political office, is a Latin American phenomenon, an unlikely event in a country with well-established, traditional parties, where even an outsider would have to win the nomination of a major party, even should the primaries make it possible for a relative unknown to gain the nomination. In fact, third-party candidates in the United States generally have been supported by a splinter group from one of the parties. However, the candidacy of Ross Perot in 1992 shows that in the context of dissatisfaction with the parties, constant criticism of Congress, and the wear of primary campaigns, an outsider can appeal directly to the electorate. In the age of television, someone with wealth and popularity in a presidential system can appeal directly to the voters without having to build a party, as he or she would in a parliamentary system.

Former U.S. vice president Walter Mondale states this difference between leadership selection in parliamentary and presidential systems: "Unlike a parliamentary system whose leaders are picked by peers who know them, we have developed a self-nomination system where almost anyone with ambition can run for President. A candidate is not required to pass any test; he or she does not need any organizational base of support; it is not even necessary for him or her to have been elected to office before."[38] The problem with such patterns is that they are based on the initial fallacy that the "best" person in the office of the president—even if he or she had more power than presidents actually have—could govern without supporters in the congress, without a pool of persons with experience in office, without the support of politicians identified with his or her positions on issues. If we can accept the assumptions of the partyless presidential election, why not apply the principle (particularly in a system of single-member plurality elections) to all representative offices? In that case we could find ourselves with legislatures of *homini* and *femine nove* without prior commitments (except those made to their voters), who after election would have to aggregate their positions into something coherent to govern. We would be back at the first nineteenth-century parliaments, where those elected had to discover their affinities by meeting in coffee houses or clubs and slowly inventing the political party.

If partyless elections seem like unsound ways of assuring good government, we might ask ourselves what kind of institutional arrangements favor them or make them less likely. I would suggest that presidentialism facilitates them and that parliamentarism makes it more difficult for them to prevail.

An institutionalized party system makes it difficult for outsiders to enter into a presidential competition and even more difficult to win the competition. The decreased institutionalization of parties after authoritarian rule in Brazil, Peru, and Ecuador, in contrast to Colombia, Venezuela, Uruguay, Argentina, and Chile, supports this conclusion. However, one could also argue that the possibility and the incentives for outsiders to enter into the presidential competition has contributed to the arrest of or destroyed incipient institutionalization in Brazil and particularly in Peru.[39] In September 1988, once the discredit of Alán García had become irreparable, if APRA could have replaced him with another leader (as the Conservatives in the United Kingdom did with Mrs. Thatcher), the party's crisis might have been limited.[40] The not negligible institutionalization of parties in Bolivia and of cooperation among them since redemocratization might be threatened in the near future by the outsider, antiparty candidacy of Max Fernández.

Plebiscitary Leadership: Delegative Democracy

O'Donnell has noted that presidential elections, particularly in those cases that fit his model of "delegative democracy," are strongly individualistic but more in a Hobbesian than a Lockean variety: voters, irrespective of their identities and affiliations, are supposed to choose the individual who is most fit to take charge of the country's destiny. In his essay, "Delegative Democracy," he writes: "Delegative democracies are grounded on one basic premise: he or she who wins a majority in presidential elections (delegative democracies are not very congenial to parliamentary systems) is enabled to govern the country as he (or she) sees fit, and to the extent that existing power relations allow for the term he has been elected."

The plebiscitary character of many presidential elections, the polarization and emotionality surrounding them, the appeal beyond and sometimes above party, the sometimes uncontrolled promises made, lead often to extremely high rates of approval after the election. Approval may be as high as 70 and even 80 percent of the electorate. Such rates are not likely in parliamentary systems, in which voters identify with the parties of the opposition and the leader of the opposition continues to occupy a position of leadership. By contrast, the defeated presidential candidate often is reduced almost to the rank of a private person. The starting popularity ratings of a number of presidents and prime ministers show this pattern.

At the same time, failure and loss of support of a president is not cushioned by party loyalty. He or she is held personally responsible, and therefore we find drops in approval in the polls to very low levels, lower than most prime ministers on the way to defeat. Presidents suffer the wildest swings in popularity, as O'Donnell writes: "Today they are acclaimed as providential figures, tomorrow they are cursed as only fallen gods can be."

As examples of that dynamic in public opinion of presidents when they face difficult challenges, such as the economic crises in Latin America (inflation, the debt problem, and so forth), we might refer to opinion about Presidents Alfonsín of Argentina and Alán García of Peru. In May 1984, 82 percent of the population in greater urban centers expressed a positive opinion of Alfonsín. By August 1987 that figure had been reduced to 54 percent, and in April 1989, shortly before the May presidential election, to 36 percent. Even so, the president was always more favorably evaluated than the government, which moved from 45 percent in May 1984 to 27 percent in August 1987 and 9 percent in April 1989. Alán García, upon entering office in September 1985, enjoyed 90 percent approval; one year later in September 1986, his approval was 70 percent; in October 1987, it was 44 percent; in October 1988, 16 percent; and in January 1989 it reached a low point of 9 percent.[41]

In contrast, support for Prime Minister Adolfo Suárez never reached such high levels in spite of his role in the transition to democracy, but it also did not fall as ver- tiginously. At the high point in April 1977 when the transition to democracy seemed assured, it was 79 percent, and before the June 1977 first free election it was 67 per- cent, although the vote for his party, the UCD, was only 34.7 percent. By October 1978 it had dropped to 50 percent, and by December 1979 to 35 percent. By June 1980 it had fallen to 26 percent. The drop reflected the internal crisis of the UCD, the im- pact of Basque terrorism, and the economic crisis, and it ultimately led to Suárez's resignation in February 1981.[42]

Approval of Chancellor Konrad Adenauer started in the last quarter of 1949 at 33 percent. By the end of 1950, it was 24 percent. It started to move up in 1951 and 1952, rose sharply in 1953 and reached 57 percent in the last quarter, moved down in 1954, rose again in 1955 to 55 percent, and then hovered over the next years a little above 40 percent (with a low of 41 percent in 1960). The founder of the Federal Republic of Germany never could attain the massive support that Latin American presidents enjoyed, but he never experienced a great drop either, although conditions were more favorable for him to do so.[43]

General de Gaulle, despite his undoubtable charisma in the period from July 1956 to his resignation in April 1969, also never reached the level of approval of the Latin American presidents. Only a few times did the practically monthly surveys of the IFOP show a positive response of more than 70 percent (a maximum of 74 percent was reached in 1960); most of the time it was more than 50 percent and quite often more than 60 percent. In 1963 it dropped a few times to between 43 and 48 percent and was at 54 percent in May 1968 and at 53 percent at the time of his resignation.[44]

Are Presidential Governments Stable and Parliamentary Cabinets Unstable?

In the vast majority of presidential systems the president appoints his cabinet without congressional input, and the same is true for the dismissal of cabinet mem- bers.[45] The "advise and consent" role of the U.S. Senate limits the president's choice, but ultimately the choice belongs to the president and not to Congress. The president might not get the most wanted cabinet member, but he will get someone he wants. In Korea since 1987 the prime minister is proposed by the president and confirmed by the legislature. He then appoints his ministers, but he is not elected by the legislature, nor does he subsequently need its confidence. He remains the president's prime minister. In the Philippines, cabinet nominations are subject to approval by the Congressional Commission on Appointments, consisting of the president of the senate and twelve members of each chamber, elected according to the proportional representation of parties in the chambers.

The power of approval in these cases does not make the legislature in any way re- sponsible for the appointment, but it allows the legislature to frustrate the president. The U.S. "advise and consent" role is the exception rather than the rule. Korea (as of 1987), Nigeria, and the Philippines also deviate from the predominant pattern. Significantly two of these countries have experienced strong U.S. influence. Even so, since only the president has the power of dismissal, the system is closer to "pure" presidentialism than to a semipresidential, semiparliamentary system.

The free choice by a president of his collaborators, the opportunity to dismiss them whenever their advice becomes undesirable, and their incapacity in such a case to return to the parliament with an independent power base is likely to discourage strong-minded, independent men and women from joining a presidential cabinet and making a commitment to politics. In a parliamentary system, those leaving the cabinet might use their position as parliamentarians to question the policies of a prime minister in the party caucus, in legislative committees, and from the benches in the parliament. A president can shield his ministers from criticism much more than a prime minister, whose ministers may have to confront the parliament's questions, interpellations, and censure, when the principle of division of powers is carried to its logical conclusion. Once more, practices and the relative positions of the congress and the presidency in a constitutional system can modify these implicit patterns, just as modern prime ministers and their cabinets are becoming more like presidents and their cabinets in presidential regimes.

It is often assumed that the freedom of presidents to appoint a cabinet without considering the demands of coalition parties or even powerful personalities or factional leaders in their own party assures greater cabinet stability. However, as Jean Blondel writes:

> The U.S. shares a common characteristic with the other Constitutional presidential countries, even though these countries did not normally live continuously under this regime. Ministerial duration is short in America; among Atlantic countries only Finland, Portugal and Greece had a shorter average duration of ministers than the U.S.—which, on the other hand, with ministers lasting an average just over three years, scores only a little more than the bulk of the Latin American countries, and is precisely at almost the same point as Costa Rica. Constitutional presidentialism does therefore lead, even where it has operated effectively and without hindrance, to a low ministerial duration; if the average ministerial longevity is under four years in Argentina, the Dominican Republic, Bolivia, Ecuador, Chile and Peru, it is under three and a half years in Venezuela and scarcely over two years in Colombia both of which had an unbroken period of constitutional presidentialism since the late 1950s. The average duration of ministers in Chile between 1945 and the end of the Frei presidency in 1970 was only one and a half years, although Chile had then an unbroken series of regularly elected constitutional presidents.[46]

Let it be noted that in many parliamentary regimes the prime minister or chancellor is also free to appoint his cabinet, that there is no investiture vote of the cabinet or approval of individual ministers, and that often the prime minister is voted into office first and then proceeds to form his cabinet. However, and this is the difference from a presidential system, the parliament can deny the prime minister investiture or confidence if it disapproves of his cabinet. Certainly in coalition governments the partners have a decisive say in the composition of the cabinet.

It can be argued that the game of "musical chairs" among ministers in some parliamentary cabinet governments, the *cursus honorum* in government offices culminating in ministerial appointment, does not assure experience and competence, but it seems very doubtful that the almost total renewal of government with each new president appointing his men or women is better. The fact that in the United States since 1945—with the exception of Johnson's retention of the cabinet after the assassination of Kennedy—only two cabinet members served under different presidents is striking and probably not exceptional in presidential systems. Besides, most presidential systems do not have highly trained and independent bureaucracies. They must rely on a government of "amateurs" with little time to become acquainted with the machinery of government or with policies in process and their implementation. Moreover, the experience they acquire on the job is not available to their successors.

In addition the generally more collective decision making in parliamentary cabinets provides all the ministers with some familiarity with a wide range of issues, so that when one finally becomes prime minister he or she cannot be ignorant of a series of issues. (A state governor who gains the presidency has no reason to be familiar with foreign policy, to give just one example.)

The position of ministers in parliamentary governments is quite different from that of ministers or secretaries in presidential regimes. Certain trends, however, are likely to lead toward a degree of convergence between systems that in principle are different. I am thinking of parliamentary systems with highly disciplined parties and a prime minister with an absolute majority or those that follow the model of the *Kanzlerdemokratie,* in which the prime minister is free to select his cabinet without parliamentary approval. All this together with the tendency to personalize power in modern politics (particularly thanks to television) has reduced the sense of collective responsibility and the collegial nature of cabinet government, as well as the individual responsibility of ministers. However, in parliamentary systems when the prime minister is dependent on party coalitions or heads a minority government with parliamentary approval, his relation to the cabinet is likely to be clearly different from that of a president to his cabinet.

Presidents and Vice Presidents

Among the characteristics not essential to a presidential system but found in many presidential systems is the office of vice president.

One of the more complex issues surrounding a vice presidency is the provision for automatic succession in the case of death or inability of the president, which in some cases is complicated by the fact that the automatic successor is elected separately and can represent a different political option, coalition, or party than the president. Or he may have been imposed as the running mate by the presidential candidate without any consideration of his capacity both to exercise executive power and to gain the plebiscitary support the president had at the time of his election. Brazilian history provides an example of the first situation, most recently with the succession to the presidency of Sarney after Neves, and Argentina illustrates the second situation with the succession after Perón of María Estela Martínez de Perón. Presidentialism leads to a personalization of power, but a succession between elections can lead to the highest office someone to whom neither the voters, the party leaders, nor the political elite would, under normal circumstances, have entrusted with that office.

Conflicts between presidents and vice presidents have been frequent. We only have to think of Jânio Quadros and Goulart, Frondizi and Gómez, Alfonsín and Martínez, and most recently Corazón Aquino and Laurel (who went as far as conspiring against President Aquino).

The same rigidity we noted in the fixed terms of presidents continues when an incumbent dies or becomes incapacitated while in office. In the latter case, there is a temptation to hide the incapacity until the end of the term (a temptation that incidentally also appears sometimes in parliamentary democracies). In the case of death or resignation of the president for one or another reason, the vice presidency presumably assures an automatic succession without a vacuum of authority or an interregnum. However, succession by a vice president who completes the term, which has worked relatively smoothly in the recent history of the United States, sometimes poses serious problems. The problems are particularly acute when the constitution allows separate candidacies for president and vice president. Rather than a running mate of the same party and presumably the same political outlook as the presidents, the vice president may have been a candidate of a different party or coalition. In such a case, those who supported the president might feel that the successor does not represent their choice and does not have the popular democratic legitimation necessary for the office. The alternative situation, which today is more likely—that president and vice president have been nominated in agreement—still leaves open the question of the criteria used in nominating the vice president. There are undoubtedly cases in which the vice president has been nominated to balance the ticket and therefore represents a discontinuity. In other cases the incumbent imposes a weak candidate so that the vice president might not represent a potential challenge to his power, and in still others, the incumbent makes a highly personal choice, such as his wife. Nothing in the presidential system assures that the voters or the political leadership of the country, if they had been able to, would have selected the vice president to exercise the powers they were willing to give to the president. The continuity that the automatic succession in presidential systems seems to assure therefore is sometimes more apparent than real. In the absence of a vice president with the right of succession, there is the possibility of a caretaker government until new elections, which are supposed to take place at the earliest possible date. But it is not sure that the serious crisis that might have provoked the need for succession would be the best moment to hold a new presidential election.

The Party System and Presidentialism

Several authors have noted that most stable presidential democracies approach the two-party system, according to the Laakso-Taagepera index,[47] while many stable parliamentary systems are multiparty systems. They also provide convincing arguments that presidencies function better with two-party rather than multiparty systems and describe the tension between multipartyism and presidentialism.[48]

Since with the exception of the United States, Costa Rica, Venezuela, Argentina, Colombia, and in the past Uruguay, most presidential democracies in the Americas (at least nine) are multiparty systems, it can be argued that there is no fit between the institutions and the party system. It could be argued that these countries should or could move toward a two-party system by "political engineering," for example of the electoral laws and other rules, but this seems doubtful. The Brazilian military regime attempted to impose a two-party framework but was forced to give up the idea. The electoral law enacted by Pinochet before leaving power had the same intent. South Korea, with between three and four parties in the legislature and three main contenders in the first free presidential election, has moved toward a two-party system with the fusion in 1990 of the Democratic Justice Party led by Roh Tae Woo, the opposition Reunification Democratic Party (RDP) led by Kim Young Sam, and the New Democratic Republican Party of Kim Jong Pilm (although the latent purpose was to establish a dominant party system like that of Japan).[49] It is questionable that a system in which one of two parties enjoys a large majority and is assured of gaining the presidency guarantees stability. The opposition minority, PPD (Party for Peace and Democracy) led by Kim Dae Jung, will have little chance of sharing or alternating in power. One might ask if a very polarized polity will not frustrate the opposition and contribute to unstable politics as well as opportunities for corruption in the dominant party. The situation in the Republic of Korea (where the DJP and the RDP together won 64.6 percent of the vote in the 1987 presidential election) would have differed from that of the United States, Costa Rica, and Venezuela, where on the average the president's party controls between 45.8 percent (U.S.) and 50.9 percent (Costa Rica) of the seats in the lower chambers. In the December 18, 1992, presidential election, however, Kim Young Sam was elected with 42 percent of the vote. His opponent, Kim Dae Jung, who gained 34 percent, announced his retirement from politics. The billionaire founder of the Hyundai industrial group drew about 16 percent. A two-party system seemed to emerge.

One of the paradoxes of presidential regimes in many Latin American democracies (and the Philippines) is the complaint that parties are weak and lack discipline and that representatives behave in parochial and self-interested ways. I say *paradox* because these characteristics of parties and their representatives make it possible in multiparty systems (in particular) for presidencies to work. A president without a clear majority in a multiparty situation with ideological and disciplined parties would find it difficult to govern, and even more difficult with an opposition majority in the congress. It is the possibility of convincing individual legislators, of producing schisms within the parties, of distributing pork barrels and forming local clientelistic alliances that enables a president to govern and enact his program without a majority. The idea of a more disciplined and "responsible" party system is structurally in conflict, if not incompatible, with pure presidentialism (obviously not with premier presidentialism or with the French semipresidentialism or semi-parliamentarism.)

Presidents have to favor weak parties (although they might wish to have a strong party of their own if it was assured a majority in the congress). The weakness of parties in many Latin American democracies therefore is not unrelated to the presidential system but, rather, a consequence of the system.

One might argue whether parties are essential to functioning democracies, but certainly the history of democratization has been associated with the development of parties and their legitimation. It is also true that nondemocratic regimes have been based on hostility to multipartism either through establishing a monopoly or a hegemonic "leading role" of a single party, attempting to create other forms of representation, or the outright suspension or outlawing of party activity. In parliamentary democracies even antiparty movements have to transform themselves into parties to gain access to or a share of power, sometimes like the NSDAP (Nationalsozialistische deutsche Arbeiterpartei) to destroy democracy, sometimes to participate in the parliamentary process and ultimately in government coalitions, like a segment of the "Greens" in the Länder of the Federal Republic of Germany. The antiparty stance of some Latin American presidents would be largely fruitless without building a party and searching for support across party lines. In Brazil, presidents have constantly stressed that they are independent from and above party; they have formed governments with ministers recruited from parties other than their own, even when they have made their political career in one party. No leader in a parliamentary system could win power by saying like Janio Quadros: "I have no commitments to the parties that support me—the ideas that I sustain in my campaign are mine alone." Even Hitler constantly emphasized his commitment to the "Movement." When a presidential candidate can say, "Professional politicians don't do anything except perturb Brazilian life," how can we expect the slow and continuous building of democratic parties? Who can be surprised at the constant party switching of Brazilian legislators when presidents switch parties (like Sarney) or disregard their ties to parties that elected them?

Mainwaring in his excellent analysis of the Brazilian case concludes:

The question is why presidents have opted for supra- and anti-party tactics. In part, the answer may be attributed to the individual styles of the different presidents or to Brazil's anti-organizational political culture. An essential argument here, however, is that the combination of presidentialism, a fragmented multiparty system, and undisciplined parties has made it difficult for presidents to function through party channels and has encouraged anti-party practices. It is not only personalities and political culture, but also political structures that explain why presidents have acted against parties.[50]

Presidentialism with Adaptations

The difficulties generated by the pure model of presidentialism have led in a number of Latin American countries to constitutional norms or political practices, to agreements among politicians or parties, that ignore or profoundly modify the principles of presidentialism. In some cases, as I will show, these practices have contributed to governability and prevented serious crises or the breakdown of democracy. However, in several cases they violate the spirit of presidential government, ignore or frustrate the wishes of the electorate, and have been outright undemocratic (although agreed to by democratically elected politicians) by limiting the choice of the voters. These patterns contribute to weakening the accountability we associate with democracy, particularly the accountability of political parties. They might also contribute to the cynicism of the electorate about parties and politicians, if not to its alienation and radical tendencies away from the mainstream of electoral politics (as in the case of Colombia).

Multipartism or drift toward it in a number of countries with presidential systems can lead to two responses: (1) an exclusionary policy in which the two main parties attempt to prevent the entry of other parties by sharing power and modifying the rules of the game, as in Colombia, or (2) constitutional reforms directed toward "coparticipation" or toward quasi parliamentarism, such as some patterns in Uruguay and Bolivia.

In Uruguay the complex political system has led after redemocratization to practices described by María Ester Mancebo as "from coparticipation to coalition."[51] These practices have contributed to what might be called a "nonpresidential" style of politics. They should not, however, be confused with "coalition government" in parliamentary systems.

Guillermo O'Donnell[52] independently and starting from a very different problem, has noted that Uruguay has a very different style of policy making from Argentina and Brazil. He asks

why the Uruguayan government did not adopt its own Paquete, specially during the euphoria that followed the first stages of the Austral and the Cruzado. Was it because President Sanguinetti and his collaborators were more intelligent, better economists or better informed than their Argentine, Brazilian, and Peruvian counterparts? Armed with this curiosity I went to Uruguay There I found, with no little surprise, that some high officers of the Executive complained quite bitterly about the various constraints that Congress had imposed on the much higher degrees of freedom they would have liked to have in various matters, including indeed economic policy! It happens that in this case of redemocratization, although far from being the perfect institution that nowhere is, Congress effectively came back to work at the moment of democratic installation. Simply, because of constitutional restrictions and historical embedded practices, the President does not have the power to unilaterally decree things such as the *paquetes* of the neighboring countries. The President of Uruguay, for the validity of many of the policies typically contained in those *paquetes,* must go through Congress. In other words, the elements of secrecy and surprise that seem so fundamental to the *paquetes* are *de facto* eliminated. Furthermore, going through Congress means having to negotiate those policies, not only with parties and legislators, but also with various organized interests. Consequently, against the apparent preferences of some members of the Executive, the economic policies of the Uruguayan government were "condemned" to be incremental, rather inconsistent, and limited to quite limited goals—such as achieving the decent performance we have seen, not the heroic goals which the (first) *paquetes* heralded.

I must say that it was in Uruguay that I really learned about the difference of having or not having, as a network of institutionalized powers that texture the policy making process. Or, in other words, between representative and delegative democracy.

The Uruguayan "National Intonation" and "National Coincidence" were responses to the fact that the party winning the presidency had no majority in the two houses of the congress. In 1984 the Colorados had 41 percent of the vote and 42 percent of the seats, and in 1987 the Blancos had respectively 39 percent and 40 percent. This situation is likely in any multiparty system with an electoral system not favoring the largest party very disproportionately. Presidents Sanguinetti and Lacalle both chose to respond to the situation as a parliamentary party leader would have done by expanding the "parliamentary base" of his government, although the strategies of the two men differed considerably, largely because the political contexts were different (transition and consolidation phases). The difference from a typical parliamentary coalition government was that the cabinet members were not leaders of the parties and that neither of the leaders who were the "addressees" of the "understanding" resigned the right to act as "responsible opposition." In a presidential system they were entitled to do so without causing the fall of the government. Those cabinets naturally did not receive an explicit approval in the congress. In policy making President Sanguinetti had to use his veto power frequently.

Bolivia is another country in which the pure model of presidentialism in practice has been modified in ways that are more congruent with parliamentarism.[53] A presidential system assumes that a candidate or a party aggregates a broad basis of support, preferably a majority of those voting. The *voto útil* should eliminate or weaken minor candidacies. Before the elections the weaker parties should form broad coalitions in order to improve the chances of the candidate closest to their views and ultimately to lead to a two-party format. This has not been the case in a number of countries with a presidential system. Bolivia stands out for its fragmented electoral record in presidential elections, with leading candidates gaining less that 30 percent of the vote. Loyalty to parties and leaders on historical, ideological, class, and regional bases is probably more responsible for this pattern than the provision of a decision by the Congress among the three leading candidates. The resulting stalemates in presidential selection and the impossibility for a president of governing without making alliances are contributing to the frustration and considerable volatility of voters and might in the near future facilitate the emergence of a populist candidate running against the parties. (Such a candidate might in turn be blocked by the parties with strength in the congress).

After the last two elections the candidate with the largest plurality did not become president. In the first of these elections the runner-up Paz Estenssoro of the MNR (Movimiento Nacionalista Revolucionario) was chosen, and in 1988 the third in the running, Paz Zamora of the MIR (Movimiento de Izquierda Revolucionario) won; he had the support of the second-place Banzer. This was on the basis of article 90 of the 1967 constitution, which establishes that:

> If none of the candidates for the presidency or the vice presidency obtains the absolute majority of votes, the Congress will consider the three with the largest number of votes for one or another office and make an election among them. If none obtains a majority of the participating representatives in the first round of voting there will be successive votes among the two having obtained most votes until one obtains an absolute majority in a public and continuous session. The president so elected will have a fixed term of four years without being eligible until four years after the end of his mandate.

In a political situation so basically incongruous with an ideal presidential system, Bolivian politics has been working in many ways as if it were parliamentary— with pacts (like the Pacto por la Democracia), multiparty governments, a congressional "vote of no confidence" leading to the resignation of President Siles Suazo in 1985, but without many of the characteristics of a working parliamentary system. The parties making the system work do not explicitly assume responsibility for their actions, and voters cannot make them accountable at election time. The no-reelection principle leads to a reshuffling of the "coalitions" for or after each presidential election. For example, the ADN (Alianza Democrática Nacional) led by Banzer supported the Pacto por la Democracia and MNR president Paz Estenssoro and his policies in the difficult period of economic reform but, after the 1988 presidential elections, shifted its support to Paz Zamora, the candidate of the MIR leading to the Pacto Patriótico rather than to Sánchez de Lozada of the MNR, who had been the framer of the New Economic Policy (NPE) under Paz Estenssoro. The principle of "least distance" in coalition formation did not work.[54]

In the July 1985 presidential election the leader of the ADN, the former dictator general Banzer, obtained 28.6 percent of the vote. He was closely followed by the historic leader of the MNR, Paz Estensorro, with 26.4 percent, the MIR candidate with 8.9 percent, and the Movimiento Nacionalista Revolucionario de Izquierda (MNRI) candidate with 4.8 percent. Other candidates obtained 18.4 percent, and 12.9 percent of votes were blank or void. Since none of the candidates obtained a majority the election went to the congress, where Paz Estensorro, the second-place candidate, obtained 94 votes from MNR, MIR, MNRI, and PDC members, while Banzer received only 51 votes.

In the 1988 election Gonzalo Sánchez de Lozada of the MNR was ahead with 23.07 percent of the vote; he was followed by Banzer (ADN) with 22.70 percent, Paz Zamora (MIR) with 19.64 percent, and CONDEPA (Conciencia de Patria) with 10.98 percent and IU (Izquierda Unida) with 7.18 percent. The alliance between ADN and MIR gave the presidency to Paz Zamora.

While these last two presidential elections according to article 90 of the constitution were fully congruent with politics in a parliamentary system, they ran counter to the logic of presidentialism. Given the minority vote and the small margins between candidates, however, the "parliamentary" coalition making was not illogical. The system remained presidential because, once elected, the president held office for a full term without depending on the confidence of the congress. Introducing the possibility of a vote of nonconfidence, preferably the constructive vote of no confidence, for a president elected by the congress, would transform the Bolivian system easily into a parliamentary one retaining the possibility of a popular presidential election should any candidate obtain an absolute majority.

The Myths of Presidential Leadership and Leaderless Parliamentary Democracy

One strong argument made in favor of presidentialism is that it provides for strong, personalized leadership. This argument ignores the fact that presidents very often are not strong leaders but compromise candidates. While their office endows them with considerable powers, the congress's obstruction might make their leadership impossible, and in the course of their mandate they might lose their capacity for leadership, as examples in recent Latin American history would show. My argument is that strong leadership can be found in many parliamentary systems.

We do not have to turn to the United Kingdom with its two-party system, which assured the leadership of Churchill and more recently of Margaret Thatcher. In continental multiparty systems Adenauer and De Gasperi were able to shape new democracies, and Willy Brandt with a coalition government managed to shift the policies of West Germany decisively. Nor can we ignore the opportunity for leadership enjoyed by Scandinavian prime ministers such as Branting, Tage Erlanger,[55] and Olaf Palme in Sweden, Gerhardsen in Norway, Kreisky in Austria, and Henri Spaak in Belgium, to mention some social democratic prime ministers. In the new southern European democracies, a parliamentary system made possible the leadership of Adolfo Suárez, Felipe González, and even Calvo Sotelo after a coup attempt in 1981 in Spain, of Karamanlis and Papandreou in Greece, and now the prime ministership, with an absolute majority, of Cavacco Silva in Portugal. These have not been leaderless democracies, but at the same time the failure of Suárez and Calvo Sotelo did not endanger democratic institutions, nor were they endangered when conservatives and communists united to force Papandreou's resignation.

I would argue that there is a certain convergence between parliamentary and presidential systems in the fact that, in many democracies, people increasingly vote for a party leader who can govern. They shift their support to the party that promises to sustain such a leader in power and withdraw it from a party that does not have an appealing leader to head the government. The weakening of ideological loyalties and rigidities, the erosion of "kept electorates" by a more homogenized class structure, the growing independence of voters with higher levels of education, and the use of the *voto útil* against minor parties allow strong leaders to appeal directly to the electorate at the same time as they strengthen the appeal of their party and with it their parliamentary base. In contemporary politics the use of television, which permits a leader to appeal directly to the electorate, reinforces that tendency perhaps even too much. Voters in contemporary parliamentary democracies increasingly vote for a party to assure that its leader forms a government, and they vote against the party whose leader does not enjoy their trust. Personalization of leadership makes contemporary parliamentary systems with leaders who know how to use it more similar to presidential systems but without some of the negative consequences I discussed at length in my analysis of presidentialism.

It puts some limit, however, on the capacity of an individual with no party base to appeal directly to the electorate, as shown by the failure of former president Eanes and his PRD (Democratic Renewal Party) and the difficulties that an attractive leader such as Suárez found due to the lack of a strong party's support. In parliamentary systems, to improvise a leader by means of a personal and mass media appeal such as we are seeing today in Brazil would be impossible. Contemporary parliamentary systems cannot be described as unable to produce leadership and stable governments, but they do this without losing the flexibility that I have highlighted as one of their advantages. In fact, they allow, as the long tenure of prime ministers in a number of parliamentary democracies shows, the possibility of continuity in leadership that the no-reelection principle excludes in many presidential systems.

Personalized, even charismatic, leadership is not incompatible with parliamentary democracy, but such a leader has also to gain the confidence of a party, of a cadre of politicians that will supply him with cabinet members, with leaders of parliamentary committees, and with a constant presence in society through elected officials such as governors and mayors. Such a leader in contrast to one in some presidential systems will not be isolated or surrounded only by his personal loyalist technocrats and friends. He or she will be both a national and a party leader and therefore will have more resources to use in governing effectively. I emphasize once more that this is a probability but that no system, either parliamentary or presidential, can assure capable leadership able to gain the confidence of a party and the nation.

Perhaps one of the main advantages of a parliamentary system is that it provides a much larger pool of potential leaders than a presidential system, though this is not true when, for example, a single party has a hegemonic position due to its majority. In a multiparty system in which leaders of all major parties have a reasonable expectation of becoming prime minister or of playing a leading role in the cabinet, the number of aspirants to leadership positions that will enter parliament is likely to be much larger than in most presidential systems. Moreover, in the parliamentary process potential leaders can gain a certain visibility between elections, unless the media are exceedingly controlled by the government. Different leaders can make their reputations in parliamentary debates, in motions of censorship, votes of no confidence, and other public actions. The parliament is in some ways a nursery for potential leaders. In addition, the parliamentary system does not exclude leaders who have lost power; they are likely to sit on the benches of the opposition waiting for their turn, something that defeated presidential candidates often cannot do. In a parliamentary system the leader or leaders of the opposition can make a position clear to the electorate without having to wait for a presidential campaign, which, in any event, is relatively short. They can become visible and identifiable to the voters long before an election. It is no accident that in presidential systems the candidates often do not come from the legislature but have been governors of states where they had a home base of clientelistic links and where they made a reputation. This circumstance produces the important disadvantage that presidential candidates very often have little experience in foreign policy and macroeconomic problems and very weak ties to the legislatures that will have to support their programs and policies. This is true even for the United States and probably for other federal states like Brazil and Argentina.

Many studies have shown that political careers leading to top cabinet positions and ultimately the prime ministership are a function of a combination of loyalty and competence as well as length of time in parliament. Backbenchers can occasionally attack the party leadership and particularly the prime minister and his government, but biting too often is penalized. Even in those parliamentary systems that retain the principle of freedom of conscience of the MP, members who change party are a small minority, quite in contrast to the recent Brazilian experience (see chapter 8).[56] Although the traitors are welcomed in another party they are distrusted and unlikely to make successful political careers, including, with a few notable exceptions, those who contributed to the disintegration of the UCD in Spain. While the incentive structure in parliamentary systems encourages party discipline and therefore consolidation of party organizations, presidential systems have no

such incentives for party loyalty (except where there are well-structured ideological parties). The president can provide personalized incentives to potential supporters, and the success of an individual legislator depends less on the performance of his party in power than on the strength of his more or less clientelistic ties with his constituency. That is why the United States Congress is today still one of the strongest legislatures and one in which individual members have great independence, although other factors, such as the sizable staff and resources that Congress provides to its members and the ideological diversity within the parties, contribute to the same effect.

Presidential systems can have strong parties, but the parties are likely to be ideological rather than government oriented. More often than not presidentialism is associated with weak, fractioned, and clientelistic or personalistic parties. We have only to think of the parties in Brazil, in the Philippines, and more recently in South Korea. Presidentialism might lead to the emergence of leaders, but it is unlikely to lead to party leaders able to govern with sufficient support in the congress, and very often those leaders will turn to nonparty cabinets of experts whose careers depend fully on their competence. In this context, I wonder to what extent the Peronist party can be happy with a cabinet of experts. Those who complain about the weakness of political parties and the poor quality of legislative leadership in some Latin American countries should perhaps look more seriously into the relationship between those conditions and the presidential system.

Presidentialism, Federalism, and Multiethnic Societies

It is sometimes argued that presidentialism is particularly appropriate for federal republics because the presidency can serve as a unifying symbol, especially in the absence of a monarchy, and can represent the nation as a totality in a way a parliament cannot. This argument might sound plausible, and the powerful example of the United States, which combines federalism reflected in an influential senate and a presidency, seems to support it. However, we should not forget the large number of democracies with a federal or quasi-federal structure that have parliamentary government, beginning with a country of the enormous social and cultural heterogeneity and extension of India. The Federal Republic of Germany is another example of combined federalism and parliamentarism, and in fact the Länder and their prime ministers have provided an important pool of candidates to the chancellorship of the republic. Canada and Australia are two other vast federal countries with parliamentary governments. Divergent forms of government account for some of the practical differences between the United States and Canada, particularly their respective party systems.[57] In spite of the strains between Quebec and English-speaking Canada, the parliamentary system probably has contributed to the unity of the country. Switzerland, which is probably the most federal country, not to say confederal, in Europe, has opted for a system that cannot strictly be called parliamentary, given its constitutional conventions, but that also is not presidential. Austria is another federal republic with a parliamentary system, although direct election of the president formally places it in the category of semipresidential or semiparliamentary. In addition, a number of quasi-federal regimes like the Estado de las Autonomías in Spain, the regionalized state in Italy, and the growing federalism in Belgium have developed with parliamentary systems. Certainly in Spain and Belgium the monarchy has served some of the integrative functions attributed to a presidency, and the same can be said about the governor general in the dominions, but the indirectly elected presidents of the Federal Republic of Germany and Italy have often been able to fulfill that same function without the powers normally attributed to a president in a presidential regime.

In some Latin American countries the heavy demographic weight and even greater political weight of some large states with large metropolitan areas would mean that a directly elected president would not be as representative of the whole federation as one in a country whose states were more equilibrated in population and resources. Therefore it would be doubtful to say that presidential systems serve national integration better than parliamentary systems.

One of the negative aspects of Latin American presidentialism has been the use of the power of intervention in the federal states, suspending or displacing authorities and appointing an intervenor with full powers. This practice is not inherent to presidentialism but is rather the result of certain constitutional provisions and their interpretation. Undoubtedly a central government, either a presidential or a parliamentary one, has to have some power to prevent actions by state authorities against the constitution or that represent a threat to public order. As the Argentine history shows, however, it seems dangerous to allow one person to make a decision to intervene without the possibility (except impeachment) of being held accountable by some representative body.[58] This practice has contributed much to the weakness of federalism in a number of Latin American countries. A practice that has weakened federalism in Latin America even more is the appointment of governors by the president. This procedure contradicts any idea of federalism.

The direct election of governors and their unipersonal authority is an indirect consequence, again not necessary but likely, of presidentialism. Such a system creates an inequality of representation because, in the case of multiple competitors for the office, it may deprive the majority of citizens of any chance to participate in the executive of the State, and that executive is in no direct way accountable to the state legislature.

A theme that will become more important in debates about democracy will be how democratic processes either help to solve ethnic, cultural, communal-religious, and linguistic conflicts or exacerbate them.[59] This is not the place to deal seriously with this enormously complex issue. Nor can we provide an answer to the question of presidentialism versus parliamentarism and these conflicts. We are handicapped because presidentialism has prevailed in societies that are relatively integrated ethnically and in societies where the problems mentioned have not yet erupted. For the few cases in which presidentialism has been tried in multiethnic societies—Nigeria and Sri Lanka—the experience has been short lived.

Advocates of presidentialism argue that a president who is elected by a statewide electorate can serve as a symbol of integration in spite of ethnic divisions. The success of such symbolism obviously depends very much on the method of election chosen. A simple plurality in a single election, which might assure hegemony to the largest ethnic group, certainly would not work. The Nigerians have attempted to deal with the problem in their constitution by dividing the country into relatively large, ethnically homogeneous states and requiring that a presidential candidate gain at least 25 percent of the votes in two-thirds of the states of the Nigerian Federation to assure that he does not represent any particular ethnic group or narrow coalition. The candidate must, therefore, seek support all over the country. A union of any two of the three largest groups behind a single candidate would not be sufficient support to reach the required threshold. The distribution formula assumes a territorial concentration of groups—that is, a certain level of homogeneity within areas but heterogeneity among areas. Horowitz discusses the uniqueness of the Nigerian situation and some of the difficulties in applying Nigeria's constitutional provisions elsewhere, specifically in South Africa, as well as the changes needed in the election of the legislature to compliment the election of the president.

One might object that whatever procedure is used in the election, ultimately a unipersonal executive will have to come from one of the ethnic groups and will be perceived as identified with that group. In any conflict in which his group is involved it will be difficult to convince his opponents that he stands above ethnic interests (or to forgo alleging such partisanship). Should this happen and should he fail to solve the problem, the rigidity of the fixed term of office makes it once more difficult to replace the president or to rearrange supporting coalitions. If a president, elected by whatever method, chooses to form a cabinet that neglects or is perceived as neglecting the interests of minorities, the situation cannot be changed (unless the system is premier-presidential or presidential-parliamentary, in which case there are the problems to be discussed).

In a multiethnic society without an absolutely dominant group supporting one party and obtaining an absolute majority, a parliamentary system would offer the possibility of coalition formation and consociational type of agreements, which could provide a flexible response to ethnic conflict. Not only coalition governments but external support for minority prime ministers would provide incentives for negotiation, compromise, and power sharing. Cooptation of leaders of ethnic protest would be possible. Obviously if the political leadership is not committed to the survival of a multiethnic state but to its breakup or to the hegemony of one group by any means, no democratic institutions will be able to function, neither parliamentary nor presidential. Votes then become irrelevant, and clubs rule.

Presidentialism and the Military

One argument used sometimes in favor of presidentialism is that it provides the political system with a personalized leadership that the armed forces can identify with as their supreme commander; it would be more difficult to identify with a prime minister. Such a direct relationship has existed historically between the armed forces and the monarch, and we still find traces of it in European monarchies even after democratization in Europe in the years between wars and today in Spain. Sometimes this relationship has been dangerous to democracy, as in the case of Greece, but when the monarch has been committed to it, as the Spanish king Juan Carlos has been, it can be favorable to the stability of a democracy. Presidents both in presidential and semipresidential systems have been conceived as continuators of the traditional relationship between heads of state and armed forces. This has sometimes meant a strong tendency to elect generals to the presidency, not only in Latin America but in some European countries in the interwar years, such as Finland, Poland, the Weimar Republic with Hindenburg, and Portugal both before and after the Estado Novo.

It is not always clear to what extent such a direct relationship of the armed forces to the president, particularly when he himself is an army officer, has contributed to a weakening of civilian political leadership and political parties. The political practices of the Weimar Republic, in which the high command of the army had direct access to the president without mediation by the cabinet in a semipresidential, semiparliamentary regime, have not been seen by many scholars as contributing to the stability of German democracy. In Portugal similar practices led to a peculiar dyarchy of the parliament and the military, which grew out of a pact between the parties and the MFA (Armed Forces Movement). The initial constitution-making process, which limited the powers of the parliament, and the role of the moderate military in breaking with revolutionary threats gave the armed forces a place not reserved to them in most democratic constitutions. This situation has changed only with recent constitutional reforms. In that context, the directly elected president, himself a military man, had to play an important role.[60] However, it is not assured that a civilian president in a presidential system can play the role of head of the armed forces better than the heads of the military hierarchy subordinated to the minister of defense and through him to the cabinet and the prime minister, as is the case in most democracies.

Undoubtedly, the personalization for a period of time of authority in a president who is both the head of government and the head of state—a symbolic point of reference for the nation when he enjoys widespread legitimacy and support—might be congruent with the value system of a military organization. But in the case of delegitimation and controversy surrounding the president, such a personalized relationship might prompt the military to take unconstitutional actions against the president. A less drastic response would be likely in the case of a less personalized direct and permanent relationship, as in a parliamentary system, where a minister of defense mediates between a prime minister and the armed forces.

The Head of State in Parliamentary Regimes

In analyzing parliamentary regimes—except in biographical and sometimes journalistic writings—political scientists tend to neglect the role of the head of state: monarch, governor general in the British Commonwealth countries, and president in the republics.[61] The role of heads of state is not irrelevant to our main theme because in presidential democracies this role and that of chief executive are not separated. Only if the head of state in parliamentary regimes is assumed to be a decorative figure would the absence of division between these roles in presidentialism be irrelevant. We have already noted some of the tensions generated by confusion of the roles of head of state—the dignified part of the presidential role—and chief executive and often party leader—the object of legitimate controversy and of attack by the opposition.

Without falling into a functionalist teleology—the notion that everything has to have a function, that monarchs and their "successors," the presidents in parliamentary republics, cannot be simply survivals of times past—it seems justified to enquire into these roles. There is evidence that on occasion a king can play an important, perhaps decisive, role, such as that played by King Juan Carlos of Spain at the time of the February 23, 1981, coup attempt. One might object that the king was important on that occasion only because Spanish democracy was not consolidated and the monarchy represented a "backward legitimation" derived from the Franco legacy, but I surmise that something more was at stake. We should not forget that many of the constitutional parliamentary monarchies of Europe survived the crisis of democracy in the twenties and thirties. And if presidents in pure parliamentary republics were irrelevant, it would not make sense for politicians to put so much effort into electing their preferred candidate to the office.

This is not the place to develop a detailed analysis of the roles of heads of state, but we might suggest a few ranging from the apparently trivial to the politically important. A trivial one is the assumption of a large number of "representative" and ceremonial functions in the life of modern states, from receiving credentials of ambassadors to visiting foreign countries to inaugurating meetings and buildings. These activities consume time that, in the case of presidents, is subtracted from governing. Travel abroad for a number of purposes, for which Latin American presidents usually require congressional authorization, is also time consuming. Ceremonial activities of a king or head of state outside of the daily political battles can link the regime to groups that might feel flattered and otherwise alienated, such as intellectuals, artists, and last but not least the military. One advantage is that a nonpartisan figure, if he or she is respected, makes it more difficult for public events to become occasions for delegitimizing protest.

Heads of state, perhaps because they are not pressed by daily business, can also keep informed, maintain contact with a wide range of persons, including the leading politicians, and convey their views privately but with some authority to prime ministers. In fact we know, from the example of Theodor Heuss and Chancellor Adenauer, how such a relationship can develop into one of trust and counsel.[62] No one in a presidential system is institutionally entitled to such a role.

The head of state can play the role of adviser or arbiter by bringing party leaders together and facilitating the flow of information among them. He also can serve as a symbol of national unity in ethnically or culturally divided states; if he had executive functions, this would be difficult to do. This role is one of the important functions of the monarchy in Belgium.

The combination between neutral friend to the parties and their leaders competing for power and dispenser of information and advice is not easy to maintain, and not all heads of state are up to the task. We know little about how that role is performed since discretion surrounds the activities of monarchs and presidents of parliamentary republics. However, differentiating between the roles of head of state and prime minister can be an element favoring compromise, negotiation, and moderation.[63]

Responses to the Critique of Presidentialism

Responses to the implicit critique of presidentialism in my writings have taken four basic directions: (1) admitting the arguments but citing the political culture of Latin America and the weight of tradition; (2) focusing on particular aspects of presidentialism that are not essential to it and are susceptible to reform; (3) favoring semipresidential, semiparliamentary systems; and (4) searching for innovative solutions.

There can be no question of the strength of the presidential tradition in Latin America, but to appeal to tradition could make any innovation impossible. In addition, in many countries the periods of democratic rather than authoritarian presidentialism have been short. Most presidents have been de facto governors deriving power from a coup rather than an election, or from a dubious election. The masses of people by themselves prefer a system they know to something unknown and not understood. It is the task of the elites to explain the earlier failures of presidentialism and their reasons for preferring another system. Even when people acknowledge the failure of presidentialism, as large numbers of Brazilians today do, they will not tend to choose parliamentarism (as Brazilians will be able to do in the 1993 plebiscite) unless their political leaders choose it and advocate it publicly.

The second type of response has much advanced our understanding of presidential systems. There can be no question that specific constitutional or legal reforms (particularly of electoral laws) might improve presidential systems and facilitate governability. I agree with many of them, particularly those related to the impact of the electoral cycle in presidential systems. Others, like a runoff election to avoid, in my view largely mechanically, a president with only minority support, seem more debatable.

The next section discusses, critically, the semipresidential, semiparliamentary regimes.

As to innovative solutions to the problems of presidentialism, I am not enthusiastic, although I confess I have tried to formulate some.

Semipresidential or Semiparliamentary Systems or Bipolar Executive

The success of the Fifth Republic in France has attracted the attention of scholars and politicians and has led to consideration of similar systems as an alternative to both presidentialism and parliamentarism.[64] Such a system has been described in the literature as a bipolar executive, a divided executive, a parliamentary presidential republic, a quasi-parliamentary and a semipresidential government, and most recently by Shugart and Carey as a premier-presidential system, indicating how different those systems can be both in theory and practice.[65] The list of countries that have experimented with or instituted such regimes is fairly long, and all those who write about the regimes, particularly Maurice Duverger, agree that they function very differently.[66] In fact, Arend Lijphart has argued that these systems are not syntheses of parliamentary and presidential systems but rather systems that alternate between presidential and parliamentary phases.[67]

Basically, dual executive systems have a president who is elected by the people either directly or indirectly, rather than nominated by the parliament, and a prime minister who needs the confidence of parliament. Other characteristics not always found but often associated with dual executive systems are: the president appoints the prime minister, although he needs the support of the parliament, and the president can dissolve the parliament. This is a significant break with the principle of separation of powers. In presidential systems we find this power only in the 1980 Pinochet constitution of Chile, in Paraguay (which has no history of democratic government), in Uruguay (where it exists only in very special cases and has never been invoked), and in the 1979 Peruvian pseudoparliamentary constitution. In dual executive systems, to dissolve the parliament the president needs the agreement— the countersignature—of the prime minister, but since the president names the prime minister, he is likely to find someone who will support dissolution. It was this combination of presidential power to dissolve the Reichstag and freedom to appoint a chancellor who would countersign the dissolution that led, at the end of the Weimar Republic, to the fateful elections in which the Nazis gained strength and finally, in the semifree March 1933 election, a majority. Sometimes the president can bypass parliament by claiming emergency powers and calling for a referendum. Powers assigned to the president and the prime minister vary appreciably, both legally and even more in practice, but in contrast to the monarch or the pres-

ident in parliamentary systems, the president in these systems is not a symbolic figure but enjoys potential if not actual power to affect policies and the governmental
process.)

These systems have emerged under very special and unique circumstances in
quite different countries.[68] Attention is mainly focused on the Fifth Republic, and
it is often forgotten that one of the first democracies that experimented with this
model was the Weimar Republic. It is surprising to find little attention paid to the
way that democracy operated when dual executive systems are discussed today. Arguments for the introduction of such a system were first formulated by Max Weber.
Hugo Preuss, the drafter of the Weimar constitution, followed Weber, with some
differences in emphasis. Dual executive systems used today are not very different
from those formulated in Weimar Germany.[69] Another outstanding example of
such a regime is that of Finland, while three other cases—Austria after 1929, Iceland, and Ireland—have worked fundamentally as parliamentary systems even
though they have some of the characteristics of semipresidential systems, by my
definition.[70] More recently Portugal, influenced by the French model, has attempted to introduce such a system,[71] and semipresidential systems have been discussed in Latin America in the course of recent transitions, although they have not
been institutionalized in constitutional reforms.[72] Some elements of the Weimar
experience were also influential in shaping the Spanish constitution of 1931. The
contrast between Weimar and the Fifth Republic already tells us that the relationship between this type of system and the stability of democracy is not unambigu-
ous. In all cases in which such a system has been introduced, particular historical
circumstances contributed decisively to its enactment. It should not be forgotten
that all European democracies in 1918 were constitutional monarchies, with the exception of Switzerland and France. At that point, the French Third Republic with
its *régime d'assemblée* was not an attractive model, and therefore Germany, after
abolishing the monarchy, turned to political innovation. Originally the aim of Max
Weber and others was to establish a parliamentary monarchy after the British
model. The impossibility of doing so and certain characteristics of the German
party system, the federal character of the state, and concerns about leadership in
Germany's difficult international position led to a directly elected president without abandoning the parliamentary tradition already established. A strong leader
was wanted for the new democracy, but full presidentialism with separation of
powers, as in the United States, was not considered.

The 1919 German constitution, approved in Weimar, established a semipresidential, semiparliamentary system. The president was popularly elected for a seven-
year term and could be reelected. He appointed and dismissed the chancellor, who
selected the cabinet, although the Kanzler needed the confidence of parliament.
With the signature of the chancellor, the president could dissolve the Reichstag.
Should the chancellor refuse, the president could dismiss him and appoint another
who would dissolve the Reichstag and call a new election, governing in the interim.

Naturally as long as the Reichstag was able to produce a majority supporting a government, it was not dissolved, but without a majority there was the possibility of presidential cabinets and short-lived governments, leading to repeated elections in the hope of producing a Reichstag majority. In addition the president had direct command of the armed forces and was able to give *"unmittelbare Befehle."* He also had the wide powers of article 48 in emergency situations. All these powers played an important role in the demise of the Weimar democracy.

In Finland, where many on the right wanted to establish a constitutional monarchy, the impossibility of doing so and the fear of hegemony of the left, which was distrusted, led to the peculiar compromise that has lasted until today.[73]

In many cases, as in France in 1958–62, a major factor in introducing a dual executive government was distrust of political parties, although the functioning of such a system ultimately depends on parties and the relationship between the president and the parties and the party system. The idea of a neutral power arbitrating between the parties or above them was very appealing in countries where polarization between parties made parliamentarism difficult, as was the case in Austria's constitutional reform of 1929, which was practically abandoned in 1931.

As Bartolini[74] has shown in great detail, dual executive systems have been introduced in countries that achieved their independence from another country or from a dominating power and sought a symbol of the new nation. This was to some extent the case in Finland but more particularly in Ireland and Iceland after independence. Popular legitimation was wanted to give the president in a new democracy or new state some of the dignity of the disappeared monarch.

The circumstances that led to a dual executive system in Portugal are more complex because of the uncertainties of a transition to democracy via military coup. The possibility of having a general as president to arbitrate between the legislature, representing political parties, and the Council of the Revolution, representing first the Movement of Armed Forces (MFA) and later the armed forces, is a feature of the Portuguese system that imitates the French model. Later constitutional reforms (1982) and a change in the party system (particularly when the government has majority support) has led to an increased parliamentarization of the system.[75]

The particular crisis of the Fourth Republic, brought to a head by the Algerian war and the coup of May 13, 1953, as well as the unique historical role of Charles de Gaulle led to the Fifth Republic. It could even be argued that in France and in Portugal one of the considerations for introducing a bipolar system was to assure subordination of the army to a president who had particular legitimacy with the armed forces, as was the case with Charles de Gaulle and with President Eanes.[76]

A formalistic legal and constitutional analysis of these regimes in our view does not reveal the entire truth and is even misleading. Even an analysis of actual party constellations in the assembly and of the president's support is not sufficient. The underlying and conflicting conceptions of the political system that often have led to the introduction of bipolar regimes, and the ambiguities and compromises re-

sulting from them, explain the lack of consensus in the interpretation of constitutional roles and the partisan alignments supporting the powers of the president or
the assembly and the prime minister that are reflected in the debates of constitutional lawyers and that can become critically important in a crisis of the regime.
Advocates of bipolar regimes should give more serious attention to the complex
(and well-studied) Weimar experience.

The systems that can broadly be classified as dual executive show many significant differences in powers attributed to the president by the constitution. These
powers do not always coincide with actual powers exercised at least at some stages.
As Duverger[77] notes in his discussion of seven cases, in three of them the president
plays an important role, in the fourth he could play an important role, and in the
other three his role is weak; in none of the cases is the strength of the presidency a
reflection of the formal constitutional powers given it. In addition, analysis of
Weimar by Kaltefleiter[78] and others shows how the same institution worked very
differently under different circumstances and more specifically different relationships between the president and the party system. The same can be said for the
Fifth Republic, although the fact that the president has lacked a majority in the parliament for only a short period (1986–88) makes the pattern more consistent.

As with all political institutions, it is impossible to analyze the performance of a
bipolar regime independently of the larger political system, most specifically the
party system and the complex historical situation. In fact, I suspect that this is truer
of bipolar regimes than of other types of government. It would be a simplification
to attribute the stability of the Fifth Republic in France to the introduction of a new
constitution because simultaneously an important change was introduced in the
electoral system with a shift from proportional representation to a two-round majority system (1958–86). After the return to proportional representation in 1986, a
threshold for representation was introduced. The strong electoral system, to use the
terminology of Sartori, combined with a presidential system and its institutionalization under the very personal leadership of de Gaulle, produced a fundamental
change in the party system and with it the political system. It is impossible to separate the impact of the constitutional change from the impact of the change in electoral system, but let us not forget that Michel Debré, the mastermind of the Fifth
Republic's constitution, had written that "the electoral procedure is a more serious
question than the separation of powers" and that, in contrast to Weimar, Finland,
and Austria, France initially abandoned proportional representation.

We should not forget either that the final consolidation of the Fifth Republic coincided with the historic crisis of communism, the minor ally and potential competitor with the Socialist party. In addition, once France overcame the final decol-
onization crisis under the leadership of de Gaulle, the republic has faced no
comparable crisis. In comparing the Fourth and Fifth Republics it is only fair to remember these facts and the European context after World War II, with the threat of
a potentially disloyal communist opposition and the principled opposition of the

Gaullist RPF (Rassemblement du Peuple Français) to the institutions of the Fourth Republic.

The literature on these regimes leads to the conclusion that the system can work approximating either a presidential model or a parliamentary one with a president who exercises influence but not power. This depends only in part on the institutional design and the intention of those introducing the system and much more on the party constellation in each situation. Raymond Aron in 1981 wrote, "The president of the republic is the supreme authority as long as he has a majority in the national assembly, but must abandon the reality of power to the prime minister if ever a party other than his own has a majority in the assembly".[79] This is what happened in France in 1986, in Portugal after 1982, and for significant periods in Finland. In no case has the system worked as half-presidential and half-parliamentary, with the president and the prime minister jointly heading the government. The Fifth Republic instead of semipresidential has most often been presidential and only occasionally parliamentary. Duverger reaches the same conclusion: that the Fifth Republic is not a synthesis of parliamentary and presidential systems but an alternation between presidential and parliamentary phases. Those who defend the distinctiveness of the two types of regime can argue, however, that the parliamentary mode of a bipolar system (the majority supporting the prime minister is different from the majority that elected the president) does not work fully like a parliamentary system because constitutionally the president has powers that are specific to him and because tasks may be functionally divided.

Sartori criticizes Duverger, noting that in the case of cohabitation the system does not turn strictly parliamentary because a popularly elected president retains certain powers and an autonomous legitimacy. The presidency adapts to the circumstances but does not transform itself. The problem is: will it adapt itself or embark on a conflictual course, particularly if a dissolution and new elections confirm the duality?[80]

It could be argued that the system can work as a purely presidential system with the parliament totally secondary. This would be the case when a fractionalized and ineffective parliament is incapable of supporting a prime minister. In such a situation, the prime minister would be only an alter ego of the president tolerated by the parliament. To some extent that was the situation of Brüning. As that example shows, the system then would depend on the absence of strain between the prime minister and the president, something unlikely when the president and his entourage, as in the case of Hindenburg, have an agenda that is in conflict with that of the prime minister. The system in that case does not assure government stability.

I would argue that as much or more than a pure presidential system, a dual executive system depends on the personality and abilities of the president. At the same time, the responsibility becomes diffuse and additional conflicts are possible and even likely, creating situations in which a fixed term of office compounds the problem.

It is important to analyze in some detail the situations in which the system has worked well to a considerable extent independently of the personality of the president. Kaltefleiter in his detailed analysis of the presidencies of Ebert and of Hindenburg in his first term and the commentators on the Fifth Republic have highlighted the conditions under which this has been the case. Incidentally, it is important to remember that neither Ebert nor de Gaulle were popularly elected when they first assumed their presidencies. Ebert was chosen by the legislature in an indirect election. Their initial success therefore was not due to a plebiscitary popular election that produced the leadership that Max Weber had in mind. Kaltefleiter's conclusion is that the influence of the president is primarily the consequence of support by his party and not of his office. The system does not eliminate the problems of the party system; on the contrary the party system controls the success of the system. Optimally, the president is also the leader of his party and that party has a majority in the parliament. This has been the fortunate circumstance in which de Gaulle, Pompidou, and to a lesser extent Scharf in Austria and more recently Mitterand have found themselves. One could argue that President de Gaulle was able to generate that kind of party support, but it is doubtful whether his success was due to his personal appeal in a crisis situation or to the office he held, and how much it has to be attributed to the change in the electoral system. Bipolar systems have also worked well with a president who has considerable influence on his party, as was the case with Scharf in Austria, and with a president who does not have great influence on the parties, but a structured party system is able to provide a parliament that supports the government, as has been the case with other presidents in Austria.

The situation is very different with unstructured party systems, polarized multipartism, and great party fractionalization. In such a context, a president who is also the leader of an important party, such as Ebert in his first presidency and Kekkonen in Finland, can use his position to bring the party to work with others and provide relatively stable government. However, the case of Ebert shows that such a policy is likely to erode the power of the president within his party, since inevitably his positions will not be those of a party leader. He might still exercise considerable influence on his party, as Ebert did during his second presidency and as most Finish presidents have; in this case he might govern jointly with a prime minister. The situation becomes much more difficult for a president who has no great influence in his party or any party and has to support policies with which he disagrees or else undermine the parliamentary government. In such situations when the party system is weak, even expressing an opinion that coincides with the opposition contributes to a growing crisis. The case of Alcalá-Zamora in Spain in the thirties illustrates these problems well. Presumably such a situation could be resolved by dissolving the parliament, as the constitution theoretically permits, in order to produce a majority supporting a prime minister compatible with the president. However that solution would not work if the electorate returned to power the party or coalition supporting the prime minister. In that case, the president might very well be forced to resign or grudgingly abdicate power. The incompatibility between the president with considerable powers and a parliament in which a party or parties not acceptable to him are in the majority can lead to a serious impasse generating a crisis of the political system.

Kaltefleiter refers to the situation of a stalemated, fractionalized party system that is unable to produce a government, in which case the reserve powers of the president become decisive. But the system does not become purely presidential; at most it is a constitutional dictatorship using emergency powers. Such a situation, as the second presidency of Hindenburg shows, has built-in elements of extraordinary instability because there is no real division of powers and the president cannot govern without the support of a legislature, which, however, is unable to provide support for him. The situation ends up being similar to the worst of the true presidential systems with an ineffective and rebellious congress.

In the case of Weimar, the possibility of relying on the powers of the president contributed to a disastrous outcome. It made it easier for the parties to abdicate their responsibility to provide a parliamentary government and led to the parliament's toleration of Brüning, to the successive presidential cabinets when Hindenburg withdrew support from Brüning, and then to the constant search for a majority for the presidentially appointed chancellors. Successive elections in a period of economic and political crisis allowed the Nazis to become the strongest party in the parliament and finally led Hindenburg to appoint Hitler chancellor in the hope that he and his allies would be able to obtain a majority, which they finally got in the semifree election of March 1933.[81]

(It would require a careful analysis to discover advantages of a bipolar system under the most favorable conditions, which as I have said are that (1) the president is the leader of, or a highly influential figure in, one of the major parties and (2) the party can form a coalition with an absolute majority in a parliamentary government that is able to work with the president) What are the advantages over a purely parliamentary government? They are difficult to define without entering into more details than space permits here, but presumably a bipolar system allows the president to change the prime minister and to change policies without creating a crisis in the system or even within the party that forms the government. This has been the case of Mitterand with changes in the direction of a socialist party in the parliament from interventionism to a more liberal policy. It is hard to say if such a change could have been generated within the party in the parliament in the absence of a president and therefore of the party's interest in holding together for the purpose of winning the presidency again. Some would argue that another advantage of a bipolar system is that responsibility for failure can be pushed onto the prime minister, leaving the president untouched. However, this possibility does not contribute to the emergence of responsible and cohesive parties. Some proponents emphasize that a dual executive allows the prime minister to assume a more powerful role whenever the president is unable to exercise his role effectively. This idea assumes that the president does not cling to his power and that he has no right of dissolution to use against a prime minister supported by the party that has withdrawn confidence from him.

Suleiman, in chapter 5 herein, notes that instability and inefficiency develop even when the president and the prime minister are supported by the same party or party coalition. Inevitably the president has his own staff and can develop policies that are at odds with those of his prime minister. Moreover, members of the cabinet with direct access to the president might bypass the prime minister and turn to the president to overrule the decisions of the prime minister, who then is in an embarrassing situation. The result inevitably is a lot of politicking and intrigues that may delay decision making and lead to contradictory policies due to the struggle between the president and the prime minister. The French experience under Mitterand shows that the system does not assure maximal efficacy.

In conclusion, it can be argued that a bipolar system might work, but not necessarily as its promoters intended. It can work when it becomes de facto a parliamentary system, as it has done in Ireland, Iceland, and Austria in the Second Republic, or when the party or parties supporting the president and those with a majority in the chamber are the same, and exceptionally when a very adroit politician realizes that he must permit a prime minister with majority support in the parliament to exercise power. However, bipolarity is probably not an effective system for overcoming the problems of a polarized or fractionalized party system, unless it is combined with other important circumstances, such as the electoral changes under the Fifth Republic, the historical crisis of the French Communist party, or the exceptional leadership qualities of Charles de Gaulle in the first years of the Fifth Republic. In the face of a weak or ineffective party system, contrary to what some of its proponents hoped, it is only an apparent therapy, to use the expression of Kaltefleiter.[82] It cannot overcome the weaknesses of a party system. *lt (sornlity*

The other implicit danger of an authoritarian interpretation of the powers of the president is exemplified by the way in which Carl Schmitt shifted the interpretation of the Weimar constitution. He used his notion of the *Hüter der Verfassung* (the guardian of the constitution)[83] to create the image of a leader who was above and against the parties, which ultimately led to the Führerstaat's breaking with the democratic liberal tradition. Such a danger cannot be excluded when the presidency is occupied by a populist leader who personalizes power or by a military man who can use his military constituency to consolidate his power against the legislature.

In view of some of the experiences with this type of system it seems dubious to argue that in and by itself it can generate democratic stability.[84] Some of the conditions favorable to the success of a bipolar system are to some extent the same as those that assure stable parliamentary government, namely, a parliament in which the parties are able to give support to a prime minister but with the additional condition that the prime minister can work well with the president.

Excursus: The President in the Spanish Republic, 1931–1936

The Spanish Republic (1931–36) has not been included in the analysis of semi-presidential, semiparliamentary regimes for the obvious reason that the president was not popularly elected but indirectly elected by the parliament and elected members of an electoral college. However title V of the 1931 constitution granted him powers that exceeded those of presidents in parliamentary democracies.[85] The most important was that the prime minister had to have the *double confidence* of the president and the unicameral chamber. The presidential confidence was strengthened by the fact that nonconfidence motions required an absolute majority of the chamber. Only the president could appoint and dismiss the prime minister, which meant that he could veto political leaders he considered unsuitable regardless of their strength in the chamber, but the parliament also had the power to deny its support to the president's appointee. In addition, the president had the power to dissolve the legislature twice during his mandate and to call for new elections, a faculty of which Niceto Alcalá-Zamora made use in 1933 and 1936. He also presided over cabinet meetings and intervened in them. On the other hand, the parliament convened after the second dissolution could decide whether the dissolution was necessary, and a negative vote by a majority of the legislature would lead to the president's removal (article 81). This article was applied in 1936 although the dissolution of the rightist legislature led to one dominated by the Popular Front.

It would be too complex and long to discuss the way in which President Alcalá-Zamora conceived his office, the ambiguities of the constitution, the decisions Alcalá-Zamora made, his clashes with the main party leaders, his conflicts with Prime Minister Lerroux, the presidential veto of Gil Robles (the leader of the CEDA [Confederación Española de Derechas Autónomas], the largest party in the 1933–36 legislature), the presidential government of 1935 that dissolved the Cortes, the attempt to form a center bloc led by Alcalá-Zamora in the February 1936 election, and his ouster by the Popular Front–dominated parliament on April 3, 1936. Although there is considerable debate[86] on how much the presidential component of the constitution and the personality of Alcalá-Zamora contributed to the crisis of the republic and ultimately to the civil war, there can be no doubt that the *double confidence* model contributed to the instability of the republic. To the extent that it fits into the model of premier-presidentialism, the Spanish system of these years does not support the hopes some scholars and politicians have for that type of regime.[87] It at least shows that such a model depends enormously on the personality of the incumbent (an unpredictable factor) and that it cannot serve to overcome the problems derived from a polarized multiparty situation. Significantly the immovability of a president who exercised the power to veto possible parliamentary governments and who might dissolve parliament led to discussion among the military (at the end of 1935) of intervention, and Gil Robles, the leader of the CEDA, might have acquiesced in such plans if there had been consensus, particularly if Franco, the most prestigious general, had been ready to support them.

Alcalá-Zamora during the Constituent Assembly debates already noted the ambiguities of the text. He asked: shall the president use the *Gaceta* (publication containing laws and decrees) or just wear a tailcoat? Shall he lay cornerstones or be stoned?[88]

The Dual Executive and the Military

A constitutional and political problem connected with the dual executive model that deserves considerable attention is the question of who has authority over the armed forces, the president or his prime minister. The question is particularly relevant because most democratic constitutions, even in parliamentary systems, in continuity with the traditional conception of the monarch as supreme commander of the armed forces view the president as the symbolic head of the military. There can be no question that an elected president in a pure presidential system is the head of the armed forces, even though the actual military policy making is delegated to the secretary of defense, who might or might not be a civilian and whom the president appoints freely. In a pure parliamentary system, the appointment of the defense minister or the ministers of the armed forces falls to the prime minister, who forms the entire cabinet. In fact, the exigencies of modern warfare have led to the appointment of a minister of defense rather than ministers of the three branches of the armed forces in order to assure better coordination among them. This innovation has been desired not only by civilians but by the most competent military professionals to reduce interservice rivalries and lack of coordination. One of the symbols of the supremacy of the constitutionally legitimated political authority in many democracies has been selection of a civilian minister of defense from the political leadership. This solution has not always been considered undesirable by the military because a politician can more efficiently represent the interests of the armed forces to the political leadership than one of their peers with less political skill.

A dual executive system is likely to have at least three major actors and very often four: the president, the prime minister, the minister of defense, and generally a joint chief of staff who has the immediate command of the forces. The hierarchical line that is so central to military thinking acquires a new complexity. Will the president act through the minister of defense? Or will the minister of defense establish a direct relationship with the president bypassing the prime minister and reporting directly to the president, who makes decisions without necessarily informing and obtaining the consent of the prime minister?

Such a direct, simple hierarchical relationship would be welcomed by the military. It would symbolize the distinctiveness of the military sphere and the withdrawal of military politics from broader political considerations and control by the parliament. Such a pattern would be even more likely if the minister of defense were a military person whose loyalty would not be to a political team at the head of the government but to a president–commander in chief "above parties." A president who sees himself as a representative of the nation and above parties is not unlikely to find a personal relationship with his minister of defense and through him with the armed forces, and to some extent to realize his function of moderating political conflicts and thereby consolidating the regime. In so doing, he, unwittingly perhaps, exempts the military from civilian political control.

Such a pattern is likely to lead to greater stability in the office of the minister of defense if he has the support of the armed forces' top leadership, while, in turn, his position in the cabinet might be reinforced by the trust of the president and the head of the military establishment. It was not an accident that in the Weimar Republic between 1919 and 1933 there were twenty cabinets and only four ministers of defense.[89] Once a personal relationship is established between the president and the minister of defense and the heads of the military establishment, the president is likely to see any interference in that relationship by the prime minister as undesirable and to jealously guard the autonomy of the military establishment. Such patterns would be especially congenial to a president with a military background. Such presidents have sometimes been elected in democracies where subordination of the military was a major issue or where the military could represent itself as above parties, as in the case of Hindenburg, Mannerheim in Finland, Eanes in Portugal, and last but not least de Gaulle. All of those presidents in dual executive systems enjoyed a special relationship with the armed forces.

Let us assume a situation in which the prime minister represents a different party or party coalition than the president and is able to impose his choice for the ministry of defense over the preferences of the president. Suppose that the defense minister enters into conflict with the high command of the armed forces. Is it not likely in such a situation that the top levels of the military establishment, finding the president more sympathetic to their point of view, would make use of their special relationship with the president to approach him in his capacity as commander in chief, bypassing the prime minister and the minister of defense? Such a situation would place the prime minister and his minister of defense in a very difficult position should the president attempt to use his reserve powers to propose or veto military policies and appointments.[90]

The system, therefore, involves a latent political and even constitutional crisis. Let me note that even in a constitutional monarchy like Spain, where the powers of the king are very well defined and the political responsibility for leading the country is clearly in the hands of the prime minister and his cabinet, including the minister of defense, this issue has been quite delicate. At some point the military has turned to the king directly, bypassing the political leadership. How much more would this be the case in the situation of a dual executive? The constitution for such a regime should define clearly the legal status of each executive so that their positions would not have to be resolved in a crisis situation by their respective power bases, leaving it to the military establishment to choose which of the two democratically legitimated authorities is most favorable to its interests. The dual executive model has room for constitutional ambiguities regarding one of the central issues of many democracies: the subordination of the military to the democratically elected authorities and hopefully to civilian supremacy.

Why Are Semipresidential, Semiparliamentary Solutions Attractive?

In view of these considerations we might ask ourselves why this system of dual executive, semipresidential or semiparliamentary government, or premier-presidentialism is attractive to many democrats confronted with the crisis and failures of presidentialism and unwilling to consider parliamentarism.[91] Undoubtedly, the apparent success of the Fifth Republic has generated much of the interest in this type of system, but some other cases, particularly the Weimar Republic and the elements of a mixed system, though not strictly speaking semipresidential, of the Spanish Republic in 1931–36, have been insufficiently considered. In the Latin American context, with its strong tradition of presidentialism, the introduction of a mixed system is perhaps to many an indirect, even surreptitious, way to move toward parliamentarism, assuming that parliamentary practices could be introduced while retaining the symbols of presidentialism. The mixed system is, therefore, the result of an unwillingness to dare to make a radical change in constitutional tradition. My own opinion is that the negative experience that many countries have had with presidential regimes offers an extraordinary opportunity for constitutional innovation, but this is not the consensus of politicians and constitutionalists in Latin America, although some voices have come out clearly in favor of parliamentarism.

To know better the difficulties and weaknesses of the dual executive model, let us look a little bit closer at the conditions under which such a system can be transformed into a parliamentary system, which is the aim of some of those advocating it, even when they might not confess it publicly. After all, the examples of Ireland, Iceland, and Austria show that such a development can take place. I have to confess that I do not see this as an easy political development, but I would not exclude the possibility of using the dual executive model as a transitional system that ultimately would become a parliamentary system. Such a process would require a number of conditions that, while not impossible, in my view are somewhat unlikely. They are the following: the major parties would agree on electing the president by consensus, and the president would not be strongly identified with any party and would not be eager to exercise his powers. Essentially it would involve the choice of a personality with high prestige who would be acceptable to almost everybody except those on the extremes of the political spectrum and who would be ready to act as a neutral arbitrator under extreme circumstances but who would have no ambition to exercise power. I do not think it is always easy to find a person satisfying these requirements. Besides, such an agreement or tacit understanding among the parties would not be enforceable; a major party could break it by supporting a strong candidate. With such an understanding, all the leaders of major parties, the men and women with ambition to govern the country, would run for seats in the congress and be ready to search for a majority in the legislature in order to form a government in which they could act as powerful parliamentary prime ministers, respecting the symbolic status and the influence of the president. This would be a true semiparliamentary system under the cover of a semipresidential constitution. I wonder if in Latin America the parties and the leaders with ambition to govern would be willing to forsake a competition for the presidency and to compete for power in parliament in order to gain a vote of confidence.

Even if such a "gentlemen's" agreement is reached, no one can assume that it would become an unwritten rule. Besides, an outsider, a populist candidate, could always denounce such a pact. Perhaps a suggestion of a Bolivian politician could initiate the change: require that a presidential candidate "above parties" be nominated by two-thirds of the members of the congress. Such a majority would not agree to nominate anyone with ambition to govern. But the voters would still have to legitimize that choice.

If the presidency is occupied by a powerful personality, a leader of a major party, the system is not likely to move into the parliamentary mold. If the president has support in the congress, the system is likely to remain presidential, that is, a system with implications already discussed.

Presidentialism with the "Cover" of a Presidential Prime Minister

In view of some discussions about introducing parliamentary components in presidential systems in Latin America, it is important to stress that a prime minister who heads a cabinet and directs an administration, is freely appointed and dismissed by the president, and does not need the confidence of parliament is not to be confused with the semipresidential, semiparliamentary constitutional model. Creating such an office is only a form of delegating presidential powers, which might allow the president to avoid some criticism and to displace it onto the prime minister. However, the powers of such a prime minister and his ministers would not be very different from those of secretaries in the cabinets of presidential regimes, who are given considerable autonomy to run their departments, or from the autonomy of a national security adviser who makes important decisions that are presumably reviewed by the president. In such a system, the president continues to be the only and ultimate decision maker and legitimator of decisions made by others.

The possibility that such a prime minister and his ministers might be members of the legislature does not change the situation. In fact, in some parliamentary systems ministerial office is incompatible with membership in parliament. The possibility that these officers might be subject to questions or interpellations by the parliament does not change the matter either, although it gives more power to the legislature. After all, the members of the United States Cabinet constantly appear before Congress. Only the possibility of a vote of censure obliging the president to dismiss a minister represents a true shift of power to parliament. However, as long as the president is free to appoint a successor to a dismissed minister who does not need the confidence of the chamber, the system is still basically presidential. It would be a system, however, in which the legislative majority would have the capacity to frustrate presidential policy, indirectly to veto his decisions without making the chamber and the parties of the majority responsible, particularly when the president has no power of dissolution.

The presidential power of dissolution would violate the assumptions of the separation of powers and further encourage presidential absolutism because the president's mandate would not be affected by the adverse response of the electorate until the next presidential election.[92] In fact, if the electorate were to give its support to the same party or party constellation, the president would be seriously weakened and the conflict between the president and the legislature would become even more visible and acute. Only if the president then allows the prime minister to govern will the system become semiparliamentary. His refusal to do so would probably create a serious constitutional crisis.

A presidential cabinet that might be overthrown by the legislature, without the capacity to impose its own choice as prime minister, combined with a president who lacks the power of dissolution, would be an unviable solution and less stable than separation of powers in a presidential system or the model of dual confidence of most semipresidential, semiparliamentary systems.

Such an institutional arrangement is a formula for permanent, sometimes cumulative conflict between the two powers, with no resolution. The president survives but is frustrated and sometimes increasingly stalemated, but the legislature cannot change the president's political course if he is not ready to seek a compromise.

One example of pseudoparliamentarism is provided by the Peruvian constitution of 1979. The president names the prime minister to head the cabinet, and both jointly name the ministers, but the parliament can censure the cabinet or individual ministers by simple majority vote. If the chamber votes no confidence in three cabinets, the president can dissolve the chamber, although only once per term and not during the last year of a term. The president can be weakened, and a process of confrontation put into motion, but the president remains in office for his fixed term and can continue to appoint ministers.

One of the ways in which the congress can weaken or frustrate a president without assuming responsibility for making policy (except negatively) is by censuring members of presidential cabinets and forcing their dismissal. Some legislatures have this power. The regime continues being presidential (contrary to the opinion of Shugart and Carey) because the president appoints successors to the dismissed ministers, but he cannot threaten the legislature with dissolution. This is a formula for permanent, sometimes cumulative, conflict between the two powers with no resolution. The president survives but is frustrated, and the same is true for the opposition majority in the legislature, which cannot change his political course if he is not ready to seek a compromise.

Presidentialism, Parliamentarism, and Democratic Stability

My analysis of the problematic implications of presidentialism for democracy should not be read as implying that no presidential democracy can be stable. But the odds in many societies are not favorable. It should not be read either as arguing that parliamentary democracies always assure stability, but they provide greater flexibility in the process of transition to and consolidation of democracy. Nor does this analysis indicate that any type of parliamentary regime will do. In fact, the analysis is incomplete without a discussion of the type of parliamentary regime and its particular institutional arrangements, including electoral laws, that could best achieve democratic stability.

All regimes depend, however, on the willingness of society and all major social forces and institutions to contribute to their stability. They depend also on the consensus to give legitimacy to authority acquired by democratic processes, at least for the time between elections and within the limits of the constitution. Ultimately, all regimes depend on the capacity of political leaders to govern, to inspire trust, to have a sense of the limits of their power, and to achieve a minimum of consensus. Our argument has been that these qualities are even more important in a presidential regime, where they are more difficult to achieve in such circumstances. A dependency on the qualities of a political leader, which the leader at any particular moment might or might not have, involves greater risks. My aim here has been to revive a debate on the role of alternative democratic institutions in building stable democracies.

Parliamentarism and Party System

One of the main arguments made against parliamentary systems is that they require relatively disciplined parties, a level of party loyalty, a capacity of parties to work together, and the absence or isolation of antisystem parties. There can be no question that political parties play a central role in a parliamentary system, while in a presidential system the personal leadership and charisma of a presidential candidate can presumably overcome or ignore a fractionalized and unstructured party system.[93] Let us say that party systems in parliamentary regimes have been extremely varied, ranging from two-party systems to polarized multiparty systems, and that probably the type of party system is related more to the electoral law than to whether the regime is parliamentary or presidential. It is argued that a presidential system tends toward a two-party system, but the evidence is inconclusive, particularly when we think of the case of Chile and the multiparty system in Finland, and even in France today. South Korea after its return to democracy might also be cited, although the fusion of parties could be seen as a move toward a two-party format (if it were not a search for hegemony). Although the March 1992 congressional elections confirmed the multiparty system, the presidential election of December 18, 1992, in which Kim Young Sam received 42 percent of the vote, his opponent Kim Dae Jung, 34 percent, and the outsider (the president of Hyundai), 16 percent seems to conform to the two-party format that is congenial to presidentialism.

Given the congruence of two-party systems with presidentialism, one would assume that in countries with a two-party tradition the restoration of democracy or the continuity of democratic politics should have consolidated bipartism. This, however, is not always the case: in Colombia the leftist Alianza Democrática M-19 could obtain 12.5 percent of the vote in the April 1990 presidential election and 26.8 percent of the vote in the December 1990 election to the constituent assembly. In Uruguay the recent gains by the Frente Amplio, including the mayoralty of Montevideo, have broken the two-party format. In addition party fragmentation in Brazil and Peru is greater than in the past. Multipartism is probably here to stay in Latin America, with the exceptions of Costa Rica, Venezuela, and Argentina. In cases such as Chile it is well structured and institutionalized; in others, such as Brazil, it is highly unorganized and volatile. There is no sign that the party systems are accommodating to a presidential institutional format.

The argument is made that the absence of disciplined parties, the narrow, localist interests represented by the parties or by individual deputies, and the instability of party loyalties in many Latin American countries are obstacles to the introduction of parliamentarism. The question is to what extent this kind of party system and type of parties in Latin American congresses are results of a presidential system with a weak congress, sometimes reinforced by proportional representation electoral systems. I would argue that since parties are not responsible and accountable for government stability and policy, because those are the tasks of the president, they are likely to concentrate their efforts on opposing, criticizing, and perhaps fiscalizing the executive, but not to give it support, respond to its policy initiatives, or assume responsibility for them. It is only natural that once a president is elected, parties are likely to turn to their distinctive partisan agendas in the congressional elections and, even if they were part of the president's electoral coalition, assert their distinctiveness by criticizing the president. It is also natural that, not having responsibility for national policy, they would turn to the representation of special interests, localized interests, and clientelistic networks in their constituencies. There is no reason for them to care about the success of a president from a different party or to support unpopular policies because there is no reward for doing so and, in fact, a great likelihood of being penalized. There are no incentives for party responsibility and party discipline. In fact, often a president has to turn to pork barrel and clientelistic policies to neutralize the opposition.

I would therefore argue that some of the negative characteristics of parties in some Latin American countries, both their unstructured and their undisciplined character as well as their ideological rigidity in such cases as Chile, have been reinforced by the presidential system. On the other hand, I believe, parliamentarism could change these characteristics, although perhaps not without other institutional changes. New and different incentives for parties and their leaders would, naturally, not produce change in political practices overnight.

Governing in Parliamentary Regimes

Institutions lead the same actors to behave differently; they provide incentives or disincentives for certain behavioral patterns. My assumption is that parliamentarism would impose on parties and leaders patterns encouraging greater responsibility for governance, greater accountability (except under conditions of extreme fractionalization), and at the same time the need to cooperate and compromise (except when one party gains an absolute majority). Parliamentarism also allows changes in leadership without a regime crisis and continuity without the fears associated with *continuismo* in presidential systems.

In parliamentary systems governments can demand from parties (either their own if it had a majority or those in a coalition) support in votes of confidence, threatening them otherwise with resignation in the case of lack of support and ultimately with dissolution of the legislature. The role of each party and even of each deputy would be clear to the voters, who are unlikely to sanction destructive actions by parties. The party that fails to support its prime minister would have to pay a price. In the Spanish experience in recent years, an undisciplined, faction-ridden party (the UCD) was severely punished by the electorate. In fact, one of the main reasons for the UCD's and the Communists' loss of support in 1982 was the internal squabbling perceived by the electorate, while the fact that the PSOE was able to overcome its internal tensions and to appear as a united party capable of governing gave it its victory in 1982, 1986, and 1989.[94] Logically the self-interest of parties and legislators in the majority is to assure their leader or leaders in a coalition success and stability in power. They do not always do so, but they are likely to pay a price, except perhaps where the alternative is antisystem parties or parties perceived as antisystem, as was the case in the Fourth Republic and in Italy after World War II. I would argue that there are even some dangers in party cohesion and discipline, particularly when a single party has an absolute majority. Unity might stifle internal democracy and debate, as has been the case in majority parties like the PSOE in Spain, PASOK in Greece, and the British Conservatives under the leadership of Margaret Thatcher.

Even though the self-interest of parties and their parliamentary members may be a major factor in assuring that parties perform their main function in a parliamentary democracy, modern parliamentary systems have introduced additional mechanisms to reduce the dangers of party fractionalization and government instability, which critics sometimes associate with parliamentarism.

Fractionalization of the party system is largely a function of the social structure, but a strong electoral system can reduce it considerably. Undoubtedly, single-member constituencies, in which a plurality of votes assures election, are likely to reduce the number of parties represented in the parliament, except where ethnic or linguistic minorities have an assured representation in areas in which they are numerically dominant. Such a system, however, might have the danger of polarization in societies deeply divided between Left and Right. When coalitions are allowed, the premium won by the largest plurality in polarized societies can lead to coalitions in which extremist parties condition and weaken more moderate parties. The system also might exclude from representation the minorities in ethnic linguistic areas, giving an impression of total consensus on nationalist separatist tendencies. It is no accident, therefore, that a number of Western democracies turned to proportional representation after World War I.

Proportional representation, however, does not need to be a totally weak electoral system that assures seats to minority ideological or interest-group parties and thus contributes to government instability, as in the Weimar Republic. Some systems of proportional representation and electoral devices can reduce fractionalization. Proportional representation does not have to lead to situations like those in the Netherlands and Israel, where 1 percent of the vote assures one seat. A number of parliamentary democracies have introduced a minimum threshold for representation: a certain percentage of votes, as in the Federal Republic of Germany, or a certain number of districts won, or a combination. That device presents some difficulties in multiethnic, multilingual societies such as Spain and therefore cannot always be used. Sometimes it is even inequitable; the Fifth Republic requires a 12 percent threshold. Some proportional representation systems, such as the d'Hondt system used in Spain, Greece, and Chile (1925–73), particularly in districts with few members assure a disproportionate representation to major parties and contribute to what in Spain is called the *voto útil*, that is, the tendency of voters to support parties that have a prospect of providing the government with a leader.

The argument is made that in parliamentary systems very often coalition governments are needed because no party is likely to have an absolute majority. It should be clear from the European experience that coalition governments can be stable and that, once party discipline is strongly enforced, they might allow for more democratic representation and debate than some majority governments. They may also facilitate alternation when two major parties have large and stable electorates, as is the case in Germany, where the FDP acts as a balance wheel between the Social Democrats and the Christian Democrats. However, I have to admit that government instability has been one of the strong arguments against parliamentarism and in favor of presidentialism. In making that argument, it has been forgotten that there is considerable cabinet instability in presidential systems and that in multiparty systems presidential cabinets are very often also coalition governments, although they have the disadvantage that the ministers are selected as individuals who do not necessarily commit their parties to support their policies. The image of assembly government overthrowing at whim governments associated with the Third and Fourth Republics and with Italian democracy in recent decades is not the rule in parliamentary systems, even in Latin countries. Since 1977 Spain has had only three prime ministers, in spite of considerable cabinet instability under Suárez during the period that preceded his fall. Besides, the negative image associated with cabinet instability should be corrected; it has been argued that under the Fourth Republic cabinet instability contributed indirectly to the capacity of the system to make some major decisions.[95] On the other hand, instability is often more apparent than real because the same persons occupy the prime ministership for a long time, although discontinuously, and many of the ministers stay in office after cabinet changes; even the parties occupying certain ministries are the same over a prolonged period. There is much more continuity than is apparent when we look at figures on the duration of cabinets and frequency of crises.

The experience of government instability in the Weimar Republic led the Bonn lawmakers to introduce an important constitutional innovation: the constructive vote of nonconfidence of article 67, which was repeated in article 113 of the Spanish constitution of 1978. This innovation has been discussed in proposals of constitutional reform in Portugal.[96] Let me quote the German *Grundgesetz:*

ARTICLE 67

1. The Bundestag can express its lack of confidence in the Federal Chancellor only by electing a successor with a majority of its members and by requesting the Federal President to dismiss the Federal Chancellor. The Federal President must comply with the request and appoint the person elected.

2. Forty-eight hours must elapse between the motion and the election.

ARTICLE 68

If a motion of the Federal Chancellor for a vote of confidence is not assented to by the majority of members of the Bundestag, the Federal President may, upon the proposal of the Federal Chancellor dissolve the Bundestag within 21 days. The right to dissolve shall lapse as soon as the Bundestag with the majority of its members elects another federal chancellor.

This constitutional device gives the prime minister in parliamentary systems a strong position; he or she cannot be overthrown by a purely negative majority, as happened in the Weimar Republic when Nazis and Communists made stable government impossible but were unable to provide an alternative one. In fact, the device has been criticized for the rigidity it introduces by making alternation in government more difficult.

It should be clear by now that the combination of some electoral law reforms modifying extreme proportional representation and the device of the constructive vote of nonconfidence can very much reduce government instability in parliamentary systems. It allows at the same time, a change of prime ministers without provoking a constitutional crisis or turning to such extreme measures as impeachment of a president. In parliamentary democracies, leadership crises lead to government crises and not, as in presidential systems, to regime crises.[97]

One possible advantage of parliamentarism is that the leaders of the parties who aspire to govern have an opportunity to become familiar with the issues in committees and in the major debates and to interact with each other. It has become impossible to aspire to govern a country without having been involved in the day-to-day business of politics, of legislating, debating the budget, confronting the government or the opposition. In that process leaders can emerge in the parties, a shadow cabinet might develop, and the public can slowly become familiar with the leader of the opposition before the electoral period when that leader makes a bid for the support of a party in order to gain the prime ministership. Although some people might dislike professional politicians, modern states are too complex to be governed by amateurs. The parliament can be a school, a nursery, for leaders. Members of parliament share a great deal of experiences, personal relations, and party links that can make negotiation, consensus, and accommodation between government and opposition possible when their roles are reversed.

Parliamentary Government: Prime Ministerial Government

One is tempted to characterize some of the modern parliamentary systems as prime ministerial or chancellor (Kanzler) regimes.[98] As opposed to the classical régime d'assemblée of the Third and even the Fourth French Republics, they are based on granting the prime minister the power to "determine and be responsible for general policy guidelines" (to use the words of article 65 of the German Grundgesetz). The chancellor in addition is given the power to appoint and dismiss the ministers, who conduct the affairs of their departments within the chancellor's policy guidelines. The position of the chancellor depends on the strength of the parties—his own and those entering into the governing coalition—but in principle he is more than a primus inter pares. In addition, he has a direct relationship to the electorate because the parties enter the campaign under a leader whom they propose to make a prime minister and ask for support to achieve that goal. The chancellor, as leader of the winning party, personalizes the campaign. This is not true, however, in all parliamentary systems.

Some analysts have suggested that the "prime minister" or "presidente de gobierno" in Kanzler democracy represents a certain convergence with the personalization of powers in presidentialism. This is only partly true, because ultimately the prime minister needs the confidence and support of his or her party (if it has a majority in the parliament) and, in the case of a coalition government, of his or her coalition partners. In the case of minority governments, the prime minister needs the support of parties that, without being in the government, support its policies or tolerate it. Even in the privileged position of the prime ministership, continuous attention is necessary to maintain that support, and therefore we can still speak of parliamentary government, or perhaps, to be more exact, of party-parliamentary government.

The Difficult Transition from Presidentialism to Parliamentarism

In the process of constitutional innovation in countries that traditionally have had a presidential constitution, or where an authoritarian regime enacted such a constitution, the transition to democracy takes place through the free election of a new president, presumably under the old constitution, for either a normal or a reduced mandate. This situation differs fundamentally from the one in which many Western European democracies found themselves at the moment of transition. In Western Europe, the first election after a dictatorship was for a legislature, whether constituent or not, that was free to create the new institutions without having to delegitimize a democratically elected president. The Spanish Cortes elected in 1977 as the result of the Law for Political Reform, which facilitated the transition, was in principle free to discuss any constitutional form. It even debated for symbolic reasons, though without any viability or meaning for the political process, whether Spain should be a monarchy (as the popular referendum on the Law for Political Reform had already decided in December 1976).

It is debatable if a constituent assembly or a legislature that, without being elected for that purpose, undertakes the task of making new constitutional laws or amendments can ignore the existence of a democratically elected president. This imposes a new and complex issue, the collaboration between the congress and the president. However, it seems reasonable to think that a president who has been elected as a symbol of democratic renewal will collaborate with the congress in making the new political institutions and will put his weight and prestige behind a new constitution (particularly if he cannot be reelected). The new president would not be required to relinquish power until after the approval of the new constitution according to proper procedures. And if the president makes a commitment to defend the new constitution, he or she would not be required to relinquish office until the end of a term. Let us not forget that parliamentary systems have as head of state either a monarch or a president who, generally, is elected not by the people but by a representative electoral college. A popularly elected president in such a situation, as defender and supporter of the new constitution, would be fully entitled to exhaust his or her mandate to perform the functions assigned to the presidency in the new constitution. This would be particularly true for a president elected with the support of all those wishing a transition to a fully democratic political system. Such a solution would also have the advantage of assuring a formal and symbolic continuity with past legality, while breaking with the authoritarian legacy in what is incompatible with a new democratic regime. It could then be a valuable component of what in Spain was the *reforma-pactada ruptura-pactada*. The president elected according to the existing constitutional norms before democracy would be part of the process of *reforma*, and the new constitution and the new parliamentarily supported government, part of the *ruptura* with a past that contributed to the breakdown or was the product of authoritarian imposition, as in Chile.

Conclusion

This analysis has focused on some of the structural problems inherent in presidentialism: the simultaneous democratic legitimacy of president and congress, the likelihood of conflict, the absence of obvious mechanisms to resolve it, the zero-sum character of presidential elections, the majoritarian implication that can lead to a disproportionality leaving more than 60 percent of voters without representation, the potential polarization, the rigidity of fixed terms and no-reelection rules normally associated with presidentialism, among others. It also has discussed some of the implications of presidentialism for the political culture, the party system, and the recruitment of congressional elites. Let me stress that not all of these consequences obtain in each and every case. I only argue that they are likely. Much more research is needed to prove them systematically, even though examples of these patterns come easily to mind and are documented in some of the contributions to this volume. In fact, Alfred Stepan and Cindy Skach in chapter 4 carry out the counterfactual analysis, with all of its difficulties, of what would have happened if a number of democracies had been parliamentary rather than presidential in serious crises and (as I have already done for Spain in 1977) what might have happened to some of the parliamentary democracies should they have had presidential constitutions.

I have also discussed the great variety and ambiguous character of the so-called semipresidential or semiparliamentary systems of dual executive, which have also been called premier parliamentarism and presidential parliamentarism. Those systems, as commentators have noted often, function either as presidential or as parliamentary, and can lead to conflict situations or stalemate unless the president shows extraordinary political skills and savoir faire in the case of a parliamentary majority different from the one that sustained him in his election. In fact, in the case of the Weimar Republic and the Spanish Republic in the thirties, the dual executive system led to solutions of dubious constitutionality and contributed decisively to undermining democratic institutions. I have also highlighted the particularly disquieting consequences of these systems for the relationship with the armed forces.

Finally, I have analyzed briefly some of the main objections to parliamentarism, noting how under certain circumstances they might be justified[99] but also how contemporary parliamentary democracies have overcome some of the dysfunctional consequences of extreme parliamentarism and its fractionalized party systems. I have also discussed at some length how parliamentary systems in contemporary politics can lead to the emergence of strong national and party leadership capable of governing with sufficient support under critical conditions.

There can be no question that neither parliamentarism nor presidentialism, nor a mixed system, is able to handle successfully intractable problems such as those faced today by Lebanon, Cyprus, and probably societies involved in civil war or in the problems of some African countries. Nor would I question that there are degenerate forms of both presidentialism and parliamentarism; some cases come easily to mind. I only argue that presidentialism seems to involve greater risk for stable democratic politics than contemporary parliamentarism.

Political engineers, like engineers who build bridges, should plan for the most unfavorable conditions, although we might hope they will never materialize. Doing so may be considered wasteful when the additional costs are counted, which in the case of political institution building are the costs of innovation, of challenging tradition. As the builders of bridges can never assure that the bridges will not collapse under some extreme circumstance, no constitution maker can assure that the institutions he creates will survive all challenges and dangers and assure a consolidated democracy. However, the accumulated evidence of the past in presidential systems, particularly in Latin America and Asia, and the success of contemporary parliamentary democracies in Western Europe show odds that seem to favor parliamentary institutions.

Innovation is not necessarily good, but to cling to the institutions of the past when they have failed too often and to choose not to innovate is to miss a historical opportunity. Perhaps as a citizen of Spain, where political leaders could reach a consensus to dare to create new institutions that have led to a consolidated democratic parliamentary regime, I am biased in my preferences. I think, however, that the intelligent use of historical opportunity after many failures and dictatorships is evidence that innovation is possible and can be successful. No one in Spain between 1975 and 1978 could have been sure that the experiment would be successful. However, the experience of Spain and other European democracies, particularly the German Republic, shows that innovative leadership and thoughtful constitution making can greatly help to generate the conditions for a stable democracy.

In the early stages of the Spanish transition to democracy, Adolfo Suárez, who was not yet the prime minister who would lead it, in a speech conveying openness to change, quoted a poem by a "great Spanish writer." Let me also close with the lines of Antonio Machado:

> ¡Que importa un día! Está el ayer alerto
> al mañana, mañana al infinito
> hombres de España, ni el pasado ha muerto
> ni está el mañana—ni el ayer—escrito.

[What does one day matter! Yesterday is alert to tomorrow, tomorrow to infinity. People of Spain, neither has the past died nor is tomorrow—or yesterday—written.—My translation]

Appendix

Some Considerations on Quantitative Analyses of the Stability of Parliamentary and Presidential Democracies

Although my analysis of the difference for democratic consolidation, institutionalization, and performance between presidentialism and parliamentarism was not originally based on a systematic comparison of the records of countries with one or another type of regime, several authors have provided evidence for the greater or lesser likelihood of stability and breakdown in both types. A systematic and quantitative comparison, given the problem of defining the historical period to be covered, the countries to be included, and the large number of variables that might or might not be held constant, presents enormous methodological problems.

Scott Mainwaring and Matthew Shugart[100] list 24 countries with 30 years of uninterrupted democracy between 1959 and 1989 (including India, despite the period of emergency powers). Of those 24 countries, 18 have parliamentary regimes, 3 are presidential (the United States, Costa Rica, and Venezuela), 2 are semipresidential (Finland and France), and 1 has a unique form of government (Switzerland).

Alfred Stepan and Cindy Skach[101] have focused on the 86 countries that became independent between 1945 and 1979. Among them 15 were democratic for 10 consecutive years. Stepan and Skach count 32 countries that were parliamentary the first year of independence, of which 15 were continuous democracies between 1980 and 1989. The exclusion of microstates would reduce the number of democracies (Dominica, Kiribati, Nauru, St. Lucia, and St. Vincent) but also the number of nondemocratic states (Gambia, Grenada, Mauritius, Seychelles, Tuvalu). This would mean that of 22 remaining newly independent states with a parliamentary government the first year, 10 would be continuous democracies between 1980 and 1989, and none with another type of regime in the first year.

Matthew Shugart and John M. Carey[102] have taken a different approach by listing 48 countries that had by 1990 held at least two democratic elections without breakdown. Among them they list 27 pure parliamentary democracies (strangely they do not include India), 12 presidential regimes, and 9 other types (5 premier-presidential, 2 president-parliamentary, and 2 assembly independent, using their typology of regimes). Since they classify, formally correctly, Austria and Iceland as premier-presidential, but these states function in fact as parliamentary, I would count them as parliamentary, increasing the number of parliamentary democracies to 29 and decreasing premier-presidential regimes to 3. If we isolate their 23 "third world countries" (among them Argentina, Uruguay, Turkey, together with Senegal, Botswana, and Papua New Guinea), 9 are parliamentary, 11 presidential (all Latin American except Senegal), and 3 "other" types.

Their inclusion of the "not newly independent countries," particularly the presidential or modified presidential regimes in Latin America, reduces the difference found in the Stepan-Skach analysis. The fact that fewer of the microstates (which were disproportionately democratic) are not included also affects the comparison.

Shugart and Carey rightly point out that by 1991, 11 "third world countries" with presidential regimes by their criterion were "democratic," to which one could add 3 with modified presidential systems, compared to 9 parliamentary (10 if we add India). The recent return to democracy of Latin American countries (including the somewhat dubious cases of El Salvador, Guatemala, and perhaps Honduras) explains the difference between the 9 or 10 parliamentary democracies (with at least two democratic elections without breakdown) and the [14] "presidential" democracies among the 48 countries (49 with India) considered.

However, Shugart and Carey's questioning of a relationship between regime type and democratic stability is based on an analysis of the breakdowns of democratic regimes in the twentieth century. They list a total of 40 cases of breakdown—some countries experiencing more than one—22 of parliamentary systems, 12 of presidential systems, and 6 of "other types" (1 premier-presidential [Austria] and 5 presidential-parliamentary, among which they include the Weimar Republic, Ecuador [1962], Peru [1968], Korea [1961], and Sri Lanka [1982]).

According to their data, breakdowns affected 7 parliamentary democracies (all in Europe) before World War II, 2 mixed systems (Germany and Austria), and only 1 presidential democracy (Argentina). The breakdown of European democracies is well documented, but there is considerable ambiguity about when and for how long Latin American countries could or could not be considered democratic and if and when they broke down. This explains why only Argentina is included in that period.

If we consider the period after World War II, Shugart and Carey list 14 cases of breakdown of parliamentary democracies, rightly excluding the transition from the Fourth to the Fifth Republic as a case of reequilibration and cases in which no consecutive elections were held before the breakdown, in order to eliminate newly independent countries that held a first election under the watchful eye of a departing colonial power or as a demonstration for foreign consumption. Only 1 of these 14 breakdowns happened in Europe (in Greece). The 14 breakdowns of parliamentary regimes contrast with 12 breakdowns of presidential systems and 4 of systems they call "presidential parliamentary." (The listing however omits multiple breakdowns in the same country; to have included these might have increased the number of Latin American breakdowns).

These figures would support the thesis that the type of regime makes little difference, or even that parliamentary regimes are more vulnerable than pure presidential ones. However, more information is needed either to prove or disprove such a conclusion. To begin with, how many democracies, parliamentary and presidential, were there before World War II? Latin America included 17 countries, all of them presidential—except for short interludes—before 1945. How many were by any reasonable standard democracies? How many, besides Argentina, experienced a breakdown?

When we turn to interwar Europe[103] we are dealing overwhelmingly with parliamentary democracies, except for a few semipresidential regimes: Germany and Finland and, depending on the criteria used, Austria, Ireland, and even the Spanish Republic. Of a total of 28 countries (including Turkey and Russia), 25 (or at least 22) were parliamentary. The total included 12 stable democracies and [1] countries that experienced a breakdown or a failure of democratic consolidation. Of the 2 truly semipresidential regimes, 1, the Weimar Republic, experienced a breakdown.

In that context of 15 "old states" (excluding empires) that did not experience major border changes, 9 were stable parliamentary democracies. Of the 8 new states, 5 suffered a breakdown. Democracy did not consolidate or survive in the 5 defeated empires—Russia, Turkey, Austria, Hungary, and Germany—irrespective of regime type.

Parliamentarism in interwar Europe, in contrast to postwar Europe (with the exception of Greece), did not assure democratic development or stability. Perhaps, among other factors, a learning process took place in a number of countries, and the constitutions introduced innovations contributing to postwar stability. After the war, of 14 European democracies, only 1 experienced a breakdown. I am obviously not counting countries in the Soviet orbit like Czechoslovakia (1948) or Hungary.

In that same period, of the democratic presidential regimes in states that had gained independence before 1945—whose number is more difficult to ascertain—only the United States and Costa Rica did not experience a breakdown. The number of breakdowns is certainly more than 1 if we count only Argentina, Chile, Brazil, Uruguay, Peru, Colombia, and Venezuela, leaving out more dubious presidential democracies.

The post–World War II weak parliamentary regimes, according to Shugart and Carey, are, in Asia: Burma, Pakistan (1954–77); Singapore (1972); Thailand (1976); Turkey (1980); and Sri Lanka (1970s). There are also 1 in Oceania (Fiji, 1988); 4 in Africa: Kenya (1969); Nigeria (1966); Sierra Leone (1967); and Somalia (1969); and 2 in America: Guyana (1974–78) and Surinam (1975). That makes weak parliamentary regimes in 12 countries. If we add Greece to them we have a total of 13 breakdowns and 13 (if we count Malta) stable European and 13 stable non-European (including Commonwealth countries but no microstates) parliamentary democracies. Therefore we have 13 breakdowns compared to 26 more or less stable, strictly speaking parliamentary democracies (not counting the Fourth Republic in France). This means 13 breakdowns in 39 countries.

Of the total of presidential regimes in the same period we have the United States, Costa Rica (since 1953), and Venezuela (since 1958) that have not experienced a breakdown. But at least 10 other countries (Argentina, Bolivia, Brazil, Chile, Colombia, and Uruguay, plus Ecuador and Peru, both classified by Shugart and Carey as presidential-parliamentary) experienced the demise of democracy. And that is to ignore the more dubiously democratic presidential regimes in Latin

America and the Philippines (1972); Korea (1972); and 2 presidential-parliamentary regimes (Korea, 1961, and Sri Lanka, 1982). This means that in a minimum of 11 countries (ignoring repeated breakdowns and the type of presidentialism) democracy broke down, compared to 3 fully stable presidential republics.

In summary, we have in post–World War II 13 breakdowns in 39 parliamentary democracies (defined by the criteria of Shugart and Carey, plus India); and at least 10 breakdowns among 13 presidential democracies (with some dubious cases deliberately excluded).[104]

The fact that, of those 10 countries experiencing breakdowns since 1945, at the time of writing 9 are democracies shows that democratization is possible in countries with a presidential tradition and that these 9 countries are presidential democracies. Perhaps the societies and their leadership in those presidential democracies have learned from past failures, and we might find in the future presidential systems as stable as parliamentary democracies are in Europe. However, some of the troubles in several presidential democracies in recent times—Peru, Philippines, Venezuela, Haiti, Brazil—do not argue well for those democracies. Certainly factors other than the type of regime account for difficulties, but it is not unreasonable to argue that presidentialism compounds the difficulties for reasons that are congruent with our analysis.

Notes

In making final revisions of this chapter for publication I find myself in a difficult and even embarrassing situation. My essay has been circulating in different versions since 1984, translated in Argentina, Chile, Brazil, and Italy, and widely discussed, especially in Poland. I published a shortened version, translated into Hungarian and Mongolian, in the *Journal of Democracy*. Circulation has led to a number of critical comments, a debate with my critics, and frequent friendly exchanges with colleagues. Scholars agreeing with my arguments have developed them further and provided empirical proof of them. Discussions of constitutional reform (in some of which I have participated) have taken the issues raised by my essay into account.

The question is: how much should I take all this discussion into account here? My inclination is not to enter into a careful analysis of all the arguments and evidence presented. I feel that it would not be fully fair to my critics not to publish the original text to which they responded, but at some points I refer to their critiques to clarify my own argument and in footnotes to some of the contributions to the debate. I also include additional sections not part of the original paper.

I want to thank the Wissenschaftskolleg zu Berlin, whose fellowship (1990–91) made possible work on this essay, and Rocío de Terán for her continuous assistance, Terry Schutz for her careful editing, and Terry Miller for typing and retyping of the manuscript.

1. My approach would be misunderstood if it were read as strictly institutional and even more as a legal-constitutionalist perspective. I take into account those aspects, although perhaps less than other recent writings such as Matthew Soberg Shugart and John M. Carey, *Presidents and Assemblies: Constitutional Design and Electoral Dynamics* (Cambridge: Cambridge UP, 1992), which provides for a more systematic analysis of the powers of presidents.

My focus is on the political logic of presidential systems and some of its likely consequences on the selection of leadership, popular expectations, style of leadership, and articulation of conflicts. Some of the empirical evidence is found in the chapters of this volume, and it is our hope that our analysis will generate more and systematic evidence of those aspects that cannot be found in or directly derived from the institutional norms.

2. F. A. Hermens, *Democracy or Anarchy: A Study of Proportional Representation* (Notre Dame, Ind.: Notre Dame UP, 1941); Maurice Duverger, *Political Parties: Their Organization and Activity* (1951; New York: Wiley, 1954); Stein Rokkan, "Elections: Electoral Systems," *International Encyclopedia of the Social Sciences* (New York: Crowell-Collier-Macmillan, 1968); Dieter Nohlen, *Wahlsysteme der Welt* (Munich: Piper, 1978); Douglas Rae, *The Political Consequences of Electoral Laws* (New Haven: Yale UP, 1967); R. S. Katz, *A Theory of Parties and Electoral Systems* (Baltimore: Johns Hopkins UP, 1980); Rein Taagepera and Matthew Soberg Shugart, *Seats and Votes: The Effects and Determinants of Electoral Systems* (New Haven: Yale UP, 1989); B. Grofman and A. Lijphart, eds., *Electoral Laws and Their Political Consequences* (New York: Agathon, 1986); Arend Lijphart and B. Grofman, eds., *Choosing an Electoral System: Issues and Alternatives* (New York: Praeger, 1984); and Giovanni Sartori, "The Influence of Electoral Systems: Faulty Laws or Faulty Method," in Grofman and Lijphart, *Electoral Laws and Their Political Consequences*, pp. 43–68.

3. Werner Kaltefleiter, *Die Funktionen des Staatsoberhauptes in der parlamentarischen Demokratie* (Cologne: Westdeutscher Verlag, 1970); and Stefano Bartolini, "Sistema partitico ed elezione diretta del capo dello stato in Europa," *Rivista italiana di scienza politica* 2 (1984):209–22.

4. Shugart and Carey, *Presidents and Assemblies;* Waldino Cleto Suárez, "El poder ejecutivo en América Latina. Su capacidad operativa bajo regímenes presidencialistas de gobierno," *Revista de estudios políticos* (nueva época) 29 (Sept.-Oct. 1982): 109–44. Richard Moulin, *Le présidentialisme et la classification des régimes politiques* (Paris: Librairie Générale de Droit et de Jurisprudence, 1978), is a work of scholarship in the classical legal tradition, rich in references to the constitutional texts and the academic commentaries with a wealth of information on the variety of presidential systems, the relations between executive and legislature, the role of cabinets, impeachment, party systems and presidentialism, and so forth, in the United States and other presidential regimes, particularly the constitutional history of Chile. It also includes an extensive bibliography. Only the equal treatment of the constitutions of democracies and nondemocratic regimes is disturbing.

5. G. Bingham Powell, Jr., *Contemporary Democracies: Participation, Stability, and Violence* (Cambridge: Harvard UP, 1982), and Arend Lijphart, *Democracies; Pattern of Majoritarian and Consensus Government in Twenty-one Countries* (New Haven: Yale UP, 1984).

6. The neglect until very recently by social scientists of presidentialism outside the United States is reflected in the facts that the *Presidential Studies Quarterly* from 1977 to 1992 (vols. 7 to 22) published only 3 articles on the subject; that the *Legislative Studies Quarterly* between 1976 and 1992 published none; that *International Political Science Abstracts* between 1975 and 1991 lists 141 articles on Latin America, 96 on countries outside the United States and Latin America, and 23 on general topics on the executive or the presidency.

7. Scott Mainwaring, "Presidentialism in Latin America: A Review Essay," *Latin American Research Review* 25, no. 1 (1990): 157–79, is an excellent summary of the literature and debates in Latin America. See also Arturo Valenzuela, *The Breakdown of Democratic Regimes: Chile* (Baltimore: Johns Hopkins UP, 1978). Another important survey article is: Mario D. Serrafero, "Presidencialismo y reforma política en América Latina," *Revista del Centro de Estudios Constitucionales,* Madrid, Jan.–Apr. 1991, pp. 195–233.

8. Mainwaring, "Presidentialism in Latin America."

9. Juan J. Linz, *Crisis, Breakdown and Reequilibration*, vol. 1 of *The Breakdown of Democratic Regimes*, edited by J. Linz and Alfred Stepan (Baltimore: Johns Hopkins UP, 1978); see "Excursus on Presidential and Parliamentary Democracies," pp. 71–74. It would be absurd to argue that presidents need to be elected on a first-past-the-post basis. I agree with Donald L. Horowitz, *A Democratic South Africa? Constitutional Engineering in a Divided Society* (Berkeley: U California P, 1991), that this view is an "untenable assumption about the way presidents are inevitably elected" (p. 20). He attributes such an assumption to me, but all I have done is to discuss the way in which presidents have been and are most often elected—either by a plurality in one round or in a runoff election. He rightly points out that in Nigeria in 1979 and 1983 and in Sri Lanka in 1978 and 1988 a different method of election was used, but it does not seem to me reasonable to base an analysis of presidential politics on those two cases (and a total of four elections at the time of his and my writings) rather than on the cumulative experience in Latin American republics and a few other cases.

10. The important essay by Anthony King, "Executives," in *Handbook of Political Science*, edited by Fred I. Greenstein and Nelson Polsby, vol. 5 of *Governmental Institutions and Processes* (Reading, Mass.: Addison-Wesley, 1975), pp. 173–256, limits itself to a comparison of the United States and the United Kingdom, with no reference to presidentialism outside the United States.

11. In view of the constant clamor for "strong" presidents, the popular hopes linked with "strong" presidents in many countries with presidental regimes, Shugart and Carey's finding that systems rating high in powers of the president in law making and cabinet formation have been more prone to crises is significant.

Ultimately, from its historical origins on, a separation of powers has been conceived to generate "weak" government, "checks and balances" (which can turn into "stalemates," divided responsibility, distrust between powers), just the opposite of "strong" power and leadership. No surprise that the terms of presidents who wanted to be "strong"—Vargas, Allende, Marcos, Goulart, Alán García, Aristide—ended in one or another kind of disaster. We know too little about the role of the presidency in Georgia to tell if Gamsakhurdia should be in that list, but it would not be surprising if some of the new presidents of former Soviet Union republics might not run the same fate.

See the collection of essays by Carlos S. Nino, Gabriel Banzat, Marcelo Alegre and Marcela Rodríguez, Roberto Gargozelle, Silvino Alvarez and Robert Pablo-Saba, and Jorge Albert Barraguirre, *Presidencialismo y estabilidad democrática en la Argentina* (Buenos Aires: Centro de Estudios Institucionales, 1991), esp. Carlos S. Nino, "El presidencialismo y la justificación, estabilidad y eficiencia de la democracia," pp. 11–27.

12. Klaus von Beyme, *Die parlamentarischen Regierungssysteme in Europa* (Munich: R. Piper, 1970), is a monumental comparative study of parliamentary regimes.

13. This analysis does not include pluripersonal presidentialism because of its atypical character, the unique circumstances that have led to its establishment, and last but not least its lack of success. For a discussion of plural presidencies, see Shugart and Carey, *Presidents and Assemblies*, pp. 94–105.

Advocates of collegial presidencies should keep in mind the experiences in Roman history and the analysis of George Simmel on the size of groups and decision making in addition to the contemporary failures.

14. The majority runoff has been advocated to avoid election by a small plurality, which is possible in a multiparty election, and to assure election by a majority. The system, however, as Shugart and Carey have noted, has several not so desirable consequences. First it en-

courages a larger number of candidates in the first run, discouraging the coalescence of opposing forces, so that those who place first and second can attract the support in the runoff
of those who failed and those who failed can enhance their bargaining position with one of
the two candidates in the runoff. The first candidates in this case obtain a lower percentage
of votes compared to elections by pure plurality. The second consequence is that the outcome depends on first-round contingencies. Let us remember that in 1989 some Brazilians
feared a runoff between Lula and Brizola, the two leftist candidates, if the Right had divided
its vote more than it did. To these I would add that in the runoff, the winner might receive
a vote out of proportion to his original electoral appeal that might not, however, represent
real support for him but contribute to his sense of being "elected by the people." The presidential majority in this case is as or more "artificial" than a parliamentary majority for a
prime minister heading a coalition, but it generates very different expectations.

15. Fred W. Riggs, "The Survival of Presidentialism in America: Para-constitutional Practices," *International Political Science Review* 9, no. 4 (1988): 247–78, is an excellent analysis of
"American exceptionalism." For European responses to American presidentialism, see Klaus
von Beyme, *America as a Model. The Impact of American Democracy in the World* (Aldershot,
U.K.: Gower, 1987), chap. 2, "The Presidential System of Government," pp. 33–76.

16. Committee on Political Parties of the American Political Science Association, *Toward
a More Responsible Two-Party System* (New York: Rinehart, 1950).

17. Shugart and Carey, *Presidents and Assemblies*, chap. 6, pp. 106–49.

18. President Fernando Collor of Brazil when, after introducing his stabilization plan on
television without previous consultation, he encountered congressional resistance, he
threatened congress with mobilizing the masses: "There is no doubt that I have an intimate
deep relation with the poor masses" and that congress "must respect me because I am the
center of power." Commenting on this, one of his strongest supporters, former finance minister and then senator Roberto Campos lamented: "This is juridical butchery, which lashes
confidence in the Collor plan." See *Latin American Regional Reports: Brazil Report* (RB-90-
04), 3 May 1990, p. 6, and "Mounting Criticism of Authoritarian Governments Novo Brasil
Plan," ibid. (RB-90-05), 7 June 1990, pp. 1–3, Campos quote on p. 31.

President Collor could not, with his electoral constituency, make threats against congress creditable in the way that Goulart (or Allende) could by mobilizing masses in the
Petrobras Stadium. For an analysis of the Brazilian crisis in 1964, which was also a crisis of
relations between president and congress, and the possible constitutional reform that might
have allowed Goulart's reelection, see Thomas E. Skidmore, *Politics in Brazil, 1930–1964: An
Experiment in Democracy* (New York: Oxford UP, 1967).

Alfred Stepan, ed., *Authoritarian Brazil* (New Haven: Yale UP, 1973), and "Political Leadership and Regime Breakdown: Brazil," in Linz and Stepan, *Breakdown of Democratic Regimes*, pp. 119–37, esp. pp. 120–33.

It should be noted that this sense of the "superiority" of the democratic mandate of presidents is found not only in Latin America but in other presidential democracies. For example, de Gaulle on December 17, 1969, in a speech disclosed: that the head of state has his ori-
gin in "la confiance profonde de la Nation" and not in "un arrangement momentané entre
professionnels de l'astuce" (*Le monde*, 19 Dec. 1965) quoted by Moulin, *Le présidentialisme
et la classification des régimes politiques*, p. 27.

19. Karl Marx, "The Eighteenth Brumaire of Louis Bonaparte," in *December 2, 1851. Contemporary Writings on the Coup d'Etat of Louis Napoleon*, edited by John B. Halsted (Garden
City, N.Y.: Doubleday, 1992), pp. 152–53.

20. Mattei Dogan, ed., *Pathways to Power, Selecting Rulers in Pluralist Democracies*

(Boulder: Westview, 1989), chap. 10, "Irremovable Leaders and Ministerial Instability in European Democracies," pp. 239–75.

21. The case of María Estela Martínez de Perón, vice president who acceded to the presidency after the death of her husband in July 1974 and was ousted by the March 1976 coup, is a prime example of difficulties caused by the rigidity of presidentialism. Faced with the total failure of her government in November 1975, her opponents wanted to start her impeachment. Then anticipated elections were announced for the end of 1976, but they would not presumably lead to a transfer of power. After a reorganization of the cabinet in August 1975, Christmas brought a mass resignation of cabinet members and December 29 a new demand for impeachment. Mrs. Perón's health was questioned in an effort to apply rules of incapacity. In February 1976 impeachment was again initiated and approved by the lower house but blocked in the senate. After another reorganization of the cabinet, a meeting of party leaders on March 12 was unable to come to a solution. After a coup on March 29, Mrs. Perón was ousted, imprisoned, and tried by the military regime. For a detailed analysis of this crisis, see Mario Daniel Serrafero, "El presidencialismo en el sistema político argentino" (Ph.D. diss., Universidad Complutense—Instituto Universitario Ortega y Gasset, Madrid, 1992), pp. 265–79. This thesis is an outstanding monograph on the Argentinian presidency. Unfortunately, I have not been able to incorporate many of its findings into my analysis.

At the time of writing, the crises in Venezuela involving President Carlos Andrés Pérez and in Brazil involving President Fernando Collor are further examples of the rigidity of presidentialism.

22. On the vulnerability of a single-person election to the influence of mass media, see the excellent article by Giovanni Sartori, "Video-Power," *Government and Opposition*, Winter 1989, pp. 39–53. See also Thomas E. Skidmore, ed., *Television, Politics, and the Transition to Democracy in Latin America* (Washington, D.C.: Woodrow Wilson Center Press, 1993).

23. Shugart and Carey, *Presidents and Assemblies*, pp. 87–91.

24. Adam Przeworski, *Democracy and the Market. Political and Economic Reforms in Eastern Europe and Latin America* (Cambridge: Cambridge UP, 1991), pp. 34–35.

25. Donald Horowitz, "Comparing Democratic Systems," *Journal of Democracy* 1, no. 4 (1990): 73–79, and my response on pp. 84–91. Scott Mainwaring and Matthew S. Shugart, "Juan Linz, Presidentialism and Democracy: A Critical Appraisal," in *Politics, Society and Democracy: Latin America*, edited by Arturo Valenzuela (Boulder: Westview Press, 1994).

26. Mainwaring, "Presidentialism in Latin America," has dealt extensively with the responses to the tensions between presidents and congresses in Latin America and the immobility derived from it (particularly with multipartism), pp. 167–71.

27. Quoted by Russell H. Fitzgibbon, "Continuismo in Central America and the Caribbean," in *The Evolution of Latin American Government, A Book of Readings*, edited by Asher N. Christensen (New York: Henry Holt, 1951), pp. 430–45, esp. p. 436.

28. Sung-joo Han, "South Korea: Politics in Transition" in *Politics in Developing Countries*, edited by Larry Diamond, Juan J. Linz, and Seymour Martin Lipset (Boulder: Lynne Rienner, 1990), pp. 313–50, esp. p. 321 on the mobilization against the constitutional revision that permitted a third-term presidency of Park Chung Hee in 1969. The constitutional amendment achieved by referendum provoked heavy student agitation and can be considered to have been a turning point in the government's ability to maintain the electoral support necessary to keep the president in office. Many who held a reasonably favorable attitude toward Park and high regard for his achievements were disappointed by the tampering with the constitution (p. 325).

29. Juan J. Linz, "Il fattore tempo nei mutamenti de regime," *Teoría política* 2, no. 1 (1986): 3–47.

30. Albert O. Hirschman, *Journeys toward Progress: Studies of Economic Policy-Making in Latin America* (Garden City, N.Y.: Doubleday, 1965), pp. 313–16 about "la rage de vouloir conclure."

31. Daniel Levine, "Venezuela: The Nature, Sources and Prospects of Democracy," in *Democracy in Developing Countries*, pp. 247–89, esp. pp. 256–60; and *Conflict and Political Change in Venezuela* (Princeton: Princeton UP, 1973). See also Jonathan Hartlyn, *The Politics of Coalition Rule in Colombia* (Cambridge: Cambridge UP, 1988).

32. It is significant that Robert A. Dahl, "A Bipartisan Administration," *New York Times*, 14 Nov. 1973, suggested that, during the period between Nixon's resignation and the election of a new president, a coalition government including Democrats and Republicans be created. Cited by A. Lijphart, *Democracy in Plural Societies* (New Haven: Yale UP, 1977), pp. 28–29.

33. On the method of presidential elections see Shugart and Carey, *Presidents and Assemblies:* pp. 208–25, particularly table 10.1, p. 211, which also gives the median percentage of votes for the two highest-scoring candidates. Dieter Nohlen, ed., *Handbuch der Wahldaten Lateinamerikas und der Karibik* (Opladen: Leske & Budrich, 1993), is the most complete source on election legislation, returns in presidential and congressional elections, names of parties and elected presidents for all the countries south of the Rio Grande and the Caribbean.

34. The bibliography on the Spanish transition to democracy and the first election is too extensive to list here. For references see my article "Innovative Leadership in the Spanish Transition," in *Innovative Leadership in International Politics*, edited by Gabriel Sheffer (Albany: State U New York P, 1993).

35. Comments of Prime Minister Felipe González at meeting organized by the Fundación Ortega y Gasset, Toledo, Spain, May 1984.

36. Walter Bagehot, *The English Constitution* (London: World Classics, 1955 [1887]).

37. Scott Mainwaring, "The Dilemmas of Multiparty Presidential Democracy: The Case of Brazil" (Kellogg Institute Working Paper 174, University of Notre Dame, 1992).

38. *New York Times*, 26 Feb. 1992, p. 52.

39. On the parties and party systems, see Scott Mainwaring and Timothy Scully, eds., *Building Democratic Institutions: Parties and Party Systems in Latin America* (Stanford: Stanford UP, forthcoming). Guillermo O'Donnell, "Delegative Democracy" (paper prepared for the meeting of the East-South System Transformations Project, Budapest, Dec. 1990), characterizes a "new animal"—a subtype of existing democracy, which in my view has much in common with many presidential systems, as I characterize them. O'Donnell does not, as I would, link those characteristics with presidentialism, although the empirical bases for his theoretical analysis are basically the Latin American presidential systems.

40. Peru in recent elections is an extreme example. While Fernando Belaúnde of Acción Popular (AP) in 1980 gained 45.4 percent of the vote and the candidate of the Partido Aprista Peruano (PAP) got 27.4 percent, in 1985 Alán García (PAP) gained 53.1 percent and the AP candidate ran fourth with 7.3 percent. In 1990 in the first round Mario Vargas Llosa, the candidate of the coalition Frente Democrático (FREDEMO) was running ahead with 32.6 percent of the vote. Alberto Fujimori (Cambio 90) followed him with 29.1 percent, and the PAP candidate, Luis Alva Castro, ran third with 26.6 percent. In the runoff Fujimori obtained 62.5 percent and Vargas Llosa 37.5 percent. In the election to the lower house the same year, PAP was ahead with 29.4 percent of the seats, followed by Cambio 90 with 17.8 percent and AP

with 14.4 percent, showing the disjunction between presidential and legislative votes. Subsequently in the constitutional crisis in which Fujimori unconstitutionally dissolved the congress in the *autogolpe* of April 5, 1992, he justified his action in the following terms:

> Today we feel that something prevents us from continuing to advance on the road to national reconstruction and progress in our fatherland. And the people of Peru know the cause of this stalemate. They know that it is none other than institutional disintegration. The chaos and corruption, the lack of identification with the great national interests of some of our basic institutions, such as the legislature and the judiciary, impede the government's development.

Alberto Fujimori claimed in the same manifesto: "I insist that as a citizen elected by large national majorities, I am moved only by the wish to achieve the prosperity and greatness of the Peruvian nation."

On the crisis of Peruvian democracy and the *autogolpe* of President Alberto Fujimori on April 5, 1992, see Eduardo Ferrero Costa, ed., *Proceso de returno a la institucionalidad democrática en Perú* (Lima: Centro Peruano de Estudios Internacionales, 1992).

41. Edgardo Catterberg, *Argentina Confronts Politics, Political Culture and Public Opinion in the Argentine Transition to Democracy* (Boulder: Lynne Rienner, 1991), p. 91; Apoyo, *Alán García, Vargas Llosa y la consolidación de la democracia en Perú* (paper presented at the Conference of the World Association for Public Opinion Research (WAPOR): Public Opinion and the Consolidation of Democracy in Latin America, Caracas, Jan. 1990).

42. Carlos Huneeus, *La Unión de Centro Democrático y la transición a la democracia en España* (Madrid: Centro Investigaciones Sociológicas, Siglo 21, 1985), p. 313.

43. Erich Peter Neumann and Elisabeth Noelle, *Statistics on Adenauer. Portrait of a Statesman* (Allensbach: Verlag für Demoskopie, 1962), pp. 40–44.

44. IFOP (Institut Français d'Opinion Publique), *Les français et de Gaulle*, presented by Jean Charlot (Paris: Plon, 1971), pp. 194–208.

45. Shugart and Carey, *Presidents and Assemblies*, pp. 106–30, esp. pp. 106–11, on the "appointment game" in the United States and other systems requiring legislative confirmation.

46. Jean Blondel, *Government Ministers in the Contemporary World* (Beverly Hills: Sage, 1985), pp. 122–25, 127, 129–34, 156–59, quote from p. 123.

47. Markku Laakso and Rein Taagepera, "Effective Number of Parties: A Measure with Application to Western Europe," *Comparative Political Studies* 12 (1979): 3–27. Alfred Stepan and Cindy Skach, in a paper prepared for the Third Meeting of the East-South System Transformations Project, 4–7 Jan. 1992, Toledo, Spain (updated in chapter 4 of this volume), have calculated the Laakso-Taagepera index for the "effective number of parties for forty-two consolidated democracies in the world between 1979 and 1989." Excluding the unique case of Switzerland there were thirty-one pure parliamentary democracies in this universe, six semipresidential democracies, and four pure presidential democracies. Of the thirty-one pure parliamentary systems, ten had between 3 and 7 effective partie. Of the six semipresidential systems, four had between 3 and 5. However, no pure presidential democracy had more than 2.5 effective political parties. The small cell of long-standing presidential systems with 3.0 or more effective parties is probably one of the reasons why there are so few continuous democracies with 3 or more parties (pp. 9–10). However, Chile between 1932 and 1973 was an exception; it was a presidential democracy lasting twenty-five years or more with more than 3.0 effective parties.

48. Scott Mainwaring, "Presidentialism, Multipartism, and Democracy. The Difficult Combination," *Comparative Political Studies* 26, no. 2 (1993): 198–228.

49. The political complexity of the move toward a two-party format in what was a four-party system by the founding of the Democratic Liberal party (DLP) by the former DJP, RDP, and NDRP is analyzed by Sung-joo Han, "The Korean Experiment," *Journal of Democracy* 2, no. 2 (1991): 92–104.

50. Mainwaring, "Dilemmas of Multiparty Presidential Democracy," p. 29.

51. María Ester Mancebo, "From Coparticipation to Coalition: The Problems of Presidentialism in the Uruguayan Case, 1984–1990" (paper presented at the 15th World Congress of the International Political Science Association, July 1991, Buenos Aires); Romeo Pérez Antón, "El parlamentarismo en la tradición uruguaya," *Cuadernos del CLAEH* (Centro Latino Americano de Economía Humana), 2d ser., yr. 14 (1989, no. 1): 107–33.

52. O'Donnell, "Delegative Democracy."

53. Eduardo Gamarra, "Political Stability, Democratization and the Bolivian National Congress" (Ph.D. diss., University of Pittsburgh, 1987); Laurence Whitehead, "Bolivia's Failed Democratization 1977–1980," in *Transitions from Authoritarian Rule, Latin America,* edited by Guillermo O'Donnell, Philippe C. Schmitter, and Laurence Whitehead (Baltimore: Johns Hopkins UP, 1986), pp. 49–71.

54. René Antonio Mayorga, "Bolivia: Democracia como gobernabilidad?" in *Estrategias para el desarrollo de la democracia en Perú y América Latina,* edited by Julio Cotler (Lima: Instituto de Estudios Peruanos—Fundación Friedrich Naumann, 1990), pp. 159–93; and *¿De la anomía política al orden democrático?* (La Paz: CEBEM [Centro Boliviano de Estudios Multidisciplinarios], 1991), pp. 216–75; Eduardo A. Gamarra and James M. Malloy, "The Patrimonial Dynamics of Party Politics in Bolivia," in Scott Mainwaring and Timothy Scully, eds., *Building Democratic Institutions,* forthcoming. Relevant discussions of the Bolivian political system by Eduardo Gamarra, René A. Mayorga, Jorge Lazarte, and others are in René Antonio Mayorga, ed., *Democracia y gobernabilidad en América latina* (Caracas: Editorial Nueva Sociedad, 1992).

55. The Swedish social democratic leader headed the government from 1946 to 1969, leading his party and maintaining an ideological identity while searching for consensus among political actors. See Olaf Ruin, *Tage Erlander* (Pittsburg: Pittsburg UP, 1990).

56. On the weakness of party identification and loyalty in Brazil, see Scott Mainwaring, "Politicians, Parties and Electoral Systems: Brazil in Comparative Perspective," *Comparative Politics,* Oct. 1991, pp. 21–43; and "Brazilian Party Underdevelopment in Comparative Perspective" (Kellogg Institute Working Paper 134, University of Notre Dame, 1990), pp. 21–25, 26–29.

57. Seymour M. Lipset, *Continental Divide: The Values and Institutions of the United States and Canada* (New York: Routledge, 1990).

58. Ana María Mustapic, "Conflictos institucionales durante el primer gobierno Radical: 1916–1926," *Desarrollo económico* 24, no. 93 (1984): 85–108.

59. Donald L. Horowitz, *A Democratic South Africa?*

60. One example of the potential for conflict between the president and the prime minister and his minister of defense was the case of Portugal at the time of the constitutional revision in the early eighties. When the deputies decided that the president would appoint the military officials nominated by the government (art. 136 of the 1982 text), the law based on that text was vetoed and sent back to the assembly by the president. See José Durão Barroso, "Les Conflits entre le président portugais et la majorité parlementaire de 1979 à 1983," in *Les régimes semi-présidentiels,* edited by M. Duverger (Paris: Presses Universitaires de France, 1986), pp. 237–55.

61. On the role of the head of state—monarch or president—in parliamentary regimes,

see Kaltefleiter, *Die Funktionen des Staatsoberhauptes in der parlamentarischen Demokratie*, particularly the extended discussion of the role of the king or queen in the United Kingdom. The role of King Juan Carlos of Spain, both in the transition to democracy (1975–77) and during the coup attempt in 1981, was unique. However it has to be stressed that until after the 1977 election and formally until the enactment of the 1978 constitution, he was not a constitutional monarch in a democratic parliamentary monarchy. Therefore his role as *motor del cambio, piloto del cambio, garantizador del cambio* (motor, pilot, or guarantor of the transition), according to different interpretations of his role, though of undeniable importance, does not fit into our analysis of working parliamentary systems. Although also an exception, his role in the traumatic hours following the sequester of the entire government and legislature on February 23, 1981, shows the importance of the division of roles and of the "reserve" powers of a legitimate and popular head of state. On the role of the king, see Charles T. Powell, *El piloto del cambio: El rey, la monarquía y la transición a la democracia* (Barcelona: Planeta, 1991); Vicente Palacio Atard, *Juan Carlos I y el advenimiento de la democracia* (Madrid: Espasa Calpe, Colección Austral, 1989); Joel Podolny, "The Role of Juan Carlos I in the Consolidation of the Parliamentary Monarchy," in *Politics, Society and Democracy in Spain*, edited by Richard Gunther (Boulder: Westview Press, 1992), pp. 88–112. On the constitutional status of the king, see Manuel Aragón, "La monarquía parlamentaria," in *La constitución española de 1978*, edited by A. Predieri and Eduardo García de Enterría (Madrid: Civitas, 1980), p. 414.

Spaniards today widely agree with the statement: "Without the presence and the actions of the King the transition to democracy would not have been possible." In 1983, 64 percent, and in 1985, 67 percent, agreed; respectively 19 percent and 18 percent, more or less, disagreed, and 18 percent and 15 percent had no opinion. In 1983, 86 percent agreed that "the King, in stopping the coup of the 23rd of February has gained the respect of Spanish democrats," and between 80 and 89 percent agreed with the statement: "The King has been able to gain the affection of Spaniards including those who did not see the monarchy with favor," with only 6–8 percent disagreeing.

62. An interesting document on the relation between a powerful chancellor and a highly respected and intelligent president of the republic in a parliamentary regime is: *Theodor Heuss–Konrad Adenauer: "Unserem Vaterland Zugute" der Briefwechsel 1948–1963*, edited by Rudolf Morsey and Hans Peter Schwarz with the collaboration of Hans Peter Mensing (Berlin: Siedler, 1989).

63. The logical possibility of a prime minister who is elected directly but is not head of state cannot be excluded, but it has not existed in practice. This solution has been proposed in Holland, where the monarchy would be retained, and in Israel.

64. When I wrote this essay I used the term *semipresidential* because it was the most frequently used term for the kind of government in question, particularly in the United States, where it became known through the writings of Maurice Duverger. Shugart and Carey prefer "premier-presidentialism" to describe this type of regime and offer good arguments in favor of that designation. Perhaps the expression, *dual executive systems*, would be adequate. Since my original text has been translated into several languages, I will continue to use *semipresidential*.

65. Regarding semipresidential or semiparliamentary (or dual executive) systems, apart from the works of Kaltefleiter and Bartolini already cited (and their sources), see Humberto Nogueira Alcalá, *El régimen semipresidencial. ¿Una nueva forma de gobierno democrático?* (Santiago: Andante, 1986).

66. Maurice Duverger, *Echec au roi* (Paris: Albin Michel, 1978); "A New Political System

Model: Semipresidential Government," *European Journal of Political Research* 8 (1980): 165–87; Michel Debré, "The Constitution of 1958: Its Raison d'Etre and How It Evolved," in *The Fifth Republic at Twenty*, edited by William G. Andrews and Stanley Hoffman (New York: State U New York P, 1980); Ezra Suleiman, "Presidential Government in France," in *Presidents and Prime Ministers*, edited by Richard Rose and Ezra Suleiman (Washington, D.C.: American Enterprise Institute, 1980), pp. 93–138.

67. On the "majoritarian" character of presidentialism, see Arend Lijphart, chap. 2 herein. On Lijphart, see the discussion in Shugart and Carey, *Presidents and Assemblies*, pp. 20–21.

68. Maurice Duverger, ed., *Les régimes semi-présidentiels* (Paris: Presses Universitaires de France, 1988) with essays on Portugal, Finland, France, and the Weimar republic and discussions of the papers presented.

69. For the presidency in the Weimar Republic and its origins, see Kaltefleiter, *Die Funktionen des Staatsoberhauptes*, chap. 4, pp. 130–44, with reference to the writings of Max Weber and Hugo Preuss and legal commentaries on the constitution. Regarding the functioning of the system, see the excellent analysis on pp. 153–67.

70. On Ireland see Basil Chubb, *The Constitution and Constitutional Change in Ireland* (Dublin: Institute for Public Administration, 1978), chap. 2.

71. Horst Müller, "Parlamentarismus—Diskussion in der Weimar Republik. Die Frage des 'besonderen' Weges zum parlamentarischen Regierungssystem," in *Demokratie und Diktatur. Geist und Gestalt Politischer Herrschaft in Deutschland und Europa, Festschrift für Karl Dietrich Bracher*, edited by Manfred Funke et al. (Düsseldorf: Droste, 1987), pp. 140–57. The Portuguese regime of the 1976 constitution and its successive reforms has not been incorporated into many discussions of semipresidential regimes, even though it is an extremely relevant case. Luis Salgado de Matos, "L'expérience portugaise," in Duverger, *Les régimes semi-présidentiels*, pp. 55–83, includes an interesting analysis of the voting patterns in the election of President Eanes in 1976 and 1980 (see maps on pp. 66–67) that shows radical shifts in support depending on the coalitions supporting Eanes and the larger political context. In the same volume, see Barroso, "Les conflits entre le président portugais et la majorité parlementaire." Kenneth R. Maxwell and Scott C. Monje, eds., *Portugal: The Constitution and the Consolidation of Democracy*, (New York: Camões Center, Columbia University, special report no. 2, 1991) includes comments by social scientists and politicians on the 1976 constitution and its subsequent reform.

72. Consejo para la Consolidación de la Democracia, *Reforma constitucional. Dictamen preliminar del* (Buenos Aires: EUDEBA, 1986) includes the text of the proposal and accompanying documents. The *consejo* was created by President Alfonsín in December 1985. It worked under the leadership of Professor Carlos S. Nino and submitted its report to the president on March 13, 1986.

73. In the case of Finland, there is no great clarity on the respective responsibilities of president and prime minister, although there are "reserve domains" of presidential authority. Article 33 of the constitution establishes that "the president shall determine the relations of Finland with foreign powers," which was so important in postwar relations with the Soviet Union. Otherwise the president has acted as an arbiter in crisis situations and in forming governments in a multiparty system requiring coalitions among a wide spectrum of parties. Kekkonen excluded the Conservatives in order to maintain the "red-green alliance." Perhaps more than other semipresidential-semiparliamentary regimes, the Finnish, which has a "division of labor" and multiparty coalition politics, seems to fit the concept of a "dual executive" and not to oscillate between presidential and parliamentary modes of governing.

See David Arter, "Government in Finland: A 'Semipresidential System'?" *Parliamentary Affairs* 38 (1985): 477–95; Jaakko Nonsiainen, "Bureaucratic Tradition: Semi-presidential Rule and Parliamentary Government; The Case of Finland," *European Journal of Political Research* 16 (1988): 221–49; and the reference to the Finnish case in Kaltefleiter, *Die Funktionen des Staatsoberhauptes*, pp. 167–73 and passim, and in Shugart and Carey, *Presidents and Assemblies*, pp. 61–63. See also Bartolini, "Sistema partitico ed elezione diretta del capo dello stato in Europa."

74. Bartolini, "Sistema partitico ed elezione diretta del capo dello stato in Europa."

75. The shift toward a more parliamentary system in Portugal is reflected in the constitutional reform of 1982. Article 193 of the 1976 constitution stipulated that the government was politically responsible to the president of the republic and the parliament. The new article 193 does not specify the type of responsibility, and article 194 states that the prime minister is responsible to the Assembleia da Républica, in the realm of political responsibility of the government, although article 198.2 grants the president of the republic the exceptional power of dismissing the government should it be necessary to assure the normal functioning of democratic institutions.

76. On the other hand, the fear of a military president led framers of the 1931 constitution of the Spanish Republic to make ineligible for the presidency anyone active in the military or in the reserves and anyone retired from the military for less than ten years.

77. Duverger, "A New Political System Model."

78. Kaltefleiter, *Die Funktionen des Staatsoberhauptes*, pp. 153–67.

79. Raymond Aron, "Alternation in Government in the Industrialized Countries," *Government and Opposition* 17, no. 1 (1981): 3–21.

80. Giovanni Sartori, *Seconda Repubblica? Si, ma bene.* (Milan: Rizzoli, 1992).

81. See Rainer Lepsius, "From Fragmented Party Democracy to Government by Emergency Decree," in Linz and Stepan, *Breakdown of Democratic Regimes*, esp. pp. 34–39, 45–50; Eberhard Jäckel, "Der Machtantritt Hitlers—Versuch einer geschichtlichen Erklärung," in *1933 Wie die Republik der Diktatur erlag*, edited by Volker Rittberger (Stuttgart: Kohlhammer, 1983), pp. 123–39.

82. Kaltefleiter, *Die Funktionen des Staatoberhauptes*, pp. 183–97, esp. p. 197.

83. In 1929 Carl Schmitt, one of the leading political scientists and constitutionalists of Germany, published in the *Archiv des öffentlichen Rechts* (Neue Folge) 16: 161–237, an article titled "Der Hüter der Verfassung" and in 1931 a pamphlet under the same title, in *Beiträge zum öffentlichen Recht der Gegenwart*, Heft 1 (Tübingen), offering an authoritarian antipluralistic and plebiscitary interpretation of the Weimar constitution.

84. Regarding the stability of parliamentary semipresidential regimes in Europe between the two world wars, see Linz, *Crisis, Breakdown and Reequilibration*, pp. 74–75. Of the seventeen countries analyzed before the depression, apart from Portugal, Yugoslavia, and Spain (1918–23), Germany had the greatest instability with 210 days average duration of cabinet, followed by the Third Republic in France with 239 days, Italy (1917–22) with 260, Austria with 267, and Finland with 294. After the depression, Spain with 101 days average duration, France with 165, Austria with 149, Germany with 258, Finland with 592, Estonia with 260, and Belgium with 285 are the countries with the most unstable governments of the fourteen countries that are included. Note that two of the systems with a dual executive are among the most unstable countries. In two of the countries with high government instability and a parliamentary regime democracy survived until World War II. See also Ekkart Zimmermann, "Government Stability in Six European Countries during the World Economic Crisis of the 1930s: Some Preliminary Considerations," *European Journal of Political Research* 15 (1987): 23–52.

85. Nicolás Pérez Serrano, *La constitución española* (9 Dec. 1931) (Madrid: Editorial Revista de Derecho Privado, 1932), pp. 244–74; see articles 75, 81, and 87. See Antonio Bar, *El presidente del gobierno en España: Encuadre constitucional y práctica política* (Madrid: Editorial Civitas, 1983), pp. 121–28, for a study of "rationalized parliamentarism" and the role of the president of the Second Republic.

He was elected by the members of the Cortes, a unicameral legislature, and an equal number of electors (who were directly elected by the people) for a term of six years and could not be reelected. However, the first president was elected by the legislature on December 10, 1931.

The system of dual confidence was derived from article 75: "The President of the Republic appoints and dismisses freely the president of the government, and, at his proposal the ministers. He shall dismiss them necessarily in the case that the Cortes should explicitly deny them their confidence."

86. On the working of the Spanish constitution of 1931 and the presidency, see: Joaquín Tomás Villarroya, "Presidente de la República y Gobierno: Sus Relaciones," *Revista de estudios políticos* (nueva época) 31–32 (Jan.–Apr. 1983): 71–90 (which quotes leading politicians on the "dual confidence"), and "La prerrogativa presidencial durante la Segunda República: Mediatización, *Revista de estudios políticos* 16 (1980): pp. 59–87; Stanley G. Payne, *Spain's First Democracy: The Second Republic, 1931–1936* (Madison: U Wisconsin P, 1993), describes in detail the working of the system. On the removal of the president, see Joaquín Tomás Villarroya, *La destitución de Alcalá-Zamora*, (Valencia: Fundación Universitaria, San Pablo, CEU, 1988). For the position of Niceto Alcalá-Zamora see his *Los defectos de la Constitución de 1931 y tres años de experiencia constitucional* (Madrid: Civitas, 1981, first published 1936) and *Memorias. Segundo texto de mis memorias* (Barcelona: Planeta, 1977). Javier Tusell, "Niceto Alcalá-Zamora y una crisis política en el segundo bienio Republicano," *Hispania* 33 (1973): 401–16.

87. If it did not compound confusion the system could be described as "semi-premier-presidential" because half the electors of the president were to be popularly elected (although the first president, like Ebert and de Gaulle, was elected by the legislature).

88. *Diario de Sesiones de las Cortes Constituyentes*, 3 Nov. 1931, p. 2092.

89. Karl Dietrich Bracher, *Die Auflösung der Weimarer Republik* (Stuttgart: Ring-Verlag, 1957), chap. 9 about the Reichswehr, pp. 229–84; see pp. 249–53 for articles 53 and 54 of the constitution, which required the double confidence of the Reichstag and the president for the minister of defense.

90. There is also the possibility, though it is less likely, that the top military leadership might turn to congressional leaders to oppose the president.

91. There is likely to be more experimenting with mixed formulas in view of the growing dissatisfaction with pure presidentialism and the distrust of pure parliamentarism (which not all forms of parliamentarism merit, probably), or the unwillingness to break with the tradition of presidentialism. In addition to the "premier-presidential" (semiparliamentary, semipresidential) systems we discuss, Giovanni Sartori has developed another type in "Le riforme istituzionali—Tra buone e cattive," *Rivista italiana di scienza politica* 21 (3 Dec. 1991): 375–408, with commentary by Angelo Pianebianco (pp. 409–18) and Stefano Passigli (pp. 419–40) and a rejoinder by Sartori (pp. 441–46). Also in Sartori, *Seconda Repubblica?*

The resistance to parliamentarism (in any version) and the difficulty of making the French type of semipresidential, semiparliamentary system work in view of the "plebiscitary culture" surrounding presidentialism in Latin America has led to the search for other hybrid solutions. One submitted by a working group of Bolivian political scientists and constitutionalists in collaboration with several foreign scholars (including me) to a political commission charged with making constitutional reforms might be dubbed "parliamentarized presidentialism." It does not abandon the presidentialist principle of direct popular election of a president but tries to reduce the risks and costs of "minority" presidencies. It also attempts to deal with the "rigidity" of the presidential mandate and the risk of ingovernability by making possible a constructive vote of nonconfidence in the case of minority presidents and a return of power to the electorate in case of total impasse by a qualified congressional majority, with both presidential and parliamentary elections. The project is based on the Bolivian tradition of parliamentary election of the president in the absence of a majority vote for any candidate.

The proposal starts with presidentialism as a point of departure. In fact, it retains a pure presidentialism (except that it allows for "political" rather than just criminal impeachment, *juicio político*) with one condition: that the majority of the people elect a president. Otherwise the equal democratic legitimacy of the congress enters into play; this body elects a president, choosing between the two candidates with the most popular votes the one who can form the strongest parliamentary coalition. However, the president so elected, by a minority of the electorate *and* a majority of the congress, is subject to a constructive vote of no confidence, which assures his succession by a president with majority support in the congress. In a sense the system is also an alternative parliamentarism, as Sartori's is an alternative presidentialism. The difference is that one case attempts to correct the impasses generated by presidentialism and the other, those of extreme, assembly-type parliamentarism.

92. In pure presidential systems the president cannot dissolve the assembly. There are, however, the exceptions of Paraguay (never tested under democratic conditions) and Chile in the authoritarian 1980 constitution. In Uruguay and Peru dissolution can be invoked after the congress has censored cabinet ministers or even the entire cabinet for political reasons (in the case of Peru, this must happen three times) with additional restrictions.

The possibility of dissolution by a president who stays in office may not resolve but exacerbate the conflict between the congress and the president. The electorate might return a congress that is hostile to the president, and the stalemate might be prolonged. Only if dissolution leads to the election of a new congress and a simultaneous presidential election might this risk be reduced; the voters then would have a chance to side with the president or with the opposition.

93. The preference for presidentialism and even mixed forms of semipresidential systems is often based on hostility to political parties, if not to democratic pluralism. It is not surprising that conservatives not fully reconciled to the transition to democracy in Germany (the DVP and DNVP), the Finnish conservatives, and more recently "reconstructed" communist parties or leaders in the former USSR and Mongolia should have favored a president who is presumably above parties. In addition, in a recently unified country like Germany, there was the hope of finding a "substitute" Kaiser in a federal republic or, in countries like Finland, Ireland, and Iceland, a symbol of the new national independence.

94. On this point see: Linz, "Change and Continuity in the Nature of Contemporary Democracies," in *Reexamining Democracy, Essays in Honor of Seymour Martin Lipset*, edited by Gary Marks and Larry Diamond (Newbury Park, Calif.: Sage, 1992), pp. 182–207, esp. pp. 188–90 and the studies quoted there.

95. Philip Williams, *Politics in Post-War France. Parties and the Constitution in the Fourth Republic* (London: Longmans, Green, 1954), p. 399.

96. In relation to the constructive vote of censure, see Bar, *El presidente del gobierno en España*, with reference to the works of the German and Spanish constitutionalists. Guilherme d'Oliveira Martins, Dieter Nohlen, José Juan González Encinar, António Vitorino,

José Magalhães, and Jorge Sampaio, *A revisão constitucional e a moção de censura construc-tiva* (Lisbon: Fundação Friedrich Ebert, 1988) includes chapters about the Bonn constitution and the 1978 Spanish constitution, with bibliographical references. On the use of the constructive vote of no confidence in Germany, see Lewis J. Edinger, *West German Politics* (New York: Columbia UP, 1986), p. 247.

97. The way in which parliamentary governments in Europe actually work is enormously varied, particularly in the formation of cabinets and their relation to the parliament. This is not the place to discuss that rich and complex experience; I refer the reader to the monumental work of Klaus von Beyme, *Die parlementarischen Regierungssysteme in Europa,* pt. 2, pp. 499–900.

98. Chapter 3 of this volume, by Giovanni Sartori, rightly argues against pure parliamentarism, the *gouvernement d'assemblée,* in which the parliament governs and the executive—the prime minister and his cabinet—has no authority and is unprotected against quickly shifting majorities in the assembly that cannot be made accountable.

He argues for an impure solution that he sometimes calls semiparliamentary, which sidesteps the principle of the sovereignty of parliament. My argument in favor of premier-parliamentarism, like the British or the German Kanzlerdemokratie, coincides with his, but we differ in the characterization of those regimes. In my view they are parliamentary because the election of the prime minister or Kanzler is made by the parties in the parliament and continuance in office ultimately depends on the parliament, where one wins a vote of confidence, fails to provide an alternative government, or even fears dissolution and the need to confront the electorate. Modern, rationalized parliamentary systems do not eliminate the role of parties or of parliamentarians but limit the arbitrary, irresponsible, excessive use of parliamentary power. However, the executive has to pay attention to the parliament, to his or her party or the supporters of a coalition, and therefore is not "independent" and "unaccountable" for the whole legislative period. The democratically elected "unequals" above whom or among whom he or she governs have a share in power and are potentially accountable for their use of it.

99. The Israeli parliamentary system is generally considered as a "bad" case of parliamentarism, with its highly fractionalized party system (largely a result of the electoral law), the difficulty of forming coalitions and their instability, the stalemate due to the concessions made in forming coalitions, and other problems. Reforms short of moving to a pure presidential system have been proposed, including the direct election of the prime minister. See the "Conclusion, Directions for Reform" in Ehud Sprinzak and Larry Diamond, *Israel: Democracy under Stress* (Boulder: Lynne Rienner, 1993).

100. Scott Mainwaring and Matthew Shugart, "Juan Linz, Presidentialism and Democracy," in *Politics, Society, and Democracy: Latin America. Essays in Honor of Juan J. Linz* (Boulder: Westview Press, 1994).

101. Alfred Stepan and Cindy Skach, "Meta-Institutional Frameworks and Democratic Consolidation" (paper prepared for the Third Meeting of the East-South System Transformations Project, 4–7 Jan. 1992, Toledo, Spain).

102. Shugart and Carey, *Presidents and Assemblies,* pp. 40–41.

103. Juan J. Linz, "La crisis de las democracias," in *Europa en crisis 1919–1939,* edited by Mercedes Cabrera, Santos Juliá, and Pablo Martín Aceña (Madrid: Editorial Pablo Iglesias, 1991), pp. 231–80; see table 1, p. 235.

104. Tatu Vanhanen, "Institutional Strategies and Democratization" (paper presented at the 15th World Congress of the International Political Science Association, July 1991, Buenos Aires).

Part II
The Experience of Latin American Presidentialism

6

ARTURO VALENZUELA

Party Politics and the Crisis of Presidentialism in Chile: A Proposal for a Parliamentary Form of Government

In most countries at one time or another severe political upheavals threaten national harmony, internal peace, and institutional stability. Chile, the Latin American country that stood out for its long tradition of representative democracy, suffered its most serious historical crisis with the violent overthrow of constitutional government in 1973 and the installation of an authoritarian regime lasting almost eighteen years. The military dictatorship led by general of the army Augusto Pinochet became the longest, and arguably most revolutionary, government in the nation's history.

From the perspective of Chile's military commanders, the September 1973 military coup meant the rejection not only of the Marxist experiment of President Salvador Allende, but also of the inefficient democratic regime that had failed to turn away externally inspired demagogic movements intent on destroying the nation's institutions and corroding "patriotic values." From the outset, the dictatorship expressed profound contempt for parties and politicians and the institutional arenas in which they were most visible, particularly the national legislature and local elected governments. Military leaders considered the politicians venal and self-serving—men who in their quest for power and their penchant for compromise and accommodation had manipulated a pliant and naive electorate for narrow partisan gain and ultimately had permitted the Far Left to capture the state and threaten the survival of the social order.

This diagnosis soon led the new authorities to define their mission as foundational: they would break sharply with the past. Rather than simply rectify the misguided policies of the ousted government by restoring the preexisting constitutional system, they would embark on a concerted strategy to revolutionize economic policy and implement far-reaching political and institutional changes. The two objectives would soon be viewed as closely intertwined. Economic development, spurred by the private sector and combined with the destruction of the old party system and the establishment of more authoritarian political institutions, would lead to basic changes in the very physiognomy of Chilean democracy, with far-reaching implications for the party system and the underlying political loyalties of the citizenry.

The expectation of Chile's military rulers was that a dictatorial interlude of indeterminate length would forge a wholly different country. Market forces and an open, export-oriented economy would unleash entrepreneurial skills and boost production and economic growth. In the political arena, Chile would become a society of loyal and obedient subjects, no longer riven by class or ideology. Authoritarian measures, aimed at rooting out "bad Chileans," combined with the implementation of new electoral and party rules in an economic climate of greater abundance, would eventually lead to the formation of two moderate blocs, similar to the party system of the United States.

To guarantee the emergence of this "modern, stable, and protected" democracy, the transformed party system would operate within the framework of a new constitutional order characterized by a far more powerful president, a weakened parliament, appointed rather than elected local governments, and a central role for an autonomous military establishment that was the ultimate guarantor of national security.

It is beyond the scope of this chapter to evaluate the progress made by the military regime in the economic sphere. Although it experienced several serious reversals, the government of General Augusto Pinochet succeeded in establishing macroeconomic stability and implementing extensive structural reforms that dramatically redefined the role of the state in economic development. By the end of the military government, the policy of encouraging private enterprise while opening the Chilean economy to world markets had contributed to impressive growth rates, spurred by a new and dynamic export sector. While wages and salaries remained low and many Chileans felt that they had not benefited from the economic policies of the military years, Chile ended the 1980s with one of the best economic records on the subcontinent.

But if the military government succeeded in achieving most of its economic goals, it had mixed success in implementing its ambitious objectives in the political sphere. The most dramatic evidence of the shortcomings of the regime's political strategy was the defeat of General Pinochet on October 6, 1988, in a yes or no plebiscite. The rejection of Pinochet was symptomatic of the military government's failure to alter Chile's party system fundamentally. The very politicians and parties he had sought to suppress, which were the target of almost daily diatribes, managed to put aside historic antagonisms and forge a successful campaign against a powerful government that did not hesitate to use its administrative and military control, its favorable economic performance, and the people's fear of the past as weapons to perpetuate itself in power.

Pinochet's defeat and the failure of the military government to radically transform the party system stemmed from a fundamental misconception regarding the nature of Chilean politics. In personalizing politics, in viewing their principal antagonists as venal political leaders who had misled a backward electorate, they failed to understand the degree to which Chilean party politics had penetrated society and the extent to which parties constituted powerful referents for citizens in a highly sophisticated political culture. Parties were not simply epiphenomena that would disappear under an iron hand and the exile of hundreds of leaders. They were deeply rooted in society and could survive long repression and inaction.

But the military also misdiagnosed the political and institutional dynamics that helped Chile establish a fairly long record of constitutional rule in a continent racked by authoritarian governments, and it misdiagnosed the factors that contributed to regime breakdown. It is true that the institutional system had been severely challenged before the advent of the Allende government. It is also true that the multiparty system, with its profound ideological differences, created political pressures that made it difficult to structure national policies capable of addressing the daunting problems of underdevelopment.

The configuration of party politics, however, was not solely responsible for the difficulties facing Chilean rulers. Some of the most stable democracies in the world have multiparty systems, even highly polarized party systems. In studying any political system it is not enough to focus on the party system per se. Rather, it is critical to examine the broader interrelationship between the party system and the institutional framework of government, the interplay between the political expressions of societal divisions and the formal and informal rules and mechanisms by which conflicts are resolved and public policies achieved.

It is the central thesis of this chapter that the crisis of Chilean democracy was exacerbated by the lack of congruence between the nation's competitive and polarized party system, on the one hand, and its institutional system, on the other. More specifically, the challenges of democracy in Chile were closely linked to the difficulties of making compatible a presidentialist constitutional framework, with its winner-take-all elections, and a polarized multiparty political system in which no single party (or political tendency of the Left, Right, or Center) could generate a majority to elect the president or support him in the legislature. Although coalitions were frequently created prior to the presidential race in order to maximize electoral chances, the presidential system provided few incentives for the maintenance of stable coalitions after the president took office. The result was unstable minority governments and frequent governmental paralysis. Indeed, this chapter argues that the very rules of a presidential system often generated pressures that undermined the logic of coalition formation.

What permitted Chile to weather these challenges was the existence of pragmatic centrist forces and the politics of compromise that they encouraged. The politics of accommodation, the hallmark of Chile's centrist parties, were essential to the structuring of governmental coalitions in a multiparty context marked by serious societal divisions. In this political process, a viable legislative arena was critical; it forced executives to build bridges, however tenuous, across Chile's complex partisan landscape in order to achieve a modicum of governability.

These institutions for coalition building, much vilified by both the Far Left in the late 1960s and the military authorities after the coup d'état, were not what undermined Chilean politics. The reverse is true. This chapter argues that the rigidities of presidentialism and the gradual erosion of arenas of accommodation, particularly the legislature, heightened the politics of confrontation in Chile, making it more difficult to negotiate political compromises. The failure of the constitutional architects of the military regime to understand the role of compromise in Chilean politics, combined with the Pinochet government's inability to eradicate the multiparty system, raises serious questions about the viability of the presidential system embodied in the constitution of 1980. It is ironic that the price the democratic opposition had to pay in its effort to defeat the military government at its own game was full acceptance of a constitutional order that contemplates an exaggerated presidentialist system, one with little room for the politics of compromise and coalition building, which were difficult to structure even with the more flexible presidential system of the past.

This work argues that Chileans, in the aftermath of the authoritarian interlude, should at the very least reverse the hyperpresidentialism of the Pinochet constitution and reestablish a stronger legislature capable of aggregating interests and structuring compromises. Chile requires strong and stable coalitions in order to govern a complex and modernizing society with a highly institutionalized multiparty system. Indeed, Chilean leaders should seriously consider taking an even bolder step: changing from a presidential form of government to a parliamentary or semiparliamentary form.

The first part of this chapter reviews the origins and principal characteristics of Chile's multiparty system and concludes with the failure of the military government to alter its basic configuration. The second part examines how Chilean parties structured governing coalitions in Chile's presidential system in the past and argues that the inability of the party system to generate majority coalitions contributed to a semipresidential form of government in practice, one that was unable to mitigate the sense of permanent crisis in Chilean politics. It concludes by analyzing the role of these institutional factors in accounting for the breakdown of Chilean democracy. The third and final section of the chapter argues the case for a parliamentary formula for Chile, showing how it would contribute to the structuring of more enduring coalitions while helping to moderate party extremes. A parliamentary system would provide the country with a more stable political regime precisely because it would be able to deal more effectively with the nation's competitive and polarized party system. The chapter concludes by analyzing several myths about the parliamentary system as it would apply to Chile.

The Chilean Party System

In few other countries did political parties play as prominent a role for as long a period of time as they did in Chile. Parties recruited leaders and determined policy options in Chile's powerful executive and legislative branches. Their influence extended into most interest groups, community associations, educational institutions, and even soccer clubs and churches. Candidates for union offices and high school and university leadership positions ran on party platforms, and party organizations paid as much attention to the outcome of these elections as to congressional by-elections. Parties gave political content and organizational form to deep-seated societal cleavages with referents going back to the nineteenth century.

Historical Antecedents

The development of party politics in Chile is closely associated with the development of republican institutions in the nineteenth century. After 1830 and a turbulent period of anarchy and dictatorship, the ballot box (albeit with a restricted electorate) became the sole mechanism for determining presidential and congressional leadership positions. The only deviation from this pattern came in the crisis years of 1891, 1924, and 1932, when unconstitutional governments held office for periods ranging up to five months. With the partial exception of the strong-man rule of Carlos Ibáñez (1927–32), who drew on civilian technocrats for government positions while jailing and exiling some prominent political leaders, parties were the determining political forces shaping the nation's democratic institutions, as well as critical protagonists in periods of political unrest and instability. With the return of democracy in 1990, after the authoritarian period extending from 1973 to 1989, parties reemerged at center stage in Chilean politics.

The distinctiveness of the Chilean party system in Latin America has often been noted. According to Kalman Silvert, "Chile stands alone with respect not only to the number of its political parties, but in their national scope, their high degree of impersonalism, and the way in which they fit into three major ideological groups."[1]

Federico Gil adds that the Chilean parties seemed more akin to their European counterparts in sophistication and genuine pluralism than to those of other American republics.[2] While catchall parties predominate in the Western Hemisphere, Chilean parties are much closer to the mass-based European models. In no other country of North or South America has a party system evolved with three distinct ideological tendencies, each garnering between a fourth and a third of the vote, including a Marxist Left and a political Right that are both organizationally strong and electorally oriented.[3]

While the center of the political spectrum has been occupied by parties whose fortunes have risen or fallen depending on the strength of the polls, for the most part it has been dominated by highly organized parties, which though they cross class lines, have advanced distinct ideological platforms devoid of populist or personalist characteristics typical of other countries in the region. And when the Conservative party lost its luster as the party of the Catholic faithful, a progressive Christian Democratic party—with no exact parallel in Latin America—gained national strength. Indeed, although one can argue that the Chilean party system was akin to a model European system, no individual European country, with the possible exception of the French Fourth Republic, embodied all the salient features of Chilean party politics.

The Chilean party system owes its basic characteristics to three fundamental generative cleavages that have found expression at different times in history: geographic (center versus periphery), religious (state versus church), and class (worker versus employer).[4] It is crucial, however, to stress that societal cleavages alone are not responsible for the characteristics of a given party system. Geographic, religious, and class cleavages were present in other countries, with very different results. What is determinative is not only the presence of particular societal divisions, but when and how they are expressed politically. This depends on the timing of the development of a particular cleavage and the nature of the institutional structures and political norms that channel the political forces emerging from it. These structures and rules can in turn be transformed by new political circumstances.[5]

What made the Chilean case distinctive was the way in which the first cleavage, the geographic one, was resolved early in the nineteenth century. As in the rest of Latin America, in Chile there was strong resistance to the development of a centralized secular state. This resistance stemmed from personal and family rivalries; from regional rivalries; from regional economic interests, such as mine owners in the northern provinces; and from conservative landed elites, who were jealous of their autonomy and supported the preeminence of the church on educational and social issues. Though paying lip service to some of the new republican norms, the conservative forces did not hesitate to resort to violence, notably in the civil wars of 1851 and 1859, to advance their own interests and curb central authority.

While the emerging political class in Chile embarked successfully on a program of economic development and expansion of state authority over national territory and rival groups and institutions, it also managed to defeat all armed challenges and to establish an effective hegemony over the military establishment. It did this by creating a powerful but politically subservient national guard as a counterforce to the regular army.

This meant that challengers to state authority were forced to advance their interests through ballots rather than bullets. The religious issue soon became the dominant one as the "liberal" anticlerical elites who controlled the state pushed for greater secularization, while the Conservative party and the church sought to defend the temporal influence of religious elites. But because opposition became centered in the legislature and not the battlefield, elements as diverse as the Conservatives and Radicals would eventually make common cause in attempting to settle their grievances and advance their programs. Indeed, as early as the 1870s Conservatives collaborated in the congress on common political strategy with members of the Radical party—which managed to achieve parliamentary and cabinet representation decades before their counterparts in Argentina did.[6]

The development of a strong legislature, which became the arena for forces opposing the overarching authority of the executive, exacerbated the growing conflict between the two governmental powers, each claiming democratic legitimacy. Of utmost importance for opposition elements with congressional representation was expanding suffrage and curbing official intervention in elections. As in Britain, the Chilean Conservatives from their position of strength in the countryside soon built legislative coalitions with the anticlerical Radicals and ideological liberals in seeking that goal. Majorities were eventually forged to bar presidents from a second consecutive term in office and, in 1874, to expand suffrage by dropping property requirements, a clear attempt to counteract the control the executive's agents had over the electoral process.[7]

Genuinely competitive elections and the expansion of political parties did not take place, however, until after the Civil War of 1891, a war that was the direct result of the long-standing and bitter struggle between shifting legislative majorities and recalcitrant minority executives, each jealous of its own prerogatives and each seeking to impose its will on the other. With the military defeat of the president and his allies by a broad range of political groups with majority representation in the legislature, the impasse occasioned by the separation of powers doctrine was resolved in favor of the legislature. Chile's presidents lost their ability to intervene in elections and to dominate the political process. For thirty-four years, Chile operated as a de facto parliamentary regime as shifting legislative majorities in both chambers of the congress determined the composition of presidential cabinets and government policies, while presidents pliantly followed their dictates, unable to dissolve the parliament when legislative majorities fell apart. With the shift of the political center of gravity away from the executive came the expansion of party networks outside the corridors of power and the emergence of Chile's multiparty system.

The rules of political contestation, with a central role for the parliament in the policy process, emerged before universal manhood suffrage. Political participation was a gradual process in response to the development, in Maurice Duverger's terms, of internally created parties that reached out of the legislative arena to build local and popular organizations for electoral advantage. Legislative and party politics also preceded the development of a strong state bureaucracy. Individuals and interest groups expressed their demands through parties and legislative cliques rather than directly to state agencies, or through corporatist schemes. This relationship reinforced the instrumental and even corrupt nature of the politics of the period, a politics based on logrolling and distribution of national wealth to benefit constituents and supporters; it was a system that often clashed with the ideological and principled declarations of parties and leaders. And yet it had the effect of reinforcing democracy by making parties and representative networks the fulcrum of the political process, insulating Chilean politics from the statist, corporatist, and populist tendencies of countries in which the legislative arena was weak and public agencies developed through the tuition of the executive.[8]

It was in the institutional context of the so-called parliamentary republic, one of highly competitive politics and expanding partisan organizations, that class cleavages became politically salient. The period of the parliamentary republic coincided with extraordinary changes in the levels of urbanization and industrialization, fueled by a booming nitrate economy. But while the Radical party sought to expand its base from urban professionals, teachers, shopkeepers, and skilled tradesmen (and in the south, wheat farmers) and to reach the growing industrial and mining proletariat, it failed to capture the full allegiance of these elements.

As Samuel Valenzuela has noted, it failed because the industrial climate at the time was not favorable to collective bargaining and worker unionization. Indeed, the response of the authorities was to repress the working-class movement with extraordinary brutality. Moderate politicians such as the Radicals could not represent working-class interests because they did not have a leadership capable of standing up to employer and government repression.[9]

However, as Valenzuela further notes, while union rights were limited, political rights were far-reaching. The new working-class leaders, who drew their inspiration from European anarchosyndicalism and socialism, soon discovered that while they could not press their grievances in the workplace, they could organize and run for office. The first working-class party of any note, the Democratic party (founded in 1857), elected its first candidate to parliament in 1894. Other parties soon found that electoral pacts and alliances with the new working-class group advanced their own standing vis-à-vis traditional rivals. The Democratic party allied with the Liberals and Radicals and even structured electoral pacts with the Conservative party. This willingness to ally with traditional groups led to a split in the party's ranks in 1912 and to the formation of the Socialist Workers party, which in turn led to the founding of the Communist party in 1922.

Although the Communist party rejected alliances with traditional forces, after considerable struggle it opted to pursue its objectives through electoral gains, a strategy that would profoundly mark the character of Chilean communism until the breakdown of democracy in 1973. It obtained three senators as early as 1926. And in 1938, it allied with the Radicals and the newly formed Socialist party in the successful election of a Popular Front candidate. The party continued to make electoral gains, despite efforts to ban it, until those efforts succeeded in 1948.

In sum, the competitive nature of a political system centered on the parliament permitted parties created outside the legislative arena to become incorporated into the political process.[10] To the parties that developed in the midnineteenth century in response to geographic and religious cleavages but that continued to represent elite economic interests were added parties representing the working class. Their presence on the political stage only redoubled the efforts of the traditional parties to expand their own organizational and recruitment efforts.

In writing about Europe, Lipset and Rokkan have noted that it is difficult to see any significant exception to the rule that the parties that have proved most viable are those that were able to establish mass organizations and to entrench themselves in local government structures before the final drive toward maximal mobilization.[11] This applies to Chile as well, as does their suggestion that the character of the party system remains remarkably similar to the one consolidated at the time of early suffrage expansion. If the system is competitive during suffrage expansion, the "support market" seems to become constrained, leaving few openings for new movements, although as noted below, in Chile numerous parties attempted through the years, with little success, to become established. The only notable exception to this rule was the emergence of the Christian Democrats in the late 1950s as a major party—a latter-day version of the religious issue as Catholic voters and church officials broke with the Conservative party in search of a Christian and reformist alternative to the Left.

The Party System at Midcentury

The year 1932 is a convenient starting point for describing the general configuration of Latin America's most prominent multiparty system. Chile returned to constitutional stability in that year, after an interlude in which several presidents resigned from office unable to cope with political and economic crises. In the interlude Chile experienced direct military involvement in governing the country on two separate occasions, each lasting several months.

The 1930s for Chile culminated with the election of the Popular Front and the inauguration of a series of left-of-center governments that would last until 1952, when Carlos Ibáñez's populist appeals presented the traditional party system with a brief, though significant, challenge. His ineffective government would be followed in succession by a Conservative administration under Jorge Alessandri (1958–64), a reformist government under Eduardo Frei (1964–70), and the leftist government of Salvador Allende (1970–73).

Table 6.1 gives an overview of the overall voting trends in Chile for all Chilean parties receiving more than 5 percent of the vote in elections to the chamber of deputies from 1937 to 1973. In the 1930s and 1940s, the parties of the Right had the largest plurality of support, with about 40 percent of the electorate. Unlike their French and German counterparts, and more like the Conservatives in Britain, the Chilean Right maintained a strong electoral base and long resisted fragmentation.[12]

In the 1950s and 1960s, however, rightist support began to erode and support for the Left increased steadily. Center parties obtained between 30 and 40 percent, with

Table 6.1. Elections for Chamber of Deputies: Results by Party

	Votes (% Total)	Deputies Elected	Votes (% Total)	Deputies Elected	Votes (% Total)	Deputies Elected
	1932		1937		1941	
Conservative	55,260 (16.9)	34	87,845 (21.3)	35	77,243 (17.2)	32
United Conservative						
Liberal	32,645 (10.0)	18	85,515 (20.7)	35	63,118 (14.0)	22
National						
Others	22,214 (8.1)	9				
Total Right	**110,119 (35.0)**	**61**	**173,360 (42.0)**	**70**	**140,361 (31.2)**	**54**
Radical	59,413 (18.2)	34	76,941 (18.7)	29	98,269 (21.9)	44
National Falange/ Christian Democrats						
Worker Agrarian						
Others	45,040 (13.7)	20	38,702 (9.4)	12	41,144 (9.1)	11
Total Center	**104,453 (31.9)**	**54**	**115,643 (28.1)**	**41**	**139,413 (31.0)**	**55**
Chilean Socialists			46,050 (11.2)	19	75,500 (16.8)	15
Popular Socialists						
National Progressive/ Communist Party					53,144 (11.8)	16
Others			17,162 (4.2)	6	23,702 (5.3)	3
Total Left			**63,212 (15.4)**	**25**	**152,346 (33.9)**	**34**

	Votes (% Total)	Deputies Elected	Votes (% Total)	Deputies Elected	Votes (% Total)	Deputies Elected
	1945		1949		1953	
Conservative	106,254 (23.6)	36	98,118 (21.1)	31	111,715 (14.4)[a]	18
Liberal	80,597 (17.9)	31	83,582 (17.9)	33	84,924 (10.9)	23
National						
Others	9,849 (2.2)[b]	3	13,916 (3.0)[c]	4	21,381 (2.7)[d]	4
Total Right	**196,700 (43.7)**	**70**	**195,562 (42.0)**	**68**	**218,020 (28.0)**	**45**
Radical	89,922 (19.9)	39	100,869 (21.7)	34	103,650 (13.3)	18
National Falange/ Christian Democrats	11,565 (2.6)	3	18,221 (3.9)	3	22,353 (2.9)	3
Worker Agrarian			38,742 (8.3)	14	118,483 (15.2)	26
Others	39,075 (8.7)[e]	11	60,869 (13.2)[f]	16	137,747 (17.6)[g]	21
Total Center	**140,562 (31.2)**	**53**	**376,553 (47.1)**	**67**	**382,233 (49.0)**	**68**
Chilean Socialists	32,314 (7.2)	6	15,676 (3.4)	5	41,679 (5.4)	9
Popular Socialists			22,631 (4.9)	6	68,218 (8.8)	20
National Progressive/ Communist Party	46,133 (10.3)	15				
Others	25,104 (5.6)[h]	3	5,125 (1.1)[h]	1		
Total Left	**103,551 (23.1)**	**24**	**43,427 (9.4)**	**12**	**109,893 (14.2)**	**29**

	Votes (% Total)	Deputies Elected	Votes (% Total)	Deputies Elected	Votes (% Total)	Deputies Elected
	1957		1961		1965	
United Conservative	154,877 (17.6)[i]	23	198,260 (14.3)[j]	17	121,822 (5.2)	3
Liberal	134,741 (15.4)	30	222,485 (16.1)	28	171,979 (7.3)	6
National						
Others	47,060 (5.9)[k]	7				
Total Right	**336,678 (38.9)**	**60**	**420,745 (38.4)**	**45**	**293,801 (12.5)**	**9**

Table 6.1. Elections for Chamber of Deputies: Results by Party *(continued)*

	Votes (% Total)	Deputies Elected	Votes (% Total)	Deputies Elected	Votes (% Total)	Deputies Elected
	1957		1961		1965	
Radical	188,526 (21.5)	36	296,828 (21.4)	39	312,912 (13.3)	20
National Falange/						
Christian Democrats	82,710 (9.4)	17	213,468 (16.1)	28	995,187 (42.3)	82
Worker Agrarian	68,602 (7.8)	10				
Others	87,320 (9.9)[l]	10	95,179 (6.9)[m]	12	111,275 (4.7)[n]	3
Total Center	**427,158 (48.6)**	**73**	**605,475 (44.4)**	**79**	**1,419,374 (60.3)**	**105**
Chilean Socialists	38,783 (4.4)	7	149,122 (10.7)	12	241,593 (10.3)	15
Popular Socialists	55,004 (6.3)	5				
National Progressive/						
Communist Party			157,572 (11.4)	16	290,635 (12.4)	18
Others						
Total Left	**93,787 (10.7)**	**12**	**306,694 (22.1)**	**28**	**532,228 (22.7)**	**33**
	1969		1973			
Conservative						
Liberal						
National	480,523 (20.0)	33	777,084 (21.1)	32		
Others						
Total Right	**480,523 (20.0)**	**33**	**777,084 (21.1)**	**32**		
Radical	313,559 (13.0)	24	133,751 (3.6)	19		
Christian Democrats	716,547 (29.8)	56	1,049,676 (28.5)	55		
Total Center	**1,030,113 (42.8)**	**80**	**1,183,427 (32.1)**	**74**		
Chilean Socialists	294,448 (12.3)	15	678,674 (18.4)	15		
Communist Party	383,049 (15.9)	22	595,829 (16.2)	22		
Total Left	**971,945 (28.2)**	**37**	**1,274,503 (34.6)**	**37**		

Source: Data compiled from the Dirección del Registro Electoral, Santiago, Chile.

Note: Parties listed are those that obtained more than 5 percent of the total vote in more than one congressional election.

    a. Combined votes for the Conservative and United Conservative parties.

    b. Liberal Progressive party.

    c. Includes the Traditional Conservative and the Liberal Progressive parties.

    d. National Christian party.

    e. Includes the Agrarian party, the Liberal Popular Alliance, and the Democrats of Chile.

    f. Includes the Doctrinaire Radicals, the Radical Democrats, the Democrats of Chile, the Democrats of the People, and the Christian Social Movement.

    g. Includes the Agrarian party, the National Movement of the People, Popular Unity, Action for Chilean Renewal, and the Labor party.

    h. Authentic Socialist party.

    i. Combined votes of the Conservative and United Conservative parties.

    j. United Conservative party.

    k. Includes the National and Christian National parties.

    l. Includes the Doctrinaire Radicals, the Democratic party, the Republican Movement, the Republican Movement of the People, and the Labor and Workers parties.

    m. National Democrats.

    n. Includes the Democratic, National Democratic, and National Action parties.

the notable exception of the 1965 congressional election, when the Christian Democrats alone obtained 42.3 percent of the vote, the highest total for an individual party in modern Chilean politics.

It is noteworthy, however, that as early as 1941—the first congressional election after the inauguration of the Popular Front government of Radicals, Communists, and Socialists in 1938—the Left outdistanced both the Center and the Right, obtaining 34 percent of the vote. The Communist party in particular made notable gains throughout the 1940s, at times at the expense of its coalition partners, attaining impressive victories in the 1947 local races.

Then the picture changed radically. Communist success, splits in the government coalition, and the onset of the cold war led to a ban against the Communist party in 1948 that would last ten years. In 1949, leftist support dropped to 9.4 percent, its lowest level for the period. The Left, however, gradually regained electoral strength, though it would not again attain its 1941 force until the tumultuous Popular Unity years of Allende.

During this period significant changes took place in the center of the political spectrum. The Radical party dominated Chilean politics throughout the 1930s and 1940s. By the early 1950s, however, the citizenry demanded changes, deserting the Radicals and other traditional parties for the populist appeals of former president Carlos Ibáñez and a host of smaller and regional parties. The Radicals never fully recovered, even though Ibáñez's movement proved ephemeral. They were largely displaced by a growing vote for the Left and the surge of the Christian Democrats in the center of the political spectrum. The Christian Democrats grew primarily at the expense of the Right, appealing to women voters and others prepared to follow the more progressive stands of a Catholic church that abandoned its close ties with the Conservative party in the 1950s. Between 1961 and 1973 (the last congressional election) the Right dropped from 38.4 percent of the vote to 21.1 percent, and the Radicals from 21.4 percent to 3.6 percent. The Christian Democrats went from 16.1 percent to 28.5 percent, while the parties of the Left increased their share of the vote from 22.1 percent to 34.6 percent—an all-time high.[13]

While national totals reveal the importance of these shifts, it is important to stress that they were far-reaching, affecting large as well as small communities in urban and rural areas across the nation. A detailed analysis by commune, focusing on municipal elections, which often revolved essentially around local issues, confirms a similar pattern. According to table 6.2, the National party lost an average of 14.8 percent of the vote, while the Radicals lost an average of 16.2 percent. By contrast the Christian Democrats saw their fortunes rise by 14.2 percent, while the Communist and Socialist vote increased by 6.9 percent and 7.3 percent, respectively. Minor parties increased their vote by an average of 2.7 percent. Even more dramatic is the fact that these parties increased their vote in more than two-thirds of Chilean communes, whereas the Radicals and Nationals lost an average of 17.8 percent and 16.7 percent in 268 and 263 communes, respectively. In high-gaining communes (above the national mean) the

Table 6.2. Gains and Losses of Chilean Parties by Commune, 1961–1973

	Communes in Which Party Lost		Communes in Which Party Gained		Communes in Which Party Had High Gains[a]		Average Gain or Loss in All 287 Communes
	No.	%	No.	%	No.	%	%
Communist	70	−5.5	216	10.9	89	18.9	6.9
Socialist	65	−7.6	221	11.6	86	20.4	7.3
Christian Democrats	24	−9.2	262	16.3	112	25.0	14.2
Radicals	268	−17.8	18	7.6	8	12.9	−16.2
Nationals	263	−16.7	23	7.1	9	15.4	−14.8
Others	82	−11.5	204	8.4	149	11.0	2.7

Source: Data compiled from the Dirección del Registro Electoral, Santiago, Chile.
a. High-gaining communes are those in which the party exceeded its national average.

Communists gained 18.9 percent in 89 communes, the Socialists 20.4 percent in 86 communes, and the Christian Democrats 25 percent in 112 communes. The trend in local elections showed erosion of the Right in favor of the Left and the Christian Democrats—even if in presidential elections the shift did not appear to be great and Allende won a smaller percentage of the vote in 1970 than he did in 1964.

This brief overview of trends in party support in Chile reveals two basic characteristics of Chilean party politics: its high competitiveness and its marked polarization.

Party Competition

The most striking characteristic of the Chilean party system was its competitiveness. There were no giants in Chilean party politics, no party or tendency with a clear majority. In the period 1932–73, forty-five different parties managed to elect at least one representative to the lower house of the parliament. Of these, twenty-three parties were successful in only one election, seven achieved representation in two successive elections, and four in three. Eleven parties were able to make use of Chile's modified d'Hont electoral system to elect their candidates to office for more than three terms.

Table 6.3 indicates that the number of parties was highest at times of political crisis, such as in the aftermath of the depression and in the early 1950s, when Ibáñez challenged the traditional parties with his populist appeals. Rae and Laakso and Taagepera's fractionalization indices were highest in 1932 and 1952, when seventeen and eighteen parties obtained parliamentary representation, respectively. By the 1960s the number of parties electing candidates to office had declined substantially as the four large historical parties and the Christian Democrats consolidated their positions. As the table shows, the five largest parties in Chile have in fact always commanded the lion's share of the electorate and an even greater proportion of congressional seats.

In an examination of party fractionalization in twenty-seven "stable democra-

Arturo Valenzuela

Table 6.3. Fractionalization Index, Number of Parties, and Relative Weights of the Five Largest Parties in Chilean Congressional Elections, 1932–1973

	1932	1937	1941	1945	1949	1953	1957	1961	1965	1969	1973
Rae index	.903	.865	.861	.854	.870	.929	.890	.860	.770	.815	.815
Number of parties with seats in congress	17	11	12	12	14	18	13	7	7	5	
Percentage of vote obtained by 5 largest parties	58.8	76.8	81.7	78.6	74.0	58.3	52.5	78.6	85.6	90.9	87.8
Percentage of seats obtained by 5 largest parties	74.6	76.8	87.7	86.4	81.6	70.5	77.5	83.6	95.9	100	100
Laakso and Taagera index	10.03	7.4	7.2	6.8	7.7	13.2	9.1	7.1	4.3	5.4	5.4

Source: Data compiled from the Dirección del Registro Electoral, Santiago, Chile. Rae's fractionalization index is from Douglas W. Rae, *The Political Consequences of Electoral Laws* (New Haven: Yale UP, 1971), pp. 53–58, 62. The Laakso and Taagera index is from Markku Laakso and Rein Taagera, "'Effective' Number of Parties. A Measure with Application to West Europe," *Comparative Political Studies* 12, no. 1 (1979): 3–27.

Table 6.4. Percentage of Variance (R^2) in Rae Fractionalization Index Explained by Various Socioeconomic Indicators in Selected Congressional Elections

Socioeconomic Indicators	Election Year			
	1961	1965	1969	1973
Urbanization	.07	−.003	.08	.02
Commune size	.11	−.003	.03	.04
Percentage of population in mining	.006	.01	−.001	.07
Percentage of population in agriculture	.14	.01	.05	−.003
Percentage of population in working-class occupations	.006	.006	.002	.002
Percentage of population in middle-class occupations	.002	−.007	.007	.0006

Source: Dirección del Registro Electoral, Santiago, Chile.
N = all 287 Chilean communes.

cies" in the period 1945–73, Giovanni Sartori notes that Chile ranks third on that measure, after Finland and Switzerland, with the French Fourth Republic, the Netherlands, and Israel close behind. Uruguay, the only other Latin American country in the sample, ranks nineteenth.[14]

Fractionalization in Chile was also ubiquitous at all levels—not simply an artifact of national aggregates or of voting patterns in Santiago and other large urban areas, where more than a third of the population is concentrated. Multiple regression analysis, reported in table 6.4, reveals that neither size nor degree of urbaniza-

Table 6.5. Party Competition Indices for France, Chile, and Chilean Regions in a Congressional and a Municipal Election

	Congressional Election	Municipal Election
France	3.37	1.64
Chile	3.95	3.83
Region I	3.86	3.89
Region II	3.86	3.95
Region III	4.05	3.73
Region IV	4.0	3.84
Region V	4.12	3.79
Region VI	3.92	4.10
Region VII	4.08	3.53
Region VIII	3.25	3.61

Source: Data compiled from the Dirección del Registro Electoral, Santiago, Chile. The index of party competition and the French data are drawn from Mark Kesselman, *The Ambiguous Consensus: A Study of Local Government in France* (New York: Alfred Knopf, 1967). *N* = all communes.

tion explains the level of political fractionalization. Nor do variables such as the percentage of the population employed in mining or agriculture, or the percentage of the population in working- or middle-class categories, explain any of the variance in fractionalization. What is more, party competition in Chile was as intense in national elections as it was in local ones, a phenomenon that differentiates Chile from France, where local elections fought on local issues led to considerably less fractionalization than elections for the National Assembly fought on national issues. Table 6.5 confirms this assertion by comparing an index of party competition for both kinds of elections, by commune, in Chile and in France. The same table shows that party competition was uniformly high in all of Chile's regions in both elections and that party competition in local elections exceeded the level of party competition in national elections in four out of eight regions of the country.[15]

Party Polarization

Sartori has eloquently argued, however, that fractionalization, or degree of competitiveness, while amenable to easy quantification, is not the most important characteristic of a multiparty system. Several countries such as Switzerland, Israel, the Netherlands, and Denmark have levels of fractionalization comparable to Chile's, but the ideological distance between parties in those countries is not as great. Fractionalization, thus, is independent of polarization. Chile, in Sartori's terms, can be classified along with Finland, Italy, and the French Fourth Republic

Table 6.6. Percentage of Polarized Communes and Average Vote in Polarized Communes by Tendency in 1961, 1969, and 1973

	1961	1969	1973
Percentage polarized communes (no.)	35 (102)	27 (77)	55 (158)
Percentage leftist	30.0	29.4	34.7
Percentage centrist	33.1	40.7	33.1
Percentage rightist	33.8	25	25.6

Source: Data compiled from the Dirección del Registro Electoral, Santiago, Chile.
Note: Polarized communes are defined as those in which the Right and Left each obtained more than 25 percent of the vote.

as one of the most polarized party systems in the world because of its clearly de-fined right and left poles, consisting of parties with strongly diverging policy ob-jectives including sharp differences about the very nature of the regime.[16] It must be stressed again, however, that Chile's Communist party opted early on for an electoral and not an insurrectionary route to power.

As with party competition, ideological distance is not an artifact of national to-tals, a reflection of politically homogeneous geographical areas expressing different political preferences. In any given election the degree of polarization is obviously due to the extent to which both Left and Right found support and the center par-ties managed to hold their own. This relationship can be seen during the 1960s by examining the number of communes that gave more support to both the Right and the Left than those ends of the spectrum obtained in the 1965 congressional elec-tion, the least polarized of the decade. In 1961, as table 6.6 shows, 102 communes, or 35 percent of the total, were highly polarized with electoral support for both Left and Right of more than 30 percent. The number of such polarized communes dropped to 77 (27 percent) in 1969 as the Christian Democrats managed to main-tain a large average vote. But in 1973, polarization increased sharply, with more than half of all communes registering high votes for both Right and Left. In the 1973 congressional elections the Center allied with the Right to form the Confederación Democrática (code) in opposition to the Popular Unity coalition (UP). Each side drew up a joint slate, making the polarization of Chilean politics complete.

The Heterogeneous Base of Party Support

To the dimensions of competitiveness and polarization, we can add a third fac-tor, one that is not readily discernible from voting trends over time. Though the contemporary Chilean party system was marked by a strong ideological debate re-volving around class issues, it would be a mistake to assume that the electoral bases of the parties were defined strictly along class lines.[17]

It is clear that the parties of the Left, and particularly the Communists, obtained much of their support from working-class elements, particularly miners and in-

Table 6.7. Percentage of Variance in Party Vote (R^2) Explained by Occupational Category in the 1969 and 1971 Congressional and Municipal Elections

	1969	1971
	%	
Nationals	17	16
Communists	33	32
Socialists	8	9
Christian Democrats	8	7
Radicals	7	5

Source: Data compiled from the Dirección del Registro Electoral, Santiago, Chile.
N = 287.

dustrial workers. Parties at the Right and Center clearly garnered more votes from upper- and middle-class individuals, though voting support for these parties included large percentages of working-class people. The Right was generally supported by rural workers, though the Radicals in some areas of the country had substantial rural support. Multiple regression analysis using aggregate data confirms these trends but also makes clear that working-class occupational categories did not explain a substantial amount of the variance in party vote for any party, with the exception of the Communists, whose vote was highly correlated with the incidence of mining population (see table 6.7).

Survey research supports the finding that there was substantial cross-class support for Chilean parties. As table 6.8 indicates, 31 percent of a sample of Santiago citizens identified themselves as rightists, while 24.5 percent thought of themselves as leftists. (These percentages are close to the 30 percent of the vote obtained by the Right and the 22 percent by the Left in the next congressional election in 1961. See table 6.1 above.) Table 6.8 shows that the Right as well as the Left received strong support from working-class groups in Chile. Thus, while 31.1 percent of the working class identified with the Left, 29.4 percent identified with the Right. In the upper-class category no respondents expressed preference for the Left. However, 18.2 percent of upper-middle-class respondents chose the Left, as opposed to 33 percent who chose the Right. Subsequent surveys, as well as aggregate data analysis, confirmed that distribution of Left-Right support remained surprisingly stable up through the election of Salvador Allende.[18]

The heterogeneous base of support was due in part to the strong appeal to voters on clientelistic and personalistic lines. The Right, for example, continued to draw important support from rural workers and people engaged in service occupations, on the basis of traditional ties. But heterogeneous support was also due to the continued vitality of the other generative cleavage of Chilean party politics—the religious cleavage—years after the major issues of church versus state had been resolved.

Table 6.8. Cross-tabulation of Self-identifications of Political Preference and Social Class, 1958

	Social Class										
	Upper		Upper Middle		Lower Middle		Working		No Answer		Total	
	No.	%	No.	%	No.	%	No.	%	No.	%	No.	%
Right	11	78.6	67	33.0	98	32.8	60	29.4	17	54.8	253	31.4
Center	3	21.4	63	31.0	59	19.7	19	9.6	0	0.0	144	17.8
Left	0	0.0	37	18.2	58	13.4	100	31.1	3	9.7	198	24.5
Other	0	0.0	4	2.0	4	1.3	3	0.7	1	3.2	12	1.5
No answer	0	0.0	32	15.8	80	26.8	78	29.2	10	32.3	200	24.8
Total in sample	14		203		299		250		31		807	

Source: International Data Library and Reference Service, Survey Research Center, University of California, Berkeley, 1958 Presidential Election Survey in Santiago, Chile.

Voters with strong religious identification, regardless of class station, were more likely to vote Conservative, and later Christian Democrat, than voters with more secular orientations. Since women were more likely to be religious, women voters in particular (as in many European countries) voted for the Right and the Christian Democrats. By contrast, Protestant voters and voters with weak religious commitments in different socioeconomic strata were far more likely to turn to the centrist Radicals or to the Left.[19]

The rise of the Christian Democrats with their strongly reformist appeal clearly undermined the ability of the Left to make further inroads among the more Catholic elements of the working class. But it also undermined the rightist parties by appealing to their working-class voters, particularly in rural areas. The severe loss of support that the historic Liberals and Conservatives experienced in the early 1960s led them to merge into a new party, the National party—along with a few more minor nationalist groups. The joining together of these parties, which had been separated primarily by the religious question, thrust the new party's concern for class issues to the fore, giving the Christian Democrats a greater monopoly over devout Catholics. This trend was supported by internal changes in the church, which shifted away from a close identification with the Conservative party as late as the 1950s. In the face of what it perceived as a growing challenge from the Marxist Left, the party felt it had to become more progressive.

Both of the generative cleavages (worker versus employer and secular versus religious) were expressed politically over several generations through repeated elections. These elections, which were akin to a national sport, helped to structure veritable "political subcultures" around each of the parties. On the street, in stores, in the workplace, on trains, in local clubs, unions, Catholic action organizations, masonic leagues, and countless other groups and associations, Chileans of all walks of life lived and breathed party politics. Over the years, parties structured a host of organizations, including the famous Radical and Liberal clubs and party-affiliated sports organizations, which served as much as social organizations as political ones.

In turn, political affiliations were reinforced by other societal reference groups. Thus upper- and middle-level leaders from the Socialist and Radical parties tended to go to public high schools and to send their children to state universities or the University of Concepción—while Conservatives and Christian Democrats were more likely to be educated in parochial schools and Catholic universities. Radical and Socialist political elites were much more likely to come from middle-class extraction and have "Chilean" names—while leaders of the Right and the Christian Democrats were more likely to come from professional families and have "foreign" names, although Jews were more likely to achieve leadership positions in the parties of the Left, including the Communist party. Indeed, even when significant sectors of the Christian Democratic Party broke away and veered to the Left, they formed new leftist parties and did not merge with the older, "secular" ones until after the Pinochet era.

The Communist party, in particular, developed its own very distinct subculture, one clearly reinforced by years of underground activity. More than other Chilean parties, the Communists developed a genuine working-class leadership, recruited primarily from unions and some popular organizations. Secondary associations created by the party, along with newspapers, magazines, and even folk songs and artistic expressions (embodied in artists and poets such as Violeta Parra and Pablo Neruda) helped to consolidate a strong sense of community and purpose that transcended the mere quest for votes. This does not imply that ideological considerations were unimportant. On the contrary, they were salient, helping to define a distinct world view for both militants and followers. Ideology, however, was interwoven with cultural, class, and religious differences. These factors combined to cement distinct party identities, which were passed on through generations and further reenforced by a succession of meaningful electoral contests at the center of national life. Party identification was shared most strongly by militants but extended into the wider community of supporters and voters as well.

Though powerful, party identification was not immutable. In the late 1930s, it was the youth wing of the Conservative party that led to the creation of the Falange (later the Christian Democrats), a party that in turn saw much of its youth leave its ranks to create the Christian leftist parties in the 1960s. At the same time, the Socialist party was a major beneficiary of disillusionment with the Radicals among middle-class elements coming from Chile's secular tradition. These defections, however, did not change the broad lines of Chile's political landscape; rather, they reinforced them.[20]

It is the continued existence of these subcultures—Radical, Socialist, Communist, Christian Democratic or Right—that helps explain much of the underlying

Table 6.9. Correlations between Voting Patterns for Major Chilean Parties in 1963 and 1971 Municipal Elections by Commune

	Communist	Socialist	Radical	Christian Democrat	National
Nation	.84	.53	.45	.27	.72
Major urban centers	.85	.39	.82	.49	.71
Region 1 Tarapaca-Coquimbo	.83	.60	.43	.47	.65
Region 2 Aconcagua-Valparaiso	.80	.60	.67	.27	.73
Region 3 Santiago	.83	.22	.55	.23	.64
Region 4 O'Higgins-Nuble	.74	.60	.42	.12	.73
Region 5 Concepción-Arauco	.72	.59	.47	.69	.70
Region 6 Bio-Bio-Cautin	.86	.28	.33	.03	.35
Region 7 Valdivia-Chiloe	.57	.43	.05	.12	.60
Region 8 Aysen-Magallanes	.67	.60	.24	.93	.93

Source: Electoral results available at the Dirección del Registro Electoral, Santiago, Chile.
Note: The votes for the Conservative and Liberal parties, which united to form the National party in 1965, were added for the 1963 election. Major urban centers are those with a population of more than fifty thousand, a total of forty communes. $N = 287$.

stability of Chilean voting behavior. An analysis of the intercorrelation of party vote across several elections in the 1960s shows that even in a period of significant electoral realignment, there was underlying stability in voting patterns. As table 6.9 shows, the Communists and Conservatives had the highest degree of interparty stability, with very high correlation coefficients between the municipal election of the Alessandri years and the congressional election of the Allende years—two dramatically different periods in Chilean history separated by years of significant change. The Socialist party followed with somewhat lower correlation coefficients, while the two center parties showed the lowest level of interparty stability, with one declining and the other gaining dramatically in this period.

The Survival of Chile's Multiparty System under Military Rule

In the immediate aftermath of the military coup, it became clear that the new authorities were not about to "restore order" and return the government to political leaders. Chile's military rulers were convinced that the country's problems stemmed not only from the mismanagement of a government bent on imposing a socialist alternative but from Chilean democracy itself, and especially from democratic party politics. Ironically echoing the ideological debates of the thirties, they shared the Far Left's contempt for "bourgeois democracy." They viewed politicians of all stripes as self-serving demagogues with a penchant for compromise at the nation's expense and as the principal culprits behind the country's social, economic, and political crisis. They were convinced that with the appropriate policies, the Chilean people would abandon parties and ideologies of the past in favor of a different kind of politics, a politics of nationalism, patriotism, and civic harmony, devoid of partisan conflict and division.

In attempting to consign Chile's parties and leaders to the dustbin of history, Chile's rulers, over the course of a decade and a half in office, expected to benefit from three different elements: naked repression, economic modernization, and institutional engineering. Only a few days after the military takeover, the governing junta issued a decree banning some political parties and declaring others in "recess."[21] For the next sixteen years, the party leadership struggled to survive under the longest-lasting government in Chilean history. The parties of the Left bore the brunt of the regime's fury as its leaders were killed, imprisoned, or exiled and party assets confiscated; but the center parties, including the Christian Democrats, also found their activities severely circumscribed and many of their leaders sent into exile. Only the rightist National party welcomed the prohibition of party activity and voluntarily disbanded. Although several of its leaders took positions in the government, especially in the diplomatic corps, it is noteworthy that the military did not turn to prominent National party leaders for key political posts, preferring conservative but apolitical technocrats.[22]

While repressive tactics were successful in curbing party activity, military authorities came to believe that economic and social modernization under their skillful guidance would render obsolete the conditions that spawned parties in the past. In articulating this position they found eloquent support in the team of young free-market technocrats that helped manage the economy and the state. According to the "Chicago boys," growth and access to consumer goods made possible by free-market economics would increase standards of living and undermine the allegiance to traditional parties, particularly those of the Left. Chile's polarized party system, in their view, was simply a vestige of underdevelopment and statist policies, an anachronism that would disappear with modernization.

Toward the end of the military government, the authorities also implemented a series of legal measures they hoped would guarantee the final transformation of the party system, a shift from an ideological multipartism to a moderate two-party system. These included constitutional provisions banning parties of the Left, a party law aimed at discouraging smaller parties, and a new electoral law designed to promote a two-party system while favoring the parties of the Right by creating an unusual two-past-the-post system, in which the runner-up has significant electoral advantages.[23]

Table 6.10. Percentage of Chilean Respondents Identifying Themselves as Right/Center Right, Center, and Left/Center Left between June 1990 and August 1992

	Right/Center Right	Center	Left/Center Left	Independent/None/Don't Know
June 1990	14.3	25.3	28.5	32.0
December 1990	13.4	29.9	23.7	33.1
July 1991	13.4	23.2	24.2	39.1
December 1991	21.9	30.8	23.3	24.1
April 1992	19.0	24.9	24.1	32.1
December 1992	26.9	22.4	36.7	13.9
March 1993	22.8	24.6	33.7	19.0

Source: CEP-Adimark, Santiago, Chile, March 1993.

The resurgence of a strong multiparty system in the aftermath of military rule is vivid testimony to the failure of those measures and assumptions. Following the economic crisis of 1982, party organizations once again moved to center stage and began slowly to forge a credible opposition to the military regime. The dramatic defeat of General Pinochet in the plebiscite of October 5, 1988, by a margin of 54.7 percent to 43 percent at the hands of a coalition of center left parties and the resounding success of these parties in winning the open presidential and congressional race a year later demonstrated the degree to which the party system remained a fundamental feature of Chilean society.

Public opinion surveys revealed that after seventeen years of authoritarianism, approximately 80 percent of all Chileans identified with particular political parties.[24] As table 6.10 shows, Chileans continue to classify themselves in Left-Right terms in proportions similar to those of three decades ago. In August of 1992, 22.6 percent classified themselves as Right or Center Right, 22.4 percent as Center, 31.4 percent as Left or Center Left; 23.6 percent viewed themselves as independents or refused to identify themselves with a political tendency. These percentages are not very different from the actual voting results for the chamber of deputies in 1973, the last election before the military coup, when the Left obtained 34.6 percent of the vote, the Center 32.1 percent, and the Right 21.1 percent.

Electoral analysis shows significant continuities in voting patterns as well. Timothy Scully and Samuel Valenzuela show that the results of the 1992 municipal election in Chile, in which parties were able to present candidates with greater ease than in the earlier 1990 congressional race, are congruent with historic voting patterns in Chile. In 1992 the Right, Center, and Left received 38 percent, 36.3 percent, and 24.3 percent of the vote, respectively. The average support for the same party clusters from 1937 to 1973 was 30.1 percent, 39.7 percent, and 24.2 percent, respectively. Indeed, the Christian Democratic vote in 1992 was virtually the same as the vote received by Radomiro Tomic, the Christian Democratic candidate for president twenty-two years earlier, and close to the party's totals in the 1969 and 1973 congressional races. The vote for the Left diminished by about 6 percent, from 36.2 percent in 1970 to 29.6 percent in 1992, reflecting the decline of the Radical party and the electoral misfortunes of the Communists, who had distanced themselves from a peaceful transition to democracy. As Scully and Valenzuela note, these continuities persisted despite dramatic increases in the voting public and the fact that half of the voters in 1992 had never voted before.[25]

The inability of the military authorities to eliminate the party system was due to three erroneous assumptions.[26] In the first place, although Chile experienced economic growth in the late 1970s and stronger and sustained economic recovery after 1985, they mistakenly assumed that partisan identification, particularly on the Left, could be explained solely by indicators of material deprivation and that, conversely, prosperity and improvement in living standards would of necessity undermine those attachments. Table 6.8, reported earlier, underscores the fact that the Left was supported by upper- as well as lower-income groups.

Alejandro Portes's studies have shown conclusively that indicators of poverty, low educational attainment, or frustration have not, historically, explained leftist voting in Chile. As Portes argues, identification with parties of the Left is the product of political socialization and organization, reinforced by key reference groups, such as trade unions, professional associations, and cultural and social groups. Political socialization in turn contributes to changes in world view, whereby individuals are likely to associate their own, or the country's, difficulties with structural inequities, not with their own failings. As Portes notes, the increase of the vote for the Popular Unity parties in 1973 (in relation to 1969), in a context of hyperinflation and severe deprivation, was testimony to the noneconomic calculations of most supporters of the Left.[27]

Secondly, the military authorities assumed that significant repression and the disappearance of electoral and party politics would cause political parties to disappear. Parties did not disappear, however, but maintained a presence in other spheres of civil society. In neighborhood associations, labor unions, student groups, and even professional associations, leadership positions were gradually assumed by activists with party ties. The process in Chile was similar to what took place in Spain under even more repressive circumstances. As José Maravall notes, "The emergence of the working class and the student movement [in Spain] was dependent on the underground survival of the parties of the left. Those parties provided the strategies, and the leaders, and it was the capacity of these parties to survive that kept the workers and the student resistance alive in the long and difficult period of the 1940s and 1950s, and that later rekindled the struggle."[28]

Ironically, the regime helped to ensure access to leadership positions by traditional party elements through its refusal to structure a mass-based, proregime partisan movement of its own; this refusal stemmed directly from the profound antipolitical attitudes of military leaders.[29] It is highly unlikely that any such movement would have succeeded in Chile because of the strong identification of Chileans with specific political tendencies and parties—Chile's "political landscape." No democracy that has experienced political breakdown, with the possible exception of Uruguay, had as strong and lasting a party system.

Finally, the military authorities erroneously assumed that they could transform the party system through constitutional and legal "engineering." The constitution of 1980, through article 8, had sought to outlaw the parties of the Left by declaring all persons or groups illicit, or contrary to the "institutional order of the Republic," which "propagated doctrines which are an affront to the family, promote violence or a conception of society, the State or the juridical order, of a totalitarian character or founded on class struggle." However, with Pinochet's defeat in the 1988 plebiscite, this provision was eliminated in the reforms of 1989. It was replaced by milder language that prohibits conduct or actions that do not respect the basic principles of a democratic and constitutional order.[30] Communist and Socialist party leaders previously banned regained their political rights.

The electoral law designed by the outgoing military government demonstrates the lengths to which that government went to engineer fundamental changes in the party system through legislation. The objective of the reform was to force the formation of a party system with two or three ideologically homogeneous constituency-oriented parties—the polar opposite of Chile's historical party system. The reforms were designed to guarantee the electoral success of the parties of the Right in the short term, even if they represented a minority of the population.[31]

Since it was clear from the 1988 plebiscite that the combined Right did not have more than 40 percent of the vote, the authors of the electoral reform law shied away from their preferred system, a first-past-the-post system such as the one in the United States. Although they were confident that the Right would be able to form a strong coalition, while the opposition parties would remain divided, they did not want to risk a scenario in which the opposition would gain most of the congressional seats because of their electoral advantage in the plebiscite.

According to Chile's clever alternative, parties or coalitions are required to present lists with candidates for two seats per district. The system takes into account both the votes for the total party list and the votes for individual candidates. The first seat is awarded to the party or coalition with a plurality of votes. But with a district magnitude of two, the first-place party must receive twice the vote of the second-place party in order to win both seats in the district. Thus, assuming two seats, the cutoff point that a party must reach in order to obtain at least one seat is 33.4 percent of the votes, while to obtain both seats it must receive 66.7 percent. Hence, the system favors the *second* largest vote getter. Any electoral support that the largest party may have over 33.4 percent is effectively wasted until its level of support approaches 66.7 percent. The system was designed so that the parties of the Right, with only one-third of the vote, could aspire to gaining half of the seats.

In the context of a two-coalition pattern of competition, the degree of interparty competition is relatively low if the parties have comparable support in a particular district, each being assured of winning one seat. Competition becomes centered on districts in which the largest party can expect to receive in the range of 66 percent of the votes. With more than two party lists, the threshold for the first-place party's success in gaining the second seat may be lowered because it needs only twice the vote of its nearest competitor. Of course, within the context of competition between more than two parties, the competitive dynamic changes. If several smaller parties have a similar level of electoral support, the result is a fierce competition for the second seat or, in situations of greater party fragmentation, for both first and second seats.

The military authorities assumed that the fractious opposition parties, ranging from Christian Democrats to Marxist Socialists would present multiple lists in the 1990 congressional race, proving incapable of duplicating the unity they displayed in defeating Pinochet. But in a remarkable display of party discipline, these parties were able to structure a relatively coherent common list that, despite the bias of the electoral system toward the minority conservatives, was able to win a majority of the seats in both the senate and the chamber of deputies in the December 14, 1990, congressional race.[32]

The electoral law did not lead to the elimination of Chile's multiparty system, nor did it fundamentally alter Chile's tripartite political tendencies or displace significant parties. It only forced the parties to structure coalitions that are parties in name only.[33] Indeed, despite the serious biases of the electoral law, representation in the chamber of deputies after the 1990 congressional race roughly conformed to the three-way split in Chilean politics, with the parties of the Right obtaining 38 seats, the Center 43, and the Left 29, giving the center-left government of Patricio Aylwin a solid majority.[34]

Presidentialism, Party Politics, and Coalitions in Chile

A party system cannot be understood with sole reference to the number of parties, their ideological distance, and their bases of support.[35] Any party system shapes and is shaped by the institutional context in which it operates, by the formal rules and procedures, as well as the informal political practices, that characterize all political systems. The interplay between a party system and its institutional context is critical to any analysis of the stability of democratic regimes.

Giovanni Sartori, drawing on his studies of Italian politics, has described the dynamics of polarized multiparty systems.[36] He argues that in highly polarized contexts, with a clearly defined Right and Left commanding substantial percentages of the electorate, the principal drive of the political system tends to be centrifugal. This means that the party system has a tendency to move toward the extremes, toward greater divisions in society. Unlike political systems that have avoided the emergence of clearly opposing partisan tendencies, a polarized party system has a weak centripetal drive lacking a dominant centrist consensus.

Ironically, polarized systems do have center poles occupied by one or more parties. However, Sartori argues, under such circumstances the Center does not usually represent a majoritarian tendency in its own right, but tends to be composed of centrist voters and additional fragments emanating from both left and right poles. Sartori notes that the "center is mainly a feedback of the centrifugal drives which predominate in the system" and is "more a negative convergence, a sum of exclusions, than a positive agency of instigation."[37]

Sartori's analysis is extremely helpful in understanding the Chilean case because it illuminates the repeated surge of centrist movements in Chilean politics at the expense of both Right and Left. While in Chile these movements often represented a coherent centrist program, they failed to generate an electoral majority on their own but depended on erosion from the two extremes for support. As such, the centrist tendencies were volatile, rising and falling as voters shifted to and away from leftist or rightist candidates, only to make way for new centrist coalitions. The instability of centrist movements contributed to the difficulty of structuring stable coalitions for public policy formation. The erosion of centrist consensus accelerated dramatically during the Allende years and was a major factor in the crisis culminating in regime breakdown.

The Problem of Coalitions in a Presidential Regime

Since the impact of a particular party system is dependent on the nature of the institutional structures in which it unfolds, it is crucial to stress that a polarized party system affected Chile's presidential form of government differently than the Italian polarized system Sartori studied. In Italy parties campaigned for seats in the parliament and governments were formed in the legislature after a parliamentary election, and the governing party or coalition depended on a continued parliamentary majority in order to survive. The volatility of Italian politics often brought governments down and required the structuring of new government coalitions.

In presidential systems the presidency is by far the most important political prize. By definition, presidential elections are winner-take-all contests that encourage either the creation of two-party systems or the structuring of broad alliances in multiparty systems. In Chile, the fact that presidents were required to obtain an absolute majority of the vote in order to assume office encouraged centrist candidates to attract votes from Left or Right. If no candidate obtained an absolute majority of the popular vote, the Congress designated one of the two leading candidates to be president.[38]

Since no party (or even tendency) commanded a majority, all candidates were minority candidates who sought preelectoral alliances with other parties to maximize their electoral chances. If no alliance obtained a majority, the two front-runners sought to structure winning coalitions in the congress in the aftermath of the election. Table 6.11 presents the results of all presidential races from 1932 to 1989.

Table 6.11. Presidential Elections in Chile, 1932–1989

Election	Vote	%
30 October 1932		
Arturo Alessandri Palma (PL)	189,914	54.6
Marmaduke Grove (PS)	60,858	17.7
Héctor Rodriguez de la Sotta (C)	47,207	13.8
Enrique Zañartu Prieto (PLU)	42,885	13.4
Elías Laferte Gaviño (PC)	4,128	1.2
Blank and void	902	0.3
Total votes	343,892	
Total registered	429,772	
Abstentions	85,880	20.0
Majority election		
24 October 1938		
Pedro Aguirre Cerda (PR)	222,720	50.1
Gustavo Ross Santa María (PL)	218,609	49.2
Carlos Ibáñez (Ind.)	112	00.0
Blank and void	2,559	0.7
Total voters	443,992	
Total registered	612,749	
Abstentions	168,757	27.5
Majority election		
2 February 1942		
Juan Antonio Ríos Morales (PR)	260,034	55.7
Carlos Ibáñez del Campo (Ind.)	204,635	43.8
Blank and void	1,838	0.3
Total voters	466,979	
Total registered	589,486	
Abstentions	114,979	19.7
Majority election		
4 September 1946		
Gabriel González Videla (PR)	192,207	40.1
Eduardo Cruz-Coke (C)	142,441	29.7
Fernando Alessandri (PL)	131,023	27.2
Bernardo Ibáñez (PS)	12,114	2.5
Null and void	1,525	0.4
Total voters	479,310	
Total registered	631,257	
Abstentions	151,947	24.0
Minority election[a]		

Table 6.11. Presidential Elections in Chile, 1932–1989 *(continued)*

Election	Vote	%
4 September 1952		
Carlos Ibáñez del Campo (Ind.)	446,439	46.8
Arturo Matte Larraín (PL)	265,357	27.8
Pedro Enrique Alfonso (PR)	190,360	19.9
Salvador Allende Gossens (PS)	51,975	5.4
Null and void	2,971	0.3
Total voters	954,131	
Total registered	1,105,029	
Abstentions	150,898	13.6
Minority election[b]		
4 September 1958		
Jorge Alessandri Rodríguez (Ind.)	389,909	31.2
Salvador Allende Gossens (PS)	356,493	28.5
Eduardo Frei Montalva (PDC)	255,769	20.5
Luis Bossay Leiva (PR)	192,077	15.4
Antonio Zamorano (Ind.)	41,304	3.3
Null and void	14,798	1.3
Total voters	1,250,552	
Total registered	1,497,902	
Abstentions	247,552	15.5
Minority election[c]		
4 September 1964		
Eduardo Frei Montalva (PDC)	1,409,012	55.6
Salvador Allende Gossens (PS)	977,902	38.6
Julio Durán Neumann (PR)	125,253	4.9
Null and void	18,555	0.9
Total voters	2,530,697	
Total registered	2,915,120	
Abstentions	384,424	13.2
Majority election		
4 September 1970		
Salvador Allende Gossens (PS)	1,070,334	36.5
Jorge Alessandri Rodríguez (Ind.)	1,031,159	34.9
Radomiro Tomic Romero (PDC)	821,801	27.8
Null and void	31,505	1.1
Total voters	2,954,799	
Total registered	3,539,757	
Abstentions	584,958	16.5
Minority election[d]		

Table 6.11. Presidential Elections in Chile, 1932–1989 *(continued)*

Election	Vote	%
14 December 1989		
Patricio Aylwin Azócar (PDC)	3,850,023	55.2
Hernán Buchi (UDI)	2,051,975	29.4
Francisco Errázuriz (Ind.)	1,076,894	15.4
Null and void	178,833	0.3
Total voters	6,978,892	
Total registered		
Abstentions		
Majority election		

Note: PL, Liberal party; PS, Socialist party; C, Conservative party; PLU, United Liberal party; PC, Communist party; PR, Partido Radical; PDC, Christian Democratic party; UDI, Unión Democrática Independiente; Ind., Independent.
    a. On October 24, 1946, the congress ratified González Videla as president with 134 votes; 46 votes went to Cruz-Coke.
    b. On October 24, 1952, the congress ratified Ibañez as president with 132 votes; 12 votes went to Matte, and 30 members abstained.
    c. On October 24, 1958, the congress ratified Alessandri as president with 147 votes; 26 votes went to Allende, and 14 members abstained.
    d. On October 24, 1970, the congress ratified Allende as president with 135 votes; 35 votes went to Alessandri, and 8 members abstained.

Electoral coalitions obtained majorities in the presidential races of 1932, 1938, 1942, 1964, and 1989. In 1946, 1952, 1958, and 1970, the president was selected by the legislature. In the latter cases, the congress chose front-runners because their supporters happened to garner the largest number of votes among senators and deputies.[39]

Pre- or postelectoral coalitions led to the election of centrist presidents with the support of the Left in the presidential elections of 1938, 1942, and 1946, with support from the Right in 1964, and with support from both sides in 1932 and 1952. Only on two occasions did the presidency go to a candidate of the extremes. In 1958, rightist Jorge Alessandri was elected by the legislature with centrist support, and in 1970 centrist congressmen made it possible for Socialist Salvador Allende to become president.

Once a president assumed office, however, there was no danger of the government "falling" with the erosion of his congressional support. Indeed, pre- or post-election coalitions, which were constituted primarily for electoral gain in an atmosphere of considerable political uncertainty, soon tended to disintegrate, and presidents found themselves with fewer coalition partners and minority support in the congress.

Erosion of preelection coalitions made governing extremely difficult and inevitably gave way to efforts to structure new alliances with parties and groups willing to provide congressional and political support to the executive in exchange for presidential concessions. A president was forced to seek these out because he was not able to dissolve the legislature in the case of an impasse. In concrete terms, this

Table 6.12. Cabinet Changes and Ministerial Turnovers in Chilean Presidencies

President	Interior Ministers	Partial Cabinet Changes	Major Cabinet Changes	Total Ministers	Average Cabinet Duration (mo.)	Average Ministerial Service Duration (mo.)
Arturo Alessandri, 1932–38	6	2	3	59	10	12
Pedro Aguirre Cerda, 1938–42	7	2	2	44	9	11
Juan Antonio Ríos, 1942–46	8	3	5	84	6½	6
Gabriel González V., 1946–52	4	2	2	73	7	11
Carlos Ibáñez, 1952–58	8	3	5	75	7	12
Jorge Alessandri, 1958–64	2	1	1	20	29	43
Eduardo Frei, 1964–70	3	2	1	22	31	40
Salvador Allende, 1970–73	9	1	5	65	5⅚	7

Sources: For the first four administrations data are drawn from information available in Luis Valencia A., *Anales de la república*, 2 vols. (Santiago: Imprenta Universitaria, 1951). For the rest, the *Hispanic American Reports, Facts on File*, and the *Mercurio Edición Internacional* were consulted.

meant adjustment of the presidential cabinet to reflect the new working alliance not only in the chamber of deputies but also in a senate that retained substantial powers. Although Chile, unlike the French Fifth Republic, had no formal prime minister, the minister of the interior, as head of the cabinet, was expected to be responsive to the realities of political alignments. This was vital not only for the president's program but for the continued administration of the country.[40]

With the 1925 constitution, ministers were no longer held responsible to changing majorities in either house of the parliament. However, the congress still retained the right to censure ministers, and most contemporary presidents have repeatedly faced censure proceedings designed to keep the presidential coalition honest and the congressional opposition happy. This guaranteed that ministerial appointments would go to individuals with impeccable party ties. Indeed, the parties further assured their influence by requiring that candidates for cabinet posts be given official party permission *(pase)* to serve in office. Presidents could not simply appoint militants from various party organizations; they had to bargain actively with party central committees to gain their consent. As early as 1934, the Radical party demanded, after the party had shifted to the Left, that President Arturo Alessandri replace Radical ministers with other ministers of the same party more to its liking. While the president refused, noting that the constitution gave him the prerogative of making cabinet appointments, within two years he was forced to make a deal with the Radicals and welcome them back into the cabinet.

An analysis of cabinet turnover for all presidential terms from 1932 to 1973, reported in table 6.12, shows that for most presidencies cabinets lasted an average of less than one year, and individual cabinet members usually held office for only a few months. The only exceptions to this pattern were the Jorge Alessandri administration, which enjoyed majority coalition support in the legislature, and the Frei administration, which sought to govern without a coalition, drawing on the Christian Democratic majority in the chamber of deputies. Allende's cabinets lasted less than six months, and individual ministers had a tenure of less than seven months. With the exceptions of Jorge Alessandri and Eduardo Frei, all of Chile's presidents from 1932 to 1973 had cabinets lasting less than a year in office, and four presidents had cabinets lasting less than seven months. From 1946 until 1958, presidential cabinets in Chile lasted an average of seven months—less time than half of the cabinets of the French Fourth Republic.[41]

Ideological or programmatic differences were often at the root of the many coalition shifts that led to cabinet instability. In 1941, during Pedro Aguirre Cerda's term, the Radical party ordered its ministers out of the cabinet in protest over the closing of two leftist newspapers. When the president rejected their resignations and the ministers refused to resubmit them, they were expelled from the Radical party. In the same year the Socialists left the cabinet because of a bitter dispute with the Communists. In 1947, the Liberals left the cabinet of Gabriel González Videla after the Communists made a surprising showing in municipal elections. In order to overcome political stalemates, presidents often sought prestigious nonpartisan technocrats or military officers to fill ministerial positions—a practice to which Salvador Allende repeatedly resorted—with ominous results.

But narrow political considerations were just as important in cabinet shuffles. The parties had little stake in active support for the president. Indeed, parties stood to gain more by the perception that the president had failed than that he had succeeded. Since a president could not be reelected, he did not have the political authority that comes from the possibility that he could win reelection. Even his own party found it an advantage to distance itself from him and his problems halfway through the term in order to prepare for the next candidacy. Only by proving electoral strength in midterm contests in which parties ran on their own could party leaders demonstrate their party's value for future electoral coalitions.

The frequent midterm elections for the congress and local governments were characterized by the politics of outbidding because the fate of governments did not hang on a lost vote. The fixed terms for both president and congress contributed to ·an atmosphere of stalemate and a feeling of permanent crisis, which permeated the country's politics. Moreover, party leaders in the congress had little personal incentive to collaborate with the president. They could not be tapped for cabinet posts and were often rivals of party colleagues appointed to the cabinet. They resented executive power and the frequent practice of presidents of attempting to govern by decree, a logical alternative for beleaguered chief executives tired of attempting to deal with recalcitrant legislators.

Parties went out of their way to criticize incumbents and seized on every inflationary increase, every incident of police repression, every allegation of partisan or corrupt practice in an effort to pave the way for a better showing at the polls. The rhetoric of the party-controlled press and of the skilled orators of the party leadership occasionally reached frenzied proportions. In such an atmosphere, centrist parties that shifted support from government to opposition and back suffered politically, and presidents found it difficult to adopt their programs and govern the country.

Table 6.13 summarizes the coalition patterns for all of Chile's presidencies since 1932. As the table notes, only in the 1961–63 period did a president enjoy a majority coalition. The Radical cabinets of the 1940s included parties of the Right as well as the Left. Gabriel González Videla began his administration with four Radicals, three Liberals, and three Communists in his cabinet. The president even sought to bring Conservatives into the government, but they balked at the Communist presence. González would end his term with the outlawing of the Communist party and a significant shift to the Right.

Independent Carlos Ibáñez del Campo had an even more difficult time structuring his government. He never managed to form a viable majority coalition in the congress. His initial support came from a fraction of the Socialist party and an array of surge parties, including his own Agrario Laborismo, which was formed to support his populist candidacy. Throughout his presidency the influential Radical party prohibited its members from joining the cabinet, and the former general failed to persuade the parties of the Right to enter into a governing coalition. The failure of the Ibáñez administration set the stage for some of the radical party shifts that would occur in Chile under the successive administrations of the rightist Alessandri, the reformist Frei, and the Socialist Allende.

In a real sense, the effort to return Chile to a presidential form of government with the 1925 constitution failed. The Chilean system was a semipresidential one; it lacked the formal guarantees provided by parliamentary rules and procedures aimed at generating executive authority from majority support. Presidents whose own parties were not large enough to give them majority electoral support or a majority in the congress had to continually engineer working coalitions with other parties in order to survive. History shows that they were repeatedly frustrated by the aura of instability and permanent crisis that this bargaining process gave Chilean politics.[42] It is no accident that at one time or another, most recent Chilean presidents extolled the example of President Balmaceda who, in 1891, committed suicide after losing a civil war to his congressional rivals.

The formula of the second round, incorporated in the Pinochet constitution of 1980 to replace the practice of having the congress select a president in the absence of a majority vote, does not resolve the basic problem. Although it is true that a second round permits a candidate to receive a majority of the vote, this does not mean that he has majority support for governing. The coalition structured around the second round is by definition a temporary coalition of convenience; losing candidates and their voters are forced to choose their second preference among the two

Table 6.13. Chilean Presidents, 1932–1992: Electoral Coalitions and Congressional Support

President	Years	Coalition Parties	Senate		Chamber	
Arturo Alessandri Palma (Liberal), 1932–38	1932–37	Liberal, Democrat, Democratic, Radical Socialist, Social Republican, Conservative	Liberal Democrat Radical Socialist Conservative Ratio:	6 7 4 10 27/45	Liberal Democrat Radical Socialist Conservative Ratio:	21 18 8 34 81/142
	1937–38	Liberal, Conservative, Democrat, Radical	Liberal Democrat Radical Conservative Ratio:	10 4 11 12 37/45	Liberal Democrat Radical Conservative Ratio:	34 10 31 36 111/146
Pedro Aguirre Cerda (Radical), 1938–41	1938–41	Popular Front (Radical, Communist, Socialist, Democrat, and Radical Socialist)	Radical Socialist Communist Democrat Ratio:	10 4 1 2 17/45	Radical Socialist Democrat Ratio:	30 17 10 57/146
	1941	Radical, Socialist, Democrat (Popular Front dissolved)	Radical Socialist Democrat Ratio:	12 5 2 19/45	Radical Socialist Democrat Workers Ratio:	44 15 9 2 70/147
Juan Antonio Rios Morales (Radical), 1942–46	1942–45	Chilean Democratic Alliance (Radicals, Socialists, Communists), Falangists	Radical Socialist Communist Ratio:	12 5 4 21/45	Radical Socialist Communist Falangist Ratio:	44 15 15 3 77/147
	1945–46	Chilean Democratic Alliance, Falangists	Radical Communist Socialist Authentic Socialist Democrat Ratio:	12 5 2 2 1 22/45	Radical Communist Socialist Democrat Falangist Ratio:	40 15 6 8 4 73/147
Gabriel González Videla (Radical), 1946–52	1946–48	Radicals, Liberals, Communists	Radical Liberal Communist Ratio:	12 10 5 27/45	Radical Liberal Communist Ratio:	40 34 15 89/147
	1949–50	National Concentration (Radical, Conservative, Liberal)	Radical Traditional Conservative Liberal Democrat Ratio:	13 6 12 1 32/45	Radical Traditional Conservative Liberal Democrat Ratio:	6 21 33 6 66/147

Table 6.13. Chilean Presidents, 1932–1992: Electoral Coalitions and Congressional Support *(continued)*

President	Years	Coalition Parties	Senate		Chamber	

González *(continued)*	1950–52	Social Sensibility (Radical, Falangist, Democrat, Social Christian)	Radical
			Falangist
			Democrat
			Social
			  Christian
			Ratio:
				13
				1
				1
				
				2
				17/45
					Radical
					Falangist
					Democrat
					Social
					  Christian
					Ratio:
						6
						3
						6
						
						1
						26/147

Carlos Ibáñez del Campo (Independent), 1952–58	1952–53	Agrarian Labor, Popular Socialists, other left and right fragments	Agrarian Labor
			Popular
			  Socialist
			Ratio:
				3
				
				3
				6/45
					Agrarian Labor
					Popular
					  Socialist
					Ratio:
						14
						
						6
						20/147

	1953–57	Agrarian Labor, other shifting support (Popular Socialists in opposition)	Agrarian Labor
			People's
			  Democratic
			Labor
			Independents
			Ratio:
				6
				
				1
				1
				3
				11/45
					Agrarian Labor
					People's
					  Democratic
					Labor
					National
					  Christian
					Others
					Ratio:
						27
						
						5
						5
						
						4
						8
						49/147

	1957–58	Agrarian Labor	Agrarian Labor Ratio:	4 4/45	Agrarian Labor Ratio:	13 13/147

Jorge Alessandri Rodríguez (Liberal), 1958–64	1958–60	Parts of Agrarian Labor and Democrats, Republican Movement, National People's Movement, Social Christians, Liberal (informally), Conservative (informally), Independents	Agrarian Labor
			  (dissidents)
			Democrat
			Republican
			  Movement
			Liberal
			Conservative
			Independent
			Ratio:
				4
				
				1
				
				1
				9
				6
				2
				23/45
					Agrarian Labor
					  (dissidents)
					Democrat
					Liberal
					Conservative
					Ratio:
						3
						
						1
						29
						22
						59/147

	1961–63	Liberal, Radical, Conservative	Liberal
			Radical
			United
			  Conservative
			Ratio:
				9
				13
				
				4
				26/45
					Liberal
					Radical
					United
					  Conservative
					Ratio:
						28
						39
						
						17
						84/147

	1963–64	Liberal, Conservative	Liberal
			United
			  Conservative
			Ratio:
				9
				
				4
				13/45
					Liberal
					United
					  Conservative
					Ratio:
						28
						
						17
						45/147

Eduardo Frei Montalva (Christian Democrat), 1964–70	1964–65	Christian Democrat	Christian
			  Democrat
			Ratio:
				
				4
				4/45
					Christian
					  Democrat
					Ratio:
						
						23
						23/147

	1965–69	Christian Democrat	Christian
			  Democrat
			Ratio:
				
				13
				13/45
					Christian
					  Democrat
					Ratio:
						
						82
						82/147

Table 6.13. Chilean Presidents, 1932–1992: Electoral Coalitions and Congressional Support *(continued)*

President	Years	Coalition Parties	Senate		Chamber	
Frei (continued)	1969–70	Christian Democrat	Christian Democrat Ratio:	13 13/45	Christian Democrat Ratio:	55 55/150
Salvador Allende Gossens (Socialist), 1970–73	1970–73	Popular Unity (Socialists, Communists, Radicals, MAPU, API[a])				
Patricio Aylwin Azócar (Christian Democrat), 1990–	1989–	Coalition of parties for Democracy	Christian Democrat Party for Democracy Radical Socialist of Chile Others (prodemocracy) Ratio:	13 4 2 1 2 22/47	Christian Democrat Party for Democracy Radical Socialist of Chile Left-wing Independents Ratio:	13 17 5 6 6 72/120

Sources: For congressional data, Walter H. Mallory, ed., *Political Handbook of the World: 1932–1962* (New York: Harper & Row), *Political Handbook and Atlas of the World: 1963–1967* (New York: Harper & Row), and *Political Handbook and Atlas of the World: 1968* (New York: Simon & Schuster); Richard P. Stebbins and Alba Amoia, eds., *Political Handbook and Atlas of the World: 1970* (New York: Simon & Schuster), and *The World This Year: 1971–1973* (supplements to the *Political Handbook and Atlas of the World: 1970* (New York: Simon & Schuster); Arthur S. Banks and Robert S. Jordan, eds., *Political Handbook of the World: 1975* (New York: McGraw-Hill); Arthur S. Banks, ed., *Political Handbook of the World: 1976–1979* (New York: McGraw-Hill), and *Political Handbook of the World: 1984–1991* (New York: CSA Publications); Arthur S. Banks and William Overstreet, eds., *Political Handbook of the World: 1980–1983* (New York: McGraw-Hill); for the makeup of coalitions, Lia Cortes and Jordi Fuentes, *Diccionario político de Chile* (Santiago: Editorial Orbe, 1967) and Reinhard Friedmann, *1964–1988: La política chilena de la a a la z* (Santiago: Melquiades, 1988).
  a. MAPU, Movimiento de Acción Popular Unitario; API, Acción Popular Independiente.

front-runners. The situation is particularly delicate if both candidates entering the second round represent the same poles, or if they represent opposite poles, of the political spectrum.

After the race is over, there is no guarantee that the agreement between the winning candidate and his new supporters will endure, or that his support will translate into support in the parliament. Presidents elected in second rounds are more likely to disdain parliamentary accords than those selected by the congress because they soon forget about their minority status in the first round and think of themselves as genuine representatives of the popular will. Such an attitude can only exacerbate the tension between a president and a legislative body in which he does not enjoy the support of a majority.[43]

The Game of Political Concessions in Chilean Politics

And yet, this description of the workings of presidential politics in Chile captures only a part of the overall picture. While the collapse of party agreements, the censure of ministers, and the sharp disagreement over major policy issues captured the headlines, the day-to-day political transactions were characterized by compromise, give-and-take, and a profound respect for the institutions and procedures of constitutional democracy. Indeed, Chilean democracy would not have lasted as long as it did had coalition politics not permitted the structuring of working arrangements that responded to the demands placed on the government by highly mobilized and competitive political forces.

Over the years agreements were structured that permitted implementation of such far-reaching policies as state-sponsored industrial development; national educational, welfare, and health care systems; a university system with few equals on the continent; an elaborate collective bargaining structure; price control and wage readjustment mechanisms; agrarian reform; and nationalization of copper. All of these measures were the product not only of the executive but of innumerable working groups that cut across the party spectrum. Some were ad hoc and informal; many others were mandated by law, among them such bodies as the boards of government agencies and the all-important commissions of the senate and chamber of deputies, where fundamental legislation was hammered out.

But working relationships also revolved around more mundane, if no less important, matters. Party leaders and congressmen from particular regions or provinces often joined hands, regardless of party affiliation, in pressing for initiatives of benefit to constituents—a new road, a dam, a special piece of legislation earmarking revenues for development projects or proclaiming a special holiday for a favorite son. Indeed, all party leaders, elected and nonelected, spent most of their time attempting to respond to demands from groups and individuals for such things as pensions for widows, jobs for school teachers, social security benefits for a trade group, wage readjustments for union groups. Much of the work involved serving as intermediaries before government agencies too overburdened to effectively respond to the public.

Chilean party politics was thus characterized not only by sharp disagreements in ideology and program, but by compromise and cooperation to achieve joint policy objectives and respond to demands from constituents, both organized and unorganized. This pattern of political give-and-take can be attributed to three factors that are mutually reinforcing: the imperatives of electoral politics, the existence of a pragmatic center, and the viability of representative institutional arenas for decision making.

The Chilean party system was characterized by relatively cohesive and highly ideological parties. But it must be remembered that their principal function was to participate in the country's continuous stream of elections. Municipal, congressional, and presidential elections, all held in different years, forced the parties to devote the bulk of their energies to candidate selection and electoral campaigning. Electoral success, in a country where elections had been held for generations, was as valued an objective as ideological purity. This was the case not only because all parties sought to gain elected representatives but also because elections helped to define the value of a party for coalition formation. Elections were also instrumental in determining the internal correlation of forces within parties. Selected representatives invariably carried a great deal of weight in party circles, and the ability of a particular faction to obtain the largest number of officials strengthened its claim in party caucuses and congresses.

Chile's proportional representation system only reinforced the importance of elections for internal party competition and for cross-party bargaining. The lack of cumulative voting meant that while each party presented a list that could include as many candidates as there were seats, voters could vote for only one of those candidates. The total vote for all candidates on each list was used to decide how many seats a particular party could fill. This effectively meant that candidates ran not only against rivals on opposition lists but against "coreligionists." Before the electoral reforms of 1958, the order of placement on the list, which was decided by party officials before the election, determined which candidates were elected—meaning that a candidate toward the bottom of the list might not be seated even if he gained a greater number of votes than someone above him. His success, however, put pressure on party leaders to take him or his faction into greater account in subsequent contests. After the reforms, the candidates who gained the largest number of votes were seated, and the number of seats the party won was determined by the strength of its ticket. This change turned the election simultaneously into an intraparty primary and a general election.[44]

Bargaining, however, went on historically not only within parties but also across parties. Before 1958 joint lists made up of very disparate parties were not uncommon as parties sought to maximize their voting success in different areas. After 1958, joint lists were outlawed, and parties made regional and even national pacts to support each other's lists in areas of mutual strength by not presenting competing lists. While most pacts were structured by parties that were ideologically similar, it was not uncommon to find pacts that spanned the full breadth of the spectrum. In addition, voters often found that their votes for a particular candidate on a list might lead to the seating of a candidate of a completely different party or ideological tendency, in a pattern strikingly similar to that followed in Uruguay under the double simultaneous vote system.

The importance of the electoral process inevitably meant that parties had to pay primary attention to particularistic and clientelistic criteria as they reached beyond the faithful to party identifiers and potential voters. The multiple-member district system and the large number of parties meant that voters had to choose from a large number of candidates. It also meant, however, that congressional candidates could be elected with a relatively small number of votes. The average number of votes per candidate in the 1969 congressional election, for instance, was 4,200–3,700 if the Santiago area is excluded. This only reinforced the importance of direct personal appeals. Candidates for congressional seats in larger communities made use of lower-level brokers, such as municipal councilmen, in consolidating their own voting strength. Local brokers, in return, expected help in delivering concrete benefits to their own supporters. These benefits could only be assured by maintaining good contacts in the capital, many of which crossed party lines. The centralization of government structures and decision making, as well as the scarcity of resources in Chile's inflationary economy, only reinforced the importance of such brokerage. Brokerage would have been meaningless, however, had elected representatives not had access to resources.

The second factor that reinforced a pragmatic dimension in Chilean party politics was the existence of viable representative institutions with significant policy-making roles. The foremost among these was the Chilean congress. The congress was the locus of compromises on major legislation, as well as the key arena for processing such important matters as a budget and legislation on wage readjustments, perhaps the most crucial public policy measure in an inflationary economy. Congress's law-making, budgetary, and investigatory powers provided the clout for cross-party agreements, as well as the influence individual congressmen needed to attend to the constituency-related duties that were fundamental for reelection. The Chilean congress was the foremost arena for expression of major policy positions and disagreements; it was also the fundamental locus for fusing divergent objectives into common public policies.

This aggregation process—the structuring of broad coalitions as well as alliances on particular measures—was, in turn, made possible by a third feature of Chilean politics alluded to earlier: the existence of flexible center parties capable of forming alliances with the Left on some matters and with the Right on others. As noted above, there were no giants in Chilean politics. No party or tendency had a decided majority. Compromise and accommodation would not have been possible without the flexibility provided by center parties, notably the Radical party, which inherited the role of the nineteenth-century Liberals as the fulcrum of coalition politics. The fact that presidents were, for the most part, members of centrist parties or attempted to project an above-parties posture (for example, Jorge Alessandri or Carlos Ibáñez), only helped to counteract the centrifugal tendencies of the party system and to reinforce the bridging mechanisms of Chilean politics. Chilean presidentialism was viable in large measure because the party system encouraged clientelistic politics and alliance formation on matters of lesser importance while retaining a highly ideological and programmatic posture.[45]

The Breakdown of Democracy in Chile: The Limits of Presidentialism

As noted above, Chile's military authorities placed the primary blame for regime breakdown on Chile's democratic system, and particularly its competitive and polarized party system. In other words the Chilean breakdown was the inevitable result of the very physiognomy of the party system. Comparative evidence, as well as evidence from the Chilean case discussed below, raises serious questions about this assumption. There is little direct relationship between the characteristics of the party system per se, whether multiparty and polarized or not, and the incidence of regime breakdown.

The Comparative Evidence

The argument that multiparty systems are less stable or effective than two-party systems has been effectively challenged in studies of European parties, particularly in those including smaller European democracies. Such studies have demonstrated that multiparty systems are associated with successful democratic governance.[46] Indeed, multiparty systems are the norm among stable democracies, and two-party systems clearly the exception.

While empirical studies have suggested that party systems with significant "extremist parties" are more likely to experience reduced cabinet durability and greater executive instability, it does not follow that polarized, multiparty systems are more prone to regime breakdown than countries with catchall nonideological parties.[47] G. Bingham Powell, after examining the stability of a wide range of regimes, underscores this point by noting that "once one controls for level of economic development, the type of party system shows no relationship to regime durability or overthrow." If anything, he adds, regime breakdowns are more likely to occur in "non-extremist party systems" of the "aggregative majority" type (such as those found in the United States, Canada, the Philippines, and Turkey) than in "extremist party" systems with strong antisystem parties (such as Japan, Denmark, Finland, Italy, and Chile).[48]

Indeed, nonideological, catchall party systems are the norm in Latin America. And yet, only one or two countries on the continent have had as strong a record of democratic rule as Chile has. Multiparty countries like Ecuador, Peru, and Brazil have been characterized by diffuse, clientelistic parties, but their record of democratic continuity has been decidedly mixed. And two-party or one-party dominant systems with ideologically centrist orientations have not fared particularly well. The Colombian case illustrates the extent to which party competition can lead to extraordinary violence and breakdown even in the absence of a multiparty, polarized system, defined in ideological terms. In Argentina, a one-party dominant system was not capable of structuring a governing consensus but instead led to extreme praetorianism.[49]

Uruguay is the best comparative case for questioning the notion that the nature of the party system is directly related to democratic breakdown. Like Chile, Uruguay established one of the longest-lasting democratic regimes in the third world. But unlike Chile, its party system consisted of two loosely structured, clientelistic parties with moderate policy objectives. These parties were capable in principle of structuring a governing consensus, and yet Uruguayan democracy broke down in 1973, the year of the Chilean military coup.

Ironically, military leaders in Uruguay have also attributed that country's political breakdown to its party and electoral system. By contrast with their Chilean counterparts, however, they find fault with precisely those features of the Uruguayan system that Chileans extoll for their country. Uruguayan parties are criticized for forcing into a two-party mold a range of different ideological viewpoints better expressed in a multiparty system. And Uruguayan parties are seen as clientelistic and diffuse, too concerned with electoral objectives and willing to compromise at the expense of principle.[50]

If regime breakdown in Chile and Uruguay resulted from party systems, and the party systems were mirror opposites of each other, an explanation based on party system characteristics as defined is not particularly credible. It would border on the logical fallacy, *post hoc, ergo propter hoc*, in which it is assumed that because a certain phenomenon (the nature of the party system) preceded a subsequent phenomenon (regime breakdown), the former necessarily caused the latter.

Although the particular configuration of a party system is not in itself the cause of regime breakdown, party system variables may indeed play a role, even a central one, in the crises of democratic regimes. In both Uruguay and Chile, party leadership bore a heavy responsibility for the final outcome, and parties often sought to accommodate narrow group stakes over broader regime stakes. And in both cases, features of the party system, such as clientelism or polarization, provided important constraints on the space for maneuvering. But in neither case was the outcome inevitable. As noted below in more detail with respect to the Chilean case, the behavior of leaders and followers and the dynamics of interparty interaction may have constituted important contributory variables to regime breakdown; they were not, however, necessary or sufficient ones.

Party Politics and Regime Breakdown in Chile

As noted above, a party system is more than the sum of individual parties, their degree of coherence, ideological distinctness, and mobilization of followers in electoral contests. It also involves the complex interplay of parties in the broader political system, an interplay that is conditioned by formal rules and structures as much as by informal practices and agreements. Chile's polarized multiparty system cannot be understood without reference to the system of bargaining and accommodation that took place in arenas ranging from local elections to the national legislature within the context of a presidential system.

Several developments led to the progressive erosion of Chile's system of accommodation.[51] Some of these developments include reforms enacted to institute greater efficiency and rationality in politics and decision making. Thus, in 1958 a coalition of the Center and Left enacted a series of electoral reforms that included the abolition of joint lists. This reform ended the long-established system of political pacts noted above—a system that permitted parties of opposing ideological persuasions to structure agreements of mutual electoral benefit. While it succeeded in making preelectoral arrangements less "political," it eliminated an opportunity for cross-party bargaining.

More significant were reforms aimed at curbing congressional powers in order to provide executives with greater authority to address Chile's chronic economic problems. With the creation of the Budget Bureau in 1959 and the introduction of planning and budgeting methods, congressional prerogatives in the allocation of fiscal resources were restricted. Under the administration of Eduardo Frei (1964–70), when Frei's Christian Democratic party controlled the chamber of deputies the executive went even further, vetoing congressional efforts to earmark very small portions of the budget for particular projects, a traditional source of pork barrel and an important instance of cross-party logrolling for regional initiatives.

The most serious blow to congressional authority came with the constitutional reforms enacted by the Christian Democrat and rightist National parties in 1970, the last year of the Frei administration. Among other provisions, the reforms prohibited congressional amendments not germane to a given piece of legislation and sanctioned extensive use of executive decrees to implement programs approved by the legislature in very general terms. It also barred the congress from dealing with all matters having to do, for example, with social security, salary adjustments, and pensions in both the private and public sectors—the very heart of legislative bargaining on redistributive issues.[52]

Both the Christian Democrats and the Nationals assumed that their respective candidates would easily win the presidency in 1970. Ironically, with Salvador Allende's victory both parties became opposition forces, inheriting a weak legislature with essentially negative powers and facing an executive even less committed than previous ones to seek compromise and accommodation with legislative leaders. In the name of political efficiency, Chile's elites had reduced the importance of the congress, the principal arena of accommodation and thus accentuated the confrontational quality of Chile's polarized party system.

These changes in the rules of the game coincided with, and indeed are partly explained by, other far-reaching changes in Chilean politics, the most notable of which was the rise in the 1960s of a new center party with a markedly different political style. Unlike its predecessors, the pragmatic Radicals, the Chilean Christian Democrats conceived of themselves as an ideologically driven reform movement, a genuine alternative to both Marxism and economic liberalism. As a new centrist alternative to both extremes, they believed that they would succeed in capturing the allegiance of a majority of the electorate, drawing from both sides of the political divide.

The Christian Democrats succeeded in capturing the presidency in 1964 with an absolute majority of the votes as the parties of the Right, fearful of a leftist victory, endorsed Eduardo Frei's candidacy. The following year, drawing on the coattails of the new president's victory, the Christian Democrats managed the best showing of any single Chilean party since the adoption of the 1925 constitution. Once in office, heartened by their electoral success, they moved quickly to implement a far-reaching reform program. Inspired by experts and technocrats and their own "communitarian" ideology, they disdained the traditional give-and-take of Chilean politics. Although the Christian Democrats succeeded in implementing many of their proposals, they antagonized all of Chile's political forces on the Left, Right, and Center. They were particularly hard on the centrist Radicals, refusing overtures for collaboration and dismissing or bypassing Radical functionaries in the bureaucracy. The Christian Democrats had displaced the Radicals as Chile's center party but were less tolerant of clientelistic and logrolling politics and less disposed to serve as a bridge across parties and groups. The Christian Democratic posture added to the growing radicalization of groups on the Left (particularly in the Socialist party) in the aftermath of the Cuban revolution and the heightened resentment among rightists, who felt betrayed by their 1964 presidential candidate.

Had the Christian Democrats succeeded in becoming a genuine center majority, the increased political conflict would not have had serious institutional repercussions. Despite vast organizational efforts, extensive use of government resources and programs for partisan advantage, and extraordinary levels of foreign aid, Frei and his collaborators did not succeed in breaking the tripartite division of Chilean politics. As a result, even when it became apparent that they could not win the 1970 presidential elections on their own, they were unable to structure a preelectoral coalition with either the Right or the Left. The bulk of the diminished Radical party joined in support of the candidacy of Socialist Salvador Allende, who surprised most pollsters by edging out rightist Jorge Alessandri by a plurality of 36.2 percent to 34.9 percent in the three-way race. Christian Democrat Radomiro Tomic came in third with 27.8 percent of the vote. Allende won, despite the fact that he received a smaller percentage of the vote than he did in his losing campaign against Frei in 1964. The results vividly illustrated the continued division of the Chilean electorate into Left, Right, and Center tendencies and the difficulties of structuring majority coalitions.

Because Allende had failed to gain an absolute majority of the vote, the election was thrown into the congress. Extraordinary pressure both inside and outside Chile was placed on the Christian Democratic leadership to back Alessandri, the runner-up, in the congressional balloting. The Christian Democratic party leadership, however, had shifted to the Left in the waning months of the Frei government, and Tomic had closer personal affinities with Allende than with Alessandri. Although survey research showed that Christian Democratic voters preferred Alessandri as a second-choice candidate to their own standard bearer, Christian Democratic leaders in the congress prevailed on their colleagues to ratify Allende's presidential bid. It was the first time in Chilean history that the Left captured the nation's highest office.[53]

The president's minority status, and the lack of majority support in the congress for the parties of his coalition, meant that Allende, like other presidents before him, would have to tailor his program to the realities of coalition politics in order to succeed. More to the point, he would have to retain the majority coalition that had permitted his election in the legislature by retaining the support of the Christian Democrats.

Pursuing a strategy of compromise and coalition building, however, was now more difficult than ever. Important elements in the Popular Unity (UP) coalition, particularly Allende's own Socialist party, were openly committed to revolutionary transformations in the socioeconomic order and basic changes in the institutional framework of Chilean politics, clearly disdaining the politics of accommodation with the "bourgeoisie" and forgetting that Allende had been elected by little more than a third of the electorate. Making matters worse, the presidential coalition itself was unwieldy and fractious, with parties and groups competing for spoils and patronage as much with one another as with the opposition.

Like most presidents before him, Allende soon forgot that he was a minority president who owed his election to the concurrence of opposition forces. He believed he represented the will of the majority over the partial interests of groups representing the status quo, groups with exaggerated representation in the parliament, the courts, and other areas of Chilean public life. As he noted in his victory speech in the National Stadium, "After their struggle to overcome the capitalist system which exploits them, the masses have reached the Presidency of the Republic. . . . Here a whole people has succeeded in taking into its hands the control of its own destiny in order to march by democratic means toward socialism."[54]

Like his immediate predecessor, he was convinced that during his six-year term he could transform his minority status into an overwhelming majority for his UP coalition, breaking the historic deadlock of Chilean politics. After all, he was in charge of Chile's powerful executive branch, and the logic of history was on his side. Most Chileans were poor or lower middle class and would soon leave their parochial political loyalties behind as they came to understand the meaning of the country's revolutionary process. He and his associates firmly believed that Chile was "the first nation in the world called upon to set up a second model for transition to a socialist society," one based not on violent confrontation with the reactionary classes but on the actions of free citizens through the ballot box. By the end of his term, Chile's masses would be squarely on the side of the revolution.[55]

The new president improved his electoral support in the nationwide municipal contest of 1971. But rather than interpreting the results as the "honeymoon surge" that frequently characterized the first "midterm" election after a presidential contest, the UP coalition saw the results as a renewed mandate for change.[56] The coalition parties redoubled their effort to employ executive authority to implement basic transformations in society, intent on capturing the allegiance of those Chileans who had voted for the opposition. The Far Left, in particular, pressed for dramatic action: more redistributive measures, more expropriations of rural properties, and more takeovers of industrial firms, the profits of which would permit the state to cover its dramatically increasing expenditures. As a result of these unilateral measures, the Christian Democratic party moved from cautious support for the government to vocal opposition.

With executive measures taken in the absence of majority support in the legislature, political conflict soon turned into constitutional impasse. Ill-conceived redistributive and stimulative economic policies in turn led to skyrocketing inflation, massive budget deficits, and serious problems of distribution. Government actions were radicalized by the strong reaction of increasingly mobilized upper- and middle-class groups and foreign adversaries, who often resorted to sabotage and subversion in an effort to destroy the Popular Unity government. In this climate of growing suspicion and violence, the lines of communication between leaders and followers in the opposing parties eroded further, accentuating the divide of Chilean politics. Allende found it increasingly difficult to govern in the face of a concerted opposition of Christian Democrats and rightists in the legislature and the exigencies of a complex coalition in which he was the final arbiter. Policy continuity was severely undermined by shifting cabinets and ministers lasting only weeks in office.

The constitutional conflict between president and legislature became focused on legislation introduced by the Christian Democrats to regulate the "areas of the economy." This measure, which would have guaranteed private property and barred wholesale expropriations, envisioned a substantial state sector, a mixed sector, and other forms of property, such as cooperatives and worker-owned enterprises. It was apparent to moderates in both the government and the opposition that the only way to save Chilean democracy was for Allende to come to an understanding with the Christian Democrats on this critical issue. The UP government did not have the votes in the legislature to enact its program through law, and many Christian Democrats were committed to significant social and economic transformations.

Efforts at compromise, which came close to fruition on two separate occasions, were undermined by the fact that incentives for cooperation were far weaker than those for noncooperation. Although many Christian Democrats would have welcomed some formula to reduce tensions by working with Allende, the right wing of the party was skeptical of any concessions that they feared would strengthen the government and permit it to move ahead with its socialist agenda to the detriment of the country. But purely electoral considerations were as important. Party leaders were concerned about the political implications of collaborating with the government, fearing that if they did not stand up to the Popular Unity government, they would risk losing the support of vast sectors of Chile's middle and lower classes to the more militantly anti-UP parties of the Right. This internal division led to further erosion of the Christian Democrats as a centrist force. The approaching congressional race of March 1973 placed strong pressure on the party to guard its electoral fortunes.

By the same token, militants in the UP feared that any compromise with the

Christian Democrats would derail their own strategy of forcing irreversible changes through executive action and that they would lose a "historic" opportunity to conquer quickly the loyalty of the masses and successfully confront the country's privileged minority. For other leaders and parties in the UP electoral considerations were also important. The coming congressional races presented a real opportunity to show the country and the world that the majority of the people were indeed committed to revolutionary change. Why bargain with Christian Democrats and dilute popular enthusiasm when the congressional race would give the UP the majority it needed to implement its policies in the congress?

The failure of the two branches of government to compromise was aggravated by the hostile relation between the executive and the courts, which the UP considered biased toward the protection of property rights. Allende appointed military commanders to his cabinet as a neutral buffer to maintain order until the elections of March "resolved" the political impasse.

But the March elections did not provide a solution. Chilean voters gave the UP a few more seats but not enough to give the government a working majority. The opposition parties, though united in a common front, failed to gain the two-thirds majority needed to impeach the president. Unless the moderates on both sides of Chile's divide succeeded in structuring a regime-saving compromise, there would be no constitutional resolution to the crisis. Allende had not yet reached the midpoint of his six-year term. A desperate president appeared willing to compromise, but the Christian Democrats, now under the leadership of their right wing simply did not trust him or the UP. They feared that the president would only stall for time to build the groundwork for an unconstitutional seizure of power.

The president, in turn, had little reason to trust his closest interlocutors in the opposition because he knew that some of them were resigned to a military solution. The center groups and moderate politicians on both sides, who had it in their grasp to find regime-saving solutions, abdicated responsibility in favor of narrower group stakes and short-term interests, thus further aggravating tension and reducing institutional channels of accommodation. The armed forces, caught in the middle, were accused on a daily basis of cowardice for giving the government room to survive and not taking matters into their own hands. The involvement of "neutral powers," such as the courts and the military, only served to politicize those institutions and pave the way for the military coup that destroyed the very institutions of compromise and accommodation that the moderate political leaders had professed to defend. It was only a matter of time until they moved to destroy Chilean democracy.[57]

The perennial conflicts of Chilean presidential politics came to their sharpest crisis during the Allende government. Earlier presidents had had great difficulty governing. Chile's multiparty system provided minority presidents with minority support in the legislature, forcing the creation of preelectoral and postelectoral coalitions. But opposition parties had few real incentives to maintain electoral coalitions, particularly since they were primarily motivated by the desire to win the next presidential race and obtain policy objectives, not simply governmental representation. The dynamics of this system of double-minority executives had a devastating effect in the polarized atmosphere of the Allende presidency, in which political struggles translated into increased polarization and institutional conflict with no clear institutional solution. Allende as a minority president was incapable of structuring a majority coalition in the parliament to implement his policies and yet was able to make use of ample executive authority to implement many of his measures. When the legislature balked at cooperating with the president, reacting strongly to what they viewed as a clear usurpation of executive authority, Chile's presidential constitution provided no mechanism to resolve the impasse except to wait for the next election in the hope that the voters would provide a solution. The lack of an electoral solution, combined with a fixed presidential term, meant that there was no constitutional solution to the crisis of Chilean politics.[58]

Had Chile had a parliamentary formula, the executive would have had to structure viable and continuing majorities to rule, or at least would have had to preside over a minority government enjoying majority support for key legislative measures. A coalition between Allende and the Christian Democrats, under a parliamentary framework, would have been based on a different political calculus. The moderates on both sides would have had stronger incentives and greater maneuvering room to work out agreements. Christian Democrats would have shared government responsibility. Change clearly would have been far more drastic than what the Right was prepared to accept but far less dramatic and totalistic than that envisioned by the Far Left.

Should a coalition between Allende and the Christian Democrats have failed, the Christian Democrats would have had a capacity to structure a government with the Right. That development would have forced the resignation of Allende, on the very hypothetical assumption that he would have presided over the coalition. The government would have fallen, not the regime. The underlying conflicts in Chilean society during the 1960s and 1970s would still have placed enormous pressures on whatever government was in office. However, rather than facing increased polarization, which reduced the scope for moderate politics, the centrist leaders would have had much more leeway and the system as a whole would have had institutional solutions for resolving political deadlock. In Chile, the logic of presidentialism in a minority government simply led to a spiral of polarization that left the country with little alternative to a military coup.

The Chilean breakdown was a complex dialectical process, one in which time-tested patterns of accommodation were eroded by the rise of a Center unwilling to bridge the gap between extremes and by the disuse of institutional arenas of accommodation in the name of technical efficiency. It was also the product of gross miscalculations, extremism, narrow group stakes, and lack of courage in key circumstances. Breakdown may not have been inevitable. While human action was severely circumscribed by the course of events and the structural characteristics of Chilean politics, there may have been room for choice, for leadership willing to prevent the denouement. And yet, the institutional parameters of Chilean politics provided increasingly narrower options for a fundamental solution to the crisis that would have prevented regime collapse.

Conclusion: A Proposal for Parliamentary Government in Chile

This chapter implies that the viability of political regimes cannot be judged on the basis of the party system alone, just as it cannot be judged on the basis of the institutional dimension alone. As such this view differs not only from the assumptions of the Chilean military, who felt that by changing the party system they could resolve the underlying institutional constraints in Chilean politics. It also differs from academic studies that emphasize strong parties as mechanisms for controlling political mobilization and thus for establishing political order. The Chilean case is not one in which weak parties were unable to cope with the rising political demands of an increasingly mobilized population. The reverse is true. Heightened political mobilization was the product of the increased strength of Chile's major parties, which were spurred on by the outbidding of the Christian Democratic and Allende years. It is not the strength of parties per se that contributes to a stable democratic order. Rather, democratic governability depends on the successful expression of societal divisions through the party system within a framework of institutional and constitutional order.[59]

The key to understanding Chilean politics, even after a lengthy authoritarian interlude, is the existence of several important political currents with strong party representation and clear Left, Center, and Right referents. The challenge for strengthening Chilean democracy is not the illusory and counterproductive attempt to destroy the party system or change the underlying ideological attachments of voters. The military government clearly failed in this endeavor. The challenge for Chile is to structure mechanisms to bridge the centrifugal realities of Chilean politics and to achieve a minimum consensus on the rules of the game and the policies required to govern the country. This can only be achieved by strengthening the institutional arenas of accommodation capable of providing channels for political expression, compromise, and effective government with either the overt or tacit support of congressional majorities.

The starting point must be a recognition of the continuous crisis of presidentialism in Chile. As argued above, all Chilean presidents who have governed since the party system was configured in the 1920s, including Carlos Ibáñez and Jorge Alessandri, who ran as independent candidates "above" party politics, found that governing the country was extraordinarily difficult. Presidents were invariably elected by minorities or by coalitions that disintegrated after the election and faced little support or outright opposition in the congress.

Paradoxically, the response to this problem of governance in Chile has been to seek an increase in presidential power. The resolution of the country's pressing social and economic problems, it is argued, requires strong leadership—a leadership that is thwarted by the narrow, partisan interests represented in the legislature. Chilean history before the breakdown of 1973, however, shows that an increase in presidential power only aggravates the problem by reducing arenas of accommodation and making executive-legislative confrontations more bitter. Indeed, the stronger the power of the presidency as a separate constitutional actor, the greater the disincentives for structuring support among parties and groups jealous of their autonomy and future electoral prospects. One can argue that in Chile there has been an inverse correlation between the power of the presidency and the success of presidential government. The stronger the president, the weaker the presidential system.

In view of the notable success of the government of President Patricio Aylwin since the reestablishment of democracy in March of 1990, it is legitimate to ask whether this generalization still holds true. Although Chile's democratic parties were able to defeat General Pinochet in the 1988 plebiscite and to triumph over the candidates of the Right in the 1989 presidential and congressional races, they were not able to change fundamentally the constitutional legacy of the military government. This legacy is, above all, one of hyperpresidentialism, with little room for the legislature in policy making.

The Aylwin government's achievements in restoring social peace and promoting increased economic prosperity are not, however, due to constitutional structures inherited from the dictatorship. The government of the Concertación may arguably be the most successful government in contemporary Chilean history precisely because it is the first coalition government that has maintained unity of purpose throughout the presidential term. Like several of its predecessors, the Aylwin government resulted from a preelection coalition of the Center Left that managed to obtain a majority of the vote. But Aylwin has been able to count on the strong support of the parties of the Concertación from the very outset. The result has been remarkable cabinet and ministerial stability and a willingness on the part of legislators to approve government laws as dictated by the leadership of the Concertación. Equally as important as legislative acquiescence has been the willingness of party militants and followers in local party organizations and in societal groups such as labor unions and neighborhood associations to accept the moderate policies of the government without pressing for more radical solutions.

The government of the Concertación has clearly benefited from the internal changes in the Chilean Left, which preceded but were reinforced by the collapse of socialism and which contribute to a marked decline in the polarization of Chilean politics. Its task has also been facilitated by the favorable economic situation of the country at the time of the transition. But the unity of the coalition—its willingness to set aside partisan, personal, and ideological rivalries—was assured by the real fear of authoritarian reversal on the part of leaders who had learned the painful way that only unity could defeat the longest and most powerful authoritarian regime in the nation's history.

The fact that General Pinochet had commanded more than 40 percent of the vote in the 1988 plebiscite was also a clear warning that Chileans feared a return to the confrontational and chaotic politics of the past and that important forces in Chilean society were more comfortable with dictatorship than with democracy. The continued presence of General Pinochet as commander of the army during the entire Aylwin government was a stark reminder of this fact and a powerful incentive to retain a common sense of purpose in the face of opposition forces in the congress and other institutions of society. Ironically, this unity would not have been possible had Chile's parties been as weak and ephemeral as the military leaders thought they were. The very strength of Chile's parties, their extraordinary ability to establish common programs and common strategies to win elections, also made it possible for them to form a viable governing coalition that overcame the institutional rigidities inherited from the past.

It is doubtful, however, whether the unity forged in the struggle against authoritarianism will survive the transitional democratic government. The "politics of forced consensus," as a leading figure in the Concertación called the coalition government, was already showing signs of wear by the beginning of the third year of the Aylwin government.[60] Members of the congress chafed at their lack of significant input into decision making, complaining that all agreements were reached by a small group of government and party leaders in Santiago. Middle-level leaders in all parties openly complained that high-ranking party leaders in cabinet posts and other government positions were forcing measures on party followers without taking their views into consideration. More significantly, party leaders and militants throughout the country increasingly balked at having to contain their own political ambitions so that leaders could structure party lists designed to beat the opposition within the difficult strictures of the military government's electoral law.[61]

At the same time, the unity of the Concertación was significantly challenged by the upcoming presidential election of 1993. Socialists began to argue that they should not continue to play second fiddle to the Christian Democrats; that if the coalition was a true coalition, they deserved the presidency in the next race. Even if they conceded that the presidency was a remote possibility for their party, they feared that unless they ran their own candidate, they risked losing their identity in relationship to the Christian Democrats.

The runoff election, contemplated in the 1980 constitution, which replaced the congress's role in selecting a president in the absence of a candidate with an absolute majority of votes, only added to the logic compelling separate candidacies. The Socialists argued that they could present their own candidate, on the basis of a prior agreement with Concertación partners that whoever reached the second round would be supported by the other. Even a losing candidacy would enable the

Socialists to present a distinct party profile and have their own presidential candidate "pulling in" Socialist congressional candidates. The Christian Democrats, fearful of the consequences of the breakdown of the Concertación and confident of their victory in the presidential race, threatened to abandon any agreement on a joint congressional list if the Socialists refused to back their candidate in the presidential race.

Separate presidential candidacies would clearly place enormous strains on the coalition agreement. A presidential race focused on the personality of the candidate would inevitably lead to antagonisms and tensions between leaders and followers. A particularly acrimonious race, may make it difficult to rebuild a viable governing coalition even if the losing coalition partners are forced to vote for their potential allies as the lesser of two evils. The runoff could also have unintended consequences if both candidates in the second round are from the Concertación. This would force the Christian Democrats to appeal to the Right to defeat their Socialist partner, thus destroying the center left coalition and inaugurating a much more precarious center right one. While the victor in a second round may appear to be a majority president, he and his party probably would not command a majority in the legislature, where the perennial problem of coalition formation in Chilean politics would be reopened.

It is likely that the Concertación will avoid separate candidacies in the 1993 presidential race in an attempt to preserve the coalition beyond the Aylwin government. Over the long run, however, other issues are likely to drive the alliance apart. As time passes and the legacy of authoritarianism fades, the parties will need to address a host of social and moral questions that remained dormant under authoritarianism. These include issues such as contraception, abortion, divorce, and the role of women in society, issues that the Catholic church, historically close to the Christian Democrats, is placing in the forefront of its own agenda.

The Socialists are more likely to side with businessmen, who are conservative on economic issues but liberal on moral questions, than they are with the Christian Democrats on matters of "family values." Ironically, as Chile becomes more "modern," it is likely to face a gamut of policy concerns that may break down the alliance patterns of the past. Under such circumstances, the strong presidentialism of the Pinochet years will only exacerbate the difficulties of coalition formation and the prospects for stable democratic rule.

Given Chile's history and the continued reality of its multiparty politics with three distinct political tendencies, Chileans should seriously consider establishing a parliamentary form of government. A parliamentary system is characterized by executive authority generated through majority support in the parliament and responsible to the parliament. Thus, if a parliamentary majority shifts, the executive must reflect that shift by selecting a new prime minister and cabinet or calling elections to determine a new parliament. All parliamentary systems have a head of state as well as a head of government. While the president (or monarch) in a parliamentary system has few powers, he or she can play an important role as a symbolic, "above-politics" leader—one who can perform an important mediating role in times of crisis.

The establishment of a parliamentary system in Chile would have three distinct advantages. In the first place it would diffuse the enormous pressures for structuring high-stakes coalitions around a winner-take-all presidential option, which by definition encourages polarization in the Chilean context. Chile's transition back to democracy is challenged by the rigidity and uncertainty of an electoral option with only one possible winner, who would hold office for eight years. Secondly, a parliamentary form of government would eliminate the paralyzing stalemate and confrontation that have characterized executive-legislative relations in twentieth-century Chile. The country would not have to live with the rigidity of a commitment to a failed administration that no longer enjoys a working majority. The dramatic cases of Siles Suazo of Bolivia and Alfonsín of Argentina, presidents who had to resign before their terms were completed, creating significant constitutional uncertainty, are dramatic illustrations of this point, as are the cases of Sarney in Brazil and García in Peru, failed presidents who stayed in office despite their loss of popular confidence and parliamentary support.

In the third place, a parliamentary system would contribute to the further moderation of Chilean politics. Given many of the similarities in the platforms of the parties of the Left and the Christian Democrats in 1970, it is likely that a coalition between Center and Left would have continued had the system been a parliamentary one. But it would have continued with the realization of Allende and his collaborators that change had to remain limited lest the support of the Christian Democrats be withdrawn and the government fall.

At the same time, the executive under a parliamentary framework could not have embarked on a strategy of taking over sectors of the economy solely through executive action because all such measures would have required approval of parliamentary majorities. Thus, moderate sectors on both sides of the political divide would have been strengthened and a centripetal drive toward coalition and compromise, rather than a centrifugal pattern of conflict in search of maximalist solutions, encouraged.

In a parliamentary system, because governments would have been structured in the parliament, centrist options would have been encouraged. Congressmen faced with the possibility of losing their seats in a new election have significant incentive for structuring working coalitions. Indeed, the internal correlation of forces within parties would have shifted in favor of elected members of parliament rather than party leaders outside of government. What Chile needs is precisely a system of governance that encourages the formation of broad centrist tendencies and not one in which the centrist forces are drowned out by the logic of the extremes. It also needs a system in which working majorities can be structured and a president seeking from a minority position to interpret the national will can be avoided.

While it is true that parliamentary systems such as Italy's may appear to be unstable, it is not the regimes per se that are unstable. A parliamentary system, like any other, reflects the underlying societal divisions manifested in party politics. Parliamentary systems with two parties or with several moderate ones may be more stable than multiparty ones that are polarized, but the crises of parliamentary systems are crises of government, not of regime. Chile might experience frequent government changes as each of the parties in its three political tendencies jockeyed to generate working majorities. But, as in Italy, the parliamentary framework would permit an adjustment of governments without bringing the country to the brink of institutional collapse.

Indeed, the generative cleavages that led to the creation of Chile's multiparty, polarized system are far more comparable to those found in Europe than to those found in the exceptional case of the United States. It is not illogical to think that Chile should therefore consider turning to the most widely used system of governance among democratic regimes, a system of governance that has worked well in societies with comparable political cleavages and traditions. All of the stable multiparty democracies in the world are parliamentary regimes.

Nor does the argument that Chile's experience with parliamentary government between 1890 and 1924 failed undermine the argument for a parliamentary system in the 1990s. While it is true that parliamentarism has a bad image in Chile, it does not fully deserve such an image. In the context of the times, Chile's parliamentary period was one of the most successful republican governments in the world. Furthermore, Chile never had a parliamentary system in the full sense of the term. The "Parliamentary Republic" was simply a presidential system in which the president deferred to an extraordinary degree to majorities in both houses of the parliament, but executive authority was not generated in the parliament, nor could the parliament be dissolved and elections called in the absence of viable majorities. Chile's parliamentary government stemmed directly from the crisis of presidentialism in the nineteenth century, which led to the Civil War of 1891 and illustrated the lengths to which political elites would go to solve the problem of divided government.[62]

In the aftermath of Chile's greatest political crisis in history, it is clear that the country's democratic leadership rejects many undemocratic features of the Pinochet constitution of 1980 and is uncomfortable with the excessive presidentialism envisioned by that document. The Concertación platform, and interparty agreements made before the coalition assumed power in March of 1990, called for significant constitutional reforms, including the gradual implementation of semipresidential or parliamentary practices moving toward a change of regime.

These plans were soon abandoned for fear of antagonizing the military, and in the realization that major constitutional reforms would be difficult to achieve, given rightist control of the senate, and could jeopardize more attainable reforms such as the reestablishment of elected local governments and reforms of the judiciary. At the same time, however, some leaders in the executive branch came to like the extensive presidential prerogatives in the Pinochet constitution and attributed governmental success to those powers, forgetting the importance of coalition politics and party discipline as the essential building blocks of the Concertación effort. If Chile is to continue to prosper under democracy, coalitions like the Concertación need to develop in the future. Since they are far more likely to develop under the institutional rules of parliamentary government, Chilean political elites should, once again, give renewed attention to the still pending constitutional reforms.

Notes

An earlier version of this article was published under the title "Orígenes y características del sistema de partidos políticos en Chile: proposición para un gobierno parlamentario," *Estudios públicos*, no. 18 (Fall 1985), pp. 88–154. A subsequent version was presented at the conference on "Presidential or Parliamentary Democracy: Does It Make a Difference?" organized by Juan Linz and me and held at Georgetown University on May 14–15, 1989, with support from the Ford Foundation. I am grateful to Hugo Castillo and Randy Kindley for their research assistance and to Juan Linz and Scott Mainwaring for their comments.

1. Kalman H. Silvert, *Chile: Yesterday and Today* (New York: Holt, Rinehart & Winston, 1965), p. 99.

2. Federico Gil, *The Political System of Chile* (Boston: Houghton Mifflin, 1965), p. 244.

3. There is a surprising lack of general studies of party systems in Latin America, but see Ronald H. McDonald and J. Mark Ruhl, *Party Politics and Elections in Latin America* (Boulder: Westview, 1989); Jean-Pierre Bernard et al., *Guide to the Political Parties of South America* (Middlesex, U.K.: Penguin, 1973). A useful review, which lists some of the single-party monographs, is Mary Jeanne Reid Martz, "Studying Latin American Political Parties: Dimensions Past and Present," *Journal of Latin American Studies* 12, no. 1: 139–67. For a comprehensive party-by-party description see Robert J. Alexander, *Political Parties in the Americas: Canada, Latin America and West Indies*, 2 vols. (Westport: Greenwood, 1982). Kenneth Janda's massive *Political Parties: A Cross National Survey* (New York: Free Press, 1980) includes information on ten Latin American countries, though curiously Costa Rica, Brazil, Chile, Colombia, and Argentina are missing. On Chilean parties see the classic study of Alberto Edwards and Eduardo Frei, *Historia de los partidos políticos chilenos* (Santiago: Editorial del Pacifico, 1949.) Other helpful studies include Germán Urzúa Valenzuela, *Los partidos políticos chilenos* (Santiago: Editorial Jurídica, 1968); Sergio Guilisaste Tagle, *Partidos políticos chilenos* (Santiago: Editorial Nascimiento, 1964); Gil, *The Political System of Chile*. A useful summary reference on Chilean parties, which must be used with caution because of frequent errors, is Lía Cortés and Jordi Fuentes, *Diccionario político de Chile* (Santiago: Editorial Orbe, 1967).

4. This account draws substantially on Arturo Valenzuela and J. Samuel Valenzuela, "Partidos de oposición bajo el regimen autoritario chileno," *Revista mexicana de sociología* 44, no. 2 (April–June 1982), reprinted in *Chile 1973–198?*, edited by Manuel Antonio Garretón (Santiago: Facultad Latinoamericana de Ciencias Sociales, 1983) and in revised form in *Military Rule in Chile: Dictatorship and Oppositions*, edited by J. Samuel Valenzuela and Arturo Valenzuela (Baltimore: Johns Hopkins UP, 1986). The framework is informed by the discussion of the generation of the European party systems found in Seymour Martin Lipset and

Stein Rokkan, eds., *Party Systems and Voter Alignment: Cross National Perspectives* (New York: Free Press, 1967). Rokkan's extensive work on the extension of electoral participation and party formation is compiled in part in his *Citizens, Elections, Parties* (Oslo: Universitetsforlaget, 1970). See in particular "Nation Building, Cleavage Formation and the Structuring of Mass Politics," pp. 72–144. A useful review of the literature on parties with a brief application to the Chilean case is Carlos Huneeus, "Los partidos políticos y la transición a la democracia en Chile hoy," *Estudios públicos*, no. 15 (Winter 1984): 57–88. I am grateful to Samuel Valenzuela for our rich collaborative work over the years, which informs many insights in this chapter.

5. The problem of sequence and timing of political crises has received considerable attention in the literature. For a discussion of this phenomena in relation to parties, see the concluding chapter in Joseph Lapalombara and Myron Weiner, eds., *Political Parties and Political Development* (Princeton: Princeton UP, 1966). Historical treatments of European and U.S. cases from this perspective can be found in Raymond Crew, ed., *Crises of Political Development in Europe and the United States* (Princeton: Princeton UP, 1975). For a valuable critique, see Robert T. Holt and John E. Turner, "Crises and Sequences in Collective Theory Development," *American Political Science Review* 69 (Sept. 1975): 969–94.

6. The Chilean Radical party was founded in 1863 and achieved cabinet representation for the first time in 1875. See Luis Palma Zuñiga, *Historia del Partido Radical* (Santiago: Editorial Andrés Bello, 1967.)

7. The key role of suffrage and of the Conservative party in the establishment of democratic institutions is discussed in J. Samuel Valenzuela, *Democratización vía reforma: la expansión del sufragio en Chile* (Buenos Aires: Ediciones del Ildes, 1985). See also Arturo Valenzuela and Samuel Valenzuela, "Los origenes de la democracia: reflexiones teóricas sobre el caso de Chile," *Estudios públicos*, no. 12 (Spring 1982): 5–39. This article was published in English as a working paper of the Latin America Program of the Woodrow Wilson International Center for Scholars (Washington, D.C.) under the title, "The Origins of Democracy: Theoretical Reflections on the Chilean Case."

8. See Arturo Valenzuela and Alexander Wilde, "El congreso y la redemocratización en Chile," *Alternativas*, no. 3:5–40. For a revisionary discussion of the period of the parliamentary republic see Julio Heise González, *Historia de Chile 1861–1925*, vol. 1 (Santiago: Editorial Andrés Bello 1973); vol. 2 (Santiago: Editorial Universitaria, 1982.) See also Arturo Valenzuela, "Politics, Parties and the State in Chile: The Higher Civil Service," in *Bureaucrats and Policy*, edited by Ezra Suleiman (New York: Holmes & Meier, 1984.)

9. See Samuel Valenzuela, "Labor Movement Formation and Politics: The Chilean and French Cases in Comparative Perspective, 1850–1950" (Ph.D. diss., Columbia University, 1979).

10. The classic distinction was made by Maurice Duverger in his *Parties politiques* (Paris: Armand Colin, 1951.)

11. Lipset and Rokkan, "Cleavage Structures, Party Systems and Voter Alignments," in *Party Systems and Voter Alignments*, p. 51.

12. The electoral weakness of the German and French Right, which led to an asymmetry toward the Center and Left, is noted by Lipset and Rokkan.

13. I compiled all data in this article from raw electoral data in the Dirección del Registro Electoral, Santiago, Chile. For an excellent study of the "Center" in Chilean politics see Timothy Scully, *Rethinking the Center: Party Politics in Nineteenth- and Twentieth-Century Chile* (Stanford: Stanford UP, 1992.)

14. Giovanni Sartori, *Parties and Party Systems: A Framework for Analysis* (Cambridge: Cambridge UP, 1976), p. 313. The actual average fractionalization scores for the period

1945–73 are: Finland, .804; Switzerland, .801; Chile, .796; France IV, .790; Netherlands, .787; Israel, .784. Denmark had a score of .755, while Italy's was .721. An intelligent study that calculates the fractionalization index while testing Douglas Rae's findings for the Chilean case is M. Teresa Miranda, "El sistema electoral y el multipartidismo en Chile," *Revista de ciencia política* 4, no. 1 (1982):59–69, 130–38.

15. For an elaboration of this point, see Arturo Valenzuela, "The Scope of the Chilean Party System," *Comparative Politics* 4, no. 2 (Jan. 1972). Further, examination of the socioeconomic correlates of party competition supports the findings reported in table 6.4 with fractionalization. In Chile smaller and more socioeconomically backward communities were as likely to be competitive as larger, more modernized ones—strongly suggesting that party system variables were not closely linked to socioeconomic determinants. These findings refute an influential body of literature in the social sciences which has sought to establish that relation and suggests that political phenomena were independent variables in their own right. See for example S. N. Eisenstadt, "Social Change, Differentiation and Evolution," *American Sociological Review* 29, no. 3 (1964):375–87. This theme emerges again later in a discussion of the support for particular parties.

16. See Sartori, *Parties and Party Systems*, pp. 310–15.

17. Several studies of varying quality have examined the socioeconomic correlates of party voting in Chile. For a sampling see Glaucio Ary Dillon Soares and Robert L. Hamblin, "Socio-economic Variables and Voting for the Radical Left in Chile, 1952," *American Political Science Review* 61 (Dec. 1967): 1053–65; Maurice Zeitlin and James Petras, "The Working-Class Vote in Chile: Christian Democracy versus Marxism," in *British Journal of Sociology* 21, no. 1 (1970): 16– 29; Steven Sinding, "The Evolution of Chilean Voting Patterns: A Reexamination of Some Old Assumptions," *Journal of Politics* 34 (Aug. 1972): 774–96; Robert Ayres, "Electoral Constraints and the Chilean Way to Socialism," in *Chile: Politics and Society*, edited by Arturo Valenzuela and J. Samuel Valenzuela (New Brunswick: Transaction Books, 1975), pp. 30–66; Arturo Valenzuela, "Political Participation, Agriculture and Literacy: Communal versus Provincial Voting Patterns in Chile," *Latin American Research Review* 12, no. 1 (1977): 105–14; Daniel Hellinger, "Electoral Change in the Chilean Countryside: The Presidential Elections of 1955 and 1970," *Western Political Quarterly* 31, no. 2 (1978): 253–73. The classic study in the Siegfried tradition remains Eduardo Cruz Coke, *Geografía electoral de Chile* (Santiago: Editorial del Pacífico, 1952) updated as *Historia electoral de Chile 1925–1973* (Santiago: Editorial Jurídica de Chile, 1984.) See André Siegfried, *Tableau politique de la France de l'ouest sous la Troisième République* (Paris: Librairie Armand Colin, 1913).

18. See James Prothro and Patricio Chaparro, "Public Opinion and the Movement of the Chilean Government to the Left," in *Chile: Politics and Society*, edited by Arturo Valenzuela and J. Samuel Valenzuela (New Brunswick: Transaction Books, 1976).

19. There is some research on women and the religious dimension of the vote in Chile. See Patricia Kyle and Michael Francis, "Women at the Polls: The Case of Chile, 1970–71," *Comparative Political Studies* 11, no. 3 (Oct. 1978); Kenneth P. Langton and Ronald Rapoport, "Religion and Leftist Mobilization in Chile," *Comparative Political Studies* 9, no. 3 (Oct. 1976); Lucy C. Behrman, "Political Development and Secularization in Two Chilean Urban Communities," *Comparative Politics* 4, no. 2 (Jan. 1972); Steven M. Neuse, "Voting in Chile: The Feminine Response," in John Booth and Mitchell Seligson, *Political Participation in Latin America* (New York, 1978).

20. The interplay of cultural and ideological dimensions as they relate to generative cleavages over time is an area that requires research. In fact there are few good studies of Chilean parties. Most focus on a chronology of events or shifts in party positions, or they

are semipolitical ideological tracts by party leaders. No studies focus in a systematic way on organizational variables or on the crucial dimension of relations between leaders, middle-level officials, militants, and voters. No studies have been conducted on the historicity of party alternatives, such as those done for Scandinavia by authors like Rokkan or Valen. Standard studies for Chilean parties include for the Left: Julio Cesar Jobet, *El Partido Socialista de Chile*, 2d ed., 2 vols. (Santiago: Ediciones Prensa Latinoamericana, 1971); Alejandro Chelén Rojas, *Trayectoria del socialismo* (Buenos Aires: Editorial Austral, 1967); Hernán Ramirez Necochea, *Origen y formación del Partido Comunista de Chile* (Santiago: Editorial Austral, 1965); Ernst Halperin, *Nationalism and Communism in Chile* (Cambridge: MIT Press, 1965); Paul Drake, *Socialism and Populism in Chile* (Urbana: U Illinois P, 1978). For parties on the Right see Ignacio Arteaga Alemparte, *Partido Conservador XVI Convención Nacional, 1947* (Santiago: Imprenta Chile, 1947); Marcial Sanfuentes Carrión, *El Partido Conservador* (Santiago: Editorial Universitaria, 1957); José Miguel Prado Valdés, *Reseña histórica del Partido Liberal* (Santiago: Imprenta Andina, 1963). There are no good studies of the National party. A very insightful study into the Chilean right is Robert Kaufman, *The Politics of Land Reform in Chile 1950–1970* (Cambridge: Harvard UP, 1972). For the Radical party see Luis Palma Zuñiga, *Historia del Partido Radical;* Florencio Durán Bernales, *El Partido Radical* (Santiago: Editorial Nascimiento, 1958). On the Christian Democratic party see Leonard Gross, *The Last Best Hope: Eduardo Frei and Chilean Christian Democracy* (New York: Random House, 1967); George Grayson, *El Partido Demócrata Cristiano Chileno* (Buenos Aires: Editorial Francisco de Aguirre, 1965); Jaime Castillo Velasco, *Las fuentes de la Democracia Cristiana* (Santiago, Editorial del Pacífico, 1965); and Michael Fleet, *The Rise and Fall of Chilean Christian Democracy* (Princeton: Princeton UP, 1985.) There is no good study of the Ibáñez phenomenon or of Agrario Laborismo, except Patricio Dooner, "La segunda administración de Ibáñez," *Estudios sociales*, no. 43, pp. 83–113. An excellent book of essays reviewing the evolution of Chilean politics and party politics is Tomás Moulian, *Democracia y socialismo en Chile* (Santiago: FLACSO, 1983).

21. Parties were originally banned by Decree Law 77 in September 1973. Restrictions aimed at the Christian Democrats were adopted in Decree Law 1697 of 1977. The constitution of 1980, approved by plebiscite, had a provision (article 8) aimed at permanently banning parties of the Left by proscribing parties of a "totalitarian" character or those that ran counter to "family" values. The text of article 8 noted that "any act of a person or group aimed at propagating doctrines which challenge the family, advocate violence or a conception of society, of the State or of the judicial order, of a totalitarian character or founded on class struggle, is illicit and contrary to the order of the Republic. Organizations and movements or political parties which because of their ends or because of actions by their adherents tend toward those objectives, are unconstitutional." Article 19 adds, "All associations contrary to morality, public order, and the security of the state, are prohibited." See Luz Bulnes Aldunate, *Constitución política de la República de Chile: concordancias, anotaciones y fuentes* (Santiago: Editorial Jurídica de Chile, 1981.)

22. The only significant exception to this generalization was the brief period in 1983–84 when, after widespread riots and a dramatic weakening of the regime's fortunes, General Augusto Pinochet turned to Sergio Onofre Jarpa, former president of the National party, to serve as minister of the interior and help buy time for the military government.

23. The law regulating political parties is Organic Constitutional Law no. 18,603 published in the *Diario oficial* of 23 March 1987. The electoral law is Organic Constitutional Law no. 18,700, published in the *Diario oficial* on 6 May 1988, followed by several modifications in subsequent issues.

24. Public opinion survey conducted by CEP-Adimark, August 1992. I am grateful to Roberto Mendéz, director of Adimark, for making available survey results from a sample taken in Santiago and other major cities.

25. See Scully and Valenzuela, "From Democracy to Democracy: Continuities and Changes of Electoral Choices and the Party System in Chile," in *Democracy, Politics and Society: Latin America—Essays in Honor of Juan Linz,* edited by Arturo Valenzuela (Boulder: Westview, 1994). As the authors note, this continuity is at the level of tendencies represented by certain large parties in each of the Left-Right clusters, such as the Christian Democrats in the Center, the Socialists on the Left, and National Renewal on the Right. There is, however, considerable shift among parties themselves, as there always was in the Chilean party system; this shift results from internal party divisions, the rise of new leadership, and the waning of party fortunes.

26. J. Samuel Valenzuela and I, writing in 1980 at the height of the success of the military government's economic measures and at a time of broad skepticism among democratic leaders and intellectuals about the survivability of the Chilean party system, predicted that parties would survive the authoritarian interlude. See "Partidos de oposición bajo el régimen autoritario chileno." For a different focus see Manuel Antonio Garretón, *El proceso político chileno* (Santiago: FLACSO, 1983).

27. See Alejandro Portes, "Occupation and Lower Class Political Orientations in Chile," in Valenzuela and Valenzuela, *Chile: Politics and Society.* See also his "Status Inconsistency and Lower-Class Leftist Radicalism," *Sociological Quarterly* 13 (Summer 1972): 361–82, and "Political Primitivism, Differential Socialization, and Lower-Class Leftist Radicalism," *American Sociological Review* 36 (Oct. 1971): 820–35, both of which are based on his Chilean study. For comparative evidence supporting this point, see Portes, "Urbanization and Politics in Latin America," *Social Science Quarterly* 52, no. 3 (1971).

28. José Maravall, *Dictatorship and Political Dissent* (London: Tavistock, 1975), p. 166, cited in Valenzuela and Valenzuela, "Partidos de oposición."

29. See Karen Remmer, "Public Policy and Regime Consolidation: The First Five years of the Chilean Junta," *Journal of Developing Areas* 13 (July 1979).

30. For a discussion of the constitution of 1980 and the reforms of 1989, including a complete text of the original and amended document, see Francisco Geisse and Jose Antonio Ramirez Arrayas, *La reforma constitucional* (Santiago: CESOC, Ediciones Chile-America, 1989).

31. For academic articles stressing the theme of party legislation as a vehicle for creating a moderate party system see Hernan Larraín, "Democracia, partidos políticos y transición, el caso chileno," and Juan Irarrazaval, "Democracia, partidos políticos y transición," *Estudios públicos,* no. 15 (Winter 1984).

32. Arend Lijphart underlines the point that there is no simple causal relationship between electoral law and party system characteristics. The relationship is in fact a mutual one; over time two-party systems see it in their interest to retain the single-member district system while multiparty systems choose to retain the proportional representation system. See Arend Lijphart, *Democracies: Patterns of Majoritarian and Consensus Government in Twenty-one Countries* (New Haven: Yale UP, 1984), p. 158. In examining the Chilean case, Teresa Miranda also emphasizes that the electoral system as such was not a determinative factor. Indeed, she notes that the decline of fractionalization in the 1960s occurred despite the fact that a similar electoral system was used throughout. See Miranda, "El sistema electoral," pp. 68–69. Electoral systems may reinforce certain party patterns over time, but they are not determinative.

33. In an earlier version of this chapter, I predicted that Chile's electoral law would not simplify the party alternatives but rather would lead to the creation of electoral blocs that retained individual party identity. See Valenzuela, "Origenes y características del sistema de partidos políticos en Chile." A similar phenomenon occurred in Israel and France, where parties were replaced by large blocs or federations, although in the French case it can be argued that a more substantial change in the party system accompanied (although it may not have been directly caused by) electoral reform. See Jonathan Mendilow, "Party Cluster Formations in Multi-Party Systems," *Political Studies* 30, no. 4:485–503. The only exception to the generalization that individual parties were not fundamentally affected by the law was the Communist party, whose political strategy during the period of regime liberalization proved counterproductive to the party's subsequent electoral fortunes.

34. These results from the Chilean case support Arend Lijphart's contention that in sharply divided societies, a two-party majoritarian option may in fact place greater strains on the political system than a multiparty option. Citing the case of Austria as an example, he notes that the two-party system in that country constrained the process of cooperation and understanding at the elite level rather than facilitating it. This was the case because the two-party structure thwarted the proper representation of important segments of society. According to Lijphart, a multiparty system is better able to reflect societal interests clearly and separately and thus facilitates elite compromise and accommodation. Mendilow makes a similar point when he argues that the "clustering of parties," as in Israel and France, rather than leading to the stability envisioned by Otto Kirchheimer's "catchall parties," is "liable to render the entire party system unstable." See Lijphart, *Democracy in Plural Societies: A Comparative Exploration* (New Haven: Yale UP, 1977), pp. 62–64; Mendilow, "Party Cluster Formations," p. 486.

35. These introductory paragraphs are drawn from Arturo Valenzuela, *The Breakdown of Democratic Regimes: Chile* (Baltimore: Johns Hopkins UP, 1975), pp. 6–7.

36. See Sartori, "European Political Parties: The Case of Polarized Pluralism," in Lapalombara and Weiner, *Political Parties and Political Development;* also Sartori, *Parties and Party Systems.*

37. Sartori, "European Political Parties," pp. 156, 164.

38. See articles 63–65 of the 1925 constitution. The 1980 constitution (articles 26 and 27) eliminated the provision requiring the congress to select the president in the absence of an absolute majority of the vote by substituting a runoff election among the two front runners.

39. Several commentators have noted that giving the front-runner a majority in the congress was part of Chile's "tradition." While the front-runner carried greater authority than the runner-up, in all races many supporters of the runner-up voted for their own candidate.

40. This point is made in Arturo Valenzuela, "Politics, Parties and the State in Chile."

41. For a table denoting the duration of cabinets during the French Fourth Republic, see Duncan MacRae, *Parliament, Parties and Society in France 1946–1958* (New York: St. Martin's Press, 1967), p. 218. There were many more cabinet ministers in France than in Chile because of the larger size of the cabinet and the very short duration of some ministries. See Phillip M. Williams, *Crisis and Compromise: Politics in the Fourth Republic* (Hamden, Conn.: Archon Books, 1964), pp. 494–95.

42. In the French Fifth Republic, the loss by the president of a majority in the National Assembly created a significant challenge for the regime. However, as Aron noted, even before "cohabitation," under the French parliamentary formula the loss of presidential support in the legislature would lead to regime alternation as a strong presidential system would give way to a "parliamentary" pattern of government. See Raymond Aron, "Alternation in Government in the Industrialized Countries," *Government and Opposition* 17, no. 1 (1982).

43. While Chile has no experience with the second round, the cases of Brazil and Peru under Collor de Mello and Fugimori are instructive. In both cases presidents that represented clear minorities in the first round believed that they were representative of national majorities and were reluctant to build bridges to parties with majority strength in the parliament. Collor finally did seek to structure such a coalition after two years in office, but it was too late to weather accusations of corruption. Fugimori reacted to his congressional difficulties by closing down the congress with support from the military, an action similar to that of President Terra in Uruguay in 1935.

44. See Mario Bernaschina C., *Cartilla electoral* (Santiago: Editorial Jurídica de Chile, 1958) and Alejandro Silva Bascuñan, *Tratado de derecho constitucional*, vol. 1 (Santiago: Editorial Jurídica de Chile, 1963). For the 1962 electoral law and 1965 and 1968 modifications, see Antonio Vodanovic, ed., *Ley general de elecciones* (Santiago: Editorial Nascimiento, 1969). The 1970 reforms are discussed in Guillermo Piedrabuena Richards, *La reforma constitucional* (Santiago: Ediciones Encina, 1970).

45. Chilean parties combined both an ideological and programmatic orientation and a more clientelistic orientation. Wright distinguishes the "rational efficient" from the "party democracy model," the former oriented to winning elections, the latter to attaining ideological purity. See William E. Wright, "Comparative Party Models: Rational Efficient and Party Democracy," in *Comparative Study of Party Organization* (Columbus: C. E. Merrill, 1971). For the now classic distinctions along these lines see Duverger, *Les parties politiques*, and Otto Kirchheimer, "The Transformation of the Western European Party System," in Lapalombara and Weiner, *Political Parties and Political Development*. An excellent study that stresses the dual objectives of electoral success and ideological purity is Samuel Barnes, *Party Democracy: Politics in an Italian Socialist Federation* (New Haven: Yale UP, 1963).

46. See Lijphart, *Democracies*, p. 111. See also Lawrence C. Dodd, *Coalitions in Parliamentary Governments* (Princeton: Princeton UP, 1976).

47. For the argument that multiparty systems may have higher levels of cabinet or government instability, see Dodd, *Coalitions;* G. Bingham Powell, "Party Systems and Political System Performance," *American Political Science Review* 75 (1981): 861–79; Michael Taylor and Valentine M. Herman, "Party Systems and Government Stability," *American Political Science Review* 65 (1981): 28–37. Lijphart, *Democracies*, also makes this point; see p. 110. It is critical, however, to distinguish between instability of government and instability of regime.

48. G. Bingham Powell, "Party Systems," p. 868. For a fuller treatment see his *Contemporary Democracies: Participation Stability and Violence* (Cambridge: Harvard UP, 1982).

49. On parties in various Latin American countries, see McDonald and Ruhl, *Party Politics*. On Argentina, see the paper by Marcelo Cavarozzi, "Los partidos argentinos: subculturas fuertes, sistema débil" (paper prepared for the workshop on Political Parties and Redemocratization in the Southern Cone, Woodrow Wilson International Center for Scholars, Washington, D.C., 16–17 Nov. 1984).

50. See chap. 7 herein.

51. This section draws extensively on Arturo Valenzuela, *The Breakdown of Democratic Regimes: Chile*, 2d ed. (Baltimore: Johns Hopkins UP, 1978).

52. See Arturo Valenzuela and Alexander Wilde, "Presidential Politics and the Decline of the Chilean Congress," in *Legislatures in Development: Dynamics of Change in New and Old States*, edited by Joel Smith and Lloyd D. Musolf, (Durham, N.C.: Duke UP, 1979). For an analysis of the 1970 reforms, see Eduardo Frei et al., *Reforma constitucional 1970* (Santiago: Editorial Jurídica de Chile, 1970.)

53. Valenzuela, *Breakdown of Democratic Regimes*, pp. 48–49, 65.

54. Salvador Allende, *Chile's Road to Socialism*, edited by Joan Garcés (London: Penguin, 1973), pp. 56–57, 66. This is a collection of Salvador Allende's speeches. See also Regis Debray, *The Chilean Road to Socialism: Conversations with Allende* (New York: Vintage, 1971). See also Salvador Allende, *Su pensamiento político* (Santiago: Empresa Editora Nacional Quimantú, 1972) and Patricio Quiroga, ed., *Salvador Allende: Obras escogidas (1970–1973)* (Barcelona: Editorial Crítica, 1989).

55. See Allende's first speech to the congress in Allende, *Chile's Road to Socialism*, p. 140 and passim.

56. Eduardo Frei and his Christian Democrats had also misinterpreted the off-year election of 1965, using the results as an excuse to break the tacit coalition with the Right and forge ahead, despite minority support in the senate.

57. *Neutral powers* is a term used by Juan Linz. See his pathbreaking study, *The Breakdown of Democratic Regimes: Crisis Breakdown and Reequilibration* (Baltimore: Johns Hopkins UP, 1978).

58. The serious dispute over the legislation regulating the "areas of the economy" was submitted to the Constitutional Tribunal for arbitration. Torn asunder by the polarized political atmosphere, however, the tribunal, issued an ambiguous ruling and thus abdicated its responsibility to resolve the conflict. In the absence of a constitutional solution to the impasse in Chilean politics, and in an atmosphere of increased confrontation, Allende finally resolved to call a referendum on his government, one that was preempted by the military coup of September 11, 1973. Had Allende lost the referendum, he presumably would have resigned, paving the way for a constitutional solution. Had he won the referendum, however, Chile's political system would still not have afforded a solution to the crisis because the legislature would have remained in the hands of the opposition. Short of presidential capitulation, there was no real mechanism for resolving a fundamental conflict between an executive with minority support in the legislature and the legislature.

59. See Samuel Huntington, *Political Order in Changing Societies* (New Haven: Yale UP, 1968).

60. Talk by José Antonio Viera Gallo, president of the Chilean chamber of deputies, Georgetown University, June 26, 1991.

61. These observations are based on my interviews over the last two years with members of the Chilean senate and chamber of deputies and with party leaders. The difficulties facing the Concertación as a result of these political problems are discussed in Arturo Valenzuela, "Political and Economic Challenges for Chile's Transition to Democracy," in *In the Shadow of the Debt: Emerging Issues in Latin America* edited by Robert Bottome et al. (New York: Twentieth Century Fund Press, 1992).

62. On the Chilean Parliamentary Republic, in addition to the study by Julio Heise González mentioned in note 8, see the classic three-volume work by Manuel Rivas Vicuña, *Historia política y parlamentaria de Chile* (Santiago: Editorial Nascimiento, 1964). For a revisionary treatment, see Arturo Valenzuela, *Political Brokers in Chile: Local Government in a Centralized Polity* (Durham, N.C.: Duke UP, 1977), chap. 8.

7

LUIS EDUARDO GONZÁLEZ

AND CHARLES GUY GILLESPIE

Presidentialism and Democratic
Stability in Uruguay

THIS CHAPTER is concerned with the effect of political structures—and, more specifically, of the presidential institution—on democratic stability.[1] In it we take *democracy* to mean polyarchy in Dahl's sense (Dahl 1971) and *political structures* to include (1) institutional features of the polity in the political sense (e.g., whether the system is unitary or federal) and (2) purely political features (e.g., the nature of the party system). These features become political structures only if they are institutionalized in the sociological sense of the word. Hence they involve observable regularities in the behavior and expectations of political actors.

This approach does not cover all the institutional dimensions of democratic stability; instead it focuses on perhaps the easiest part. It excludes specifically the effects on democratic stability of new political institutions and the short-term consequences of political engineering. Such narrowing of the attention, however, facilitates a little theoretical thinking regarding usually intractable counterfactual considerations; this is so simply because by definition the setting includes stable political structures that in the short run do not depend on the will of the actors.

Nevertheless, theoretical simplicity tends to be associated with practical difficulties. The single most important part of an empirically based discussion of democratic stability is perhaps the study of cases of instability, that is, the histories of democratic breakdowns. But at least until recently, political processes tended to be neglected in the analysis of democratic breakdowns (Linz 1978, 39). Furthermore, when authors did analyze those processes they emphasized the strategies followed by political actors and the eventual patterns that emerged from their choices rather than the politicostructural constraints on those strategies and choices. More generally, in past studies of democratic breakdowns the term *structural problems* normally meant "socioeconomic problems." The political structures of a very young democracy are bound to be somewhat fluid: the instauration of polyarchy is by definition a discontinuity that deeply affects the preexisting political system. When a democracy is born at least some of the critical rules of the political process change, and with them all the other components of the system change to some extent as well. This helps to explain the absence of political structures from the literature on democratic breakdowns for, as Dahl has pointed out, almost all those breakdowns occurred in regimes that had lasted less than one generation (Dahl 1985, 39).

Writings on Latin America certainly confirm Dahl's arresting general rule. What is more, politicoinstitutional factors per se—irrespective of whether they are related to political *structures*—are also missing in Latin American literature. They tend to be neglected in favor of other levels of analysis more rooted in the problems of economy and society. This does not necessarily involve a social or economic reductionist bias. Although the problems analyzed are as varied as the dynamics of class struggles and party competition, the role of fiscal crisis, development bottlenecks, and international economic linkages, or the process of expanding the role of the military, the analyses tend to share the assumption that the persistence or destruction of political regimes is largely determined by factors external to them. Internal, institutional factors are generally ignored.

More particularly, executive-legislative conflict, which has long been recognized as a factor in the breakdown of democratic regimes, has been scarcely considered by students of Latin America. This neglect is especially unfortunate. For, on the one hand, nearly all Latin American nations have adopted constitutions based on the separation of powers, modeled on that of the United States. On the other hand, they have also adopted a peculiar combination—unlike that of the United States—of presidentialism with proportional representation as the basis for legislative elections. Thus, from the successful American combination of presidentialism and simple majority voting, they took one solution but not the other.

This neglect of institutions is unsatisfactory, particularly as the consolidation of new or restored democracies under difficult constraints has become one of the central problems of the whole region. A first step toward a solution may well be to consider democratic breakdowns in comparatively structured, consolidated regimes. At a minimum this should clarify conceptual problems, and in some cases it may even contribute to better constitution making, or at least to more informed decisions that incorporate greater awareness of the conditioning effects of institutions.

These reflections lead us to underscore the relevance of the Uruguayan case with regard to the study of presidentialism. For, as Dahl observed on the Uruguayan coup of 1973, "Uruguay may be the *only* instance in which a relatively long-standing democratic system has been replaced by an internally imposed authoritarian regime" (Dahl 1985, 40). Uruguay thus provides an exceptional opportunity to study the eventual effect of politicostructural factors on democratic stability.

This chapter probes the impact of presidentialism on the two democratic breakdowns Uruguay experienced in the twentieth century. First it analyzes the nature of Uruguayan presidentialism—or *quasi* presidentialism, a more precise term encompassing the whole history of Uruguayan democracy. Then it discusses the 1973 military coup and, more briefly, the 1933 civilian-led coup in order to point out several common patterns—particularly the importance as mediating factors of the nature of the party system, the electoral law, and the resulting composition of the legislature. Before concluding we take a brief look at the emerging state of affairs since the democratic restoration of 1985.

Constitutional Instability and Stable Quasi Presidentialism

For much of this century, Uruguay has been the stablest democracy in Latin America. Two of its largest parties, the Blancos and Colorados, are among the oldest in the world, their roots going back more than a century and a half. For this reason they are often called the "traditional parties," though since 1971 their duopoly has been challenged by an alliance of leftist parties known as the Broad Front. However, the very permanence of Uruguay's traditional parties, which still won nearly 70 percent of the vote in the 1989 elections, serves to underline the instability of Uruguayan constitutional arrangements. The 1918 constitution was the second in the country's life; the first, founding constitution was enacted in 1830. Since 1918, however, the constitution has been reformed in 1934, 1942, 1952, and 1966.[2]

Apart from giving birth to democracy, the 1918 charter introduced a novel form of executive, very largely as a result of the ceaseless campaigning of former Colorado President José Batlle y Ordóñez. During the years between his first presidential term (1903–7) and his second (1911–15), Batlle had traveled in Europe, where he had been struck by the Swiss form of government; upon his return, he announced his conversion to the principle of collegial executive authority. As it happened, his reforming zeal frightened the opposition and split his own Colorado party, much of which mistrusted his huge political power and ambitious ideas. Thus it was that the constitutional convention elected in 1917 contained only a minority of *Batllistas:* in order to press his proposed reform he had to severely compromise with rival Colorado fractions.[3]

The 1918 constitution introduced a dual executive: there was still to be a directly elected president, but the authority of the chief executive was largely confined to matters concerning public order, defense, and foreign affairs. Beside him, a nine-member National Council of Administration had collective responsibility for domestic policy: education, social security, public works, and so forth.[4] The other concession won by the combined opposition within Batlle's own party and the Blanco party was that there would be guaranteed representation for the minority party in the council. Given that there was also a team of ministers with specific portfolios under the council, this arrangement provided the maximum opportunity for jurisdictional disputes and conflicts. It lasted until 1933, when under the impact of the Great Depression and the worldwide tide of fascism, Uruguay's elected president unilaterally abolished the 1918 constitution. He thereupon persecuted progressive rivals within his own Colorado party and proceeded to reintroduce a unipersonal presidency with the support of some Blancos (Taylor 1952; Nahum et al. 1989).

Toward the end of the thirties pressure built up for a return to a more open system: this was achieved by General Baldomir's so-called good coup in 1942. In 1952 a fully collegial executive was constructed, in the hope that this would guarantee the future of Uruguay's relatively harmonious political order (Fitzgibbon 1952; Vanger 1954).[5] However, the decade of the 1950s was a time of precipitous economic decline for what had become South America's most prosperous and egalitarian nation, and what some consider the region's first "welfare state."[6] In 1958 the Blancos won control of the executive for the first time in almost a century and proceeded to attempt a program of economic stabilization backed by the International Monetary Fund (IMF). They found the political costs too heavy to bear and consistently undermined their own austerity plans. By the 1960s, many Uruguayans blamed the peculiar multiperson executive for the country's mounting inflation and declining prosperity.

The 1952 constitution had been only narrowly approved by the people when submitted for ratification in a plebiscite, and by 1958 conservative sectors of the Blanco party swung back in favor of presidentialism. In that year, and again in 1962, they succeeded in getting a proposed constitutional amendment restoring a single-person executive onto the ballot. Both times the amendment was unsuccessful. However, newspapers and the media began to take up the issue as the 1960s wore on, and in the middle of 1965 Senator Jorge Batlle, leader of the dominant "Fifteenth List" fraction of the Colorados, called for immediate discussions on constitutional reform. The following year, leading sectors of the Colorado party held joint talks, which led to the drafting of a new constitution. A campaign to collect signatures to get the new proposal on the ballot was soon successful, even though sectors of the party refused to back the new idea.

In the meantime the Blancos had been drawing up their own proposal for a new constitution. Ultimately, the party split over the proposals: the most conservative sectors continued to favor the original Blanco project, while other sectors reached a compromise deal with the Colorados on a joint reform. In the subsequent elections voters also had a third option promoted by a leftist alliance grouped around the Communist party. The principal difference between the modified Colorado proposal, known as the Interparty Project, and the hard-line Blanco version was that the latter would have given the president far greater powers to dissolve the congress and call new elections. The Interparty Project finally won the support of 62 percent of the voters in the 1966 election, and it came into force in 1967. Suspended during the authoritarian regime (1973–84), it is once more in force now.

Below this agitated surface at least one keystone of the Uruguayan institutional

Table 7.1. Main and Secondary Components of Presidential and Parliamentary Systems

	Presidential Systems	Parliamentary Systems
Main components		
Direct election of head of government	Yes[a]	No
Head of government also is chief of state	Yes	No
Legislature cannot oust head of government	Yes	No
Secondary features		
Head of government may dissolve legislature	No	Yes
Ministers responsible before the legislature	No	Yes

a. Although U.S. voters choose an electoral college, this has ceased to be a deliberative body, and the system operates like, and is perceived by voters to be, one of direct election.

setting has remained constant since the birth of democracy: the "quasi presidentialism" of the Uruguayan constitutional tradition. This political structure has deeply shaped Uruguayan ways of doing politics. The essential characteristic of a presidentialist system is that the president is a directly elected chief of state who also governs (Sartori 1982, 310).[7] It can be added that the president cannot be removed by the legislature except in truly extraordinary circumstances, as with impeachment in the United States—a weighty procedure that cannot be the result of a disagreement on policies. Other characteristics are also more or less typical of presidentialist regimes, though none has the central, defining role of those mentioned above. For example, ministers are not supposed to be removable by the legislature; theoretically they are truly "secretaries" of the president. Table 7.1 contrasts these features of presidential and parliamentary systems.

From the beginning, Uruguay's constitutional framework exhibited, in varying degrees, several of the secondary traits usually attributed to parliamentary systems (see table 7.2). Under democratic regimes the legislature has usually had the right to interpellate and sometimes even to remove ministers. For that reason it has been said that the Uruguayan system has a strong parliamentary basis, and it has even been called a quasi-parliamentary system. Gros Espiell (1956, 90, 105 ff.) called the 1934 and 1942 constitutions semiparliamentarian, defining the systems they introduced as *rationalized parliamentarism*. Sanguinetti and Pacheco Seré (1971, 108–9) agreed with that judgment and used the term *neoparliamentarism* regarding both constitutions.

A legal approach, however, is not enough on its own to assess these matters. In its classical sense a constitution is far more than written or unwritten law; it also includes the set of expectations, mores, and institutions—in sociological terms—describing the modes by which a state is organized. According to the text of the 1830 constitution, it was *not* a truly presidential system, partly because of the position of

Table 7.2. Presidential and Parliamentary Formal Features of Uruguayan Democratic Constitutions

	Constitutions				
	1918	1934	1942	1952	1966
Main components					
Direct election of head of government	Yes	Yes	Yes	Yes	Yes
Head of government is chief of state	Yes[a]	Yes	Yes	Yes[b]	Yes
Legislature cannot oust head of government	Yes	No	No	Yes	Yes
Secondary features					
Head of government may dissolve legislature	No	Yes	Yes	No	Yes
Ministers responsible before legislature	No	Yes	Yes	No	Yes

a. Mixed form, president plus members of National Council of Administration; all are directly elected.
b. Directly elected *collective* head of government, whose (rotating) president is the titular chief of state.

the ministers and partly because the president was elected by the legislature. In practice, however, most of the time all of this was a juridical fiction. The president was a de facto first elector and enjoyed more real power than the president of any democracy.

Irrespective of the important differences in the approaches, values, and behaviors of the nineteenth-century presidents, the presidency itself became a very powerful institution. For precisely this reason, José Batlle y Ordóñez sought to destroy it, dividing its power among the members of a pluripersonal body. The 1918 constitution was a compromise solution that preserved a president deprived of some of his previous power but still in charge of the interior (including the appointment of the chiefs of policy in the *departamentos*), defense, foreign affairs, and, to some extent, finance as well.[8] As an additional precaution Batlle y Ordóñez used his great political weight to prevent really popular politicians from becoming candidates, in order to reduce the prestige attributed to the presidency and, presumably, the risks that would result from too many power resources clustering in the presidency. All told, he failed. "Immediately after his death it became clear that the majority of his party had forgotten his views on the nature of the presidency" (Lindahl 1962, 203–4). Batlle died in 1929; four years later a democratically elected Colorado president headed a coup and then reformed the 1918 constitution.

The 1934 and 1942 constitutions can be viewed as neoparliamentary systems, for although they established a single popularly elected chief of state and government and abolished the National Council of Administration, they also gave the legislature the power of censuring ministers and the president the symmetrical power of dissolving the legislature and calling general parliamentary elections—provided that less than two-thirds of the General Assembly had voted the censure. If the General Assembly resulting from that election maintained the censure, then the president as well as the ministers would fall. The president thus partially resembled a prime minister in a parliamentary regime. Nevertheless, these theoretical possibilities remained untested; under the 1934 and 1942 constitutions dissolution never occurred. In practice it would have been extremely difficult to achieve; it should be remembered that after 1942, in particular, the Colorados were the predominant party: massive Colorado defections would have been needed to oust any Colorado president.[9] In fact, the presidency was, if anything, *more powerful* than during the so-called quasi-presidential system of the 1918 constitution.

Limiting the powers of the presidency was actually one of the motivations behind the 1952 reform. The 1952 constitution was made possible because the politicians who promoted it sought three different but not contradictory goals: some of them were true believers in the virtues of the pure *colegiado* finally established by the new constitution; others sought to expand opportunities for the runner-up party to participate in and control the administration; and still others saw in the reform the only legally available way of blocking another Batlle, Luis Batlle Berres, from acceding to a powerful presidency. This latest Batlle, nephew of Don José, was expected to be a presidential candidate and the likely winner of the coming election (Gros Espiell 1956, 114, 116; Sanguinetti and Pacheco Seré 1971, 7–8). The 1952 constitution satisfied all three groups. It could not prevent the electoral victory of Batllism, but it left Luis Batlle with considerably less power. In a nutshell, the new constitution instituted a ceremonial chief of state renewed every year and a four-year collective chief of government, the *colegiado;* the chief of state was simply the presiding member of the nine-person *colegiado*. In a further weakening of the government, the collegial executive lost the right to dissolve the parliament (Sanguinetti and Pacheco Seré 1967, 108). Batlle Berres in fact became the first among nine equals. The 1952 constitution thus produced the weakest chiefs of state since 1918. It would have been far more difficult for a member of the *colegiado* to head a coup like that of President Terra in 1933; had Batlle y Ordóñez been alive, he would doubtless have seen this as one of the most significant virtues of the *colegiado*.

As mentioned above, the crisis that began around the midfifties drove many politicians to think that the virtues of a diminished risk of authoritarianism no longer outweighed the shortcomings of government by committee. These feelings led to the interparty agreement that finally produced the 1966 constitution, which makes the presidency a more powerful institution than in any of the constitutions since 1918. The president, as in classic presidentialism, is a directly elected chief of state who also governs. His mandate is expanded to five years, and he may no longer be removed by the legislature for political reasons, as the 1934 and 1942 texts at least theoretically allowed. The new document also augments the president's powers in various significant ways: apart from the points mentioned above, it increases executive control over autonomous parastatal enterprises (article 197) and the budgets of other agencies and ministries. It also gives the president the right to send bills to the parliament with a "declaration of urgency" (article 168, section 7), which means that if parliament fails to reject the bill within specified time limits it automatically becomes law.

A leading constitutional lawyer favorable to the new charter summed up the alleged benefits of the changes: "The reestablishment of the Presidency of the Republic, prolongation of the governmental period to five years, and the increase in governmental and administrative duties in the hands of the executive . . . will modernize our system of government along the lines of current trends in the great democracies."[10] In particular, the new centralized executive is able to press forward with the coordination of different agencies on the basis of five-year plans, supposedly preventing "autonomous feudalities" from standing in the way of the collective welfare. As had often been the case, the French experiences of the Third and Fourth Republics were foremost in Uruguayan minds.

The 1966 constitution gives the president the right to call new legislative elections when a minister or ministers are censured by the parliament. When a minister is subject to a vote of censure in either house, a joint session of both houses (known as the General Assembly) must be called within forty-eight hours. If this body repeats the vote of censure by a majority of less than two-thirds, the president may refuse to accept the minister's dismissal. The General Assembly is then summoned into a renewed session, but if the censure motion is now repeated by a majority of less than three-fifths, the president may choose to override it and dissolve the parliament. Thus far the provisions are similar to those of the 1934 and 1942 constitutions, but a major difference is that in the event that a newly elected parliament reaffirms a vote of censure of the entire cabinet, the president is not forced to resign with the council of ministers as had previously been the case. This means that Uruguay has adopted a hybrid form of executive-legislative relations that lacks rigid separation of powers and has created a stronger presidency than the United States has.

To argue that the resulting system is neoparliamentary, as do Sanguinetti and Pacheco Seré (1971, 114), because the legislature may censure ministers is a misleading overall assessment of the situation. It is true that the legislature, unlike the U.S. legislature, may remove ministers for political reasons, but the president of the United States may not dissolve the legislature, whereas the Uruguayan president may. Furthermore, the position of the Uruguayan president is stronger than that of a prime minister: the president remains in charge during the whole of his mandate, no matter how difficult a time his ministers may have with the legislature. Hardly discussed at the time but later to prove of the utmost importance was section 17 of article 168, which allows the president to "take prompt security measures in grave and unforeseen cases of foreign attack or internal disorder." Similar provisions had existed in earlier constitutions.

The procedure to invoke a dissolution was initiated on just one occasion, in 1969. The General Assembly censured a minister, but the president rejected that decision. An absolute majority of the assembly was against the minister, but the majority was not enough to supersede the presidential veto. When that veto came to a vote, however, many Colorados voted *against* their own government for tactical reasons in order, by surpassing the three-fifths threshold necessary to override the veto, to block a dissolution and new legislative elections.[11] Distinguished commentators concluded that "the special characteristics of the vote and the absence of a general election did not oblige a change of policy. [This] was reasserted by the President" (Sanguinetti and Pacheco Seré 1971, 118–19). The president had thus to change his minister but not to change his policy, even though he was without a legislative majority. The opposition in fact accepted its defeat at least partly because it was already unsure—the exact word is perhaps "frightened"—about how far the president was willing to go to assert his views. A system that works in this manner simply cannot be called "neoparliamentary" in any meaningful sense.

To sum up: under democratic governments Uruguay has always been a *quasi-presidential* system—"quasi" due to the secondary traits typical of parliamentary systems it has exhibited most of the time, some of which still remain. From a formal, juridical point of view, this statement is debatable when applied to the 1934 and 1942 constitutions (see table 7.2); the systems in those cases might properly be called quasi-*parliamentary* systems. However, this generalization is valid only for the years 1942–52 because the period 1933–42 was an authoritarian *situation*, in Linz's sense,[12] instead of a democracy. This is not, however, the really important point: our judgment on the nature of the system must take into account actual practices and institutionalized behavior no less than the legal framework. When this is done, it may be clearly seen that, given the party system and actual political practices and expectations, the presidents envisaged by the 1934 and 1942 constitutions were just that—presidents. It should be noted, finally, that both the 1933 and 1973 coups occurred under the most decidedly *presidential* versions of Uruguayan quasi presidentialism. In fact, the parliamentary features of the current constitution, that of 1966, dilute the separation of powers of the classical model—that of the United States—by *increasing* presidential power; the legislature can sack ministers but not the president or his policies, whereas the president in certain circumstances may dissolve the legislature.

The 1973 Coup

The first president the Uruguayans elected, in 1966, under the current constitution was a Colorado moderate, former General Oscar Gestido. He faced a legislature in which his party had a very narrow majority, but his own sector of the party was rather weak. The reason that Gestido was elected was that his fraction had formed an alliance with another fraction of the party, his group providing the presidential candidate and the other group the candidate for mayor of Montevideo. Each of these groups controlled half the senators and half the deputies of their combined sector, but even together these two fractions accounted for less than half the Colorados' seats. The rival fraction led by Senator Jorge Batlle (known as the

Table 7.3. Election Results and Distribution of Seats (1966)

Major Parties and Fractions	Absolute Votes (1,000)	Seat Share (%) in General Assembly
Colorado party	608	51
Gestido/Pacheco	262	25
Batlle	211	18
Vasconcellos	78	5
Michelini	48	3
Blanco party	497	42
Echegoyen	231	19
Gallinal	171	15
Heber	95	8
Christian Democrats	37	2
Communists	70	5
Total votes cast	1,232	100

a. The General Assembly is a joint meeting of the two chambers—the House of Representatives, 99 members, and the Senate, 31. It is particularly important in executive-legislative relations. The political composition of each chamber, both elected by proportional representation, is very similar to that of the 130-member General Assembly.

Fifteenth List) actually had more votes than either of the two groups that backed Gestido, taken on their own. And on the left of the party were other smaller fractions led by Senators Vasconcellos and Michelini. The defection of the latter alone was enough to rob the president of his majority in the parliament (table 7.3); as it turned out, the leading Colorados were to face even more widespread revolts within their party.

This state of affairs was a more or less direct consequence of the peculiarities of Uruguayan electoral law. Its major components, which have been in force at least since 1942, and some of them since the beginning of the century, are (1) a simple plurality decides which party wins the executive; (2) parties present preprinted and closed lists of candidates; (3) proportional representation (PR) applies in the election of both chambers (a modified d'Hondt system); (4) all elections (executive, legislative, local) occur together; and (5) party votes are summed by the method of "double simultaneous vote" (DSV). The DSV—which is the truly exotic practice—allows the fractions of each party to present competing lists at each election. The votes for each party are pooled to calculate that party's share of the seats, and then the seats are divided proportionally between the different fractions. The workings of this complex system are most easily grasped with regard to presidential elections. Each party may present several candidates (usually around three or more), and victory goes to the one with the most votes from the party with the most votes. This amounts to a form of simultaneous primary, but with the oddity that voters are never quite sure who their ballot might help to elect.[13]

President Gestido died in December 1967, after only eight months in office. Before his death the Colorado progressives had left the cabinet because of disagreements on the handling of strikes. Gestido was immediately replaced by his vice president, Jorge Pacheco, a less well-known and less popular figure. As president, Pacheco responded to the growing social tensions manifested in labor conflicts, student protests, and guerrilla violence by attempting a tough law-and-order stance. Lacking a majority in the National Assembly, he faced the problem of forming a stable cabinet, but rather than seeking a coalition or a political agreement, he increasingly appointed *pachequista* technocrats and businessmen to ministerial portfolios. Parliament retaliated by holding up legislation and using its powers to interpellate and censure ministers.[14] The president increasingly began to rule by decree in order to force through the measures for maintaining law and order and the reforms he favored. Laws and administrative acts that did not have the backing of a majority of the congress were simply imposed under the very vague constitutional clause permitting the president to take "prompt security measures."

Originally intended to counter states of internal disorder, the security measures were first invoked by Pacheco to decree the abolition of Uruguay's postwar system of wage councils at the height of crucial wage negotiations between unions and employers in 1968. Instead of the existing system of tripartite bargaining, Pacheco decreed a temporary wage-price freeze, and set up the National Prices and Incomes Board. Subsequently, the measures were renewed almost without interruption until the military coup of 1973. Under the pretext of these blanket powers, disguised laws as well as administrative acts gushed forth. Not only were suspected terrorists detained, leftist magazines closed, and so forth, but the system of pensions and social security was also reformed and centralized under executive control, prices and wages were fixed, and the press was censored with regard to the reporting of terrorist activity.

The government was in a deadlock—at least according to the constitution. President Pacheco and his successor, Bordaberry, "overcame" the deadlock at the cost of ignoring the constitution and generating a political crisis of confidence that, in the end, also terminated democracy. Pacheco could not pass his legislative agenda; he risked a defeat at the hands of the opposition because even the rebels in his own party would have joined against him. Thus he relied instead on decree powers that were constitutionally very dubious. On more than one occasion Parliament voted to lift the "prompt security measures," the umbrella under which Pacheco governed by decree, but the president merely decreed them again at once.[15] Beyond the letter, the spirit of the constitution was no longer respected. Pacheco's congressmen stayed away from the legislature for absurdly long periods in order to prevent the reaching of a quorum that might have led to further votes to lift the so-called prompt security measures (Kerbusch 1969, 213; McDonald 1972, 31). As cited above, a good indicator of the political and constitutional confusion came when Batlle's sector voted to censure one of Pacheco's ministers merely in order to ensure that the

Table 7.4. Election Results and Distribution of Seats (1971)

Major Parties and Fractions	Absolute Votes (1,000)	Seat Share (%) in General Assembly
Colorado party	682	42
Pacheco/Bordaberry	380	28
Batlle	243	13
Vasconcellos	49	1
Blanco party	669	40
Aguerrondo	229	11
Ferreira	440	29
Broad Front[a]	304	18
Total votes cast	1,664	100

a. Includes Communist, Socialist, and Christian Democratic parties, plus splinter fractions from both major parties.

motion was carried by more than two-thirds, thus avoiding the danger that Pacheco might finally dare to dissolve the parliament.

As is common in Latin America, the Uruguayan constitution does not allow re-election of presidential incumbents, and thus Pacheco was unable to run in the 1971 elections. Instead he chose a relatively unknown figure, Juan María Bordaberry, to run as his proxy. Bordaberry had not always been a member of the Colorado party and had little popular support of his own. Various explanations have been given for the decision to offer Bordaberry the nomination of the leading sector of the Colorado party: some argue that Pacheco wanted to avoid the emergence of any serious rival, others that he thought Bordaberry's very unpopularity might aid his referendum campaign to allow reelection of presidential incumbents. In all events, by a hair-thin majority, the Colorados beat the Blancos in the 1971 elections, and Bordaberry was elected. The result was so close that, to this day, some believe it may have been obtained by fraud (Franco 1984). Whatever the case, table 7.4 shows that the balance of power in the new legislature inaugurated in March 1972 was held by the newly formed leftist alliance known as the Broad Front. The governing party, the Colorados, had become a minority within the legislature.

In the wake of the election, President Bordaberry sought to form a coalition government with the leading Blanco senator, Wilson Ferreira, but failed: the differences between the president and the progressive Blanco were too large. Instead, Bordaberry was forced to form a government with the minority right wing of the Blanco party. This solution was at once popularly dubbed the "little pact."[16] Parliament was more docile under Bordaberry than under Pacheco, partly because the survival of democratic institutions began to appear imperiled under the climate of growing violence and political polarization in the country. Following the Tupamaros' attempt to launch a major guerrilla offensive, the Blanco party supported the passage of a draconian Law of State Security and Public Order, which among other things suspended the civil rights of terrorist suspects and permitted press censorship, thus legitimating such measures, which had hitherto been decreed under the dubious guise of "prompt security measures."

By mid-1972 the undermining of democratic institutions had brought on an open struggle between politicians and the military for the first time in this century (Kaufman 1978; McDonald 1975). When the military launched a campaign against alleged political corruption they arrested Colorado Senator Batlle and held him for several days, leading his sector to withdraw from the government. A senate commission began to investigate the use of torture by the security forces charged with defeating urban guerrillas. Congressmen met with threats and noncooperation as a result of their investigations of military dealings with the Tupamaros. Finally, in February of 1973, when the armed forces rebelled against the president's choice of defense minister and demanded a role in overseeing the government, all but the closet allies of President Bordaberry refused to come to his aid. In fact there is now evidence that leading Blancos and even Colorados were trying to force him to resign so that the vice president might take over.[17] Isolated politically, President Bordaberry agreed to the military's demands and subsequently allied with their campaign against the parliament.

The military's major demand by the middle of 1973 was that Parliament lift the immunity from prosecution of a leftist senator whom they accused of links to the Tupamaros guerrillas. Believing that once they gave in to military threats they might as well cease to exist, the majority of congressmen resolutely refused to comply. On June 27, 1973, Bordaberry declared the National Assembly "suspended," and the army invaded both chambers.

The 1933 and 1973 Breakdowns Compared

This is not the place for a general explanation of the 1973 and 1933 coups.[18] Several writers have probed social and economic arguments that are undoubtedly relevant for that purpose. Here it will suffice to note that both coups were preceded by deep crises that had important *external* components. In 1933 it was the aftermath of the 1929 Wall Street crash; in 1973, more indirectly, it was the protracted crisis of the import-substituting industrialization process, similar to though more acute than that experienced by Argentina at about the same time (O'Donnell 1978). For all their importance, however, it is unclear whether these crises *determined* the breakdowns. The dismal Uruguayan economic performance, by comparison with *all* other semi-industrialized countries during the two decades preceding the 1973 coup, suggests that external constraints were not the only causes of the breakdowns. The inability of political elites to confront those crises appears to have played an important role as well.

That collective "inability," in turn, may be seen in different ways. On the one hand, it can be put down to plain incompetence. This cannot be ruled out, of course, but it seems a poor explanation: first, those same elites had been comparatively successful in the past; and second, particularly with regard to the 1973 breakdown, since the denouement of the crisis was so long in coming—about fifteen years—we would have to assume that leaders were *consistently* unqualified during a whole generation. On the other hand, the account of the previous section suggests a more sensible alternative: perhaps there was something in the Uruguayan way of doing politics that hindered the process of finding and sustaining policies capable of reversing crises as severe as those of 1933 and 1973—at least within a democratic order.[19]

Consider, first, the government deadlock preceding the 1973 coup mentioned above. There was no stable legislative majority; without it, it was impossible to maintain controversial policies—and the kinds of policy capable of successfully confronting a long, hard crisis must be controversial. That lack of a majority, in turn, stemmed from three facts. First, under democratic conditions *inter*party government-sharing agreements have been exceptional in Uruguay. Since 1918, there has been nonparty government during the authoritarian situation of the years 1934–42, during the year preceding the 1973 coup, and during the subsequent authoritarian regime itself; outside of these periods government was always *party* government.[20] This is an important point because in the Uruguayan tradition the term *coparticipación* (coparticipation) has several different meanings and is sometimes understood as the opposite of party government.[21] For the present purposes it will suffice to point out that Uruguayan democratic governments have always been party governments, whatever the level of *coparticipación* that may have existed. This left the task of forming majorities to individual parties. Except during brief periods, however, the major parties enjoyed almost equal levels of popular support, thus making clear majorities difficult to obtain. Second, even if they had a majority, Uruguayan major parties have always been *fractionalized*. As has been seen, the *sublema* (the legal name of a party fraction) within the winning *lema* (party) wins executive power. In the four elections from 1958 through 1971 those winning *sublemas* obtained between 43 and 58 percent of the votes their *lemas* received, which amounted to 21 to 27 percent of all voters. What is more, those *sublemas* were further subdivided among different lists for the senate and, even more, the lower chamber. In 1971 Pacheco's *sublema* won the presidency (the candidate was Bordaberry), obtaining 56 percent of Colorado votes, which amounted to 23 percent of all voters. Nevertheless, the *sublema* included three lists for the senate, two of which obtained seats, and thirteen lists for the house in Montevideo alone, two of which obtained seats. Even that 23 percent of the total vote, then, was *not* a single bloc, but an alliance of subfractions each of which considered that its share of power should be no smaller than its share of the electorate. Furthermore, because the core constituencies of the main fractions within each major party have usually been different, covering a wide spectrum of interests (Aguiar 1977, passim), either party was bound to find internal opposition capable of blocking almost any conceivable policy bold enough to confront the crisis. Those who felt reluctant to pay a disproportionate share of the initial cost of the new policies could, and did, react quickly to stop the unjust role their own party was assigning to them. The interplay of subfractions *within* the fractions opened even more room to internal blockages. Thus, the inner structure of the two major parties also tended to block the kind of policy making necessary to fight the crisis. *Third,* and finally, before the 1972 coup the *fragmentation* of the party system (i.e., the dispersion of voters among different options), though still low in comparative terms, began to increase substantially. A cursory comparison of tables 7.3 and 7.4 shows that while in 1966 the winning party—the Colorados—had a very unstable majority, by 1971 they risked losing even the basic two-fifths plurality (40 percent) necessary to maintain presidential vetoes and, if need arose, to dissolve the legislature, an extremely important bargaining chip for the president.

All these features of the parties and party system were scrupulously translated into *parliamentary* traits by the proportional representation system. Since *any* of these factors considered in isolation could produce a stalemate, the result of their simultaneous cumulative action was a powerful force toward political deadlock. Nevertheless, such a situation did not necessarily lead to a total blockage; at least in theory, a series of short, unstable governments could have tried different approaches, some of which could have resulted in significant improvement. A further factor canceled even this possibility, however: Uruguayan quasi presidentialism froze the stalemates generated by the structure of the parties and of the party system. That freezing effect of quasi presidentialism—or, since 1966, of plain presidentialism—on political stalemates has at least two dimensions. The first and most obvious is that election dates are fixed: in Uruguay neither presidential nor legislative elections have ever taken place, under democratic governments, outside their legally preestablished dates. The stalemate produced by any election was thus frozen during the four-year presidential term (five since 1966) between elections.

The second dimension to the freezing effect of quasi presidentialism concerns its lack of flexibility for coalition making. Parties entering a governing coalition they do not lead necessarily take some risks beyond the ordinary attrition of governing. If things go well they do not receive much of the political credit, but if things go wrong as a result of actions they do not control, they may have to take part of the blame. The mechanics of a parliamentary system, however, provide a crucial resource to coalition partners: they are not powerless vis-à-vis the prime minister because they in effect own a share of the prime minister's position equal to their own share of the votes of the coalition in the legislature. The prime minister is always politically responsible, and a no-confidence vote can terminate his or her tenure. The power of the members of the coalition is thus directly expressed in a highly visible indicator: their share of the seats of the governing coalition. The vulnerability of a prime minister acts as a guarantee for the other members of the coalition, reinforcing or even replacing mutual trust among top politicians who are, by definition, adversaries. This guarantee is always *zero* in a presidential, or quasi-presidential, system. A president is not the *primus inter pares* a prime minister is and cannot be replaced because of disagreements on policies, whatever their intensity. Replacement of the president can be achieved only by a truly politico*criminal* procedure such as impeachment. Such a procedure is never part of normal political life, and not every system is strong enough to absorb it. The institutional position of a president thus necessarily implies that the minority partners in a governing coalition have to participate in a subordinate position that is politically damaging for them and that they lend political capital without any guarantee.

The argument so far has stated that certain features of the Uruguayan polity—the structure of its major parties and the nature of the party system, coupled with traditions of party government and of proportional representation in legislative elections—complicated the task of confronting the crises of the early thirties and the sixties because they precluded the formation of stable legislative majorities. This was indeed the case before the 1933 and 1973 democratic breakdowns. The rigidities of the Uruguayan presidential tradition made things far worse: first, because in critical circumstances they froze minority governments that obviously were going nowhere for four- or five-year periods; second, because they seriously contributed to blocking interparty coalitions capable of sustaining government majorities.

These "systemic," so to speak, negative effects of presidentialism are not the only ones relevant for the present purpose. Others are directly linked to the position of the central piece of the system—the president. In a presidential polity with a structured party system, as in Uruguay, the absence of legislative majorities normally means that the president commands a *plurality*—the one that put him or her into office in the first place—confronting a more or less divided opposition. In certain circumstances the resulting deadlock may pose a serious risk for democratic stability; the Uruguayan experience illustrates some of those circumstances.

The country's two democratic breakdowns in this century occurred when men of weak democratic faith became president. Although these men had the direct personal support of only a quarter of the electorate or less, they felt that the system blocked their presidential rights and duties and began to ignore the rules, opening the road to authoritarianism. The importance of personal attributes—underscored by the obvious fact that most Uruguayan presidents since 1918 did not stage coups—should not obscure the fact that Terra,[22] Pacheco, and Bordaberry were indeed *presidents*. In at least partially consolidated polyarchies, the institutional position of the president conveys a mix of resources and pressures that is by definition unique. He has material means, institutional resources, personal legitimacy, and when lacking parliamentary support, arguments that provide him with a ready-to-use rationalization for his potential antisystem behavior. A prime minister lacks the relative independence from the legislature of a president and the legitimacy that results from being directly chosen by the whole electorate, and if leading a minority government, he or she is subject to clearly defined rules governing the situation. In particular, a minority government can endure only as long as the majority allows. The simple fact that a president is at the same time chief of state and chief of government gives presidents—ceteris paribus—more power than prime ministers. Still, the difference between them does not boil down to power differentials. The presidential position also involves a greater expectation of leadership, irrespective of the political context; there is no king or experienced, trusted leader behind him. Presidents not only have more power but also more pressure to deliver. Hence major difficulties may arise in the case of minority governments: their rules are well defined in parliamentary systems but not in presidential ones. The prime minister of a minority government has an explicit caretaker role, yet this is not true for presidents in a comparable situation.

The peculiar combination of the powerful institutional position of a president with a weak *political* position—as happens when an incumbent president has no real chance of leading a legislative majority—is thus a risk-prone configuration. When this arises in a context of social and economic crises and increasing political polarization, the fate of democracy may well depend on the personality of the main political actors. There is no need for a truly ideologically undemocratic president, such as Bordaberry, for a breakdown to occur; it may suffice that in the president's perception his substantive duties (his "mission") far outweigh certain "merely procedural" rules. Probably Terra's history belongs to this last type. In either case, the logic of the situation will likely force a final confrontation between president and legislature. Chances are that the defender of democracy of last resort will be the legislature.

The Uruguayan record fits this model very well. Both Gabriel Terra in the early thirties and Juan María Bordaberry forty years later acted like and were seen as presidents, but they probably were the politically *weakest* presidents of this century, especially Bordaberry. Neither could lead even his own theoretical fraction of the party, much less the whole of the party. Both confronted severe crises. In 1933 and 1973 the breakdowns followed clashes between the legislature and the president, and in both cases parliamentary majorities denied the presidents what they were asking for; the legislatures appeared as an obstacle to presidential will; and their last sessions before their illegal dissolutions—which marked the end of the respective crises—recorded their anti-authoritarian stance. Although inefficiently and too late, the legislatures stood for democracy against presidents who did not. The two coups thus exhibited a Weimar-like path during which parliamentary majorities—those that were to stand for democracy in the final confrontation—proved unable to stop presidents whose antidemocratic behaviors were increasingly clear. This points once more to a crucial difference between presidential and parliamentary regimes: a no-confidence vote and the replacement of the chief of government by a more trusted leader could have taken place at an earlier stage than that of the final conflict between the president and the legislature, lowering the risk of breakdown.[23]

Table 7.5. Election Results and Distribution of Seats (1984)

Major Parties and Fractions	Absolute Votes (1,000)	Seat Share (%) in General Assembly
Colorado party	778	42
Pacheco	184	7
Sanguinetti/Batlle	592	35
Blanco party	661	35
Ortiz	83	1
Zumarán	554	34
Civic Union	48	2
Broad Front	401	21
Total votes cast	1,886	100

Institutional Deadlock under the Restored Democracy

The authoritarian regime that began in June 1973 imposed eleven harsh years on Uruguay. It had no important, enduring political successes; its major victory, the defeat of the Tupamaros and other smaller guerrilla groups, was accomplished in 1972, before its birth. It experienced two large political defeats: a plebiscite in 1980 rejected a constitution proposed by the military, and the 1982 "internal elections" within the major parties legalized a democratic civilian leadership as the only legitimate interlocutor with the military. After complicated negotiations, the country held a general election in November 1984. The parties campaigned rather freely, but the elections were not open: there were forbidden candidates, the most important of whom was the main Blanco leader, Wilson Ferreira. Ferreira would have had a real chance of victory had he been allowed to run, but he could not even campaign for his party because the military jailed him until after the election.[24]

The 1984 elections brought a return to civilian government, to the politicoinstitutional status quo ante—the 1986 constitution—and to democracy. The Colorados again won the election with almost exactly the same share of the vote as in 1971, but this time it was their moderate Batllist sector that put up the candidate with the most votes, Julio María Sanguinetti. The election thus produced a president far closer to the center of gravity of the legislature than that of 1971 (table 7.5).

The new president offered the opposition a "national unity" government, including cabinet posts, but only the Civic Union—a small Catholic party of the political center—accepted. Two Blancos also entered the cabinet as "technocrats." They did not represent their party, but symbolized the "governability" the Blanco leader Ferreira promised his party would maintain. The president said then that his cabinet was one of national *intonation:* not what he had asked for, but still better than an all-Colorado cabinet. Sanguinetti's administration brought repeated cycles of moderate confrontation and compromise between executive and legislature. The most important bones of contention between administration and parliament proved to be the behavior of the police and the interior minister, the enactment of the budget, and the granting of an amnesty to military officers accused of past human rights violations. In the case of the controversy over police brutality toward a student sit-in in which members of parliament were beaten, the president used the threat of early elections to shield his interior minister from censure. In the struggle over the budget, which was heavily amended by the opposition, the president vetoed the revised clauses and thus precipitated a mini constitutional crisis. Nevertheless, when the Supreme Court ruled that he had overstepped his powers, he backed down and reached a compromise.

The crisis over the military's refusal to face trial in civilian courts, where private citizens had brought actions accusing various officers of torture, kidnapping, and presumptive murder, soon broke up the mood of political consensus, giving rise to a bitter three-cornered struggle. The combined opposition first threw out the government's proposed immunity law. The Blanco party then introduced a far tougher law, which would mainly have absolved those military who had violated human rights while carrying out orders from above. This compromise was defeated by the bilateral opposition of the Left (which thought it too weak) and the ruling Colorados (who thought it too harsh). With only days to go before the first scheduled appearance in court by an officer who openly threatened not to testify, the Blancos introduced a third bill, one granting effective immunity to all those accused of past violations of human rights. Known as the *Ley de Caducidad* (Statute of Limitations) this third bill received the support of the government and became law just before Christmas 1986 (Gillespie and Arregui 1989, 1990).

Passage of amnesty for the military closed the cycle of Uruguayan politics that had begun with the Naval Club Pact of 1984: the Left returned to its traditional role of militant opposition and began to collect signatures for an initiative to repeal the new law. The bulk of the Blanco party under Wilson Ferreira embarked on a path of more moderate opposition, disputing with the ruling Colorados the center ground of Uruguayan politics with an eye to the 1989 elections.[25] After a long and often bitter process that took two years, the signatures to repeal the *Ley de Caducidad* were collected and counted by electoral authorities, and the law itself was finally brought to a referendum in April 1989. The law was upheld by 57 percent of voters; however, in the country's capital—Montevideo—56 percent of valid votes were cast against the amnesty. In an important sense the referendum prefigured the end of the transition itself: everybody accepted the final result as the people's will, and the last major political problem inherited from the authoritarian regime was thus solved.

The following months were increasingly dominated by the electoral campaign preceding the November national elections. The incumbent party, the Colorados, chose the candidate of its then majority fraction—the Batllists—in an open pri-

Table 7.6. Election Results and Distribution of Seats (1989)

Major Parties and Fractions	Absolute Votes (1,000)	Seat Share (%) in General Assembly
Colorado party	597	30
Pacheco	289	13
Batlle	292	17
Blanco party	766	40
Lacalle	445	28
Zumarán	101	1
Pereyra	219	11
New Space	177	8
Broad Front	418	22
Total votes cast	1,971	100

mary contest conducted in May and won by Senator Jorge Batlle. Pacheco again headed the ticket of the conservative Colorados. A third, small Batllist candidacy led by former labor minister Fernández Faingold then emerged as a result of disagreements with Jorge Batlle. Within the Blancos the selection of candidates was easier. Ferreira had died before the referendum, and his successor was Zumarán, the man who ran as Ferreira's proxy in 1984. Zumarán positioned himself at the center of the party; at his left was Pereyra, the Blanco leader who was against the amnesty, and to his right Lacalle, who was not unlike Sanguinetti five years before: a moderate, sensible young man. On the Left the Broad Front broke down in early 1989: on the one hand, a moderate wing that became known as the *New Space* (consisting of the Christian Democrats, the former Colorado "Ninety-nine List" and, later, the Civic Union), and on the other hand, a majoritarian, radical wing that retained the original label *Broad Front* (Communists, Socialists, and all other former members, plus for the first time the Tupamaros). The breakdown occurred in spite of the unifying effect of the referendum, which was firmly supported by the whole Left.[26]

The November 1989 elections, this time entirely free and open, concluded the transition from authoritarianism to democracy (see table 7.6). The incumbent party lost a full ten points of the vote, about half of which were won by the victorious Blancos, and particularly by the winning fraction within them, that of Lacalle. Considering its previous share of the electorate, however, the net winner of the election was the Left. On the one hand, though divided into two alliances—or perhaps partly thanks to this very division—the whole of the Left obtained as many votes as the Colorados at the national level. On the other hand, the Broad Front won the local election in Montevideo, where Tabaré Vázquez, a young, respected socialist physician of working-class background became *intendente* —something less than a provincial governor, since Uruguay is a unitary state, but more than just a city mayor. Both results were absolute firsts in Uruguayan political history.

The newly elected president looked for legislative support before assuming office, as Sanguinetti did in 1985. Yet he carefully avoided using the same words: Sanguinetti had called for a "national unity government," whereas Lacalle favored a "European-style coalition." The different wording was not a mere disguise. Lacalle was far clearer and more explicit about what he was asking for: the standard deal—as in a *parliamentary* system—of a would-be prime minister from a party lacking legislative majority. He was willing to give a lot in exchange—so much, in fact, that some reluctant Colorados (most important among them Batlle) suggested they would not be able to reply to his offer because what it amounted to was still unclear: Lacalle insisted the details had to be decided *with* his coalition partners.

Like Sanguinetti, Lacalle obtained less than he had asked for. His "national coalition" became a "national *confluence*."[27] Still, observers and participants alike agree that he obtained more than Sanguinetti. The new cabinet included four Colorado "technocrats"; though doubling the Blanco participation in Sanguinetti's first cabinet, they still, at least theoretically, did not represent their party, and their actions would not bind it. Besides cabinet-level Colorado participation, a basic agreement was reached on some central policy matters and, accordingly, on a package of laws to be passed during the first months of the new administration, beginning on March 1, 1990. How firm those agreements were, and how long they would survive, remained to be seen.

Conclusion: Reconsidering Parliamentarism?

This essay has two different varieties of concluding remarks. On the one hand, the Uruguayan experience allows some tentative generalizations for more comparatively oriented reflections. Since the birth of Uruguayan polyarchy by 1918 the country has confronted two major crises, both characterized by social and economic problems and increasing political polarization; in both opportunities democracy broke down. During the years immediately preceding those breakdowns a certain combination of politicoinstitutional factors blocked effective policy making when it was most needed. These factors included fractionalization of the major political parties (coupled, since the early seventies, with increasing fragmentation of the party system); direct translation of these features into the political composition of the parliament due to proportional representation in legislative elections; and a tradition of party government. The obvious result was lack of legislative majorities to decide upon and maintain policies bold enough to confront the crises. Presidentialism, though per se not necessarily connected to any of those factors, made things far worse. For during full four- and five-year periods it froze governments that were clearly unable to cope with the situation; furthermore, it hindered the formation of interparty coalitions to obtain governing majorities.

Two other important negative effects of presidentialism were directly linked to the position of the president. First, the blocked situation just described meant that policy disagreements between president and opposition very easily became institutional conflicts between the legislature and the president. The second negative effect stems from the obvious fact that a president with no legislative majority is a *politically weak* president. But the *institutional* position of a president is strong: ceteris paribus, a president is more powerful than a prime minister.[28] An institutionally powerful but politically weak president is in an unstable position: the pressure on him to deliver is blocked by his political weakness. The blocking agent, besides, appears directly personified in the legislature.

Whenever the context fits the pattern described in the two preceding paragraphs, democratic stability may heavily depend on haphazard factors such as, for example, the personality of the president. For a breakdown to occur it is not even necessary that the president be committedly and ideologically undemocratic. A strong sense of mission may be enough. Sartori writes that the position of the president in the governing bloc is critical for the stability of a highly polarized polity: if the president is to the right of a right-wing block, or to the left of a left-wing block, then it is likely that further polarization will develop and that the system will approach breakdown (Sartori 1982, 311). This hypothesis fits very well both Terra's and Bordaberry's positions, and it is probably directly linked to the sense of mission mentioned above. This seems particularly clear in Bordaberry's case (Bordaberry 1989).

Uruguayan political history does not show that presidentialism alone causes the breakdown of democracy. It does show, however, that in certain critical circumstances presidentialism greatly contributes to that breakdown. It cannot show, but it does suggest—in our view strongly—that a parliamentary system would considerably diminish the risks of breakdown. This suggestion is based upon counterfactual considerations but also, at least in certain cases, by very direct hints from the events leading to the breakdown (e.g., the attempt to oust Bordaberry).

Though our case study alone leads us thus far, two additional considerations should be added. First, the crises that led to breakdown were rare but not abnormal; in fact, they may be comparable in several respects to the current "lost decade" for development and the burden of external debt in many a developing country. This adds a different dimension to the whole discussion. Second, the present argument is more against presidentialism than in favor of a parliamentary system. The ideal comparison would be a case of democratic breakdown in a parliamentary polity no less structured and consolidated than Uruguay was in the early seventies.[29] Such a case does not exist, though in principle nothing prevents it from occurring. We cannot state positively whether that nonexistence results from pure chance or because such breakdowns are far more unlikely in parliamentary systems. On purely theoretical grounds we are thus in a position similar to the classical one of too few cases and too many variables. Policy making, however, has different rules; it cannot wait for further evidence to develop. From that point of view

Table 7.7. Should the Constitution Be Reformed?

	Broad Front	Blancos	Colorados	All[a]
Percent favoring change	90.0% ($n = 10$)	40.0% ($n = 15$)	44.4% ($n = 18$)	56.6% ($n = 46$)
Specific reforms:				
Parliamentary system with executive responsible to legislature	100.0	50.0	38.5	62.9
Retention of National Security Council with advisory role alone	11.1	40.0	35.5	36.1
Collegial executive with opposition participation	11.1	40.0	33.3	25.7
An end to the ban on reelecting presidents	11.1 ($n = 9$)	25.0[b] ($n = 10$)	21.4 ($n = 12$)	25.7 ($n = 35$)

Note: Respondents were asked: "With the transition to democracy safely assured, should there be any reforms to the constitution?" Obviously the balance of opinions among the respondents depends on the proportions of people interviewed from each party. Gillespie tried to interview politicians in rough proportion to the electoral strength of their party, but the final sample inevitably overrepresented the minor parties. For a later survey on congresspersons' attitudes to decentralization, see Equipos (1988).
    a. Includes a Patriotic Union and three Civic Union leaders.
    b. $n = 8$.

we believe that our case strongly contributes to the line of proparliamentary reasoning Linz began to develop more than ten years ago.[30]

At the beginning of the democratic restoration the attitudes of political elites on the subject of parliamentarism were relatively open. In interviews with leading politicians during 1984 Gillespie raised the issue of constitutional reform; his results are shown in table 7.7. A majority of all politicians interviewed favored at least some constitutional changes once a transition to democracy was safely assured, though there was noticeably greater enthusiasm for revisions among the leaders of the Left. In particular, the single most favored reform was precisely a "parliamentary system with executive responsible to legislature." There is a certain ambiguity to these answers, since many politicians believe the 1966 constitution to be semiparliamentary already. All in all, however, the answers suggest a cautious but slightly favorable predisposition to parliamentarism.

These results are now ten years old, but in spite of incremental improvements, the main social and economic problems still exist. In broad terms the fractionalization of the major parties looks as healthy or unhealthy as ever and the fragmentation of the party system—as measured by *any* of the well-known indexes available for that purpose—has steadily increased (tables 7.5 and 7.6). Obviously the potential for a politicoinstitutional stalemate keeps pace with the increasing fragmentation of the party system. Things did not go awry after 1985 to a large extent because Sanguinetti was neither Bordaberry nor Terra; he was an experienced, democratic politician of the political center. As of 1990 the short- and medium-run forecasts are similar because the same description fits Lacalle's personality.

This rather gloomy landscape nevertheless shows two interesting new developments: On the one hand, both Sanguinetti's (essentially failed) and Lacalle's (just beginning) openings toward extraparty alliances will add valuable experience on the subject to a rather scarce pool. On the other hand, the electoral growth of the Left suggests that an Allende-like situation—a highly motivated plurality that forms a minority government—might not be far away; in fact, this almost happened in Montevideo in the 1984 election, and it finally did happen in 1989. At least some politicians are surely thinking about the best ways to prevent this situation from occurring at a national level—that is, to prevent a government by a simple plurality of the radical Left.

If the main arguments of this essay are right, the status quo does not favor the prospects for Uruguayan democracy. Given the beliefs of political elites and the recent developments just mentioned, some politicoinstitutional changes may be in the making. Yet there are not many democratic ways of preventing government by simple pluralities without preventing any government at all; a parliamentary system is perhaps the best, though it is by no means certain that Uruguayan politicians would choose that alternative.[31] If they do, even though the motives for the eventual changes may be politically biased, the final results may help democracy. Mechanisms that prevent government by a mere plurality of the radical Left would also work to prevent government by the radical Right. While such debates may remain very abstract to the general public, there is no doubt that they are beginning to preoccupy Uruguay's political elites and social scientists.[32]

A large part of the educated Uruguayan political elite has traditionally tended to believe, and still does, that parliamentary systems are intrinsically better institutionally but that a mixture of tradition and idiosyncrasy makes presidentialism best fitted to the country's needs. In order to combine the best of both worlds, the approach has often been to add a little of the first to the second. This has not produced the desired results; as one observer dryly noted regarding the workings of presidentialism since 1967, while "the country is never without a government, it is often without a workable government" (Kerbusch 1969, 216–17). Thus, the time seems ripe for abandoning incremental tinkering with presidentialism in order to try a bolder approach.

Notes

1. Many ideas in this chapter are drawn from Gillespie (1991) and González (1991).

2. We leave aside the Institutional Acts of the 1973–84 authoritarian regime because the 1985 democratic restoration saw a return to the 1966 constitution. Neither the 1934 nor the 1942 reforms were conducted according to the existing laws, although the 1942 reform can be described as undoing the situation created by the 1933 coup. In spite of their origins, however, both reforms contributed in enduring ways to Uruguayan constitutional law.

3. Throughout this chapter we refer to competing currents within political parties as fractions because the alternative term, *factions,* has unintended pejorative associations.

4. Members of the National Council of Administration were elected by thirds every two years, like U.S. senators (Lindahl 1962).

5. The presidency was this time completely replaced by a nine-member National Council of Government dominated by the winning party but with three seats assigned to the runner-up. Its presidency rotated yearly among the members of the majority.

6. At the end of the nineteenth century, the per capita wealth of Uruguay was estimated to be about the same as that of the United States (Franco 1975).

7. A distinct chief of government may exist as long as he or she is explicitly subordinated to the president, who has the ultimate executive responsibility.

8. A special majority of two-thirds within the National Council of Administration—the pluripersonal component of executive power—was necessary to supersede the president's veto power.

9. Between 1933 and 1942 dissolution would have been even more difficult because of the peculiar composition of the senate and the electoral abstention of the main opponents of the de facto regime.

10. Alberto Ramón Real, cited in Sanguinetti and Pacheco Seré (1971), p. 30.

11. This strange maneuver was in their interest because they represented fractions of the ruling Colorado party, which stood to lose votes at the elections.

12. It was, in other words, not a fully fledged authoritarian regime.

13. Differing views on Uruguayan electoral law may be found in the compilations by Franco (1986) and Nohlen and Rial (1986). González (1988) examines the combined effects of electoral law *and* quasi presidentialism on the party system and on democratic stability.

14. Apart from Colorado feuding and parliamentary harrying of the government, no less than five ministers were forced to resign as a result of the actions of the Tupamaros urban guerrillas: in some cases because the terrorists uncovered corruption, in others because of the failure of the security forces to maintain law and order (Rouquié 1973, 17).

15. Nevertheless, the parliament did not always oppose Pacheco's security measures. For example, right-wing Blancos assured the passage of a twenty-day suspension of all personal liberties in the wake of the kidnapping and execution of U.S. police advisor, Dan Mitrione, by Tupamaros guerrillas in 1970 (McDonald 1971, 121).

16. Besides its ideological feasibility, it may also be noted that the "little pact" was a minimum winning coalition—as table 7.4 shows.

17. Had he been a prime minister it seems obvious he would have been deposed.

18. Different though not necessarily contradictory views on the 1933 coup may be found in Taylor (1952), Nahum et al. (1989), and Reyes Abadie (1989). Gillespie (1984; 1987, chap. 3) reviews alternative explanations of the 1973 coup and provides references.

19. The military regime of 1973–84, however, did no better.

20. During the 1934–42 authoritarian situation there was a peculiar coalition between a governing Colorado fraction led by President Terra and the Blanco majority led by Herrera. In 1972 there was a pact between the Colorado majority and the Blanco minority. And during 1973–84 there was military rule with civilian collaborators from the right wings of both traditional parties—who, however, acted "personally," without formal decisions or support from their respective fractions.

21. Coparticipation is the Uruguayan practice of offering the opposition a share in government spoils; it should not be confused with consociation in Lijphart's (1969) sense.

22. Terra was a democratically elected Colorado-Batllista president who led the 1933 coup.

23. As mentioned above, some influential Colorado and Blanco leaders attempted to

force Bordaberry to resign in order that his vice president, Sapelli, might take over. Sapelli was more respected than Bordaberry and did not follow the president after the coup.

24. González (1983), Gillespie (1986), and Rial (1986) discuss these three major political events (those of 1980, 1982, and 1984, respectively) and provide further references. As the leader of the Broad Front, Liber Seregni could make speeches, though he, too, was not authorized to run.

25. The sector of the Blancos led by Senator Pereyra did, however, support the Left's efforts to repeal the amnesty for the military.

26. Nevertheless, when González in 1987 analyzed the Uruguayan party system mainly on the basis of survey data collected in 1985, he considered the Broad Front as two relevant political actors, in Sartori's sense, with the same dividing line observed later in the 1989 split (González 1988).

27. The literal phrase used, *Coincidencia Nacional,* has unfortunate connotations in English; another rendering would be "National Coinciding."

28. This does not mean, of course, that all presidents are more powerful than every prime minister. It merely says that, other things being equal, of the two formal positions described in table 7.1, that of president is the more powerful.

29. An alternative would be to analyze the weathering of a similar crisis in a consolidated parliamentary system. Sweden in the 1930s and Italy in the 1970s may be two cases in point.

30. Though long circulated in unpublished form, Linz's ideas were given a wider audience in 1990 (Linz 1990; see also chap. 1). Valenzuela's essay on Chile (1985) also influenced our thinking. Mainwaring (1989) presents a strong, essentially concurrent argument on Brazil.

31. Another solution adopted in France since 1958 is to require a second runoff ballot in elections when no candidate obtains an overall majority in the first round.

32. Some of the debate can be followed in Pérez Antón (1987, 1989), Peixoto (1987, and 1988), Lindahl (1987), and Pareja (1988).

References

Aguiar, César. 1977 "Notas sobre política y sociedad en el Uruguay, 1942–62." Montevideo: CIEDUR.

Bordaberry, Juan María. 1980. *Las opciones.* Montevideo: Imprenta Rosgal.

Dahl, Robert A. 1971. *Polyarchy: Participation and Opposition.* New Haven: Yale UP.

———. 1985. *A Preface to Economic Democracy.* Berkeley: U California P.

Drake, Paul, and Eduardo Silva, eds. 1986. *Elections and Democratization in Latin America, 1980–85.* San Diego: Center for Iberian and Latin American Studies.

Equipos Consultores Asociados. 1988. "Opinión de los parlamentarios uruguayos sobre la organización territorial des estado." *Cuadernos del CLAEH* nos. 45–46.

Fitzgibbon, Russell H. 1952. "Adoption of a Collegiate Executive in Uruguay." *Journal of Politics* 14: 616–42.

Franco, Rolando. 1975. "¿Battle: el gran responsable?" *Nueva sociedad* no. 16, pp. 34–47.

———. 1984. *La democracia a la Uruguaya.* Montevideo: El Libro Libre.

———, ed. 1986. *El sistema electoral uruguayo: peculiaridades y perspectivas.* 2 vols. Montevideo: Fundación Hanns Seidel.

Gillespie, Charles. 1984. "The Breakdown of Democracy in Uruguay: Alternative Political Models." Wilson Center Latin American Program Working Paper no. 143. Revised version in *Uruguay y la democracia,* edited by Charles Gillespie, Louis Goodman, Juan Rial, and Peter Winn. 3 vols. Montevideo: Banda Oriental.

————. 1986. "Activists and the Floating Voter: The Unheeded Lessons of Uruguay's 1982 Primaries." In Drake and Silva (1986).

————. 1991. *Negotiating Democracy: Politicians and Generals in Uruguay*. New York: Cambridge UP.

Gillespie, Charles, and Miguel Arregui. 1989, 1990. "Uruguay." *Latin America and Caribbean Contemporary Record, VI and VII*. New York: Holmes & Meier.

González, Luis E. 1983. "Uruguay, 1980–81: An Unexpected Political Opening." *Latin American Research Review* 18:3.

————. 1991. *Political Structures and Democracy in Uruguay*. Notre Dame, Ind.: Helen Kellogg Institute for International Studies, U Notre Dame P.

Gros Espiell, Héctor. 1956. *Las constituciones del Uruguay*. Madrid: Ediciones Cultura Hispánica.

Kaufman, Edy. 1978. *Uruguay in Transition*. New Brunswick: Transaction Books.

Kerbusch, Ernst J. 1969. "Uruguay in der Verfassungskrise." *Verfassung und Verfassungswirklichkeit* 4.

Lijphart, Arend. 1969. "Consociational Democracy." *World Politics* 21 (Jan.): 2.

Lindahl, Göran G. 1962. *Uruguay's New Path*. Stockholm: Library and Institute of Ibero-American Studies.

————. 1987. "El presidencialismo en América Latina y Uruguay." *Cuadernos del CLAEH* no. 43.

Linz, Juan J. 1978. *Crisis, Breakdown and Reequilibration*. Baltimore: Johns Hopkins UP.

————. 1990. "The Perils of Presidentialism." *Journal of Democracy* 1 (Winter): 1.

McDonald, Ronald H. 1971. "Legislative Politics in Uruguay." In *Latin American Legislatures*, edited by Weston H. Agor. New York: Praeger.

————. 1972. "Electoral Politics and Uruguayan Political Decay." *Inter-American Economic Affairs* 26 (Summer): 1.

————. 1975. "The Rise of Military Politics in Uruguay." *Inter-American Economic Affairs* 28:25–43.

Mainwaring, Scott. 1989. "Institutional Dilemmas of Multiparty Presidential Democracy: The Case of Brazil." Paper presented to the 15th International Congress of the Latin American Studies Association, Miami.

Nahum, Benjamín, et al. 1989. *Crisis política y recuperación económica: 1930–1958*. Historia uruguay, vol. 7. Montevideo: Banda Oriental.

Nohlen, Dieter, and Juan Rial, eds. 1986. *Reforma electoral*. Montevideo: Ediciones de la Banda Oriental.

O'Donnell, Guillermo. 1978. "State and Alliances in Argentina, 1956–1976." *Journal of Development Studies* 15:1.

Pareja, Carlos. 1988. "Asignaturas pendientes en el debate de la reforma política." *Cuadernos del CLAEH* no. 47.

Peixoto, Martín. 1987. "El debate político en el Uruguay." *Cuadernos del CLAEH* no. 43.

————. 1988. "¿Parlamentarismo y presidencialismo: dónde están las diferencias?" *Cuadernos del CLAEH* no. 47.

Pérez Antón, Romeo. 1987. "¿Parlamentarismo como alternativa? El caso de Uruguay." *Cuadernos del CLAEH* no. 43.

————. 1989. "El parlamentarismo en la tradición constitucional uruguaya." *Cuadernos del CLAEH* no. 49.

Reyes Abadie, Washington. 1989. *Historia del Partido Nacional*. Montevideo: Ediciones de la Banda Oriental.

Rial, Juan. 1986. "The Uruguayan Election of 1984." In Drake and Silva (1986).

Rouquié, Alain. 1973. "L'Uruguay de M. Pacheco à M. Bordaberry." *Notes et Etudes Documentaires* (23 Mar.), nos. 3973–74.

Sanguinetti, Julio María, and Alvaro Pacheco Seré. 1971. *La nueva Constitución.* Montevideo: Alfa. (A 1967 edition has slightly different pagination.)

Sartori, Giovanni. 1982. *Teoria dei partiti e caso italiano.* Milan: Sugarco Edizione.

Taylor, Philip B. 1952. "The Uruguayan Coup d'Etat of 1933." *Hispanic American Historical Review* 32 (no. 3): 301–20.

Valenzuela, Arturo. 1985. "Orígenes y características del sistema de partidos en Chile." *Estudios públicos* no. 18.

Vanger, Milton I. 1954. "Uruguay Introduces Government by Committee." *American Political Science Review* 48 (no. 2): 500–13.

8

BOLIVAR LAMOUNIER

Brazil: Toward Parliamentarism?

Having chosen a president through direct elections, after fifteen years of "transition," Brazil now clearly begins a regressive counting toward the final choice of its form of government. The constitutional congress elected in 1986 debated this issue for almost two years and opted at the end for the presidential system. But for a variety of reasons to be discussed later on, that decision has been regarded as provisional; the congress itself defined it this way when it included in the transitional clauses *(Disposiç Æes Transitórias)* of the constitution of 1988 an article determining that the final choice will be made by a plebiscite in 1993. In other words, we are not here dealing with an academic hypothesis but with a constitutional fact. Explicitly scheduling a plebiscite, the congress has said that the process of institutional revision is still underway. This definition of the situation has impacted upon the calculations of political actors throughout this period.

The five-year term of Fernando Collor de Mello, the first president popularly elected since 1960, is thus the political and time frame for a decisive debate between presidentialists and parliamentarists. The outcome may be influenced by the president's cautiously parliamentarist preference and, more likely, by his performance. Confronted with the imperatives of fighting soaring inflation and reforming the public sector, Collor de Mello's failure will be no less a determinant than his eventual success. But other factors linked to Brazil's institutional history and to present perceptions about the country's political structure and needs will also carry weight.

On a broader historical canvas, it seems plausible to assert that Brazil is presently undergoing a process of institutional rearrangement as important as those that took place in the 1840s and again after the Revolution of 1930. In that first case, the crowning of Pedro II, then a fifteen-year-old adolescent, was the key to ending a series of armed rebellions and stabilizing a quasi-parliamentary monarchy that would last for another half-century. In 1930, the armed movement that brought Getúlio Vargas to power reversed the excessive federalism of the First Republic (1889–1930) and paved the way for Brazil's economic and political modernization. In the 1840s, there was no significant republican alternative, and hence no presidentialist proposals. What was at stake was rather the degree of autonomy of the provinces within the unitary empire and the prerogatives of the parliament vis-à-vis the monarch, who personally exerted a fourth power (the *poder moderador*). In the third decade of this century, on the contrary, the parliamentary hypothesis was weak. The evils of the First Republic, especially backland bossism, were invariably imputed to the importation of the North American constitutional model, to federalism and liberalism, or to "politics" pure and simple. True, demands were often and strongly vocalized in liberal democratic language (electoral reform, the secret vote), but the key to progress, within the ideological climate of the times, was protofascist: centralization, strengthening the federal government and the executive, increasing the presence of *técnicos* at all levels of the governmental structure, and eventually schemes of corporatist representation.[1]

Today's Brazil seems to be living through changes as important as those but with radically different content. More than at any other moment in the country's history, the elites seem increasingly convinced that democratic consolidation is the only route toward modernity, and that stability and governability may depend crucially on the institutional choices under way. The debate between presidentialism and parliamentarism has thus gained a salience it has not had since the early days of the republic, and it is a lot more central than in the other Latin American countries.

Unique in Latin America because of its monarchical and parliamentary experience of the nineteenth century, Brazil seems also unique for its recent transition to democracy. One aspect of the transition was the formal calling of a constitutional congress, which engaged the country for almost two years in a full constitution-making process. The strength of the parliamentarist demand in the last few years is undoubtedly linked to this fact. Yet there is substantial evidence, at least at the elite level, that demand grew remarkably after the adoption of the constitution. In 1987–88, let us recall, the issue of the incumbent president's term of office interfered powerfully with the debate on the form of government. President Sarney's struggle to confirm a five-year term led to a confrontation with those proposing four years and direct elections at the end of 1988. The president managed to put together a broad coalition against parliamentarism and for presidential elections in November of 1989. Fearing that presidential elections on short notice or a change toward parliamentarism would introduce intolerable uncertainties in a country already threatened by economic chaos, sizable portions of the business community and the military backed the president's position. After one year, that negative evaluation no longer commanded the same consensus. Ungovernability became the catchword throughout 1989. The advances made by the Left in the municipal elections of November 1988 brought the fear that the presidential election scheduled for one year later would have two leftist candidates in the second round, adding to the general atmosphere of instability. Several factors, from the plebiscite scheduled for 1993 to the reevaluation of President Sarney's claims to the quick erosion of President Collor's authority have thus contributed to keep the presidentialist/parliamentarist debate afloat.

On the other hand, it would seem naive to ignore the enormous difficulties that lie ahead. There is, first of all, what has been called the country's "presidentialist tradition." Second, there is a doubt about parliamentarism in a country with proverbially weak parties and without a professional bureaucracy. Memories of the parliamentary experience of 1961–63 can also be counted as a negative factor. Improvised as a means to overcome the impasse created by President Quadros's resignation and the military veto against Vice President João Goulart, that experiment has since been described as a failure. Fourth, and finally, there is the coexistence within the parliamentarist demand of potentially conflictive preferences, from "pure" parliamentarism to various "mixed" formulas.

The objective of this chapter is thus to examine this institutional change *en train de se faire*, reviewing some of its historical origins, its foundations in the recent redemocratization process, and alternatives to it in the near future. The first part provides an overall review of the political system from 1889 to the military takeover of 1964, with especial attention to the idea of a "presidentialist tradition." The second deals briefly with the military regime (1964–85) but concentrates on President Sarney's "New Republic" and especially on the growth of the parliamentarist demand since the constitutional debate of 1985–88. At the end the alternative parliamentary formulas now being considered are sketched, on the assumption that a successful transition toward parliamentarism largely depends on the sedimentation of a viable preference among the relevant elites.

Brazilian Presidentialism, 1889–1964

"Tradition" is one of the main arguments against changing institutional structures from presidentialism to parliamentarism, or vice versa. Regardless of how tradition is interpreted in each case, political scientists recognize that established structures have a weight of their own. Long experience with parliamentarism makes presidentialism unlikely in countries like Turkey and India. Conversely, in Latin America, resistance to parliamentary proposals is largely grounded in the fact that the subcontinent has been presidentialist for a long time.

But what exactly should we understand by a "presidentialist tradition"? Is it simply a matter of time? Or is it rather the fact that these countries never experienced parliamentarism (or experienced it a long time ago, under very different conditions, as in the case of Brazil)? Is the weight of the tradition duly "discounted" by the perception that the historical record has been punctuated by instability and democratic breakdowns?

An important question here is to what extent we are really talking about a sequence of historical facts (a succession of presidential governments) or about a certain reading of the political culture. There is, of course, a broadly shared interpretation of Brazilian (and Latin American) political culture as being inherently authoritarian, meaning that there is a "craving" for hierarchy and personalistic leadership. The corollary is normally that presidentialism (or dictatorship) is more congruent with this sociological substratum, which would repudiate "impersonal" institutional forms like parliamentarism as alien. A rigorous study of this family of hypotheses and research designs capable of evaluating their empirical significance for the choice between presidentialism and parliamentarism would of course be desirable. Are all Latin American cultures alike in this regard? If it is true that such authoritarian traits reflect a long history of inequality and patron-client relationships, are they resistant to change even in the highly urbanized, media-intensive society that is now emerging throughout Latin America? What proportion of citizens uphold hierarchical or personalistic views of public authority? What is the context and depth of such views—are they deep-seated propensities, or do they reflect an understandable demand for more effective government, regardless of institutional form?

There is, however, a more sophisticated formulation of the "requisites" that presidentialism is supposed to fulfill or have fulfilled, thus becoming a tradition. It deals with government structures as such, rather than with cultural determinants. This sort of inquiry is felicitously phrased by Lawrence Whitehead:

> It is probably true that a sovereign parliament should be more flexible, more accountable, and more responsible to regional and other differences of interest, than a fixed term directly elected President, or a mixed system. It might nevertheless be argued that in at least some Latin American countries it would be better to sacrifice a certain measure of flexibility, accountability and responsiveness in order to accommodate the programmatic unity and persistence required to overcome deepseated obstacles to development. National integration has frequently been achieved by means of a strong executive authority. The same institutional structure could be desirable to overcome acute regional or social inequalities, or to promote rapid economic transformation. Parliamentarism may be better at equilibrating an established and broadly satisfactory status quo than at building a new order.[2]

The key words here are clearly "programmatic unity and persistence," which in turn suggest requisites such as stability, effectiveness, and legitimacy. Does Brazil belong to that subset of Latin American countries in which presidentialism might be superior in terms of these criteria? On the face of it, it seems hard to maintain that presidentialism has earned uniformly high scores on these three measures over this first century of republican government. Leaving aside minor episodes, it seems sufficient to point out that there were three major violent interventions (1930, 1937, and 1964). Taken together, these three instances led to thirty-two years without regular competition for the supreme executive position, and it is worth noting that the first four (1930–34) and the last twenty-one (1964–85) began with presidential succession crises. In 1930, the incumbent president (Washington Luís) was over-thrown by a movement led by the defeated candidate (Getúlio Vargas). Getúlio stayed four years as chief of the provisional government; he was then elected (con-firmed as president) by the Constituent Assembly but established a dictatorship (the Estado Novo) from 1937 to 1945. When he came back to the presidency through direct elections in 1950, his government was subject to intense opposition, ending in a serious political and military crisis that led to Getúlio's suicide on August 24, 1954. Jânio Quadros, elected in October 1960, resigned less than a year later, in Au-gust 1961. The inauguration of Vice President João Goulart was vetoed by the mil-itary, and the country came close to a civil war. An improvised parliamentary for-mula—the same that many consider to have been a "failure"—allowed Jango to take office as chief of state. But Jango maneuvered to regain full presidential pow-ers and finally succeeded through the plebiscite of January 6, 1963. Fourteen months later (March 31, 1964), he was ousted by the military. Brazil then entered its longest period of authoritarian military rule, which ended only with the (indirect) election of a civilian, Tancredo Neves, in January 1985.

By the most generous counting, then, one-third of this century of presidential-ism has fallen short of constitutional normalcy and stability. However, to be re-garded as decisive, this sort of evidence must be submitted to a rigorous critique—that is, to counterfactual arguments showing that the outcome would have been better under parliamentarism. This is a formidable task, which I only occasionally tackle here. A prerequisite for such an analysis, I think, is a broader analytical cri-terion on the basis of which the presidentialist tradition can be grasped as a whole and as a response to the triple requisite of stability, effectiveness, and legitimacy. By this I mean a more substantive conceptualization going beyond the usual formal criteria (such as the fixed term of office and the combination of the roles of chief of state and chief of government) by means of which we define presidentialism. It is not so much presidentialism as a system of institutional rules but the etiology of presi-dential authority that I have in mind here. The latter question leads me to consider Whitehead's "programmatic unity and persistence" as a form of power that needs to be created rather than as a constant or as a natural consequence of the fixed term.

The key to presidential authority in the sense stated above, in my view, is the plebiscitarian nature of the office. The source of the authority we are talking about is diffuse support by a broad national constituency. Prime ministers may enjoy such support in addition to parliamentary confidence, but the way in which presi-dents are chosen is designed to make them independent of parliamentary confi-dence and capable, in theory, of pitting that diffuse support against parliamentary pressure or resistance. The plebiscitarian assumption of Latin American presiden-tialism is as clear as the one articulated by Max Weber when he favored a "charis-matic" (directly elected) chief of state in Germany.[3] It is, nota bene, the idea of a charismatic office and not simply a search for occasional charismatic incumbents. Except for the North American case, which always included a strong emphasis on checks and balances and federalism as counterweights to presidential power, and despite variations in time and space, modern presidentialism seems to be preeminently a charismatic conception of authority. In Latin America, as in Weber's thought, the presidential office is the focus of very contradictory expectations. It is seen simultaneously as a stabilizer and a destabilizer. Appealing directly to the masses, especially the urban masses, Latin American presidents are supposed to attract a formidable volume of diffuse support and thus free themselves from oligarchical and clientelistic demands that would otherwise block the modernization drive and eventually impair the functioning of the state. At the same time, they are expected to be engines of social change, acting as creative destabilizers vis-à-vis settled ways and routines. Newly elected presidents are invariably seen as formidable moving forces, bearers of a substantive mandate for major social change, a means to break the resistance of tradition, oligarchy, clientelism, imperialism, and what not. This, as Linz has noted, leads them to claim superior legitimacy, as if their legal and ethical status were higher than the legislature's. Without the plebiscitarian expectations underlying that claim, may I add, presidentialism would not be nearly as strong as it is in Brazil, and generally in Latin America.

The problem, of course, is that plebiscitarian expectations are only one of the sources of presidential authority within a democratic constitutional framework. There is also the whole constellation of regional, sectoral, economic, and other interests, represented in various ways and degrees in the legislature and through interest group pressure. Electoral campaigns are heavily plebiscitarian, but organizing and running governments are a different matter. So we can say that effective presidential authority emerges (when it really does) from a complex and potentially contradictory movement: a plebiscitarian election, which individualizes and concentrates power in one person, and henceforward the adjustment of that person to a depersonalizing political and institutional framework. While campaigning the future president may say anything he wants, but after election he must be the head of a viable governing coalition. The problem with regard to the "programmatic unity and persistence" to which Whitehead refers is that it is not a "given" but an aspiration that national leadership should always fulfill this difficult combination of stabilizing and reformist roles. A thorough reexamination of the presidential tradition should therefore distinguish among several (interrelated) questions. In the early stages of state building and democratic development, the question is: Can presidential leadership really emerge in the absence of a national electorate capable of propelling it to plebiscitarian heights? As society becomes more complex and democracy allows for an enormous diversity of pressures, the paramount query becomes: How in fact do presidents try to govern? What kind of coalition do they try to build? How do they manage to respond to conflicting interests and at the same time try to assert a measure of autonomous, generalized power?

In the following subsections I argue that there was a time in Brazil, up to the Revolution of 1930, when the presidential system was primitive and weak because it lacked the plebiscitarian "push" of a numerous national electorate. The office was finally expanded and strengthened by Getúlio Vargas between 1930 and 1945, but it is crucial to inquire how much of that expansion was due to the plebiscitarian energy assumed in the theory of presidentialism. After World War II, an electorate capable of providing plebiscitarian support began to emerge and the development of mass communications gradually allowed instant contact with the mass public. Far from consolidating the system, these developments seem to have made Brazilian presidentialism utterly unstable: the difficulties related to "depersonalization" became glaringly obvious.

The First Republic (1889–1930)

Despite some resistance from monarchists and parliamentarists, the presidential model was chosen in the early days of the republic and remains the basic feature of the Brazilian institutional system. The liberals who hoped for something similar to the North American model and, on the other extreme, the intellectuals and young military officers who saw the new regime as a step toward a "republican dictatorship" based on Auguste Comte's teachings soon discovered they had created something very different. For a period of forty-one years, the presidential government of the First Republic proved to be stable but also a primitive and eminently oligarchical form of authority.

The relative stability of the First Republic was a direct reflex of the country's low level of social mobilization (in the old Deutschean sense). Presidential successions were relatively normal to the extent that they took place within an oligarchical condominium. Conflict was intraelite, mostly regional, only occasionally expanding to the numerically small urban middle sectors. It was certainly not a lapse of mind that led Dunshee de Abranches, then a federal deputy, to write that the chamber of 1896 was the power "in charge of making the next president."[4] Formally elections were direct, but the candidate nominated by the consensus of congressional leaders and accepted by the incumbent would fatally become the latter's successor. And, indeed, Prudente de Moraes had been elected president in 1894 without opposition, with 94 percent of the vote; Campos Sales (1898) and Rodrigues Alves (1902) would get more than 90 percent; Afonso Pena (1906) would climb to 98 percent. The only reservation to be expressed about these figures is that they deserve the same confidence generally accorded statistics of the First Republic, to wit, none. And this again serves to reiterate my point that intraelite conflict, though serious, did not extrapolate to the field of electoral competition. Plebiscitarian push, the crucial prerequisite of a presidential system, was clearly absent.

The first reasonably competitive presidential election took place in 1910: the so-called civilianist campaign of Rui Barbosa against a military officer, Marshal Hermes da Fonseca. Hermes won with 57 percent of the vote, but it is necessary to point out that even at this point voters amounted to only 3 percent of the total population. In 1919, with the death of Rodrigues Alves, a special election had to be called, with Epitácio Pessoa standing for the "ins" and Rui Barbosa again for the "outs." Epitácio had 71 percent of the total vote, but turnout was even lower, with the voters amounting to less than 2 percent of the total population. In 1922, in a very tense election, Arthur Bernardes beats Nilo Peçanha at the ballot box (56 percent) but faces the first of a series of rebellions undertaken by young military officers (the *tenentista* movement). The state of siege was not lifted during Bernardes's whole term of office. Luís Carlos Prestes, a rebellious young officer, undertakes a long march across the country (the "Prestes column") and becomes a national hero. The creation of the Brazilian Communist party (to which Prestes would later adhere) and labor unrest also signaled that the oligarchical condominium was losing its grip on the country. Among intellectuals, the *castilhista*, positivist authoritarian credo was clearly on the rise. In short, alternative routes to power, all of them with plebiscitarian undertones, were quickly seducing would-be political actors.

In 1926 the candidate of the "ins," Washington Luís, still draws 98 percent of the vote, but his attempt to control his own succession, four years later, was doomed to bring about the downfall of the First Republic. His nominee, Júlio Prestes, got 58 percent of a voting body now reaching the unprecedented figure of 6 percent of the total population, but instead of him it is Getúlio Vargas who takes office in 1930, as military chief of the revolution. It is worth noting that even this last election pitted entire states against others, rather than reflecting widespread competition among a national electorate. Júlio Prestes had an average of 85 percent of the vote in the states where he won; the oppositionist Getúlio Vargas carried only three states (Rio Grande do Sul, Paraíba, and Minas Gerais), but had the same 85 percent in them. Political conflict took place among states, hence among regional oligarchies, not among different sections of an autonomous electorate.

If plebiscitarian push was not forthcoming, where did the presidents of this period get their support? Historians seem generally agreed that the key was an arrangement called "politics of the governors" *(política dos governadores)*, framed by Campos Sales (1898–1902). It was in essence an institutional pact by means of which the states (especially the two largest, Minas Gerais and São Paulo) supported the president of the republic (who had, needless to say, predominated in the nomination process), and the president, standing for the whole federal government, reciprocated by refraining from any interference in the internal affairs of the states. In other words, stability was bought at the price of not taking up the active reformist role that presidentialists regard as one of the superiorities of the system. The virtually unanimous evaluation among historians is that the "politics of the governors" had disastrous consequences for the course of Brazilian political development because it legalized an oligarchical single party within each state and dramatically retarded the growth of a national electorate. Dissidents in each state had to choose between being coopted by the dominant group and facing dire consequences. At the federal level, the "politics of the governors" was based on an unabashed resort to what came to be known as "beheading" *(degola)*, that is, nonrecognition by the proper congressional commission of the election of any deputies considered distasteful to the dominant coalition who happened to have won at the ballot box. The consequence, it goes without saying, was that no stable opposition ever took shape during the First Republic, let alone stable national parties, since the very existence of the latter would imply a certain degree of independence of the legislature vis-à-vis the executive.[5]

Lacking a national electorate and institutionalized opposition, the country recognized conflicts only when they appeared in the guise of serious dissensions among the large states. This is why the "politics of the governors" is often described as the functional equivalent of the "moderating power" exerted personally by the king during the nineteenth century. Just like the royal power, the scheme articulated by Campos Sales meant that the apex of the system (the presidential office) was not really subject to political competition; quite the contrary, it functioned as the regulating power that set (and restricted) the scope of the electoral process. But since that regulating power, unlike the monarch, had to be chosen every four years by those whom it was supposed to regulate, it had to allow the regulated extensive autonomy, a broad gray area between the private and public spheres, petrifying rather primitive forms of domination at the state and local levels. With the downfall of the First Republic, who would fulfill the function until then ascribed to the "governors" scheme? One is tempted to say the armed forces would, but the fact is that they did not at that moment possess the organizational strength and the separate identity required for that role. The military would emerge with such characteristics at the end of World War II, not before. For the time being, the embryo of a new centralization, namely presidential charisma, lay dormant within the oligarchical system itself.

The Getulian Cycle (1930–1954)

The Revolution of 1930, which brought Getúlio Vargas to power, expanded the presidential office and identified it with a project of state building, economic modernization, and national assertion. The achievements of the Getulian cycle can be measured not only through indicators of industrialization but also by the lasting presence of some of the institutional arrangements then established, such as the proportional electoral system initially introduced by the electoral code of 1932 and the corporatist model of interest representation that took shape toward the late thirties.

My historical argument, to repeat, is that the "charismatic" leadership implicit in Brazilian (and Latin American) presidentialism is hard to come by, and dangerous when it does come. This section looks at the very special circumstances under which this form of authority first appeared in Brazil.[6] The fact is that Vargas's rise to power was not preceded by anything even remotely resembling "charismatic" leadership. The previous section established that plebiscitarian electoral support was out of the question, given the low level of social mobilization, the underdevelopment of communications, widespread poverty, and the practical restrictions on the suffrage then prevailing—not to mention that Getúlio actually lost the election of 1930. The revolutionary movement itself was undertaken by dissident elite groups, not by a broad mass movement. Vargas's position as military chief was a consequence of political arrangements that reserved that position for the governor of Rio Grande do Sul, and not of a particularly buoyant personality or leadership style, which in fact he had not developed at that time.

How then did Vargas become a national leader of the first magnitude? The answer is clearly that he consolidated that condition step by step, capitalizing partial victories and especially the substantive results of a variety of governmental policies. Ex post factum, all of this undoubtedly amounts to an epic change, a turning point in the evolution of Brazilian governmental structures: a veritable cycle of state building, or state founding. We can argue forever whether the skill that Getúlio Vargas demonstrated in this process was in some sense an expression of "charisma," but the point I am making is simply that there was no prior plebiscitarian or mass identification capital on which he could draw. The perception of Vargas as a statesman expressed a gradual understanding and an a posteriori acceptance of policies conceived and implemented by a small circle up to 1937, and indeed by a dictatorial regime from 1937 to 1945. If any remarkable personality trait were to be emphasized during Vargas's first few years in power, it would be rather his cautious style and his sober evaluation of the distance between the protofascist rhetoric of a "strong state" and the reality of the country at that time. In other words, we are here dealing with a case of legitimation through substantive results, or effectiveness, and not with charismatic leadership in the usual meaning of the term. The newly expanded presidential office grew stronger as it proved capable of gradually strengthening the central government vis-à-vis regional oligarchies, of containing the disruptive impact of the international financial crisis on the country, of redirecting the Brazilian economy toward industrialization, and generally of introducing new regulations in a number of spheres.[7]

Saying that the Getulian cycle derived a great deal of its strength from policy effectiveness or substantive results leads of course to a different understanding of the etiology of presidential authority. In my interpretation, plebiscitarian push is neither a necessary condition for the emergence of effective leadership nor a sufficient one for its continuity. If the Getulian cycle began with a central power that was more apparent than real, without the charismatizing force of a strongly mobilized electorate, without strong national parties, without a modern and cohesive military organization; if at its inception it was in fact based on an extremely conflictive coalition of elite groups, it does then seem that the personal and institutional requirements implicit in the theory of charismatic presidentialism seem implausible in this major case. After a while, Getúlio Vargas did assert his personal power, expand the presidency, and capitalize on the diffuse support accruing to a major mass leader, but he brought none of these resources with him when he arrived in Rio de Janeiro in October of 1930.

The interpretation of the Vargas cycle I am putting forward is that his leadership grew gradually, and that it grew as he gave effective responses to an unusually broad policy agenda (a veritable "state-building" cycle). There were, on one hand, demands that had been ripening for a long time (e.g., electoral reform, labor unions) and that could be implemented immediately, with important gains in legitimation. And there were, on the other hand, other policies, such as trade negotiations and incentives to import-substitutive industries, which had to be undertaken as short-run responses to the economic crisis, some even without a clear perception of their indirect effects. Military victory against the counterrevolution backed by the state of São Paulo in 1932 also helped to increase Vargas's stature considerably. From 1935 to 1938, tough repression against communist and *integralista* rebellions also provided ample room for Getúlio Vargas to assert his personal power and engage in an organized propaganda effort centered on the cult of his own personality. In short, substantial results were achieved simultaneously in a variety of arenas, from infrastructural to symbolic ones. The enhancement of the presidential role, hence of Vargas's "charismatic" leadership, was coextensive with the formulation, implementation, and glorification of those various policies. The expansion of the central state machinery and of the public sector, as an abstract proposition, had itself become a legitimating symbol, given the widespread perception that liberalism and extreme federalism had led to virtual anarchy. In practice, that expansion meant adopting specific policies the effect of which was to expand social and political rights, to contain right- and left-wing extremism, and to redirect the economy toward nationalism and industrialization. Striving for economic autonomy was also linked to growing concerns with military security and national (cultural) identity. Personal power, charismatic leadership, and the like are therefore names that we give to a complex process: the successful articulation of this broad policy agenda and of the political coalition capable of putting it into effect.

The reasoning just sketched suggests that the thirties and forties were a turning point in Brazilian history. It can only be compared, as a cycle of institutional growth, to the pacification of the country in the 1840s, which allowed for a period of prosperity and a reasonably stable, quasi-parliamentary monarchy. At the end of Vargas's Estado Novo, in 1945, that exceptional set of circumstances had clearly come to an end. From Vargas's return to power in 1950 until the early sixties, diffuse support through plebiscitarian mobilization was theoretically available but proved utterly insufficient for, if not incompatible with, political stability. The overall results are well known: a serious political and military crisis led to Vargas's suicide in 1954; his political heir, Juscelino Kubitscheck, was reasonably successful in promoting industrialization but unable to ensure continuity through the election of his successor. Elected to the presidency in October of 1960, the oppositionist candidate, Jânio Quadros, resigned in August 1961, paving the way for a series of crises that ultimately led to the democratic breakdown of March 31, 1964.

The "Democratic Experiment" (1945–1964)

The conclusion of the preceding sections is clearly that presidentialism was not subjected to a real test, in Brazil, until the end of World War II. If our emphasis on plebiscitarian "push" is accepted, the political system of the First Republic (1889–1930) hardly meets this defining criterion of a presidential system, given its totally oligarchical character and the minuscule proportion of the potential electorate actually voting. The first "Getulian" period (1930–45) began revolutionary and ended dictatorial. From 1945 to 1964, the social, economic, and institutional structures of the country became more modern and complex. Electoral participation grew slowly (13 percent of the total population in 1945, 22 percent in 1960), but elections became competitive and truly national in scope. There emerged, unmistakably, a "political market." Presidents had to seek both popular (plebiscitarian) and coalitional (congressional, interest group) support, thus bringing the contradictory character of the presidential process glaringly to the surface. Reviewing this Brazilian "experiment in democracy," as the period 1945–64 has been called, is thus crucial for my argument.[8] Why were Getúlio Vargas, Jânio Quadros, and João Goulart—three out of the five presidents of the period—unable to complete their terms of office? Was such instability due to the presidentialist system as such, or to a different or more complex combination of causes?

Let us first look at that emerging political market. Since 1964, a favorite explanation of the crisis of "populist democracy" (as that period is often called) has been the emergence of the urban masses as a decisive political actor. Presidential candidates, so the argument goes, were now forced to appeal to a poverty-stricken and demanding urban electorate, which in fact became the pivotal part of their national constituency. This led them to "populism," that is, to embrace reformist symbols and proposals, obviously with varying degrees of sincerity and without firm linkages with organized sources of support. Once elected, they had to face a national legislature that was both powerful and responsive to an opposite constellation of interests and expectations. The constitution of 1946, in line with Brazilian institutional tradition, provided for a senate, in which all states were equally represented, and a chamber, in which the smaller states where clearly overrepresented.[9]

There is a lot to be said for this hypothesis, but it clearly needs complementation as an account of the instability of Brazilian presidentialism under the "populist republic." First, there is the demographic fact. Urban population, defined as the proportion living in towns and cities above twenty thousand, was only 15 percent in 1940, 20 percent in 1950, and 30 percent in 1960. Populist politicians might (and did) play games with the growing plebiscitarian potential of the cities, but trusting it blindly—and here the word "market" is quite to the point—would certainly have been a mistake: this was a potential available to and contested by a number of populist entrepreneurs. Remaining at a very aggregate level, a number of sociological tracts on populism have failed to underline the extent to which "intrapopulistic" competition made for instability. It was now much easier for a variety of enterprising politicians to feed themselves on mass politics, but more often than not this meant competition among would-be charismatic leaders (generally presidential candidates) as well as vetoes of the incumbent's attempts to capitalize on that potential. Brazil, let us recall, is a federation, with distinct political subsystems in the different states. Rapid change made it possible for such careers to emerge at least in the most populous states. São Paulo, for example, had been becoming highly urbanized and industrialized since the interwar period. Not by chance, a former *interventor* (appointed governor) of the time of the Estado Novo, Adhemar de Barros, emerged as a key vote getter after 1945. When Getúlio Vargas started playing with his checkerboard with an eye on the elections of 1950, one of his first moves was a mutual support/nonaggression pact with Adhemar de Barros. In like manner, presidential candidates, state governors, and even mayors of capital cities would often drain off some of the plebiscitarian water on which presidents depended in the ensuing years.[10]

One obvious question here is why couldn't political parties channel or somehow circumscribe intrapopulistic competition. The role of political parties in Brazil is a complex story, to which I will return. Let us now look only at the early days of the populistic republic. It was Getúlio Vargas himself who had the idea of trying to ensure the continuity of his developmental project by creating two distinct and to some extent conflictive political parties: the PSD (Social Democratic party), representing the more conservative wing, notably landowning interests and the electorate of small towns and rural areas, and the PTB (Brazilian Labor party), combining the whole system of state-controlled labor unions with nationalist industrialists who had prospered under the Estado Novo.[11] This strange-bedfellows arrangement has been subjected to a variety of analyses, some underlining its unsurpassable sagacity, others its congenital impossibility. Some mutual misgivings were indeed visible from the beginning. Picking a candidate in 1949–50 was for the PSD a thorny dilemma. The final choice, Cristiano Machado, a colorless politician from Minas Gerais, was perfect for a party intent on avoiding division but unbecoming for a party intent on winning. As the campaign unfolded and Vargas, supported by the PTB, appeared a likely winner, PSD leaders quickly began to "Christianize" the party's candidate. *Christianizing* (obviously after the candidate's name) became a popular term in Brazilian politics, meaning more or less the opposite of *bolting*—that is, abandoning one's own candidate and supporting the opponent, but softly, always keeping the appearance that the former commitment still holds. Valenzuela has suggested that this sort of behavior is exacerbated by presidentialism, and he may well be right. With so much at stake (the zero-sum nature of presidential contests), party unity becomes particularly difficult to sustain when defeat looms ahead. Sizable portions of the PSD-PTB alliance would again "Christianize" Marshal Henrique Lott in 1960, when Jânio Quadros began to appear unbeatable. Followers of "Jango" (Lott's running mate) and of Quadros actually created a number of "Jan-Jan" electoral committees, splitting the ticket to bring about an ominous partnership (Quadros/Goulart).

What about the UDN (National Democratic Union), the liberal opposition to the Estado Novo, personification par excellence of the anti-Vargas sentiment? With due allowance for the fact that Brazilian parties have not been very ideological, UDN opposition to Vargas was based on a recognizable set of ideological orientations. *Udenismo* stood for an elitist, status-conscious, change-resisting, middle-class outlook, and this was true at the national as well as the provincial levels. Conservative landowners were probably as influential in the UDN as in the PSD, but the UDN's business connections were generally internationalist, at a time when nationalism and industrial protectionism were on the rise. Government intervention and state enterprise, expanded by the Varguista coalition of technocrats, leftists, and military nationalists, were generally resisted by UDN leaders. Recent studies have suggested that the policies actually implemented by Vargas's second government were not as statist/nationalist as many have thought, but defeated Udenistas certainly expected them to have that character. Here, in this game of appearance and reality, is perhaps where the key to the whole Getulian tragedy lies. Politics, as we have suggested, was becoming plebiscitarian, or populistic, a trend the UDN abhorred out of both style and interest. Udenistas diffusely felt that deep—one is tempted to say holistic—differences about the future of Brazilian society were staked on a method—plebiscitarian elections—whose reliability they were far from convinced of.[12]

Needless to say, ideological conflicts of this sort are not a rare phenomenon. Why did they seem especially difficult to manage during Vargas's second government? Why did they keep fermenting until the final explosion? Dahl's concept of peaceful contestation seems useful here. There are polities, or stages in the development of a given polity, where a disposition to accept the adversary as a legitimate contender in a peaceful game is simply absent. In such stages and polities, the divide between politics and war is quite narrow. Perhaps the oligarchical system of the First Republic, the Revolution of 1930, and then Vargas's Estado Novo retarded Brazilian political development on that dimension. Or perhaps we are dealing here with something that deserves a specific label. Seen as a sociopsychological process, I submit, plebiscitarian personalist identification has a negative face, an equally personalized antagonism that, lacking a better term, I propose to call rejection of the person. In the case of Getúlio Vargas (as well as of Perón and many other Latin American charismatic leaders), past wrongdoings, the dictatorship, policy disagreements, changes that many abhorred, in short, a variety of causes that the literature has amply documented, condensed themselves to arouse that kind of rejection. The zero-sum atmosphere of a presidential election undoubtedly made the hated figure more threatening and the rejection more rancorous.

The kind of political hatred we are talking about can be dangerous in a country where "peaceful contestation" is not yet clearly established. Let us recall that the elections of 1945, held immediately after Vargas's deposition, had themselves been preceded by a series of negative circumstances. Sensing the approaching end of the dictatorship, Vargas maneuvered to stay in power through some sort of pseudo election. One maneuver was the incentive he gave to the *queremista* movement (from the slogan "Queremos Getúlio," meaning "We want Getúlio to run and thus remain president"). Hastily organized, the election was fought between two high-ranking military officers, Marshal Eurico Dutra for the PSD (with Vargas's decisive endorsement at the last minute) and Brigadier Eduardo Gomes for the anti-Vargas UDN. During Dutra's government, Vargas showed up only a few times at the senate and then studiously confined himself to his fazenda in Rio Grande do Sul. In February of 1949, he exceptionally gave an interview, admitting he would run in 1950: "Yes, I will come back," he told journalist Samuel Wainer; "I will come back, but not as a politician: as a mass leader." Tancredo Neves was probably alluding to this interview a few years ago when he coined a curious verb to reinterpret Vargas's decision. According to Tancredo, Vargas had "plebiscited" his past; plebiscited, that is, the fifteen years he had held power, including the seven years as dictator. He plebiscited them and gained the approval of 49 percent of the voters, 1.5 million more than the UDN candidate, Eduardo Gomes. The context of Vargas's plebisciting was, however, a rancorous one. One quote may suffice as illustration. On June 1, 1950, four months before election day, the journalist Carlos Lacerda, on his way toward becoming a major UDN leader, wrote in his Rio-based newspaper: "Mr. Getúlio Vargas, senator, must not run for the presidency. If he does run, he must be defeated. If he wins, he must be prevented from taking office. If he does take office, we must resort to revolution to prevent him from governing."[13]

If our previous analysis is right, Vargas's "charisma" was to a large extent a product of his governing effectiveness between 1930 and 1945. By 1950, of course, he could command a formidable amount of diffuse support. But even his mythological prestige had to be sustained against bitter opposition and growing social demands by policy results, the congruence of which was bound not to occur this time around. Extremely serious conflicts had surfaced in every policy arena.[14] Regulative policies now were no longer virtually consensual laws, like the electoral code of 1932, or policies capable of creating new bases of support, like the paternalist/corporatist labor laws, but rather antistrike legislation, which cut deep into his own coalition, or laws relating to foreign capital and profit remittances, which pitted nationalist and internationalist positions violently against each other—under the oversight, let us add, of a press freed from dictatorial censorship. In the accumulative arena, instead of a consensus forced by the war situation upon a small group of policy-makers, the country now witnessed mobilization on highly divisive issues, such as the creation of Petrobrás (the governmental monopoly on oil).[15] Redistributive measures were equally unlikely to bolster a wide consensus behind Vargas.

Wages had to be kept down as a means to control inflation, obviously with the resistance of the now much stronger labor unions. From 1953 on Vargas began court-
ing organized labor through his minister of labor, João Goulart. His decision to
grant a substantial wage increase on May 1, 1954, already looked like a desperate attempt to mobilize mass support against a business and military opposition well on
its way to becoming open conspiracy. But populistic plebiscitarian support was not
really there, and an attempt to mobilize it quickly alienated part of the support Vargas did have within the elite. Isolated, hounded, humiliated, he committed suicide
on August 24, 1954.

Juscelino Kubitscheck (1955–60), regarded as a Vargas heir, was elected by the
PSD-PTB alliance, with João Goulart as his running mate. In 1955, cleavage between those two spiritual families, one broadly *Varguista* and the other anti-Vargas
was again in the air. But Vargas's suicide had performed the miracle of revitalizing
the popular base of *Varguismo*, now represented by the alliance PSD-PTB. Indirectly it had also forged military support for the alliance. Marshal Lott's so-called
prolegality coup *(golpe da legalidade)*, which formally speaking amounted to the
deposition of two successive presidents, paradoxically ensured that the elections of
1955 would be contested normally and that the winner, Juscelino Kubitscheck,
would in fact take office.[16]

Elected with only 35 percent of the vote, and a modest 12 percent in the country's
major state, São Paulo, Juscelino wielded power judiciously, without plebiscitarian
raptures. Time showed that Kubitscheck's economic policies were generally acceptable to the UDN. Adopting a more receptive attitude toward foreign investment
(e.g., the automobile industry) and fostering a national mystique of modernization
and economic growth, Juscelino Kubitscheck largely disarmed the time bomb of
anti-Varguista resentment. Vis-à-vis the legislature, Juscelino made the most of the
"consociational" features of the system (more on this below), seeking multiparty approval for his proposals. Of course, these strategies achieved stability at a price. His
opponents seized on the claim that modernization was only a facade for patronage
and corrupt payoffs. Some pointed to the freezing of a conservative status quo with
regard to the agrarian structure and to labor relations in the countryside. Confronted with these contradictions and with the emergence of a truly national electorate, the end of Kubitscheck's term dramatically illustrates the weakness of diffuse
support for elected presidents and the extent to which it can be mobilized against
them; indeed, it showed the limits of the underlying faith in the charismatization
of presidential authority through substantive policy results. Juscelino staked everything on economic growth and on the climate of optimism he had skillfully created. But rising inflation and a reduction of the growth rate again accentuated divisions in the country, as the electoral campaign began. Juscelino chose not to
engage his prestige fully in the presidential succession, but the defeat of the PSD-
PTB candidate, Marshal Henrique Lott, in the elections of 1960 was an unmistak-
able setback for him. First, the landslide in favor of Jânio Quadros meant that a

large proportion of the electorate endorsed the charges of mismanagement and corruption levied against Kubitscheck during the campaign. Second, it was a coup de grâce for the PSD-PTB alliance, on which he depended to come back in 1965 and, according to some interpretations, on which the stability of the whole political system was based. From this point on, ideological differences began to sharpen between Vargas's two creatures.[17]

Jânio Quadros was the clearest example of the plebiscitarian entrepreneur, the antiestablishment, antiparties, modernizing demagogue. With some literary abuse, we may perhaps say that Quadros's plebiscitarian shock was just too much. The freest and most truly national of the four contests of the period, Quadros's election led to a series of unfortunate developments: his own resignation in August of 1961; the military veto of the inauguration of João Goulart as vice president; the latter's inauguration under a hastily improvised parliamentary formula; an unstable government; growing ideological polarization in the country; a plebiscite determining return to presidentialism in January 1963; and finally the military takeover of March 31, 1964, which would last for twenty-one years. Why did it happen?

A look at the institutional parameters complements the analysis presented so far. Quadros's election, as has been said, was a plebiscitarian shock of formidable proportions, dramatizing the weakness and fragmentation of the Brazilian party system. There are, about this question, two main lines of interpretation. One stresses the low level of prior party institutionalization and argues that other party-weakening factors were at work in the post-1945 institutional system. Party formation at the beginning of the "democratic experiment" took place in an organizational space already heavily occupied by executive bureaucratic or alternative representative structures, such as corporatism. The presidential system itself, federalism-cum-financial-dependence of the member states on the central government, plus the very permissive model of proportional representation, made party development even more difficult. Rapid social change and the emergence of a highly competitive political market thus "prematurely" weakened the largest parties; by 1960 the PSD, on whose shoulders the responsibility for institutional stability was primarily placed, was itself badly divided. Under Goulart (1961–64), instead of acting as buffers, the party system and the national legislature began to reflect and exacerbate the ideological polarization going on in society at large.[18]

The other line of interpretation says that there was nothing inherently wrong with the electoral and party systems. The difficulty lay in the coalitional nature of Brazilian presidentialism, that is, in the fact that all presidents of the period under consideration resorted to "grand coalitions" as a means to ensure both regional and party support in the legislature. Coalitions much larger than those needed for a legislative majority tended to reduce government effectiveness and to raise payoff costs intolerably (clientelism). "Under presidentialism," writes Abranches, "unstable coalitions can directly affect *(atingir)* the presidential office."[19]

This interpretation implicitly says that a mechanism (large coalitions) designed to stabilize may itself become a cause of instability. This may be true under specific circumstances, but it would seem more accurate to say that coalitions had to be large exactly because the parties were too weak to counteract the divisive forces of federalism, of presidential (and gubernatorial) executivism, and of a rapidly changing sociopolitical context. Neither can it be taken for granted that effectiveness was uniformly low throughout the period; it certainly was not, if we judge in terms of government-induced industrialization. Finally, it seems also difficult to reconcile the low-effectiveness hypothesis with the abrupt nature of the three crises analyzed here, namely, Vargas's suicide, Quadros's resignation, and Goulart's overthrow.

Twenty-eight years later, former president Jânio Quadros was still offering vague allusions to "concessions he would not make" as the explanation for his resignation.[20] We probably will never know what "hidden forces" he was talking about on August 25, 1961. He might be referring to the congress; to members of the UDN itself, such as Carlos Lacerda, who by then were violently attacking his "independent foreign policy"; or to a combination of these. Why couldn't he, with a massive 48 percent of the nominal votes in a three-candidate, single-ballot election get at least the same level of legislative cooperation that Kubitscheck had? Why couldn't he wait until the legislative elections of 1962 and then try to win a congressional majority? The answer to these questions, aside from personality traits, is clearly that Jânio's belief in plebiscitarian charisma had gone a bit too far. Enchanted by de Gaulle's nascent Fifth Republic, he seems to have thought that resignation would produce a resounding plebiscitarian acclamation, conferring superpowers on him. It did not.

An obvious institutional difficulty in the 1945–64 "democratic experiment" was that the constitution of 1946 did not require that presidential and vice presidential candidates belong to the same party. The election of 1960 thus produced a dangerous result: conservative (?), UDN-backed Quadros as president, and the Varguista João Goulart, with left-wing support, as his vice president. On August 25, 1961, the congress accepted the president's resignation at once, defining it as a unilateral decision, and thus emptied the plebiscitarian commotion that Quadros might be seeking. Goulart, then visiting China, was the successor. This is where Quadros's military ministers came in. Goulart's brother-in-law, Leonel Brizola, then governor of Rio Grande do Sul, organized a military resistance in his home state. Parliamentarism was on the way out.

The parliamentary experiment of 1961–63 is often asserted to have been a failure. This may well be so, if the expectation was that it would do more than avoid a civil war. At that time, an articulate parliamentary demand did not exist in Brazil. There were isolated proponents of parliamentarism in the national legislature (see below), but the constitutional amendment of 1961, devised and introduced by political leaders who had little or no commitment to parliamentary government, was only a way out of the emergency. Improvised, lacking any prior debate or preparation, going against the grain of those plebiscitarian times, it was evidently taken as provisional.[21] So, the "failure," if failure there was, can hardly be explained by the specific features of the parliamentary model of 1961. Perhaps a handful of constitutional lawyers can remember the exact details of the formula then adopted. I have never heard of a political scientist discussing them in the classroom. Yet the specific architecture of that parliamentary experiment does seem relevant for Brazil's current debate, so I will come back to it in the second part of this chapter.

Would it have been different if Brazil had adopted a parliamentary system in 1945? In the early days of the so-called populist republic, as I have pointed out, rancor against Getúlio Vargas and diffuse, but deep, policy differences might have impaired either system. Would Getúlio "plebiscite" his dictatorial past running for the presidency, or would he seek to become prime minister? The former course would certainly represent a danger for a dual executive, parliamentary system. As to the prime ministership, Getúlio's chances would depend on an assiduous presence in the congress and on his ability to overcome resentments. Instead of coming back "as a mass leader," he would try to do it as a strong congressional leader. Under these hypotheses, a parliamentary system might have been less traumatic and, judging from Kubitscheck's more parliamentary style, just as effective with regard to development policies.

How about 1961–64? Here again, a lot would depend on the method by which the chief of state was chosen, and on the extent of his prerogatives. We may assume, however, that a parliamentary system adopted in 1945 would have already arrived at stable definitions in this respect. Jânio's plebiscitarian shock would seem less likely. His resignation (from the presidency) would again be less traumatic; instead of an unacceptable vice president, another election would be called, or the congress would choose a successor indirectly. If he resigned from the prime ministership, we would be facing a routine change in parliamentary systems. As to Goulart, we may reason by analogy to the case of Vargas. Ideological polarization plus rancorous opposition to the person are dangerous in any system. Let us recall, however, that Jango ran twice for the vice presidency, balancing both Juscelino's (1955) and Lott's (1960) tickets. In neither opportunity did he have Getúlio's stature as a plebiscitarian candidate against the whole establishment. In this respect he was far inferior even to Jânio Quadros. As a candidate for the prime ministership, he would be even weaker; if eventually he arrived there, he would carefully avoid drifting toward the left, pulled by plebiscitarian competitors. In this case, the outcome would certainly have been better: the 1964 breakdown might have been avoided.

The Parliamentarist Demand

In the first part of this chapter I traced the broad outlines of presidentialism in Brazil, showing that it evolved from an oligarchical condominium to an unstable combination of extreme plebiscitarian and consociational features. Here I attempt to explain the growth of the parliamentarist demand and specify what competing parliamentary formulas may eventually command significant support. Brazil had a quasi-parliamentary system under the nineteenth-century monarchy, but only now, after one hundred years of a republic, did a strong parliamentarist demand emerge. How can we account for this fact?

Background

The parliamentary conception of government died out quickly as the republican regime established in 1889 consolidated itself. The main reason for decline was undoubtedly its identification with the monarchy. The Federalista party of Rio Grande do Sul, for example, had a noted parliamentarist and prominent member of the last monarchical cabinet—Gaspar da Silveira Martins—among its leaders. An extremely bloody civil war broke out between federalistas and Comte-inspired republicans in 1893. Martins's acceptance of a federative but parliamentary republic was suspected of insincerity and restorationist intentions.

Under the First Republic, as suggested, the issue of parliamentarism could hardly arise, given the dominant concern with strengthening the presidency, and central authority generally, over regionalism. Yet consociational features already existed in embryo. The first constitution (1889) had established a very decentralized federation, the four-year presidential term without reelection, and a bicameral national legislature. After the Revolution of 1930, the latent paradox unfolds: political institutions become more plebiscitarian (the Getulian cycle) but, at the same time, more consociational. Starting with the electoral code of 1932, the constitutions of 1934 and 1946 and evolving political practices would consolidate that model. From then on, in democratic periods, the Brazilian political system has preserved those initial features and reinforced them with proportional representation, multipartism and "grand coalitions." Thus, an explicit parliamentarist demand was weak for many decades, but the consociational features of the system have always provided a space for its lingering presence.

Another important factor here was the fear of Vargas and Varguismo on the part of the UDN (National Democratic Union) and of liberal politicians in some smaller parties. This sort of conservative or antipopulist liberalism generally fell short of parliamentarism, but its sustained critique of plebiscitarian presidentialism probably helped a small group of parliamentary devotees to sustain their own fight. The most persistent spokesman for the latter group was Raul Pilla, a federal deputy from Rio Grande do Sul. Pilla was constantly reelected by the tiny Partido Libertador and belonged to the same spiritual family as Assis Brasil, one of the main drafters of the electoral code of 1932.[22]

Pilla's preaching was in the air in 1961, when parliamentarism was improvised as a solution to the impasse over João Goulart's taking office. According to the Ato Adicional then adopted, a plebiscite would be called in 1965, nine months before the expiration of Goulart's term as chief of state. If that plebiscite decided for the continuation of parliamentarism, succeeding presidents would be elected indirectly by the congress; in like manner, the member states would adapt their constitutions to a parliamentary structure, once incumbent state governors completed their terms of office. In other words, the improvised dual executive system of 1961 was positioned to evolve toward "pure" parliamentarism—on paper, at any rate.[23]

With the military takeover of March 31, 1964, the parliamentarist demand vanished from view, for obvious reasons. But even here, it is worth recalling that military authoritarianism in Brazil did not go as far as abolishing the legislature altogether. Existing parties were declared extinct, but only one year and a half after the coup, two "provisional organizations," which became ARENA (Alliance for National Renewal) and MDB (Brazilian Democracy Movement), were permitted to function as parties. Indirect presidential elections were simply a means to extract civilian legitimation for military nominees, but legislative elections did take place at all three levels, thus providing some room for the opposition to survive.[24]

The problem, of course, was that parliamentarist demands became "unreal" under such a militarized atmosphere. The priorities of the opposition (guerrilla movements aside) in its various shades were rather to reestablish the rule of law, to do away with casuistic electoral legislation, to prevent human rights violations—especially after 1967, when left-wing armed groups began to act and harsh repression became widespread. The Brazilian military did not establish a dictatorship as closed as that of Pinochet in Chile, but neither did they come up with a consistent plan of political reform. Indirect elections for the presidency, state governorships, and major mayoral offices were reminiscent of old UDN preaching; toying with the idea of a two-party system may also have had the same inspiration, but the proportional electoral system was kept at all three levels. Centralizing tax resources at the federal level and stripping the congress of any real influence over their global allocation, the authoritarian process had far-reaching consequences, cutting deep into congressmen's traditional role orientations. To a far greater degree than in pre-1964 legislatures, they became low-level procurators of narrow regional or municipal interests, coming to Brasília to expedite specific appropriations rather than to legislate or represent broad political claims.

Plebiscitarian practices and expectations began to grow sharply as support for the military regime began to dwindle. After 1974, a turning point, senatorial elections in the major states became clearly plebiscitarian, expressing the enlarged scope of oppositionist sentiment. In 1979, the Amnesty Law allowed pre-1964 politicians to return from exile, most notably Leonel Brizola, now the only surviving heir of the old Varguista tradition. More decisively still, the heterogeneous front that opposed the military regime finally achieved complete unity in 1984, by means of the *diretas-já* (direct elections now) campaign. The purpose was to pressure the congress to approve a constitutional amendment abolishing the electoral college that would choose President Figueiredo's successor in January 1985. What those huge rallies in all major cities demanded was primarily redemocratization, but direct presidential elections then became a symbol of the democratic struggle, thus indirectly revitalizing the plebiscitarian substratum of presidentialism.[25]

The congress did not approve the *diretas-já* amendment. The return to civilian government finally took place through the electoral college itself, with the election of Tancredo Neves as the first civilian president after twenty-five years. By this time, Tancredo Neves was definitely committed to calling a constitutional congress. In his inaugural speech, Tancredo would already announce the creation of a drafting commission headed by a senior politician and jurist, Afonso Arinos de Melo Franco, a former Udenista and noted parliamentarist. But Tancredo entered the hospital on the eve of the inauguration and died thirty-seven days later, without taking office. It thus fell to President José Sarney, Tancredo's vice president, to appoint the Provisional Commission for Constitutional Studies, or Afonso Arinos Commission (he did this only in August of that year) and formally call the constitutional congress through an amendment approved by the congress in February of 1986. When the commission began to work, the Sarney government was in dire straits, and this in theory might have weakened the presidential mystique and led to a parliamentarist proposal; but the congress was no less discredited and the two governing parties (PFL—Liberal Front party and PMDB—Brazilian Democratic Movement), which were badly split, produced the opposite expectation.

From the Arinos Commission to Sarney's Day After

The fifty-member commission finally appointed by President Sarney in August 1985 had a solid majority of jurists, many of them with significant direct political experience; but it also included important businessmen, like the São Paulo industrialists Antônio Ermírio de Moraes and Luís Eulálio Vidigal, the latter being at that time the president of FIESP—the powerful São Paulo Federation of Industries; renowned social scientists and writers like Celso Furtado, Hélio Jaguaribe, and Jorge Amado; respected labor representatives such as José Francisco da Silva, of the Confederation of Agricultural Workers, and Walter Barelli, of DIEESE, a São Paulo–based research center supported by the unions; a handful of religious, women's, and ethnic representatives. Some of the members held ministerial positions at that time: Celso Furtado himself (culture), Paulo Brossard (justice) and Rafael de Almeida Magalhães (social security). Célio Borja, a noted jurist, was then a personal advisor to the president and was later appointed to the Supreme Court.

This commission of "notables," as it was often called, was widely resented as an intrusion into the sphere of the constitutional congress to be elected at the end of 1986, and thus became extremely controversial. At the beginning, it was often criticized by the press and "civil society" spokesmen as an official body that could only come up with progovernment proposals, which in turn meant cosmetic modifications of the constitutional status quo. As time went by, there was a sharp reversal, and the commission came under fire from the conservative press and business representatives as being too liberal (progressive), overly nationalistic, or outrightly utopian. With regard to the form of government, however, the commission was from the very beginning divided into four groups:

1. *Pure presidentialists*—those who would basically go back to the 1946 constitution

2. *Pure parliamentarists*—those preferring a system with an indirectly elected chief of state, possibly after the West German model

3. *Mild parliamentarists*—a few who would accept the figure of a coordinating minister *(Ministro-Coordenador)*, or at the most a cabinet under strong presidential influence (Finnish model), but not really a prime minister dependent on parliamentary confidence

4. *Dual executive parliamentarists*—those who would settle for a system like the French, or the Portuguese, provided that the mechanism by which the prime minister and his sphere of prerogatives were chosen were more clearly parliamentarist than in those two models

Some circumstances of the commission's debate should be noted at this point. Some of the "pure parliamentarists," such as the minister, Brossard, and the jurist, Borja, clearly did not press their case strongly enough. This may have been because of their loyalty of office to President Sarney or, more likely, to an evaluation that pure parliamentarism was simply not a viable position at that time. The climate created by the *diretas-já* campaign had seemingly made it impossible for anyone to defend the indirect election of a chief of state. It is worth noting that the commission took up this matter under the strong impact of the Cruzado plan, a stabilization scheme based on a price-and-wage freeze that had propelled President Sarney's prestige to unprecedented heights. Opposition to parliamentarism in the press and the dilemma of "cohabitation" finally brought to France by the 1986 elections could also have led the commission to a pure presidentialist position. Yet the draft finally approved and taken to President Sarney in September 1986 was basically the "dual executive" position sketched above, a French/Portuguese model with a strong "German" complement insofar as party and electoral regulations were concerned. The choice of a parliamentary system (although one retaining a directly elected president with substantial powers) was allegedly one of the reasons why President Sarney shelved the commission's report instead of sending it officially to the constitutional congress for its future debates.[26]

The struggle over the exact legal profile of the constitutional congress was going on as the Afonso Arinos Commission proceeded with its work. A number of "civil society" organizations, with substantial backing in the congress, collided head-on with President Sarney's proposal, the former demanding an "autonomous" assembly and the latter establishing that the constitutional congress would be the National Congress itself; that is, the deputies and senators to be elected in November 1986 would meet unicamerally and decide by simple majority while making the constitution and would remain afterward in their usual capacity as legislators. One

Table 8.1. General Results of 1986 Elections by Party (absolute figures)

| | State Governorships | Congress | | State Assembly |
		Senate[a]	Chamber	
PMBD	22	38	261	448
PFL	1	7	116	233
PDS	—	2	32	80
PDT	—	1	24	63
PT	—	—	16	39
Other Left	—	—	9	8
Other Right	—	1	29	67
Other	—	—	—	15
Total	(23)	49	(487)	953

a. Renewal of two-thirds of seats in twenty-three states and first senatorial election in Brasília (Federal District).

of the objections made to Sarney's proposal (which was favored by most politicians) was that the regular congress would be chosen together with state governors. This would place the dispute in an "executive" context and empty it of any constitutional debate. Another fundamental fact of this period, as noted above, was the Cruzado plan, which gave enormous authority to the president for some months and thus unequivocally affected the results of the election. The governing parties, especially the PMDB (Party of the Brazilian Democratic Movement) won twenty-two out of twenty-three state governorships and the absolute majority in both senate and chamber (see table 8.1). This enormous *inchaço* (swelling) of the PMDB and the almost complete lack of constitutional discussion during the campaign were initially detrimental to the constituents' legitimacy; worse still, they were felt to have dropped a black box over Brasília: 559 gentlemen whose constitutional ideas were unknown, to put it mildly.[27]

Yet, some sounding of the congressmen's preferences, already at the end of 1986, suggested that parliamentarist demands were not as insignificant as many would have thought. The weekly magazine *Veja*, for example, concluded from a survey that President Sarney might be able to confirm a five-year term as he wanted, but as head of state in a parliamentary system. Equally significant, some staunch parliamentarists, capable of exercising substantial leadership among their peers, had been elected; one of them was Afonso Arinos himself, now a senator from Rio de Janeiro. As the congress's debates went on, the positive effects of the Cruzado plan vanished completely, bringing President Sarney's popularity and his government's effectiveness squarely to the ground. The parliamentarist position then began to grow in the same proportion, bringing together convinced supporters of cabinet government and others who saw it as a means to shorten Sarney's term, or at least of replacing him as chief of government by a prime minister. The issue became entangled, as pointed out before, with the president's term of office, and thus pressures and favors from the executive undoubtedly contributed to the final defeat of parliamentarism. The antiparliamentary coalition was, however, much broader. When the Systematization Commission sent to the plenary a report recommending parliamentarism and a four-year term for President Sarney, it probably made a major mistake. Potential presidential candidates immediately rolled up their sleeves, adding to the presidentialist pressure. High-ranking military spokesmen publicly expressed their preference for the existing system. Fearing instability, major business leaders claimed that parliamentarism would make the stabilization effort more difficult; fearing a loss of power under a parliamentary regime, state governors mobilized opinion against the proposed change; obedient to their historical faith in the plebiscitarian presidency, the Brizolistas (PDT—Democratic Labor party) closed ranks for presidentialism, despite their frontal opposition to Sarney. Even the PT (Workers party), which claims to be the truly modern Left, gave fifteen out of sixteen votes to presidentialism. On March 22, 1988, the final vote was taken: the parliamentary proposal was defeated by 344–212. Some weeks later Sarney saw his fifth year easily confirmed. The parliamentarists, in turn, succeeded in their proposal that a plebiscite be held in 1993, thus preventing total closure of the form of government issue.

The stabilization effort did not become more effective after the congress approved both presidentialism and President Sarney's fifth year. On the contrary, inflation rates went on soaring and reached the unprecedented level of 50 percent a month in December 1989. Throughout 1989, with the country under the threat of hyperinflation, elite opinion became increasingly convinced (see survey evidence below) that Sarney's fifth year had not strengthened the government's hand against inflation. Some business sectors actually came to fear presidential discretion, convinced that inflation would get out of hand if for some reason Sarney fired his last finance minister, Maílson da Nóbrega. This rather dramatic scenario was heavily compounded by the presidential campaign itself. The possibility of a leftist president, and even of a second round contested between two leftist candidates, Lula (Workers' party) and Brizola (Democratic Labor party), undoubtedly intensified the turbulence in the economy and added to the fear of imminent ungovernability. Subjective as such evaluations inevitably are, they seem to have a bearing on the presidentialist-parliamentarist debate. For many members of the antiparliamentarist coalition of 1988, effectiveness did not increase as they hoped, and stability could have been seriously endangered.[28]

Reasons for Parliamentarism

A more analytical survey of the arguments for parliamentarism along Brazil's republican history is useful at this point. Clearly enough, the recent transition from authoritarianism brought in its wake a denser concern with political institutions in general. The idea that democracy must be consolidated, and that some institutions may help and others hinder consolidation, attracts far more attention today than in the past. For the Left, until recently, this sort of reasoning was at best irrelevant and "superstructural," at worst decidedly reactionary. Why then did the parliamentarist demand grow in Brazil in the last few years?

A preliminary answer would be that when a serious concern with political institutions begins to develop, the country's prior experience with parliamentarism becomes more important. There is, so to speak, a revalorization. One effect of that prior experience is that the presidential-parliamentary issue remained important in some circles (constitutional lawyers, politicians, some journalists), who managed to preserve a certain "literature" about it. In moments of crises, the parliamentary alternative tended to be retrieved, with greater or lesser realism. Scattered devotees constantly mobilized their resources to keep abreast of developments abroad and to bring old writings back into circulation.[29]

A second reason would be the growing perception that the rigidities of presidentialism grow increasingly dangerous as society becomes more complex. It seems worth noting that Tancredo Neves, sincerely or not, had already emphasized this argument in his inaugural lecture as prime minister, at the University of Minas Gerais:

The very expediency with which the cabinet attacks the most diverse questions, some of which have been pending for years, documents the incapacity of former presidential governments to deal with them, or even to define them conclusively. . . . [Under presidentialism] there were abundant political crises, including the last one, which gave rise to the parliamentary regime. If it has not yet demonstrated other virtues, this regime has been successful in the considerable tasks of keeping political and social forces in balance and reestablishing peace and order. From another point of view, a growing pluralism in Brazilian society would seem to recommend that fundamental decisions be made through a congress and through a collegiate system of government, in order to prevent, in a political crisis or situation of social tension, anxiety, radicalism or overriding executive power from destroying the democratic regime itself.[30]

The members of the Afonso Arinos Commission (see above) were impressed by professor Hélio Jaguaribe's historical arguments. Jaguaribe's contention was that contemporary Brazil witnesses the exhaustion of a model that was sketched by the military presidents in the early days of the republic but came to full fruition with Getúlio Vargas. This model, typical of Latin American presidentialism, is based not only on a positive evaluation of the fusion of state and governmental roles in the president, but in fact on the assumption that the latter must be a shaker and mover, an agent of modernization, a manager of the accumulative process, and an engine of social change. The historical record, according to Jaguaribe, has shown this combination of roles to be impossible. In Brazil, change-oriented presidents have suffered from severe instability and stabilizing presidents have been reactionary. Only parliamentarism can reconcile the two halves because it confers the stabilizing function on one magistrate (the chief of state) and the change-oriented role on another (the chief of government, or prime minister).[31]

This line of reasoning can be complemented by another set of historical arguments. As I have tried to show in the first part of this study, the growth of plebiscitarian presidentialism is directly linked, in the Brazilian case, to the growth of the public sector or, more broadly, to a whole cycle of state building, which involved a more active role for the state in the economy and greater legitimacy for its regulatory role vis-à-vis capital and labor, not to speak of the modernization of the armed forces and the tutelary role they took up henceforward. This broad change was in line with worldwide economic and ideological trends, that is, with the demise of old-fashioned, gendarmelike conceptions of liberalism. Enlarging the scope of the presidential office was part and parcel of that larger process.

After the constitutional congress of 1987–88, the growth of the parliamentarist demand was fostered by widespread concern with ungovernability and by fears arising from the electoral (presidential) campaign itself. The ungovernability argument emerged in close connection with the Sarney government's inability to deal with spiraling inflation but quickly came to cover a wider area. Three points, besides inflation, should be noted here. First, after a period of resistance against its allegedly utopian features, business and other elites began to realize that the constitution of 1988 had come to stay. Under the new constitutional text, the congress has a strong role in the budgetary process, from the initial "directives" (which must be in a specific law) to final approval. Legislative authority was established over a broad range of economic and administrative issues that previously fell under executive discretion. These new constitutional provisions mean that governability vitally depends on executive-legislative cooperation. The perception that this revitalization of congressional power is irreversible tends to increase the salience of the parliamentary alternative.[32]

A second point is that this formally powerful congress is presently perceived as an incompetent and wildly clientelistic body. Before the constitution was completed this perception obviously worked against parliamentarism, but after its adoption, the issue became how to change the congress's structure and behavior in the next few years. If the legislature is going to have such an active role, then it must somehow be made coresponsible for the concrete tasks of governing. It is worth noting that a number of economists, including former ministers of finance, have come to support parliamentarism as a by-product of their search for a stronger antidote to corporatism. Convinced that sectoral demands have become far more articulate then in the past, they tend to see it as one of the main causes of the country's virtual ungovernability. It is of course true that a variety of organized interests have successfully pressured both the executive and the congress in recent years. The new constitution has extended the right to unionize and other labor guarantees to previously unorganized sectors—the civil service is a case in point—and lifted the traditional ban on strikes in the so-called essential services.

Needless to say, concern with executive-legislative relations works the other way around, too. Public sector reform and economic restructuring have come to be seen as the sine qua non for development and even social peace, but it seems increasingly clear that rigid separation of powers compounds rather than helps solve that problem. From this perspective, the Brazilian situation is certainly more dramatic than that of Argentina, for example, given the inchoate and highly fragmented nature of the party system. Elected by a tiny party (see below) and unable to put together a consistent congressional basis, Collor runs the risk of becoming a lame duck less than two years after his spectacular victory at the ballot box.

But the main perception bearing on the presidentialism/parliamentarism debate has to do with the plebiscitarian substratum of presidential authority per se. As stressed before, the effectiveness of presidential power is largely a function of diffuse support, and hence of the extent, consistency, and stability of the president's popularity. In a highly inflationary economy, that form of support tends to erode quickly. The collapse of the Cruzado plan and Sarney's subsequent unpopularity—not to speak of Argentina's President Alfonsín's and Bolivia's Siles Suazo's departures before the end of their legal terms of office—have hammered this danger home rather forcefully. In a system that depends vitally on the president's popularity, for policy effectiveness as well as for institutional stability, the idea that the popularity cycle is ever shorter must be a matter for serious concern. Can the double-ballot method, ensuring an absolute majority for the president, solve that problem? This, of course, was and is the hope of many a presidentialist in Brazil, but the first experience with that method, in 1989, left some room for doubt.

Collor versus Lula: Chronicle of a Confrontation Foretold

The Brazilian electorate numbered 16 million in 1960, when Jânio Quadros was elected; in November/December of 1989, 82 million were eligible to vote, and 75 million actually went to the polls to choose between Fernando Collor de Mello (PRN—party of National Reconstruction) and Lula (PT—Workers' party). The first direct election since 1960, this was also the first experience with double balloting in Brazil. For many years, this innovation was demanded as a way to ensure stability and enhance the president's legitimacy.

The presidential campaign of 1989 actually began twelve months before, in the municipal elections of 1988. Lula's PT and Brizola's PDT (Democratic labor party) came out of that contest showing substantial results. Together, these two parties were now the governing force, at the local level, over some 23 percent of the Brazilian population, an unprecedented figure for the Left in Brazilian electoral history; more than that, they now controlled some of the country's major cities, including São Paulo, Rio de Janeiro, Porto Alegre, Vitória, Santos, and Campinas. With the

Table 8.2. Brazilian Presidential Elections, 1989: Comparison between Pre-election Polls and Actual Results

	Polls			Official Results	
Candidates	June	Oct.	Nov. 10	1st Ballot (Nov. 15)	2d Ballot (Dec. 17)
Collor (PRN)	42	26	27	28.52	42.75
Brizola (PDT)	11	15	14	15.45	—
Lula (PT)	7	14	15	16.08	37.86
Covas (PSDB)	5	9	11	10.78	—
Maluf (PDS)	4	9	9	8.28	—
Ulysses (PMBD)	5	4	4	4.43	—
Aureliano (PFL)	2	1	—	0.83	—
Afif (PL)	1	5	5	4.53	—
Freire (PCB)	1	2	2	1.06	—
Caiado (PSD)	1	1	—	0.68	—
Others	—	1	3	2.92	—
Blank/null	7	—	3	5.66	4.99
Undecided (abstentions)	14	—	7	11.94	14.40

Sources: Datafolha, June, October, and November 10 polls; TSE (Superior Electoral Court), official results.

federal government plagued by the imminence of hyperinflation and the two largest congressional parties (PMDB and PFL) in utter discredit, the image of a left-leaning election, and possibly of a second round between Lula and Brizola, began to haunt the Brazilian "establishment." This sort of apprehension became even sharper as time went by and Mário Covas, of the PSDB (Brazilian Social Democratic party), regarded as a moderate center-left alternative, kept scoring modestly in the polls.

If the Lula/Brizola scenario did not materialize, the reason was that since March the former governor of a tiny northeastern state, supported by an ad hoc party, the PRN, began to prove himself a remarkable vote getter. His support skyrocketed to more than 40 percent in the polls in May, and thus Brizola remained frozen in the neighborhood of 15 percent, with all the other candidates trailing way behind. When the official TV campaign began, on September 15, many still thought that Collor's advantage would collapse. But it didn't, and from that point on it became clear that the second balloting had become Collor against "somebody else." Table 8.2 compares preelection polls with the actual results of the first and second rounds. Clearly, at least four candidates (Brizola, Lula, Covas, and Maluf) could have been Collor's opponent, but Brizola's remarkably faithful voters in Rio de Janeiro and Rio Grande do Sul and the PT's cohesive party organization were decisive assets. With Lula's victory over Brizola (by a narrow margin), the stage was set for a dra-

Table 8.3. Seats in Federal Chamber and Presidential Votes in First Balloting by Party, 1989

	Chamber Seats, March 1987	Chamber Seats, July 1989	Votes in 1st Balloting, 1989
PMDB	53.6	39.7	4.43
PFL	23.8	20.8	0.83
PDS	6.6	5.8	8.28
PDT	4.9	5.6	15.45
PT	3.3	3.2	16.08
PRN	—	2.6	28.52
PSDB	—	9.0	10.78
Others	3.8	13.3	15.63[a]

a. Includes abstentions, null, and blank votes.

matic play. On one side was Collor, with no real party or organized societal network behind him. His strength was, firstly, the advantage he already had in the polls and in the first balloting, and secondly, the widespread perception and fear of the PT as too far to the radical Left. On the other side was Lula, a former metal worker and union leader, now the PT's hope of winning the presidency. The first poll after the first ballot showed a 52–38 split for Collor, a difference many had expected would be larger at that point. As subsequent soundings indicated consistent reductions in Collor's lead, the campaign pitched to a highly emotional tone and quickly acquired the overtones of a Right-Left confrontation.

How did the two-round method fare in this case? Can we regard it as a substantial boost to stability and governability, or was it further proof that Brazilian presidentialism is "irreformable"? A totally negative evaluation on the basis of a single case would be premature, but it does seem clear that the double-ballot method fell short of the high expectations that led to its adoption The idea that the second balloting forces the two main contenders to tone down their appeals in order to win a moderate or "centrist" vote seems clearly unwarranted in a country with steep income differentials and persistent inflation. A number of factors, including the personality of the candidates, may make for a polarizing, rather than a centripetal, logic. Secondly, the notion that consistent governing alliances arise from the electoral alliances mobilized by the two final contenders is just as fictional. In the Brazilian case, this hypothesis seems precluded by the inchoate nature and highly fragmented character of the party system. Table 8.3 compares party strength (seats) at the start of the constitutional congress (1986) and in June of 1990 with the popular vote in the first round of 1990. The picture seems clear enough. The enormous erosion of the PMDB and PFL (the governing alliance of Sarney's "New Republic") contrasts with the PT's and PDT's strong showing, not to mention Collor's PRN, which simply did not exist in 1986.

The combination of double balloting with such a party system (and permissive party legislation) actually encourages fragmentation, given the incentive to "go it alone" that all parties perceive in the first round. In the second, a few weeks later, even electoral alliances may be difficult, with no guarantee of permanence or of governing consistency. Indeed, President Collor's lack of parliamentary support and the extreme volatility of the electoral alliance that brought him to power was always manifest. His electoral strength in the second round (and the same applies to Lula) was largely based on negative votes, that is, on voters who first of all wanted to prevent the other guy from being elected. Despite these patently negative aspects of the 1989 experience, faith in double balloting is intense in Brazil. Many believe that it will always strengthen a president's legitimacy, to the point of counteracting the negative effects of ideological or rancorous polarization. From this point of view, it seems worth remembering that Getúlio Vargas almost won the absolute majority in a single run, in 1950, and fell dramatically in 1954; Juscelino Kubitscheck had only 35 percent of the vote in 1955, with a modest 12 percent in Brazil's economic heartland, São Paulo, but managed to finish his term of office normally. Limited as they certainly are, these examples suggest that plebiscitarian legitimation cannot perform miracles.

Survey Evidence

The choice between presidentialism and parliamentarism is among the most complex questions posed to common citizens in opinion polls. In Brazil, however, a number of surveys have tried to measure popular preferences on this issue. During the parliamentary experiment of 1961–63, more than two-thirds of the voters said on at least one occasion that they would rather return to presidentialism.[33] Since the mid-1980s, the constitution-making process and the growing concern with ungovernability under both Sarney and Collor have made that issue a lot more salient. The number of surveys has thus increased remarkably, and so has their impact on public debate.

The key question, of course, is whether survey results on such a complex issue can be trusted. The average voter's ability to apprehend the meaning and context of the form of government issue is often questioned. This sort of argument forgets, however, that Brazil's 85 million voters have already been asked to come to the polls to make that choice in a "real-life situation": the plebiscite scheduled to take place on September 7, 1993. This is a constitutional fact, not an academic proposal. The specific wording of survey questions does seem to influence results (see below), but the main difficulty is that the issue is in fact new to both voters and polling institutes.

Surveys taken at the time of the constitutional congress (discussed below) suggest that the distribution of preferences regarding the form of government can be strongly influenced by the changing fortunes of the president and other political leaders, as well as by the country's broader psychological context. The overall economic situation, adverse electoral results, and other factors affecting the popularity of the president or the image of legislators and political parties can lead to important fluctuations in popular opinion. Both Sarney (in 1986) and Collor (in early 1990) climbed to unprecedented heights in popularity, as long as their economic shocks were believed to produce quick positive results. During these honeymoons, the legislature was relentlessly attacked by the media as anachronistic, clientelist, and corrupt, appearing in a number of polls as one of the least esteemed institutions in the country. A standard objection to changing the form of government thus became: "How can there be parliamentarism with such a congress?" Yet in July 1991 the São Paulo Institute of Social and Political Studies (IDESP) asked voters in Rio de Janeiro and São Paulo which one they trusted more, the president or the congress: the result was a 48 percent to 28 percent margin in favor of the congress, with the remainder trusting neither (18 percent) or unable to answer (6 percent).

After a few months of apparently crushing success, in early 1990, Collor's popularity fell abysmally. Lacking a parliamentary basis and unable to set up a coherent strategy in the minority, he entered his second year seen as a helplessly ineffective leader. Disenchantment with the administration became intertwined with pessimism over the country's future. Desperate protest may partly explain why support for monarchy as against republic—another issue to be decided in the 1993 plebiscite—began to appear less negligible than expected, scoring more than 10 percent in several polls. Also worth noting here is that the gubernatorial and legislative elections of October 1990 were rather adverse to both President Fernando Collor and parliamentarism. Leonel Brizola, a vocal adversary of the president's liberalizing economic policies, won a stunning victory as governor of Rio de Janeiro and imposed himself as one of the main pillars in the president's power scheme. Orestes Quércia, former governor of São Paulo, managed to name his successor and to take up the presidency of the largest congressional party, the PMDB, now in opposition to Collor. Antonio Carlos Magalhães, a strong man under the military governments and minister under Sarney, was elected governor of Bahia. All three men, staunch presidentialists, aspire to succeed Collor in 1994. Despite these complex and contradictory factors, survey results show that parliamentarism has become an important current of opinion in Brazil.

Table 8.4 compares twelve surveys taken since 1986. Research approaches, as pointed out, have varied a great deal. The two samples interviewed by IDESP were intended to represent the electorate of the cities of Rio de Janeiro and São Paulo only. The first interview was in August of 1986, between the end of the Arinos Commission and the beginning of the electoral campaign for the constitutional congress. The second, with the same kind of sample, was in July/August 1991. In both, only respondents who claimed to know the difference between presidentialism and parliamentarism were asked to state their preference. The "Don't know/not sure" column at the right indicates those who did not know which system they favored. With this approach we can be reasonably sure that only about one in every four

Table 8.4. Mass Preferences on the Form of Government from Twelve Surveys

	Presidentialism	Parliamentarism	Don't Know/Not Sure	N
IDESP (1)				
1986	14	10	76	1349
1991	36	32	32	1030
IBOPE (2)				
June 1989	26	18	56	3753
August 1991	46	26	28	3650
Gallup (2)				
July 1987	44	33	23	1917
November 1987	49	32	19	2555
March 1988	51	31	18	2771
Datafolha				
May 1987 (3)	39	54	7	4122
September 1987 (4)	36	43	21	5622
November1987 (5)	42	43	15	4755
April 1991 (6)	35	53	12	5149
September 1991 (2)	32	52	16	7018

Note: Numbers in parentheses identify the samples interviewed as follows: (1), Rio de Janeiro and São Paulo; (2), national; (3), eight capital cities; (4), eleven capital cities; (5), nine capital cities; (6), ten capital cities.

voters in Brazil's two major cities were in a position to make the choice at that time—76 percent did not really know what the interviewers were talking about or could not make up their minds.

The approach of the Brazilian Institute for Public Opinion Research (IBOPE) can be considered to have a similar effect to IDESP's in its tendency to produce a high percentage of "don't knows." But this survey elicited the "don't know" response by means of the wording of the question itself: "In your opinion, which is the best regime of government for Brazil: parliamentarism or presidentialism, or do you not yet have a sure opinion on the issue?" In 1989, the Sarney government was trying to get a lease on life, but the country was staking its hopes on the direct presidential election to be held in November. The two national samples interviewed in that year were somewhat more presidentialist than parliamentarist, but the striking fact was the absolute majority of "don't knows." In the 1991 survey, presidentialists still outnumbered parliamentarists by a wide margin, but the percentage without opinion had dropped sharply.

In the Gallup polls, interviewers were instructed to read a short definition of presidentialism and parliamentarism and then ask the respondents' opinion. In a literal (and thus a little odd) translation, the text was as follows: "Presidentialism is the system in which the president presides and governs the country. Under the parliamentary system the president presides and the deputies and senators elect a prime minister to govern. Which (of the two systems) do you think is better for

Brazil?" As table 8.4 shows, the percentage of "don't knows" was a lot smaller than in both IDESP and IBOPE surveys. The presidentialist advantage was not spectacular, but it is worth noting that it tended to increase somewhat between July 1987 and March 1988. These were the crucial months when the constitutional congress outlined its parliamentary proposal and President Sarney mounted a major offensive against it, with significant support from the mass media.

Datafolha's approach is similar to Gallup's—an explanation of the two systems is imbedded in the question. Like Gallup, Datafolha also found a weakening of the parliamentary preference between May and November of 1987. However, two out of three polls taken during this period showed an advantage (albeit small) for parliamentarism. This may have been due to slight differences in question wording or to the fact that the samples represented only some major capital cities. Yet in 1991 a solid parliamentary advantage—20 and 18 percentage points, respectively—was found in two national samples. In the last one, in early September, the question (literally translated) read as follows: " Are you in favor of presidentialism, which is the present system, in which the president alone is the chief of government and thus chooses the ministers, or of parliamentarism, a system in which the president shares the chieftaincy of the government with a prime minister, who appoints the ministers?"

Despite possible technical shortcomings, the results shown in table 8.4 seem to allow two main conclusions. First, an important learning process seems to have taken place over the five years from 1986 to 1991. This is suggested by the IDESP/IBOPE technique, which shows a substantial reduction in the "Don't know/not sure" category over that period. Voters seem better informed or more willing to state their preferences in 1991. Second, the stereotype of an authoritarian presidentialist political culture is not supported. The presidentialist advantage that appears in some (not all) of the surveys reported here is substantial, but it is not the landslide one would infer from some culturalistic tracts. If the plebiscite had taken place in September 1991, parliamentarism would have been favored by a minimum of 25 percent (IBOPE) and eventually by half (Datafolha) of the voters.

A major premise of this chapter, however, is that a successful transition toward parliamentarism requires more than a majority at the ballot box. It will depend on the sedimentation of that preference among relevant elite groups. To what extent are these groups willing to support such a change? Here again, some figures may be useful. Table 8.5 compares the results of three recent elite surveys, two by IDESP and one by the newspaper *Gazeta Mercantil*. The first was taken between November 1989 and June 1990, that is, roughly between the presidential election and the failure of President Collor's economic megashock. A structured questionnaire was submitted to 450 elite respondents in eight groups, as follows: 76 businessmen, 34 labor leaders, 26 associational leaders, 34 journalists, 78 intellectuals, 26 public sector managers, 108 politicians, and 68 high-ranking officers of the navy and air force. As shown in table 8.5, parliamentarism was favored by 69 percent and presidential-

Table 8.5. Elite Preferences on the Form of Government from Three Surveys

	Presidentialism	Parliamentarism	Don't Know/Not Sure	N
IDESP 1989 survey of 8 elite sectors[a]	30	69	1	450
Gazeta Mercantil 1990 survey of businessmen[b]	29	68	3	766
IDESP 1991 survey of the National Congress[c]	26	68	6	469

a. The sample included 76 businessmen, 34 labor leaders, 26 associational leaders, 34 journalists, 78 intellectuals, 26 public sector managers, 108 politicians, 68 navy and air force officers.
b. The survey was a mailed questionnaire.
c. The sample included 80 percent of the national legislature (deputies and senators).

ism by 30 percent. Except for the military officers, among whom presidentialism had 55 percent of the preferences, there was a solid majority of parliamentarists.

The results above have been thoroughly confirmed by subsequent surveys. In August of 1990 the São Paulo-based *Gazeta Mercantil* reported that parliamentarism was favored by 68 percent of businessmen from all over the country who responded to a mail survey. It is worth noting that this figure did not reflect disenchantment with the Collor government or opposition to its economic measures: 78 percent of the respondents said their business had been directly affected by the government's stabilization measures (freezing of financial assets); 69 percent recognized that the economy was in a recessive process; 78 percent had voted for Fernando Collor in 1989; 65 percent would vote for him again (22 percent would not).

If the preference for parliamentarism in the *Gazeta Mercantil's* sample of businessmen seems unrelated to Collor's handling of the government up to that time, this is probably less true among congressmen. In the national legislature, Collor's alledged preference for parliamentarism probably had no effect, but his policies and especially his aggressive style have certainly helped convince congressmen of the dangers of presidentialism. A survey sponsored by IDESP succeeded in interviewing 469 out of 584 deputies and senators in June 1991. As table 8.5 shows, no less than 68 percent of them declared a parliamentarist preference against 26 percent who stayed with presidentialism and 6 percent without opinion.

Alternative Models

A successful transition to parliamentarism largely depends on the sedimentation of a viable preference among the relevant elites. The central issue here is undoubtedly the contrast between "pure" and "mixed" parliamentarism, meaning by the latter a system in which the chief of state is directly elected and retains substantial prerogatives. The proponents of parliamentarism are generally aware that mixed formulas cannot completely do away with the tensions arising from the divided sovereignty of presidentialism; yet the majority leans toward such formulas, either because it sees them as more advantageous in other regards or because of the recent revitalization of plebiscitarianism through the *diretas-já* campaign. A long presidentialist tradition undoubtedly creates difficulties for a full transition, despite the qualifications I have presented with regard to the concept of tradition. Unless the ongoing debate significantly changes Brazilian perceptions, it seems therefore more likely that the transition, if it does occur, will be to or at least through a mixed system.

The Ato Adicional of 1961, as pointed out above, was rather incongruous, since its real aim was to provide a way out of the impasse created over Goulart's rise to the presidency. If the plebiscite originally scheduled to take place in 1965 had confirmed parliamentarism, the system would then be different; most notably, future chiefs of state (presidents) would be chosen indirectly by the congress. From this point of view, it is noteworthy that both the Afonso Arinos Commission (1985–86) and the constitutional congress itself settled on less parliamentarist proposals that were closer to the French and Portuguese models.

Some difficulties of the French model have been recurrently noted. Diluting or depersonalizing the plebiscitarian energy attracted by a directly elected president will always be a difficult process. A power-seeking president will be tempted to use that political capital in competition with the prime minister. Regardless of his intent, economic hardship may lead the electorate to transform him into a channel of diffuse protest. Depending on the extent of his role as commander of the armed forces and on whether he has an explicit constitutional role in economic policy making, the dual nature of the system may endanger stability. Such objections notwithstanding, hybrid models of this sort seem increasingly attractive in Brazil. Is there a positive justification for this, or must we defend it simply as the art of the possible?

Let us note, first, that the proposals that have been considered in Brazil, since the Afonso Arinos Commission, tend to be more clearly parliamentarist than the French model insofar as the choice of the prime minister is concerned, since in the latter the president actually appoints the prime minister unilaterally (article 8). In addition, the French president presides over the council of ministers (article 9). Secondly, even under the present presidential system, the Brazilian constitution does not include legal provisions of last resort like article 16 of the French or article 48 of the Weimar constitutions. Thirdly, if a European reference is needed, the Arinos proposal and subsequent trends in congressional opinion should more appropriately be called Franco-German because they seek to reinforce the party system and the legislature in various ways, including the adoption of an electoral system roughly like the German mix. Finally, it can be argued that that direct election of the president would function as a counterweight to the disproportionate influence presently exerted by the less populous states in the Federal chamber of deputies and to the decentralizing features of the federal system more broadly.

Conclusion

On April 21, 1993, 55 percent of the Brazilian electorate voted for presidentialism, 25 percent voted for parliamentarism, and 20 percent cast null or blank votes. Can the arguments developed in this chapter accommodate these results? Why didn't parliamentarism fare better? Two broad observations seem in order—one about the plebiscite itself, another about its aftermath.

My first observation concerns the apparent contradiction between the plebiscite results and the survey data. In 1991 parliamentarist strength was estimated by IBOPE and IDESP at between 26 and 32 percent and by Datafolha at better than 50 percent (see table 8.4). The large difference between Datafolha and the others seems to be largely attributable to the wording of the question. A number of both elite and mass surveys conducted between mid-1991 and December 1992 confirmed substantial support for parliamentarism, and this trend was clearly associated with the sharply negative evaluation of President Collor's performance. An IDESP survey of congressional opinion during the second semester of 1991 showed only 6 percent of deputies and senators rating President Collor's administration as "good" or "excellent" and 71 percent inclined toward parliamentarism. Beginning in May 1992, the charges of corruption that ultimately led to the president's impeachment gave further impulse to parliamentarism. An IDESP survey of the public at large showed that the parliamentarist option was most attractive to voters who were strongly opposed to Collor. In the same survey, however, four-fifths of interviewees said they wanted to vote directly for the head of government, indicating that a "pure" parliamentarist proposal would stand no chance at all.

The crucial factor behind the plebiscite result was that the presidentialists managed rapidly and surely to depict the parliamentarist proposal (an admittedly hybrid one) as an attempt to "deprive" the voters of their basic right to vote directly for the head of government. In the first few days of the campaign, when the three "fronts" addressed the electorate through the official radio and TV network, the presidentialists used this theme aggressively and obtained an early substantial lead in the polls that practically defined the final result and demobilized a large number of possible parliamentarist militants.

An adequate understanding of the reversal must, however, give due weight to several other contributing factors. (1) On October 12, 1992, the main symbol and articulator of the parliamentarist campaign, Deputy Ulysses Guimarges, died. (2) The final vote against Collor in the senate created widespread feeling that the crisis was over and that a successful impeachment had shown the virtues of presidentialism. (3) On the heels of this "triumph," Collor's successor, President Itamar Franco, enjoyed tremendous good will and popularity. (4) A sharp reversal of the parliamentarist inclination of the PT (Workers' party) followed popularity ratings showing Lula the strongest contender for the presidency in 1994. (5) The legislature had a negative public image. (6) The majority of the press was against the plebiscite on the grounds that time was short and the issues too complex and that "merely" institutional issues should not be given precedence over urgent social and economic difficulties. The parliamentarists were thus left without media support in their effort to motivate the voters and to promote debate on their proposal. It is noteworthy that in São Paulo, where debate was more fertile than elsewhere in the country, presidentialism enjoyed only a 10 percentage point advantage.

My second set of observations concerns the "day after." Surprisingly, immediately after the presidentialism landslide in the plebiscite, President Itamar Franco met a barrage of criticism and even suggestions that he should step down and allow the congress to name another president for the remainder of his term. The climate was so negative that a democratic breakdown was widely predicted. Rightly or wrongly, the idea that the person of the president is an obstacle to good governance made a strong comeback. Now it was Itamar Franco's "ill temper," just as it had been Collor's "political isolation" (and later corruption) and, before that, Sarney's clientelism. The diagnoses are sufficiently varied to suggest that it is all a matter of bad luck. Three weeks after the plebiscite, the prestigious weekly *Veja* ran a cover story, "The Crisis and the Man," playing on a classic slogan of Sarney's time, "the crisis is the man." (In Portuguese, the two phrases differ only by an accent that converts the single letter *e* from "and" to "is.")

In May 1993, President Franco was being universally applauded for appointing Fernando Henrique Cardoso as finance minister, and the country's optimism seemed suddenly rebuilt. A major São Paulo-based newspaper *(O Estado de São Paulo)* actually said in a headline that Cardoso was being appointed "with the powers of a prime minister." The question that remains is whether Brazil's ups and downs are exclusively a matter of luck or perhaps also of institutional imperfection.

Notes

1. On the Brazilian monarchy in general, see Eul-Soo-Pang, *In Pursuit of Honor and Power: Noblemen of the Southern Cross in Nineteenth-Century Brazil* (Tuscaloosa: U Alabama P, 1988). On its political and institutional features, José Murilo de Carvalho, *Teatro de sombras* (São Paulo: Editora Vértice, 1988). For a broad survey from the empire to the recent military governments, Peter Flynn, *Brazil: A Political Analysis* (Boulder: Westview, 1979).

2. Lawrence Whitehead, "Presidentialism and Parliamentarism: A Comment" (paper submitted for discussion at the Latin American Regional Institute on Comparative Constitutionalism, ACLS, Punta del Este, Uruguay, 3 Nov. 1988), p. 15.

3. Weber's conception of the plebiscitarian/charismatic president and its influence on the Weimar constitution are discussed by J. P. Mayer in *Max Weber and German Politics*, 2d ed. (London: Faber & Faber, 1956), pp. 98–109. See also Weber's 1917 essay: "Parlament und Regierung im Neugeordneten Deutschland" (published in Portuguese by Abril S.A., São Paulo, series *Os Pensadores*, 1980).

4. C. A. Dunshee de Abranches, *Como se faziam presidentes* (Rio de Janeiro: José Olympio Editores, 1973), pp. 9–10. "Direct elections—wrote a former UDN deputy and constitutional lawyer—was for forty years the greatest enticement *(engôdo)* of our institutions"; see

Prado Kelly, *Estudos de ciência política* (São Paulo: Edições Saraiva, 1966), 2:9–10. For electoral figures, B. Lamounier and Judith Muszynski, "Estatísticas eleitorais brasileiras," *Textos IDESP*, no. 34 (São Paulo).

5. See Dunshee de Abranches, *Como se faziam presidentes*; Afonso Arinos de Melo Franco, *História e teoria dos partidos políticos no Brasil*, 2d ed. (São Paulo: Editora Alfa-Omega, 1974), pp. 54–78; Maria do Carmo Campello de Souza, "O proceso político-partidário na Primeira República," in *Brasil em perspectiva*, edited by Carlos Guilherme Mota, 3d ed. (São Paulo: Difusão Européia do Livro, 1971).

6. There is considerable literature on Getúlio Vargas. Especially useful here is Paulo Brandi, *Getúlio Vargas: Da vida para a história*, 2d ed. (Rio de Janeiro: Zahar Editores, 1985); see also John Foster Dulles, *Vargas of Brazil, A Political Biography* (Austin: U Texas P, 1967).

7. Electoral reform was directly linked to bloody conflict in Vargas's home state. Assis Brazil, a political opponent of Vargas in Rio Grande do Sul, was included in the revolutionary cabinet and entrusted with direct responsibility in the elaboration of the electoral code of 1932. See J. F. Assis Brazil, *Democracia representativa: Do voto e do modo de votar* (Rio de Janeiro: Imprensa Oficial, 1931). On corporatist legislation, see J. F. Oliveira Vianna, *Problemas de direito sindical* (Rio de Janeiro: Max Limonad, 1943); P. Schmitter, *Interest Conflict and Political Change in Brazil* (Stanford: Stanford UP, 1971); Amaury de Souza, "The Nature of Corporatist Representation: Leaders and Members of Organized Labor in Brazil" (Ph.D. diss., MIT, 1978).

8. Thomas Skidmore, *Politics in Brazil, 1930–1964: An Experiment in Democracy* (Oxford: Oxford UP, 1967).

9. See Celso Furtado, "Obstáculos políticos ao desenvolvito econômico do Brasil," *Revista civilização brasileira* 1965, no. 1; Celso Lafer, *O sistema político brasileiro* (São Paulo: Editora Perspectiva, 1975); Abdo Baaklini and Antonio Carlos Pojo do Rego, "O presidencialismo na política brasileira," *Revista brasileira de ciência política* 1, no. 1 (1989). On the composition of the Federal Chamber (article 58 of the constitution of 1946), Maria do Carmo Campello de Souza, *Estado e partidos políticos no Brasil* (São Paulo: Editora Alfa-Omega, 1976), chap. 4; Gláucio A. D. Soares, "El sistema electoral y la representación de los grupos sociales en Brasil," *Revista latino-americana de ciência política* 2, no. 1 (1971); Wanderley Guilherme dos Santos, *Crise e castigo* (São Paulo: Editora Vértice, 1987).

10. On *adhemarismo*, see Regina Sampaio, *Adhemar de Barros e o PSP* (São Paulo: Global Editora, 1982); John French, "A ascensão de populismo adhemarista em São Paulo," *Textos IDESP*, no. 19 (São Paulo, 1987). On the relationship between Getúlio and Adhemar, see Brandi, *Getúlio Vargas*, chap. 6; Samuel Wainer, *Minha razão de viver* (Rio de Janeiro: Editora Paz e Terra, 1989).

11. On the 1945–64 party system, see Gláucio A. D. Soares, *Sociedade e política no Brasil* (São Paulo: Difel, 1973); Campello de Souza, *Estado e partidos*; Lúcia Hippólito, *PSD—De raposas e reformistas* (Rio de Janeiro: Editora Paz e Terra, 1985); Maria Vitória Benevides, *A UDN e o udenismo* (Rio de Janeiro: Editora Paz e Terra, 1981); Antônio Lavareda, *A democracia nas Urnas* (Rio de Janeiro: Rio Fundo/IUPERJ, 1991).

12. Brandi, *Getúlio Vargas*; Celina D'Araújo, *O segundo governo Vargas* (Rio de Janeiro: Zahar Editores, 1982).

13. On the 1950 elections, see Brandi, *Getúlio Vargas*, chap. 6; Skidmore, *Politics in Brazil*, pp. 72–80. For Tancredo Neves's analysis of Getúlio's return to power and his last years, see Valentina de Rocha Lima, *Getúlio: Uma história oral* (Rio de Janeiro: Editora Record, 1986), pp. 163–95.

14. The concept of policy arenas was suggested by Theodore Lowi in his well-known ar-

ticle in *World Politics* 14 (1964). In that article, he sketched a classification in three main arenas—redistributive, distributive, and regulatory. I am suggesting here a fourth arena, the accumulative, corresponding to the locus of the main investment decisions. In a country with a large entrepeneurial public sector, like Brazil, this seems to be an important distinction.

15. The UDN went to the extreme of supporting a complete government monopoly on oil, contrary to its ideology, in order to embarrass Vargas, who had proposed a mixed company. "This surprising UDN position had a clear political dimension, admitted by the party's own deputies," see Brandi, *Getúlio Vargas*, p. 255.

16. Vargas's successor, Vice President Café Filho, was apparently scheming against Kubitscheck's taking office. On November 3, 1955, he requests a leave for medical treatment. The presidency is then occupied by the president of the chamber, Carlos Luz, ostensibly anti-Kubitscheck, who is then deposed by General Lott on November 11. The next in line is a *pessedista*, Senator Nereu Ramos. Café Filho leaves the hospital on November 22, but Nereu is confirmed in the presidency by the chamber, with army backing. Details in Skidmore, *Politics in Brazil*, pp. 149–54. On the Kubitscheck government, see Celso Lafer, "The Planning Process and the Political System in Brazil: A Study of Kubitscheck's Target Plan" (Ph.D. diss., Cornell University, 1970); Maria Vitória Benevides, *O Governo Kubitscheck: Desenvolvimento econômico e estabilidade política* (Rio de Janeiro: Editora Paz e Terra, 1976).

17. On the erosion of the center represented by the PSD, see Lúcia Hippólito, *PSD*. Building on Sartori's "polarized pluralism," Santos stresses ideological radicalization, more than party fragmentation per se; Wanderley G. dos Santos, *Sessenta e quatro: Anatomia da crise* (São Paulo: Editora Vértice, 1986).

18. The decline of the two large "conservative" parties was stressed as early as 1953 by a UDN intellectual; Orlando de Carvalho, *Ensaios de sociologia eleitoral* (Belo Horizonte: Edições RBEP, 1958); see also B. Lamounier and R. Meneguello, *Partidos políticos e consolidação democrática: O caso brasileiro* (São Paulo: Editora Brasiliense, 1986).

19. Sérgio Abranches, "Presidencialismo de coalizão: O dilema institucional brasileiro," *Revista dados* 31, no. 1 (1988): 30.

20. Jânio Quadros, "Aprendizado de salvação nacional," *O globo*, 31 Dec. 1989. According to Baaklini and Pojo do Rego (n. 9), Brazilian presidents of this period have always been led to a strategy of dividing in order to govern: "By means of favors and threats, they have sought to keep congressional parties in a constant state of internal conflict" (p. 175). At the same time, coalitions tend to become highly unstable as congressmen seeking reelection began to oppose the president. The constitutional veto on reelection obviously aggravated this trend.

21. Despite his elegant defense of parliamentarism on the triple grounds of stability, effectiveness, and legitimacy, the first prime minister, Tancredo Neves, apparently did not favor the system. Skidmore goes as far as saying that Neves and Goulart were pursuing a deliberate plan to demonstrate the unworkability of the parliamentary system. Paulo Mercadante says that Tancredo remained "viscerally presidentialist" to the end of his life, though always avoiding saying it in public. Olavo Setúbal says that Tancredo was "attracted" to parliamentarism, but grew skeptical after the experience of 1961 on two main grounds: the legislative veto that the Ato Adicional gave to the president, seriously weakening the cabinet's legislative initiative, and the position of the president as commander-in-chief of the armed forces. The last of the three prime ministers, Brochado da Rocha, worked explicitly to advance the plebiscite required by the Ato Adicional, from 1965 to 1963. See Skidmore, *Politics of Brazil*, pp. 211–33; Tancredo Neves, *O regime parlamentar e a realidade brasileira* (Belo Horizonte: Edições RBEP, 1962); Paulo Mercadante, "Tancredo Neves, presidencialista,"

Folha de São Paulo, 24 Sept. 1987; Olavo Setúbal, oral comment in Miguel Reale, "Sistemas de governo," *São Paulo Federation of Industries/Robert Simonsen Institute* 5 (1989).

22. See Prado Kelly, n. 4; Afonso Arinos de Melo Franco and Raul Pilla, *Presidentialismo ou parlamentarismo* (Rio de Janeiro: José Olympio Editores, 1958); Miguel Reale, *Parlamentarismo brasileiro* (São Paulo: Edições Saraiva, 1962).

23. Complete text in Adriano Campanhole, *Constituções do Brasil*, 6th ed. (São Paulo: Editora Atlas, 1983).

24. For a broad review of the post-1964 regime, see Thomas E. Skidmore, *The Politics of Military Rule in Brazil, 1964–1985* (Oxford: Oxford UP, 1988); also Alfred Stepan, ed., *Authoritarian Brazil: Policies, Output, Future* (New Haven: Yale UP, 1973) and *Democratizing Brazil* (Oxford: Oxford UP, 1989).

25. On the connection between elections and *abertura*, see my "Authoritarian Brazil Revisited," in Stepan, *Democratizing Brazil* (n. 24). In Portuguese, Bolivar Lamounier and Fernando Henrique Cardoso, *Os partidos e as eleições no Brasil* (Rio de Janeiro: Editora Paz e Terra, 1975); Bolivar Lamounier, *Partidos e utopias: O Brasil no limiar dos anos 90* (São Paulo: Editora Loyola, 1989). Also Maria D'Alva Gil Kinzo, *Legal Opposition under Authoritarian Rule in Brazil* (London: Macmillan/Oxford, 1988).

26. For a detailed account of the commission's proposals with regard to the political parties and electoral system, see my paper, "Um projeto, tres utopias: Variações sobre o tema da reorganização institucional brasileira," *Textos IDESP*, no. 33 (São Paulo, 1989).

27. On the constitutional congress's debates and voting patterns, see Baaklini and Pojo do Rego, n. 9; Maria D'Alva Kinzo, "O quadro partidário e a constituinte," *Textos IDESP*, no. 28 (São Paulo, 1988); Lamounier, *Partidos e utopias* (n. 25).

28. The remarks in this section are largely based on my personal experience as a member of the Afonso Arinos Commission.

29. An opuscule by Silvio Romero, originally published in 1993 and reprinted in 1979 by the senate, is a case in point. At an abstract level, virtually all arguments for parliamentarism can be found in it: the flexibility of the parliamentary arrangement as against the fixed term; the zero-sum nature and the fusion of chief-of-government and chief-of-state roles under presidentialism, which often facilitate the escalation of political into institutional crises. Silvio Romero, *Parlamentarismo e presidencialismo* (Brasília: Senado Federal, 1978).

30. Tancredo Neves, *O regime parlamentar* (n. 21).

31. Hélio Jaguaribe, "As opções da Comissão Constitucional," *Jornal do Brasil*, 9 Sept. 1986; "O regime de poder," ibid., 28 Aug. 1987.

32. For a social scientist's interpretation of the new constitution, see Amaury de Souza and B. Lamounier, "A feitura da nova constitução: Um reexame da cultura política brasileira," *Textos IDESP*, no. 31 (São Paulo, 1989); for an outstanding detailed explanation, José Afonso da Silva, *Curso de direito constitucional positivo*, 5th ed. (São Paulo: Editora Revista dos Tribunais, 1989).

33. The IDESP 1986 poll was done jointly with Gallup. For a more detailed presentation of the data reported in this section, up to the elite survey of 1989–90, see B. Lamounier and A. Souza, "Changing Attitudes towards Democracy and Institutional Reform in Brazil," in *Political Culture and Democracy in Developing Countries*, edited by Larry Diamond (Boulder, Colo.: Lynne Rienner, forthcoming). On the first year of the Collor government, B. Lamounier, *Depois da transição: Democracia e eleições no Governo Collor* (São Paulo: Editora Sumaré, 1991).

9

JONATHAN HARTLYN

Presidentialism and Colombian Politics

In the study of democratic political regime establishment, consolidation, or overthrow, a focus on the role of political institutions has fallen out of favor in recent decades. Analysts prefer other explanatory variables such as culture, internal class formation, or international economic dependency; or, when examining political factors, they focus more on party or electoral systems. These various factors, to differing degrees, do often play a role in any comprehensive explanation of political regime change.

Yet the neglect of constitutional and institutional factors may have gone too far, even as earlier analyses of Latin America may have excessively or inappropriately analyzed these factors (e.g., Fitzgibbon 1950). Thus, Linz (1978, 1984), Mainwaring (1990), Riggs (1987), and Valenzuela (1985a, 1985b), among others, have recently argued that, whatever the merits of presidentialism in the previous century or early years of this century, in contemporary Latin America the logic inherent to presidential systems has helped create or exacerbate crises in democratic regimes.[1] Riggs notes that, with the exception of the United States, no country following a presidentialist model has been able to avoid a breakdown or significant disruption of some kind, whereas similar problems are true of only one-third of the third-world countries that adopted parliamentary constitutions (Riggs 1987, 2). Linz and Valenzuela advance their arguments against presidentialism by comparing relatively successful parliamentary regimes with failed presidential ones (marked by military overthrows) in which elections did not provide clear majorities for a single party or coherent coalition of parties: Italy with Argentina or Chile, and Spain with Chile. In his review essay on presidentialism, Mainwaring concurs with the argument that institutional analysis must be brought back and more specifically that presidentialism may negatively affect the possibilities for democratic consolidation, especially in multiparty systems; he also usefully warns of the risk of an excessive focus on institutional analysis that underplays issues of domination.

Earlier institutionally oriented analyses frequently examined the preeminence of presidentialism in Latin America and noted the inspiration derived from the constitution of the United States. Yet, at the same time, an argument was advanced that the Iberian tradition and the central role of military leaders in the struggle for independence, as well as the continent's postindependence difficulties in achieving national integration, all buttressed the logic of presidentialism in Latin America (see Davis 1958a, 12; 1958b, 255–61). These analyses often found problems with presidentialism. Lambert argued that Latin American regimes, rather than presidential systems, should more appropriately be called systems of presidential dominance because of the lack of effective legislative power (Lambert 1967, 262). Blanksten, noting the "brief and sporadic" experiments with parliamentary arrangements in Latin America, was dubious that such arrangements could generate more governable regimes in the continental context. He noted a tradition of monarchy in both Spanish and Indian cultures and a penchant for caudillo rule, and cited Simón Bolívar; "The new states of America . . . need kings with the name of presidents" (Blanksten 1958, 233–37, quote on 237; 248–51, quote on 250).

Thus, even after reviewing the perceived faults of the presidential system in Latin America, these scholars often concluded that because of cultural factors and the need to centralize power to achieve national integration, presidentialism was still the system best suited for the continent (Davis 1958, 255; Lambert 1967, 271). In other words, presidentialism was favored principally because of its perceived ability to increase state capacity and achieve national integration, rather than because it was better than alternative institutional arrangements in terms of consolidating democratic rule.

Yet at least four factors may be identified that are either inherent to or empirically associated with presidentialism in Latin America and that may have negative consequences for political regime consolidation. These factors are: the effects of attempts to check presidential abuse of power while seeking paradoxically to strengthen presidential power; the absence of a moderating power; the "winner-take-all" nature of presidential elections, with the potential for serious executive-legislative deadlock; and the polarizing potential of these elections.[2]

A major concern regarding parliamentary systems is that an absence of a clear parliamentary majority may generate tremendous governmental instability and policy drift; similarly, minorities that enable a governing majority may gain an importance disproportionate to their popular support. In presidentialism, two major contrasting fears depend on whether the president possesses a majority in the legislature or not. When the president has a congressional majority, the principal fear is of excessive, unchecked presidential power. This fear has led to efforts to control potential abuses, primarily by prohibiting reelection, though also by such measures as filibustering, judicial review, federalism, or even granting the armed forces a constitutional "moderating power." Yet, in efforts to sidestep immobilism (a consequence of executive-congressional deadlock when the president and congress are of opposite parties, or of lack of support toward the end of a president's term), or perceived congressional localism, countries have often strengthened presidential powers vis-à-vis the congress. This, in turn, has tended to shift political struggles away from electoral arenas, with potentially nefarious consequences for regime survival: presidents can become virtual or actual dictators through the use of special powers, or fears of such action may encourage other political actors to seek a military overthrow of the president. The potential for these actions is increased by the fact that presidential systems usually lack a symbolic head of state (either a monarch or a symbolic president), which could provide flexibility or serve as a moderating influence or unifying element in times of crisis.

Because presidential elections have some "winner-take-all" characteristics absent in parliamentary ones, increased presidential powers can often have severe polarizing consequences. Unlike prime ministers, presidents have their own independent electoral legitimacy and tend to have significant independent powers. There are also potential perceptual problems, for both the person elected president and the supportive electorate. Presidents, even minority ones, as both holders of executive power and symbolic heads of state, are more likely to perceive their election as a mandate, even as popular expectations by their supporters may also be greater due to their plebiscitarian relationship. These problems can be aggravated by the fixed-term characteristics of executive and legislative elections in presidential systems.

Because of the enhanced powers and the "winner-take-all" characteristics of the presidency, presidential elections may tend to polarize electoral outcomes unless there already is a massive societal consensus around the middle of the country's political spectrum. If significant parties on the extremes of the political spectrum exist, then coalitions may need to be structured before a presidential election, whereas in parliamentary systems they can be established after elections. And under presidentialism, it may be much more difficult to sustain these coalitions over time.

The most obvious counterargument to the assertions that presidential systems have helped foster crises in democratic regimes is that the United States, one of the most stable, consolidated democratic regimes, has a presidential system. This example suggests that societal factors such as national wealth or other political or electoral mechanisms can mitigate the problems associated with presidential systems. In the case of the United States, these include the dispersal of power through federalism, the institutional role of the judiciary, and bipartisan patterns of recruitment for executive posts and of policy formation in certain areas (see Linz 1978, 73), as well as the "catchall" nature of the parties, the centripetal two-party system, and the underlying societal consensus this reflects and reinforces.[3] The U.S. case demonstrates that arguments about the political effects of presidentialism rarely can be made in the abstract but must consider societal, political, or electoral factors that can have an impact on the dilemmas associated with presidential systems.

Following a brief historical section that sketches the constitutional evolution of presidentialism, this chapter explores how the four major problems with presidential systems identified above have appeared in democratic regimes in Colombia.[4] It also examines the party system and electoral laws and identifies the ways in which certain political mechanisms and actors have mitigated some of the more problematic elements of presidentialism as it has operated in Colombia, particularly those related to fear of permanent exclusion from power and violent responses to that fear. The power-sharing coalition National Front, established in the 1950s, provides an example of extensive interparty accommodation within a presidential system to eliminate these concerns. It illustrates how ingenious consociational mechanisms can be created even within a presidential system to try to circumscribe some of these concerns; yet it also demonstrates some of the equally negative unintended consequences engendered by these efforts.

At the same time as this chapter focuses on presidentialism, it does not argue that Colombia's current crises of governability and of violence can be reduced solely or even primarily to problems with presidentialism. Its more limited goals are first to discuss the evolution of presidentialism in Colombia and then to analyze how—in interaction with the party and electoral systems—it has engendered dilemmas and complicated efforts at political reform with pernicious effects for the Colombian regime even as the Colombian state also found itself increasingly confronted with dramatic challenges from other directions. A shift away from presidentialism was not a priority in the debates leading up to the enactment of the 1991 constitution, nor was it necessarily recommendable in the face of a perceived growing crisis in state authority and other apparently more urgent reforms of political institutions. However, as noted in the conclusion, in seeking to correct one set of excesses— such as an asphyxiating two-party system, inordinate formal presidential powers, and an extremely parochial legislature—this new constitution may have opened up other potential challenges to governability and democratic effectiveness.

Historical Background: Defining Presidential Powers

From its inception, constitutionalism in Colombia, as in other Latin American countries, has been presidential, though it has varied from the rest of the subcontinent tremendously in other respects. Following independence, monarchism had a few adherents but never gained widespread support. And Simón Bolívar's hopes for South American unity (under his leadership) also met little success. His notion of a life-term president, imposed in the constitution he wrote for Bolivia, met great opposition in Colombia. Frustrated by separatist tendencies within Gran Colombia and by resistance to his personalist rule, which led to a deadlocked constitutional convention in 1828, Bolívar in that year assumed power in Gran Colombia by decree. He resigned in despair and died in 1830, as Gran Colombia (which included what is now Venezuela and Ecuador)[5] was breaking up, after asserting that "America is ungovernable. Those who have served the revolution have plowed the sea" (see Uribe Vargas 1985, 79–115; quotation from Skidmore and Smith 1984, 36).

The subsequent history of nineteenth-century Colombia is a history of oligarchic republican rule, strong regionalism, marginal military presence, a weak and poor state, and violence. These factors enabled the gradual consolidation of two political parties in the country, in contrast to its Andean neighbors, where stronger military and state structures led to long-term caudillo rule and the absence of strong oligarchical parties. In Colombia, a series of often brutal civil wars divided the loyalty of the population between the Conservative and the Liberal parties, and it was these parties that served as the major means of national integration. Conservatives tended to emphasize close cooperation between church and state, and favored a strong, central administration and protectionism. Liberals, in turn, generally argued for separation of church and state, federalism, and free-trade economic policies. At the same time, brief bipartisan coalitions, with one party dominant, were occasionally formed during periods of political crisis, as occurred when a challenge by a military leader supported by various popular groups was beaten back in 1854, the 1880s, the 1900s, the 1930s, and the 1940s. The National Front of the 1950s was the last, the most formal, and the longest lasting of such agreements; under it, the parties agreed to share power equally (and exclusively).

Constitutional definitions of presidential powers have evolved in contradictory directions from the 1850s to the present. In the midnineteenth century, constitutionalism reflected Liberal fears of potential presidential abuse of power. This led to a sharp counterreaction in the 1880s; the 1886 constitution sought more effective centralized presidential power. More limited reforms in 1910 provided some checks on presidential power. As discussed in the next section, a 1968 constitutional reform augmented formal presidential powers, whereas the 1991 constitution has placed restrictions on them.

The Liberals emerged victorious in the 1860s from a particularly drawn-out civil war. They soon enacted a more extreme version of their 1858 constitution, which had established the short-lived Grenadine Confederation. Their 1863 constitution for the "United States of Colombia" was extremely federalist, secularist, and politically liberal (e.g., most state constitutions decreed universal male suffrage). It instituted an extremely weak presidential system, though a proposal that executive power be exercised by three ministers elected by a congress (in imitation of the Swiss system) did not prosper. Instead, presidents were elected indirectly, with each of the country's "sovereign states" receiving one vote. If no candidate received support from an absolute majority of the states, then the congress elected the president from among leading contenders. The presidential term was restricted to only two years, with no immediate reelection. The president required approval by the senate for his cabinet and other top-level appointments,[6] and presidential vetoes could be overridden by a simple majority vote in the legislature. The central government was given only limited fiscal and military powers vis-à-vis the now powerful "sovereign states"; for example, congressional authority was required for federal intervention in the states, even in the case of rebellion. Finally, the process prescribed for constitutional reform was so onerous that it essentially guaranteed the constitutional text could not be amended (Uribe Vargas 1985, 160–80; Vázquez Carrizosa 1979, 159–61).

To a certain extent, the constitution's recognition of regional autonomy made a virtue of necessity, given the central government's inability to extend effectively its control over the entire country. But recurring insurrections and civil wars, economic boom-and-bust cycles, and free-trade policies over the next several decades brought the country to the brink of economic ruin, destroyed its incipient industrial base, and impeded national integration (see McGreevey 1971, 146–81). Deeply etched into the country's memory is the notion that weak executive authority and federalism were the central culprits.

As a consequence, a centralizing reaction with bipartisan support (though primarily Conservative inspiration) gradually emerged. It eventually led to the 1886 constitution, the basic text in effect until 1991, and to a period of Conservative hegemony that lasted until 1930. The 1886 constitution imposed a unitary state, enhanced presidential powers, once again restricted suffrage, and called for a greater role for the church. Presidential powers were greatly strengthened by extending the term to six years, decreeing legislative sessions only every other year, and granting the executive state-of-siege powers and also greater appointive powers, including life-term Supreme Court judges (Uribe Vargas 1985, 191–97). Political exclusion of Liberals and conflicts over economic and political measures, though, led to one of the longest and bloodiest of the country's civil confrontations. This war consolidated the intense sectarian partisan identification throughout the country, leading to a situation in which its citizens became Liberal or Conservative as they became Colombian, by birth, and in which changing party became as unthinkable as changing nationality. Many Liberal leaders, though, following their defeat, now rejected violence as a means of promoting their aims or seeking political office.

Constitutional reform became oriented toward seeking greater accommodation and curtailing presidential powers. Following a brief dictatorial period, a new set of constitutional measures agreed to in a bipartisan fashion ushered in a lengthy period of oligarchical democracy dominated by Conservatives from 1910 until 1930; it finally broke down in 1949. The reforms of 1910 limited presidential powers and gave greater assurances to the minority party. The president's term was cut to four years, and immediate reelection was prohibited. Congress, in which the minority party was guaranteed a presence by means of proportional representation, was to meet at least annually and was to elect a presidential successor if one was needed to complete a term. Greater judicial independence and judicial review were established.

A peaceful, though incident-ridden, transfer of power from a Conservative president to a Liberal one transpired in 1930, a period in which governments in other Latin American countries were falling to military coups under the weight of the Great Depression. The transition in Colombia was facilitated by division within the Conservative party and formation of a bipartisan coalition. It ushered in a politically exclusionary "Liberal Republic" and a period of additional constitutional change and of active social and economic reform. A process analogous to the one of 1930 led to a transfer of power from a Liberal president to a Conservative one in 1946 in a more mobilized and polarized society. This set the stage for a renewed wave of tremendous violence, democratic breakdown in 1949, Conservative quasi dictatorship, an undeclared civil war between party adherents, and a military coup in 1953 with partial attenuation and transformation of the bases of conflict into banditry and revolutionary violence.

The National Front consociational (power-sharing) agreement negotiated between Conservatives and Liberals in 1956 and 1957 facilitated the removal of the military and a return to a civilian regime in 1958 while seeking to avoid a potential revival of partisan violence or radical economic transformations. As a consequence, first of massive social and economic changes and of aspects of the agreement unmet by timely and necessary political modifications, and then of complex patterns of violence generated by guerrillas, drug traffickers, and allied groups, the regime—and the state—fell under challenge in the late 1970s into a spiral of bloodshed that increased throughout the 1980s and into the 1990s. After several unsuccessful attempts at political reform, a new constitution, which combined a continuing embrace of presidentialism with substantial modifications to formal presidential powers, was agreed upon in 1991 in a remarkable convention that included former guerrillas and representatives from Indian communities as well as figures from the two traditional parties.

Dilemmas of Presidentialism in Colombia

How were the predicaments of presidentialism mitigated during the period of oligarchical democracy? What role did presidentialism play in the 1949 breakdown? P how have the problems associated with presidentialism affected the regime established in 1958 and its current predicaments with governance and reform and problems with violence and order? These questions are examined below in sections that explore in turn the various dilemmas discussed in the introduction. And in the conclusion potential problems that could emerge as a consequence of the measures seeking to curb presidential power in the 1991 constitution are considered.

Strengthening Presidential Powers versus Preventing Presidential Abuses

As the historical overview has underscored, presidentialism has been an unquestioned principle in Colombia, reinforced by the country's perceived negative experience with extreme federalism and limited parliamentarism during the second half of the nineteenth century. The perceived failures of the congress—factionalism, localism, and corruption—in the period since civilian rule was reestablished in 1958 probably reinforced this experience and facilitated the granting of additional powers to the president in the 1968 constitutional reform. At the same time, concern over possible presidential abuse of power led in 1991, as it had in 1910, to certain limitations on presidential powers.

The formal powers of the Colombian president were considerable prior to the National Front. They were much greater than the formal constitutional powers of the U.S. president (that the U.S. president is otherwise more powerful is almost too obvious to mention). As a consequence of the centralized nature of the polity, a Colombian president had massive appointive powers, whose significance was augmented by the importance of spoils and patronage to the clientelist and brokerage-oriented parties and by the absence of any meaningful civil service legislation. Presidents could appoint cabinet ministers without congressional approval and, in fact, often named congressional representatives to such posts.[7] Also significant were the ability of the president to legislate once granted extraordinary powers by the congress and to suspend laws and issue decrees under a state of siege. The ability of the executive to declare a state of siege, essentially removed in the 1863 text, was reinserted and strengthened in 1886 and modified in 1910. A president could declare a state of siege, with the signature of all of his ministers, in case of "external war" or "internal disturbance" but was required to call the congress into session within sixty days only in the case of external threat (see Vázquez Carrizosa 1979, 321–35).

Presidents used state-of-siege powers broadly to break strikes, to deal with political crises, and increasingly to legislate. Following a failed coup attempt by disgruntled Conservative military officers in 1944, President Alfonso López declared a state of siege and decreed sweeping labor legislation. As a consequence of the *bogotazo*, the days of rioting and bloodshed that followed the assassination of the Liberal populist leader Jorge Eliécer Gaitán in April 1948, President Mariano Ospina declared a state of siege and employed it to issue decrees in a wide variety of areas until it was lifted in December of that year. And, as is discussed in more detail below, facing impeachment charges in the Liberal-dominated house of representatives, Conservative President Ospina in November 1949 simply closed the congress and the departmental assemblies, imposed press censorship, and restrained the judiciary following declaration of a state of siege (see Wilde 1978, Vázquez Carrizosa 1979, 335–43).

The checks on presidential power increased dramatically as a consequence of the National Front agreement between the two parties, which became part of the constitution by means of a plebiscite in 1957 (for a detailed discussion of the process leading up to the agreement, see Hartlyn 1984). As it finally emerged, the agreement was based on the principles of *parity* and *alternation*. Absolute parity was imposed in all branches of government—for twelve years in the legislative and executive branches, proportional to congressional representation within the executive branch subsequently, and with no time limit in the judicial branch. A two-thirds majority vote was required for most legislation. In addition, the sensitive post of minister of government (through whom the president appointed all departmental

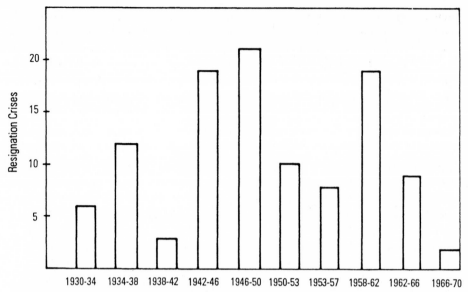

Fig. 9.1. Cabinet Changes, 1930–1970. The simultaneous resignation of several ministers is designated a "resignation crisis." Serious crises, in which five or more ministers resign, are weighted by a factor of three; less serious crises, involving three or four resignations, by a factor of two.
Source: Richard Hartwig, University of Wisconsin—Madison, unpublished paper, 1972, from data collected by the Departamento de Ciencias Políticas, Universidad de los Andes, Bogotá. Reprinted from Alexander W. Wilde, "Conversations among Gentlemen: Oligarchical Democracy in Colombia," in *The Breakdown of Democratic Regimes: Latin America,* edited by Juan Linz and Alfred Stepan (Baltimore: Johns Hopkins UP, 1978), p. 38.

governors) was to be of the opposite party of the president, as were the attorney general *(procurador)* and comptroller *(contralor),* both of whom were elected by the congress.[8] It was also agreed that in each ministry, ministers and vice ministers would be of opposite parties, and similar arrangements were provided for in decentralized agencies and at the departmental and municipal levels. Divisions within the Conservative party, which was supposed to select the first National Front president to be presented jointly by the two parties in the 1958 elections, prevented agreement on a nominee. As a consequence, a Liberal was elected president for the 1958–62 term, and the parties agreed to enact a constitutional reform (passed in 1959) to institute presidential alternation for the subsequent three terms, extending parity for an additional four years.[9] Cabinet changes were substantial during the first National Front administration but declined through the next two administrations (see fig. 9.1).

Paradoxically, even as formal presidential powers were circumscribed by parity and other National Front features, the nature of the agreement also almost inevitably led to an increase in presidential powers in order to ensure the country's governability. Immobilism, which is possible in any democratic regime, was inherent to the political formula of the National Front agreement, due not only to the specific conditions of the pact (particularly legislative parity, two-thirds majority, and presidential alternation) but also to the nature of the two parties.[10] The Conservative party began the National Front badly divided, and the Liberal party was soon to factionalize. At the same time, the requirement for presidential alternation required the parties, or at least their pro–National Front factions, to agree on an "official" candidate. Factionalization forced each president to create and recreate an effective governing coalition, so that the National Front period resembled a multiparty system. Yet at the same time, the need to present an official bipartisan National Front presidential candidate due to alternation and the absence of major ideological differences between the two polyclass parties made the regime appear to be based upon a "single" party with hegemonic aspirations (see López Michelsen 1963, 202–14). Each presidential election became in part a new plebiscite on the National Front.

The potential problems of executive-congressional deadlock in the period prior to 1968 are apparent from table 9.1, which shows that a clear two-thirds majority existed in the house of representatives only in the 1958–60 period.[11] The table also points out how anti–National Front forces increased steadily during the National Front years to around 30 percent of the seats, declined in 1968, and then jumped in 1970 back up to 33 percent. The desire for political accommodation with party factions and the search for congressional allies help explain the degree of cabinet instability during the National Front years (fig. 9.1). With the return to competitive elections and a convincing Liberal victory in 1974, opposition movements almost disappeared from the congress. Yet party factionalism meant that even presidents with ostensibly large party majorities in the congress often could not rely on them.

The solution to immobilism and deadlock was to concentrate more power in the presidency. In many critical areas, the president legislated on the basis of extraordinary powers ceded to him by the congress or by decrees emitted under a state of siege. According to the constitution, decrees issued under a state of siege could not be employed to repeal previous laws, though those "incompatible with the state of siege" could be suspended. This did not prevent the executive from emitting a wide variety of decrees affecting the economy or labor, but all such measures ceased to be effective the moment the state of siege was lifted. Thus for these measures to become permanent, the congress would need to enact legislation prior to its lifting. In the case of President Alberto Lleras (1958–62), the state of siege imposed by Ospina in 1949 was lifted in all but the three departments most affected by violence a few days after his inauguration. But the state of siege was not completely removed until January 1962 (in the meantime it had been briefly reinstated in the entire country in two different periods), following congressional approval of legislation from the Ospina, Gómez, and Rojas years.

Table 9.1. Seats Held by Party and Faction in the House (%), 1958–1974

Party and Faction	Year							
	1958	1960	1962	1964	1966	1968	1970	1974
Presidential period	A. Lleras 1958–62 (Liberal)		Valencia 1962–66 (Conservative)		C. Lleras 1966–70 (Liberal)		Pastrana 1970–74 (Conservative)	López 1974–78 (Liberal)
Progovernment								
Liberals (Oficialistas)	50	38	32	32	36	38	27	57
Conservatives								33[a]
Laureanistas	33							
Ospinistas		24	27	35	18	24	14	
Subtotal	83	62	59	67	54	62	41	90
Dissident								
Liberals								
Dissidents						8		
Belisaristas							2	
Sourdistas & others							7	
Conservatives								
Ospinistas	13							
Alvaristas		25	25		14	10		
Belisaristas							9	
Sourdistas							6	
Subtotal	13	25	20	0	14	18	25	0
Anti–National Front								
Liberals								
MRL		12	18	17	11	1		
ANAPO				0.5	2	3	13	
Conservatives								
Alzatistas or Leyvistas	4	0.6		0.5	0.5			
ANAPO			3	14	17	14	20	7
Opposition								2
Subtotal	4	13	21	32	30	18	33	9
Total[b]	100	100	100	100	100	100	100	100
Total *(N)*	148	152	184	184	190	204	210	199

Source: Registraduría Nacional del Estado Civil; *El Tiempo,* June 29, 1978. From Hartlyn 1988, 87.
a. Joint lists.
b. May not add to 100% due to rounding.

President Guillermo León Valencia (1958–62) implanted a state of siege for one week in 1963 and then again in May 1965, ostensibly to deal with student demonstrations against the U.S. invasion of the Dominican Republic. Yet after averting a potential coup crisis and a threatened national strike in January 1965, President Valencia used his state-of-siege powers to enact significant new labor legislation and a wide variety of economic stabilization measures. It was not until well into the presidency of Carlos Lleras (1966–70), when pro–National Front party factions again had the necessary votes in the congress and with constitutional reform and other permanent legislation in place, that the state of siege imposed in 1965 was lifted (December 1968).[12]

Presidential constitutional powers were further strengthened as a consequence of the enactment of the 1968 constitutional reform. President Carlos Lleras poured his energies into approval of the reform out of frustration with congressional immobilism and conviction that an active state role was needed in economic planning and social reform and that certain aspects of the National Front agreement should be "dismantled." In part, he was reacting to the political problems of the Alberto Lleras administration and to the policy drift, economic decline, and perceived presidential weakness of the Valencia administration. Bitter division within the Conservative party between Gómez and Ospina and a midterm shift in electoral fortunes from the former to the latter had led Alberto Lleras to switch his reliance in the cabinet (note the high instability in fig. 9.1) and in the congress from one Conservative faction to the other. Attempting to achieve a governing majority in the congress, President Valencia had carefully formed his cabinet by giving representation to all major party factions through the approval of their respective directorates (a process derisively called *milimetría*). Lleras noted the National Front plebiscite had not introduced a "cabinet-regime nor one led by [party] directorates," and asserted that it was necessary to "reaffirm and strengthen the presidential regime to save democracy. Weak and anarchic governments are the prelude to dictatorships" (in Ramírez Aljure 1986, 39). Yet the nature of the changes Lleras eventually enacted also reflected a preference for centralized, technocratic, rationalized planning through the executive over the more decentralized, particularistic, patronage-oriented and congressionally based spending that was common to other Latin American countries.[13]

The 1968 reform greatly strengthened presidential powers vis-à-vis the congress, especially in economic matters, a process that began with the 1886 constitution and accelerated with the closing of the congress in 1949 (see Vidal Perdomo, 1970, Findley, Cepeda, and Gamboa 1983). In 1968, the congress lost the power to initiate legislation dealing with social and economic development (except for limited pork barrel funds) or with the modification or creation of new administrative structures. Although the president's powers under state of siege were modified, a new power to legislate following declaration of a "state of national economic and social emergency" was created. The reform did seek to bolster congressional agility and increase its oversight capacity, though here the results were far short of the intentions. Growth in the size of the congress was trimmed. Efforts to improve the technical staff and administrative services of the congress failed as money earmarked for these purposes was misspent or directed to partisan purposes. And congressional representatives could not agree on the appropriate partisan and regional criteria for membership in the special permanent commission that was to examine the executive's plans and programs. The commission appeared excessively rich in patronage potential compared to all other congressional functions.

The effects of the constitutional reform were soon felt. Using new presidential powers granted with little discussion in 1968, President Misael Pastrana (1970–74) in 1972 was able to sidestep the congress completely in implementing his development plan, which was focused primarily on urban housing, and to establish by presidential decree new financial institutions whose deposits, loans, and mortgages were to be indexed to the inflation rate.[14] And in 1974, inaugurated following an overwhelming victory in the country's first competitive presidential elections in decades and with an overwhelming Liberal majority in the congress, President López enacted a major tax reform by decree after declaring a "state of national economic and social emergency" (using article 122 of the constitution created by the 1968 reform). The bipartisan nature of the reform was assured in part by the fact that executive parity was still in effect and measures decreed under article 122 required the full cabinet's signature. The executive preferred to avoid congressional debates for it feared producer associations and other groups might modify the measures (as in fact they subsequently did), and some congressional representatives were happy to have the president take the blame for the added tax burden. The Supreme Court ruled the declaration of the state of emergency was constitutional though it disallowed certain measures. Subsequent tax legislation through the congress in 1977 and 1979 largely watered down the more redistributive aspects of the initial reform.

Gradually, a more activist judiciary began to curtail certain executive powers, even as former President Lleras and other political figures protested what they considered the abuse of emergency powers. When Conservative President Belisario Betancur (1982–86), facing a Liberal majority in Congress, tried to enact a new tax reform in 1982 employing the same state of emergency powers, a Supreme Court with several changes in membership now declared it was not constitutional to do so. Betancur had no recourse but to reach an accommodation with Liberals in the congress, which led to changes in his cabinet and his governing style (as well as to a new tax law not significantly different from the one the president had originally sought to enact). Although there were no significant policy or ideological differences between the parties as such (many of Betancur's policies were opposed more by elements of his own party than by Liberals), Betancur was forced to negotiate more with the congress on legislation and to offer more in the areas of patronage and brokerage than he might otherwise have been willing to do. The trend to greater willingness by the judiciary to limit executive decree powers under both a state of siege and a state of national economic emergency increased during the subsequent administration of Liberal Virgilio Barco (1986–90).[15]

The net effect of the shift over these decades of power and functions to the executive, which suffered a slight reversal under both Betancur and Barco, appeared to be to marginalize the congress further from major decisions, reducing its functions to ones of patronage, brokerage, and management of limited pork barrel funds. From the inception of the National Front to the 1980s, the political parties lost what few links they had to mass organizations as they became dominated by regional politicians in control of small captive electorates who were convinced their electoral success required participation in government by their faction in order to gain access to resources controlled by the executive. This considerably affected the image of the congress in public opinion, even as various movements of "moral restoration" emerged, though with only limited electoral success. At the same time, the relative independence of congressional representatives from the executive and thus their obstructionist capabilities were reinforced. Through the 1970s and 1980s, presidents and national party authorities played almost no role in determining congressional, much less local, lists; given the electoral law, politicians unhappy with their placement on a list could always form a dissident list with the same party label. At the same time, information about the legislative activities of particular representatives, which could affect their electoral fortunes, was essentially nonexistent.[16]

The political regime of shared rule with its access to resources and the electoral system of high abstention made traditional, machine-oriented politicians reluctant to change the model of coalition rule. This was true even though the ostensible justification for sharing executive power, sectarian party identification potentially leading to violence, was no longer relevant in part because of the experience of coalition rule and in part due to rapid socioeconomic changes related to urbanization, increased education, and other factors. Ironically, with a return to competitive elections, opposition movements found it more difficult to gain electoral representation even as the traditional parties were increasingly incapable of channeling dissent (see the electoral results and abstention rates in tables 9.2 and 9.3).[17] The absence of effective electoral opposition led to the growth of nonelectoral opposition—more militant labor organizations, civic movements and strikes around issues such as the poor provision of public services, and guerrilla violence.

Thus, presidents continued to require use of a state of siege, increasingly though to manage student, labor, and civic unrest (see Gallón Giraldo 1979). After lifting the state of siege in December 1968, President Lleras once again implanted it in October 1969. For the next two decades, except for periods of varying length totaling less than three years, the country was under a state of siege. Probably the most dramatic use of state-of-siege powers was the enactment of a tough statute on security by President Julio César Turbay (1978–82) shortly after his inauguration. Ostensibly decreed to be employed as a tool against drug trafficking, it was employed primarily against the growing guerrilla threat and against student and labor activists. The new statute increased the powers of arrest of the armed forces and the types of crimes by civilians to be tried by military justice, lengthened sentences for such crimes as kidnapping and extortion, and limited press reports on public disturbances. An increase in military actions against guerrilla groups and allegations of human rights violations led to fears of the "Uruguayization" of the country— meaning a gradual military takeover, as in Uruguay in 1973.

But, the state of siege was lifted and thus the statute on security was automati-

Table 9.2. Electoral Results for the House of Representatives, 1935–1986

Year[a]	Liberal (%)	Conservative (%)	ANAPO (%)	Leftist Parties[b] (%)	Total Votes	Participation Rates (%)[c] A	B
1935	100	—	—	—	430,728	33.4	23.5
1937	100.0	—	—	—	550,726	32.5	28.9
1939	64.4	35.1	—	—	919,569	—	46.4
1941	63.8	35.7	—	—	885,525	—	43.0
1943	64.4	33.8	—	—	882,647	—	41.2
1945	63.0	33.6	—	3.2	875,856	38.4	39.4
1947	54.7	44.4	—	0.8	1,472,689	56.3	63.7
1949	53.5	46.1	—	0.4	1,751,804	63.1	72.9
1951	0.6	98.6	—	0.5	934,580	—	37.4
1953	—	99.7	—	—	1,028,323	—	39.0
1958	57.7	42.1	—	—	3,693,939	68.9	60.7
1960	44	41.7	—	12	2,542,651	57.8	39.6
1962	35.0	41.7	3.7	19.5	3,090,203	57.9	45.6
1964	46.2	35.5	13.7	4.3	2,261,190	36.9	31.3
1966	52.1	29.8	17.8	—	2,939,222	44.5	38.7
1968	49.9	33.7	16.1	—	2,496,455	37.3	31.0
1970	37.0	27.2	35.5	—	3,980,201	51.9	46.5
1972	46.3	30.8	19.0	—	2,947,125	36.3	32.5
1974	55.6	32.0	9.5	3.1	5,100,099	57.1	51.0
1976	52.0	39.1	3.6	4.6	3,265,974	34.5	31.2
1978	55.1	39.4	—	4.3	4,180,121	33.4	33.2
1980	54.5	38.2	—	4.1	4,215,371	33.8	32.2
1982	56.3	40.3	—	2.5	5,584,037	40.7	40.8
1984	54.4	39.6	—	2.4	5,654,436	38.0	39.8
1986	54.2	37.2	—	4.4	6,909,851	42.9	47.1

Sources: Colombia, DANE 1972, 152–54 (for electoral results and participation rates 1935–53); Colombia, Registraduría Nacional del Estado Civil, for electoral results and participation rates, column A, 1958–82; Losada 1976, 7; Losada 1979, 9n; and Losada personal correspondence for participation results, column B, 1958–86. Dix 1967, 140, for Liberal and MRL vote, 1960, 1962, and 1964. From Hartlyn 1988, 150–51.

a. In 1935 and 1937, the Conservative party officially abstained; in 1951 and 1953, the Liberal party did. Small percentages for non-Left minor candidates and blank and void votes are not included. In 1972, 1976, and 1980, the figures are for departmental assemblies (and in 1984 for municipal council) because no national elections were held in those years.

b. Leftist parties: In 1945, 1949, and 1951, the Communist party; in 1947, the Socialist party. In 1960 and 1962, the MRL; in 1964, the MRL *linea dura*. In 1974, the Unión Nacional de Oposición (UNO); in 1976, UNO and the Movimiento Independiente y Revolucionario (MOIR); in 1978, UNO, the Frente Unido del Pueblo (FUP), and Unidad Obrera y Socialista (UNIOS); in 1980, UNO, FUP, Frente Democrático (FD), Movimiento Firmes, and Coalición; in 1982, FUP, FD, Unidad Democrática, Liberal–FD, and Movimiento Izquierda Democrática; in 1984, FUP, FD; in 1986, Unión Patriótica (UP) and joint Liberal–UP lists, as Galán's Nuevo Liberalismo vote (6.6%) was included with the Liberal vote.

c. Column A is based upon estimates by the Registraduría Nacional del Estado Civil of the total number of eligible voters; Column B is based on estimates of the population eligible to vote (male and over 21, 1935–53; over 21, 1958–74; over 18, 1976–86).

Table 9.3. Electoral Results for the Presidency, 1930–1986

A. 1930–49	Liberal (%) A	B	Conservative (%) A	B	Total Votes	Participation Rates (%) A	B
1930	44.9 Olaya	— —	29.1 Valencia	25.9 Vásquez	824,530	n.a.	n.a.
1934	97.6 López	—	—	—	942,309	n.a.	n.a.
1938	100.0 Santos	—	—	—	513,520	30.2	26.4
1942	48.5 López	41.3 Arango	—	—	1,147,806	55.8	54.7
1946	32.3 Turbay	26.3 Gaitán	41.4 Ospina		1,366,005	55.7	60.2
1949	—	—	100.0 Gómez		1,140,646	39.9	47.4

B. 1958–70	Official National Front (%)	ANAPO (%)	Other (%) A	B	Total Votes	Participation Rates (%) A	B
1958	79.9 Lleras C.	—	19.8 Leyva	—	3,108,567	57.7	51.1
1962	62.1 Valencia	—	11.7 Leyva	25.9 López M.	2,634,840	48.7	38.9
1966	71.4 Lleras R.	28.0 Jaramillo	—	—	2,649,258	40.1	34.9
1970	40.3 Pastrana	38.7 Rojas	11.7 Betancur	8.3 Sourdís	4,036,458	52.5	47.2

C. 1974–86	Liberal (%)	Conservative (%)	ANAPO (%)	Left (%)	Other (%)	Total Votes	Participation Rates (%) A	B
1974	56.2 López	31.4 Gómez	9.4 María Rojas	2.6 Echeverri	0.1 Duarte	5,212,133	58.1	51.0
1978	49.5 Turbay	46.6 Betancur	—	2.4 3 candidates	1.3 Valencia	5,075,719	40.9	41.2
1982	41.0 López	46.8 Betancur	—	1.2 Molina	10.9 Galán	6,815,660	49.8	50.7
1986	58.3 Barco	35.8 Gómez	—	4.5 Pardo	0.6 Liska	7,229,937	n.a.	n.a.

Sources: Colombia, Registraduría Nacional del Estado Civil; Colombia, DANE 1972, 152; and Losada 1976, 7; Losada 1979, 9n; and Losada personal correspondence (for participation rate B). From Hartlyn 1988, 152–53.
Note: Participation rate A is based on estimates by the Registraduría of the total number of eligible voters; participation rate B is based on population estimates of the number of eligible voters.

cally repealed near the end of Turbay's term, following the surprise victory of the Conservative Belisario Betancur in the 1982 presidential elections and after one of the guerrilla groups operating in the country had suffered a significant setback. Both presidential candidates had campaigned in 1982 on a theme of "peace," seeking amnesty and political incorporation of the guerrilla groups. Illustrating commonly held views of the congress, many commentators viewed Turbay's action as a way of complicating the possibility of an amnesty under Betancur, which would now require passage through the congress, rather than simply an executive decree; in fact, the congress quickly approved one of the country's most generous amnesty laws, though its success was quite limited.

One important remaining legacy of the National Front period was negotiated as part of the 1968 reform and was a potentially significant limitation on presidential authority. This was the requirement that once executive parity ended in 1978 the party receiving the second highest number of votes needed to be offered "adequate and equitable" representation in government by the party in control of the presidency.[18] Turbay, in discussion with the Conservative directorate, gave them five of the twelve ministries.[19] Betancur, however, with a congress with a Liberal majority, brought five Liberals into his cabinet by asking them directly rather than by discussion with the Liberal directorate. Liberal party leaders, upset, called the Liberal participation "personal and technical." Subsequently, following the accommodation with Betancur after the tax reform fiasco, it was termed "cooperation with oversight *(fiscalización)*"; in Betancur's last two years, as they prepared for elections, the Liberals called it "constitutional collaboration with critical independence." In 1986, an overwhelming Liberal victory in both the congressional and presidential elections (see tables 9.2 and 9.3) led to the formation of a single-party government and an attempt to establish a "government-opposition" regime.[20] However, in spite of possessing a seemingly overwhelming majority in the congress, President Barco was unable to ensure legislative passage of numerous reform measures, including a broad-ranging constitutional reform that would have finally dismantled the last remaining remnants of coalition rule and provided additional access to opposition movements.[21]

In the 1980s, the regime would almost certainly have faced political turmoil and a growing legitimacy crisis in part because political actors had sought to justify and retain a political model—coalition rule—that no longer responded to the country's social structure. *The country's excessively strong formal presidential powers and centralized rule had clearly generated incentives encouraging the retention of the model, with negative consequences.* Yet the scope of the crisis and its effects on the Colombian state, regime, and society were all magnified by the interactive effects of escalating and complex patterns of violence.

In ironic and paradoxical juxtaposition to the president's strong formal powers, throughout the 1980s the effective power of the president in society and in relation to other parts of the state appeared more circumscribed than ever. There had been a severe deflation of state authority as a direct consequence of drug trafficking, and due to several indirect ones, such as its facilitating growing paramilitary and criminal violence as well as guerrilla activity, its regional alliances with local landowners and elements of the armed forces against leaders of popular movements and opposition parties, and the increased penetration of drug money into political campaigns (facilitated by the decentralized, clientelistic nature of the parties).[22] In spite of its near paralysis in society, the judicial branch demonstrated increased willingness to constrain executive decree powers. And for a president who ostensibly possessed a majority in the legislature, such as President Barco, the management of relations with the congress was a growing exercise in frustration due to extreme factionalism, absence of party discipline, and opposition to reform. Many of Barco's major proposed reforms failed to gain passage in the congress. In addition, there was a greater sense of corporate self-identity within the armed forces.

However, a step initiated as President Barco was in his last months in office finally enabled wide-ranging political reform to occur, in the form of a Constituent Assembly that produced an entirely new constitution. Following an informal ballot concurrent with congressional elections, Barco authorized a more formal ballot requesting a constitutional assembly cast at the same time as the presidential elections of May 1990 (which turned out overwhelmingly to favor it). Then newly inaugurated Liberal President César Gaviria called for a special election for a constituent assembly in December; this time, by a narrow vote, the Supreme Court accepted the constitutionality of the election. The decision followed a particularly difficult period for the country. Among other events, the principal Liberal contender for the presidency, Luis Carlos Galán Sarmiento, had been assassinated; the government had declared a more vigorous war against several of the major drug traffickers, who had responded with terrorist bombings and other violence; and two leftist presidential candidates had been assassinated, including the leader of the M-19 guerrillas, who had just recently agreed to lay down their arms and reincorporate themselves into the political process.

"Winner-Take-All" Presidential Elections and Potential Electoral Polarization

As Colombia became nationally integrated, though politically divided, through the two political parties in the nineteenth century, divisions within the governing party occasionally led to partial interparty alliances, though never to the successful formation of third parties. In some cases, the party out of power or elements of it sought to regain power by going to war to take advantage of divisions within the governing party. This would lead to the temporary unification of the party in government (as the Conservatives discovered in 1876–77 and the Liberals in 1895 and 1899–1902).

These "rules" were modified somewhat in the twentieth century. One reason was that the strength of the regions relative to the central government had eroded due to expanding central government revenues and expenditures compared to local ones and to regional elite migrations to the capital city. Thus, the possibility of a region rebelling against the central authority and seeking support from other regions, as had occurred in the nineteenth century, declined (Abel 1974, 308). However, divisions in the governing party and a conciliatory approach by the other party could lead to a transfer of power, though still with considerable local violence.

Transfers of power from one party to another were carried out in 1930 and 1946. In both of these elections, a moderate figure from the opposing party promising bipartisan government was able to win a narrow plurality and assume power as a consequence of divisions in the then-governing party. In both cases, the newly elected presidents formed bipartisan cabinets and faced majorities of the opposing party in the congress, in part because presidential elections were held separately from elections for the congress, departmental assemblies, and municipal councils (held on different dates every two years). National leaders could not fully control the actions of lower-level leaders on whom they depended for votes. In the years following the 1930 presidential election, which brought a Liberal to the presidency, the process of "Liberalization" of local-level public administration was often violent. By 1933, Liberals had obtained a legislative majority in the house of representatives and in many departmental and municipal legislative bodies. But violence deescalated as a consequence of the nationalist effort involved in a brief border conflict against Peru.

The "winner-take-all" nature of presidential elections had its strongest impact and presence in the area of patronage, particularly given the country's constitutional centralism and the president's expansive appointive powers. Party activists were likely to press aggressively for access to state spoils and patronage, regardless of the narrowness of the electoral victory. Sharp policy swings and policy "maximalism" as power changed hands from one party to another was somewhat less of a factor in Colombia than elsewhere, given the fact that both political parties had similar social bases of support.

Yet the Liberal reforms enacted by President Alfonso López Pumarejo (1934–38, 1942–45) helped to polarize relations between the two parties. López came to power in 1934 in elections in which the Conservatives refused to participate. Constitutional reforms focused on secularization and state interventionism in the economy, and universal male suffrage was enacted. In addition, fiscal and land reforms were passed, and labor organization was supported. However, opposition within López's own party also forced a "pause" in the reform effort. A parliamentary structure would not necessarily have had an impact on the passage of the reforms, given the Liberal majority in the legislature (and the Conservative tactic of abstention).

The nature of presidential elections and the risk of polarization inherent to them, though, is quite apparent in examining the period from 1945 to 1949. A detailed analysis of the collapse of the regime in 1949 would examine multiple political, social, and economic factors (see Hartlyn 1988, Wilde 1978, Oquist 1980). What is important to emphasize for the purposes of this chapter is the way that the "winner-take-all" characteristics of presidential elections, the fixed presidential term and timing of elections, and executive-legislative deadlock further polarized the political situation and exacerbated the crisis. The Liberals gradually became the country's majority party over the 1930s and 1940s (see table 9.2), as a consequence of urbanization, initial industrialization, Liberal sponsorship of labor organization, and other reforms. At the same time, these economic and social changes also meant that the stakes of politics increased. President López, reelected in 1942, resigned in 1945 under bitter attacks from Conservatives and from the populist wing of the Liberal party, led by Jorge Eliécer Gaitán. To deal with the political crisis, his Liberal replacement formed a "National Union" cabinet with the Conservatives.

In this context, the 1946 elections were a mirror image of events in 1930, though they occurred in a society that was far more socially differentiated and politically mobilized. The Liberal party was irreparably split, with the more traditional, regional leaders and moderate national leaders (and the Communists, pursuing a "Popular Front" strategy) supporting one candidate and the urban poor, blue-collar workers and many employees and professionals backing the emerging Liberal populist Gaitán. Just six weeks before the elections, the Conservatives nominated Mariano Ospina, a moderate figure, as their presidential candidate. He pledged to continue a bipartisan "National Union" policy from government over the opposition of more sectarian Conservative figures, such as Laureano Gómez. Ospina won a plurality of votes (see table 9.3), and formed a "National Union" government as he had promised. The Liberals continued to control the congress.

The logic of presidentialism, hegemonic politics, and partisan violence began to play itself out. At the regional level, Conservatives, following the example of the just defeated Liberals in the 1930s as well as their own past historical patterns, began removing and excluding Liberals from office. Conservatives feared that if they were to lose the presidency, they would be able to regain it only with great difficulty, if at all. And Liberals feared that Conservatives, as a minority party, would attempt to consolidate a permanent grip on power by force. Violence increased around local elections, as Liberals unified and held on to their local and national legislative majorities in 1947. The conflict intensified as it became clear that the 1950 presidential elections would be between the two polarizing figures, Gómez and Gaitán, and Liberals left the "National Union" in February 1948. There were serious doubts about the honesty of electoral procedures and whether the presidential elections would be held at all (Oquist 1980, 116–17).

Violence then exploded into near civil war after the assassination of Gaitán in April 1948 and the days of rioting in Bogotá (the *bogotazo*) and other major cities that followed. Liberals reentered Ospina's government, though only for one month. Cabinet crises and their related ministerial changes, which had begun to rise sharply in the previous administration, increased even further (see fig. 9.1). Various power-sharing arrangements were proposed, but none prospered.[23] The conflict between the two parties became a struggle between the executive and the legislature, a struggle that became even more bitter as Liberals held on to their legislative majority in the 1949 elections (see table 9.2). Liberals moved up the presidential elections and began impeachment proceedings against President Ospina. Ospina responded by declaring a state of siege, closing the congress, banning public meetings, and imposing censorship of the press and radio.

How much importance should be placed on presidentialism in explaining the 1949 breakdown? All the elements of the National Front that the parties agreed to several years later had been suggested during the various failed attempts of the 1940s. As the National Front agreement successfully (though ingeniously) built upon the country's presidentialist structure, this suggests that presidentialism was, strictly speaking, neither necessary nor sufficient for the breakdown in 1949. Yet it did exacerbate the sense of crisis in that period, unduly raising expectations and hopes of the minority Conservative leaders and followers who found themselves in "control of government" while simultaneously heightening fears of Liberals.

Under a parliamentary system, hegemonic politics in Colombia would have had a different flavor. A prime minister of the minority party could still have emerged, if supported by one or more factions of the other party, especially given Colombia's electoral system of proportional representation with multiple lists and the fact that national leaders had substantial influence over their factions in the 1930s and 1940s (which declined dramatically over the National Front years). Yet such a prime minister could only have retained power with the continued support of such factions, until or unless subsequent elections gained him a one-party majority. Social and political mobilization, violence, fraud, and coercion could still have wreaked havoc on the political regime, but the timing and nature of the crisis would have been different, and regime collapse may not have occurred.

The "winner-take-all" nature of presidentialism heightened the fears of the divided minority Conservatives and complicated the enactment of the National Front. The original National Front agreement pacted between the major political leaders, which became part of the country's constitution by means of a national plebiscite, envisioned addressing the dangers of presidentialism by perfect parity between the two parties in all branches of government for sixteen years and by depoliticizing public administration.[24] It was also agreed that a Conservative would serve the first presidential term. However, divisions within the Conservative party led to the candidacy of a Liberal for the first term and an agreement to have the congress approve a constitutional reform to institute presidential alternation for the three subsequent terms. The need to enshrine the agreement on power sharing formally as part of the constitution was a consequence of presidentialism and of the fact that national leaders could not control the drawing up of potentially victorious dissident lists opposed to the agreement.

During the National Front, the requirement of presidential alternation created its own problems for the regime. This was particularly true in the two elections in which only Conservatives, the minority party, could present candidates. In both cases, the Liberal party played a large role in determining the official National Front candidates, and in both cases the National Front faced serious challenges. In 1962, the challenge came from a dissident Liberal faction that presented its own presidential candidate, threatening a potential defeat of the National Front Conservative due to the country's Liberal majority. The Supreme Court eventually ruled that votes for the dissident Liberal candidate would be considered null and void (these are the votes reported for López in the 1962 elections in table 9.3).

By 1970, the National Popular Alliance (ANAPO), a primarily Conservative populist opposition to the National Front led by General Gustavo Rojas Pinilla (head of the military government from 1953 to 1957), had emerged as the major electoral threat to supporters of the National Front. ANAPO was strengthened by the fact that it could ambiguously present a "Conservative" presidential candidate (Rojas's party affiliation) and sharply anti–National Front legislative lists under both parties at the same time, in presidential elections in which only Conservatives could present their candidacies. The absence of Liberal candidates unquestionably strengthened ANAPO's vote, especially in major urban areas, and the movement lost the presidential election by the narrowest of margins (last-minute fraudulent additions to the official candidate's vote total probably kept the victory from ANAPO). This was the National Front's most serious crisis, and the sense of political frustration and blockage that the electoral process helped engender provided inspiration for one of the most prominent of the country's guerrilla movements in the late 1970s and 1980s. The M-19 (Movement of April 19 [1970]) took its name from the date of the 1970 elections that it considered fraudulently kept the victory from ANAPO. These kinds of problems would have been obviated in a parliamentary system, where determination of a prime minister would have followed elections (though other problems related to forming governing coalitions would have been generated).

But the central problem in Colombia toward the end of the National Front with regard to elections was not their polarizing potential due to presidentialism (cf. the case of Chile in Valenzuela 1985a, 1985b). Rather, with the blurring of differences between the two parties, the decline of sectarian identification with them, the long years of coalition rule, the nature of electoral procedures permitting each party multiple lists, and the maintenance of brokerage and clientelistic practices in a context of high abstention, the central issue was that elections were not effectively channeling political opposition.

Absence of a Moderating Power

In the process of breakdown of 1945–49, it was evident that moderate leaders in both parties lacked a unifying figure who could provide support and credence to any potential compromise. In addition, the church was essentially involved as a partisan actor in support of the Conservative party; the courts, in turn, were largely subservient to executive authority. By the time of the 1953 military coup, most major Liberal leaders were in exile. The conspiracy was fueled by Ospina and other dissident Conservatives opposed to efforts by Gómez to impose a Falangist-style constitution with even stronger presidential powers. Liberals warmly welcomed the military action.[25]

During the National Front, acute economic or political crises were managed by ad hoc decision forums or summit negotiations among national party leaders. In the 1965 crisis, which combined serious economic problems, a threatened national strike by labor confederations, and talk of a military coup led by an activist general, the industrialists' association (ANDI, Asociación Nacional de Industriales) played a key role in defusing the crisis.

In subsequent crises, former presidents have sometimes been called upon to play a mediating or supportive role. One example was when President Betancur called upon all the former presidents in attempting to deal with the takeover of the country's Palace of Justice in November 1985 by M-19 guerrillas a few months after a truce between them and the government had broken down.[26] Yet though this so-called club of ex-presidents has consisted of important leaders of both major parties, it has symbolized "national" figures only ambiguously. Ambiguously, because some of its members have still been leaders of major party factions, often with continuing presidential ambitions (only immediate presidential reelection was prohibited until 1991). In addition, as constitutional legacies of coalition rule and bipartisan exclusion of other political forces has increasingly become a topic of debate, reliance on a group of individuals that represent only the two major parties has been problematic. Thus, most recently, it has occasionally been expanded to include other elements of Colombian society. During the Barco administration, to assist in generating negotiations with the government, one guerrilla group requested the formation of a "Commission of Notables" consisting of two former presidents from different parties, a major church figure, and the president of ANDI (Bejarano 1990, 21–23). In sum, this "club," more recently in an expanded version, has on occasion provided a weak functional alternative to the potential moderating role that a "head of state" in a parliamentary regime could play. And, the recently adopted constitution, by its firm embrace of presidentialism—while seeking to curtail presidential powers, enhance the policy-making role of the congress, and weaken the two-party electoral stranglehold—also clearly rejects any formal role for a "moderating power."

Concluding Reflections

The dilemmas of presidentialism have been evident in the Colombian case. In the late 1940s, the rhythm of presidential politics in a context of a minority president with extensive appointive powers—executive-congressional deadlock, fixed terms in office, and polarization around "winner-take-all" elections—intensified the sense of crisis, which eventually resulted in a breakdown of the regime. A parliamentary regime, which could have led to a coalition government, mitigating fears of exclusion and making the sharing of spoils easier, might well have attenuated a number of these critical issues and prevented the 1949 breakdown. Yet firm judgment on this point is complicated by the existence of past patterns of intense interparty violence in the country. It is also difficult to point to presidentialism as *the* insurmountable obstacle, given the fact that successful accommodation was reached between the two parties some years later. However, that accommodation required peculiar—and eventually costly—institutional adaptations to ensure that it would function in a presidential system.

The consociational National Front agreement that facilitated the restoration of civilian rule in 1958 has been unique among consociational cases in being the only one in a presidential system.[27] Its rigidity and the method chosen to ensure that the constitution was appropriately modified (a national plebiscite) showed distrust of sectarian regional and local figures by national party leaders. It also demonstrated the willingness of the majority Liberal party, as it was out of government, to underplay its potential power and agree to grant an equal share of political power to the Conservatives in order to ensure access to the government for itself. These were issues that might not necessarily have been more easily resolvable in the context of a parliamentary regime, unless the electoral law prohibited multiple party lists. National party leaders feared that if congressional elections were held first and one party received a significant majority, it would be difficult to impose party discipline and acquire passage of a constitutional reform imposing parity. One possible solution, an extraconstitutional agreement to present joint congressional lists, would not necessarily work because the electoral law permitted those opposed to the National Front plan to present their own dissident lists (see Hartlyn 1984, 259). Thus the rigidity of the National Front agreement reflected not only a desire for demobilization following the country's intense violence but also fears of potential abuse of power by a party in control of the unitary, presidential system.[28]

The almost inevitable result of the immobilism inherent in the National Front agreement was the strengthening of formal presidential power. Combined with the fact that the agreement was constitutionally enshrined, this had several negative effects. It encouraged coalition rule longer than necessary because the benefits of participating in the executive were great and weakened the congress as a site of policy discussion and accommodation even as links between regional figures and national leaders deteriorated. This also encouraged simultaneously an increased reliance on brokerage and clientelism by regional politicians and the growth of nonelectoral opposition and tactics by increasingly frustrated groups in society. As sectarian party hatreds receded and a different kind of guerrilla violence and civic protest emerged in the late 1970s, national party leaders saw the need for political reforms and for attempted incorporation of guerrilla movements into the country's political process. However, the structure of incentives generated by coalition governments, multiple party lists, and high-abstention elections so favored regional leaders that they resisted change (a comprehensive examination would also need to consider the nature of the country's socioeconomic change, patterns of support and opposition by different social groups, movements, and organizations, and the evolution of particular guerrilla groups and the armed forces).

Institutional reform came later and for many years in more limited fashion than it should have, even as it confronted a much more complex and mobilized society, further complicated by the consequences of drug trafficking and of state efforts to combat it. The dual processes of amnesty for the guerrillas and of political reforms began somewhat separately under President Betancur but became joined by the middle of his term. Economic problems limited the government's ability to deliver on its promises of socioeconomic measures, but guerrilla groups had also been promised reforms to assure them greater political access. Laws touching on electorai reform, civil service, party structure, campaign financing, regionalization, local referendums, and access to television and public information were passed, though their impact was limited because they had been considerably weakened in passage.

The most important reforms that gained passage revolved around decentraliza-tion. Although vital, by themselves they were insufficient to stem the wave of vio-lence. Various fiscal measures increased the flow of resources to the departmental and municipal levels. And a constitutional reform calling for the popular election of mayors in 1988 gained passage. This reform was a key component of efforts to inte-grate guerrilla forces into peaceful, electoral forms of struggle. It was felt that these forces would be more willing to engage in democratic politics if they could acquire political power at the local level and have access to their own funds without com-plete dependence on the central government. For some political leaders, this reform also had the potential to strengthen the "government-opposition" form of govern-ment begun in 1986 while revitalizing the traditional parties. The possibility of gain-ing local political office encouraged Conservatives to go into opposition in 1986. Yet many amnestied guerrillas were targeted for assassination, and political violence subsequently expanded further in nature and scope. Efforts by the Barco adminis-tration to achieve more far-reaching political reforms also failed, though the suc-cessful incorporation of the M-19 and other guerrilla groups and the overwhelming popular vote in support of a constitutional assembly at the end of Barco's term pre-saged the successful passage of a new constitution, which occurred a year later.

The 1991 constitution, while sustaining presidentialism as an unquestioned principle, has instituted a variety of sometimes contradictory measures whose overall effects appear likely to weaken formal presidential powers. Measures also seek to enhance the role of the congress in policy making while reducing excesses of corruption and patronage and to reduce the control of the two traditional par-ties over the political regime.

In the new constitution, presidential powers have been restricted in several ways. Presidential reelection has been flatly prohibited. Presidential emergency decree powers under state of siege have been considerably reduced and congressional oversight enhanced, even as the length of time in which a state of siege can be in effect has also been limited. The special presidential powers regarding finance from the 1968 reform were eliminated, and the organism responsible for monetary policy has been given greater autonomy. A degree of decentralization of power has been built in by the requirement that now both governors and mayors are to be elected for three-year terms (with no immediate reelection), and some fiscal decentralization has been assured.

The role of the congress has been enhanced in several ways. First, its size has been reduced. The senate is restricted to one hundred members, to be elected in nationwide elections (two more will represent Indian communities); chamber representatives are chosen by departmental elections, and their number is determined largely by population levels. These changes should reduce the previous overrepresentation of rural regions and interests in the congress. Additionally, the congress has been given several potentially significant roles. For example, under the new constitution, it can now censure ministers, forcing their resignation by a majority vote of the full membership in each chamber. In an effort to reduce the worst excesses of both nepotism and clientelistic practices, various restrictions—such as ones related to the holding of public office in the previous year or of relatives in public office—have been imposed on those seeking to occupy a congressional seat; pork barrel funds (known as *auxilios parlamentarios*) also have been explicitly prohibited, and severe limitations on the use of funds for foreign travel have been imposed. Yet absent other measures—such as an increase in and a professionalization of congressional staffs—it is not clear that these changes will do more than change the tenor, and perhaps even increase the scope, of pork barrel politics in the country.

If the risk in multiparty presidential systems has been of extreme polarization, the problem in Colombia's two-party system has been perceived to be the opposite. These and other measures could open up a healthy political competition by weakening the historic electoral domination of the two traditional parties while also forcing them to forge more effective organizational links to groups in society. All remaining elements of coalition rule have been removed, and the judiciary has been completely revamped. Nationwide senatorial elections and restrictions on clientelistic practices could loosen the grip of the regional brokerage and machine politics–oriented figures of the two traditional parties. State financing of parties and their campaigns has now been raised to a constitutional mandate. To attempt to reduce vote buying and other fraudulent practices, a single ballot has now been required in all elections and electoral oversight has been strengthened. In addition, if no presidential candidate receives an absolute majority of votes, the constitution now calls for a second electoral round among the two top vote-getters; a vice president, who does not necessarily have to be of the same party as the president, will also be elected. Both these measures might encourage more parties and more party coalitions.

However, various elements remain that continue to favor the two traditional parties, even in their currently factionalized and clientelized state. One is the fact that voting has not been made obligatory. In high-abstention elections, this favors machine politicians, who can mobilize voters (it can also help parties or movements who receive a sudden surge of popular support, as with the M-19 in the election for the Constituent Assembly). Another is that multiple party lists are still permitted, allowing each party to present multiple candidacies.

The impact of other changes is even more unpredictable. One of these changes is that the constitution permits plebiscites, referenda, enactment of legislation by popular initiative, and recall elections. Another requires that election dates be separated. The constitution specifies that presidential elections must be held separately from congressional ones, which must be carried out on a date different from local ones. Historically, high abstention rates in local elections have tended to favor machine politicians from the two parties; however, more recently, even as that continued to be true, in some areas of heavy guerrilla presence leftist parties have done well, and in the very low turnout election for the Constituent Assembly, the M-19 lists received a plurality victory. Similarly, the polarization effect of presidential elections has usually favored widely known figures from the two parties, sometimes in partial opposition to regional party brokers. The possibility of a two-round presidential election might now mitigate this effect.

As Colombia moves into the 1990s, it faces continuing problems of governability. State authority must continue to address the challenges of drug trafficking and the paramilitary groups they spawned or fortified (even if many have been weakened or dismantled), guerrilla forces (several of which have continued blindly to insist on armed struggle, though peace talks have continued sporadically), right-wing reaction (from both within and outside the state), and continuing high levels of criminal violence.

The effort to resolve two-party conflict under presidentialism *(la violencia)* led to the excessively rigid National Front and to coalition rule that lasted far too long; the two traditional parties remained electorally dominant, but social conflict was increasingly channeled elsewhere. This social conflict engendered complex patterns of violence, exacerbated by the impact of drug trafficking and government efforts to combat it, which weakened the state. Thus, though dilemmas common to other presidential regimes were apparent in Colombia, given the country's party structure and electoral laws and multiple other problems, presidentialism has not appeared central to the current issues of governability, as could be argued has been more the case in countries with polarized multiparty systems (see Valenzuela 1985a, 1985b on Chile).

The new constitution, however, seeks to encourage further democratization by moving the country away from what has been perceived as a restrictive bipartisanship, with extreme clientelism and marginalization of the congress from central policy issues and excessive formal presidential powers (while also seeking to enhance individual rights and strengthen and reorganize the judicial branch). In these intentions it can only be applauded, even if the document is partially contradictory and both excessively broad in its claims on the state and too specific in many respects. Conflict may be perceived to increase, but if it is channeled through parties and political institutions, this would be a healthy sign in a country in which so much conflict—to put it mildly—has not been managed through democratic processes. Although it currently appears unlikely, it would be both ironic and tragic if the result were unexpectedly to be a different set of challenges to governability in the country, this time emerging more directly from the fact that presidentialism has remained an unchallenged principle in Colombian constitutionalism. Such an outcome could occur if the new potentials for executive-legislative deadlock and for the polarization of presidential elections—in the absence of an effective moderating power—were dramatically realized.

Notes

This material was prepared for a May 1989 conference on "Presidential or Parliamentary Democracy: Does It Make a Difference?" and was revised shortly thereafter. In October 1991, minor modifications were made and several paragraphs were added to the conclusion to reflect actual and potential changes due to the new Colombian constitution promulgated on July 4, 1991. I gratefully acknowledge the comments made on the initial version by several participants at the conference, particularly Michael Coppedge and Arturo Valenzuela, as well as those by Ronald Archer regarding the paragraphs on the potential impact of the 1991 constitution. Responsibility for contents remains mine alone.

1. In institutional terms, the contrast being drawn is between presidential and parliamentary systems. Parliamentary systems are normally understood to be ones in which the holder of executive power, the head of government (usually the prime minister), and his or her cabinet remain in power only with the confidence of the legislature. Thus, to a certain extent, executive and legislative powers are fused. In presidential systems, the chief executive (the president), combining the functions of head of state and head of government, is separately elected and cannot be removed by the legislature except in very unusual circumstances. Hybrid constitutions have sometimes made it difficult to categorize countries (such as the French Fifth Republic) neatly, and of course other political characteristics, such as the degree of centralization (or federalism) or the nature of the party system and electoral laws often also have profound implications regarding the nature and dilemmas of particular presidential or parliamentary regimes (see Lijphart 1984, 1–36, esp. 6).

2. These are derived principally from Linz (1978, 1984) and Valenzuela (1985a). Riggs also emphasizes that independent of executive-legislative deadlock, a legislature in a presidential system tends to have a larger and more controversial agenda as its members must make up their minds independently of the recommendations of the president. This occurs much less frequently in parliamentary systems, which tend to have more disciplined parties, though there are cases of presidential systems with strongly disciplined parties, such as Venezuela. Similarly, Riggs emphasizes that it is easier to organize and sustain political parties in parliamentary systems than in presidential ones and that an effective judicial "third branch" is essential as an umpire between the executive and the legislature (Riggs 1987, 10–14).

3. Regarding the comparatively unique characteristics of U.S. political institutions, see

Lijphart (1984): for an argument that they are both "unique" and "antique," see Huntington (1967, 93–139); for an analysis of the "paraconstitutional" practices that have helped sustain presidentialism in the United States, see Riggs (1987).

It might be useful at this point to make explicit an implicit normative implication about a preference regarding the potential trade-off between radical social change and democratic regime survival. A presidential regim₂ may lead a newly elected minority president and his supporters to believe that efforts to enact radical policy change are both appropriately supported and feasible, with potential polarizing consequences, while a parliamentary regime in similar circumstances would more likely lead to a scaling back of these expectations and to accommodation and moderation (though also possibly frustration and drift). Cf. the explanation for the adoption of presidentialism with an electoral system of proportional representation in Nicaragua's new constitution in Reding (1987, esp. 279–81). If this helps to explain why leftist groups often favor presidentialism, it is also true that rightist groups in Latin America have usually argued in favor of presidentialism because they desire a clear figure of authority at the head of the political regime. As will be seen below, however, this potential trade-off is not the central issue in the Colombian case.

4. The precise nature of Colombia's civilian political regimes has been subject to considerable academic debate. From 1910 to 1949, Colombia had an "oligarchical democracy" (Wilde 1978). Because of restrictions on majoritarian democracy imposed by the National Front agreement discussed below and because the country has been governed for most of the time since the 1940s under a state of siege, most analysts have viewed Colombia since 1958 as a qualified democracy—employing adjectives such as a "restricted democracy" *(democracia restringida)* (Leal 1984) or a "limited democratic consociational regime" currently in an uncertain process of transformation (Hartlyn 1988). Yet others have characterized it from the other side of the democracy-authoritarianism continuum as "inclusionary authoritarian" (Bagley 1984) or as in a lengthy (thirty-year) "transition" from dictatorship to democratic government, impelled by reforms of the mid-1980s (Chernick 1988).

5. The Colombian province of Panama gained its independence many decades later under very different circumstances.

6. To date, all Colombian presidents have been male.

7. Such appointees were not required to resign from the congress, as alternates *(suplentes)* replaced them in their absence. These cabinet officers often served as key liaisons with the legislature (see Archer and Chernick 1988).

8. This agreement held up until the first series of national level competitive elections in 1974 resulted in an overwhelmingly Liberal congress. Over the protests of Liberal President López Michelsen, the congress elected Liberals to both posts. During this period, the two offices often served less as a check on presidential authority for policy reasons and more as a brake on efficiency and as an important source of congressional patronage.

9. The National Front plebiscite also called for the creation of a civil service and protection of government employees covered by it. It confirmed the vote for women (first granted by the military government of General Rojas in 1954), required a minimum of 10 percent of the national budget to be spent on education, provided only per diem pay for congressional representatives rather than a salary, and stated that future constitutional reforms could only be carried out by the congress (to block future reform efforts by plebiscite) (see the text in Vázquez Cobo Carrizosa n.d., 345–47).

The 1968 constitutional reform, discussed in the text below, partially "dismantled" the National Front. It reimposed a simple congressional majority for most legislation, reinstated competitive elections at the local level in 1970 and at the national level in 1974, extended parity in the executive branch until 1978, and required the winning party subsequently to *offer* an ambiguous "adequate and equitable" representation in government to the party receiving the second highest number of votes.

10. Elsewhere (Hartlyn 1988, 75–78; 91–94), I present two other predicaments inherent to the political formula of the National Front, threatened policy incoherence and lack of popular responsiveness, and discuss various "rules of the game" that emerged to address them. One of these, discussed in the text below, is increased presidential authority.

11. The table summarizes information about the major party factions at election time. Following elections, new factions were sometimes created and old ones disbanded as congressional representatives shifted allegiances and factions occasionally changed their position. These changes are not reflected in the table.

12. A 1960 reform of the president's state-of-siege powers ironically reduced the incentives for the congress to approve legislation decreed by the executive under a state of siege. Reacting to the fact that President Ospina had been able simply to close the congress in 1949 after declaring a state of siege, the constitutional language was changed in 1960 to require the congress to be called into session ten days after a state of siege was declared and to remain in session until it was lifted (it could also now request by a majority vote in both chambers that the constitutionality of executive decrees be determined by the Supreme Court). Yet the National Front plebiscite had specified that congressional representatives were to be paid only a per diem wage for the time the congress was in session, rather than a salary. Thus, under a state of siege, senators and representatives were effectively paid much more than they would have been under normal circumstances. The 1968 constitutional reform once again specified that congressional representatives were to be paid a salary.

13. For an analysis of a similar set of changes in Chile during the Frei administration, see Valenzuela and Wilde (1979).

In the Colombian case at least, this trend was strongly reinforced by international aid agencies concerned about such things as proper identification of projects, preinvestment studies, tight institutional control, professional staffing, clear operating regulations, proper auditing, and prior review of selected loan disbursements. For them, this was best achieved by channeling funds independently from political ("partisan") influence from the congress or even from central ministries (see Hartlyn 1988, 97–102, 126–131; Cepeda and Mitchell 1980).

14. The system was known as the UPAC (Unidad de Poder Adquisitivo Constante) system. Because of the web of interests rapidly created around the new financial institutions, the subsequent president could not dismantle the system, though he did trim back its indexation features (see Findley, Cepeda, and Gamboa 1983; Hartlyn 1988, 131–34).

15. See Valencia Villa (1987). Tragically and ironically, this was occurring even as judicial capacity vis-à-vis society was largely in a state of collapse as a consequence of the violence, intimidation, and corruption generated by drug trafficking, which came on top of decades of neglect of the country's judicial system.

16. The marginal role of national party leaders and the possibility of multiple party lists presents a dramatic contrast with neighboring Venezuela, where central party authorities have been extremely powerful in determining party nominees for elected office (the *partidocracia*) and each party can present only a single list.

17. The electoral system of proportional representation by department in which parties are permitted to present multiple lists (and ballot splitting is permitted) has allowed the two major parties to accumulate many more seats than they might have had if they were allowed to present only a single list by department. When legislative parity was in effect, opposition

movements benefited from the ambiguity of ostensibly representing one of the two traditional parties with which the country's population has identified while also opposing National Front governments or policies.

After the 1974 election, there was an increase in the number of departments in which only "uninominal" lists (lists in which only the first person named was elected) were victorious; in the 1978 and 1982 elections, this was the case in roughly 75 percent of the country's departments (see Hartlyn 1988, 160–63).

18. A congressional vote in 1968 that would have led to a requirement for indefinite fixed parity in the executive branch led President Carlos Lleras, in a classic but still risky maneuver, to offer his resignation. The conditions noted in the text were the compromise eventually worked out (see also n. 10). In a 1969 message to the congress, Lleras noted that the reform as passed "frees the republic from the dangers of a collective government, lacking in unity, impotent to manage increasingly more challenging situations. . . . At the same time, it provides formulas we consider satisfactory to maintain a true national spirit in the executive branch and public administration" (cited in Latorre 1986, 80n).

19. Since the National Front began, the remaining thirteenth ministry of defense has been headed by the country's top-ranking general. Although this also resolved the issue of parity, the main objective in 1958 was to permit the armed forces to manage their own affairs in the complex transition from military rule under General Rojas to civilian government. As became particularly evident by the nature and extent of military opposition to President Betancur's efforts to seek negotiated settlements with guerrilla groups, a military head of defense also accelerated a process of growing military autonomy and corporate self-identification, which was compounded by the civilian abdication of broad areas of internal security policy to the armed forces. Following the promulgation of the 1991 constitution, and in light of the fact that cabinet ministers could now be censured by the congress and forced to resign, President César Gaviria appointed a civilian minister of defense. Time will tell to what extent this step marked a process of redefinition of civil-military relations in a more democratic direction.

20. The Liberal candidate, Virgilio Barco, had campaigned on the pledge to pursue a Liberal "government-program," which potential Conservative party collaborators would have to accept if they were to participate in government. Following their defeat, Conservative party leaders called for their party to refuse to participate in government. Technically following the constitutional requirements, Barco named three Conservatives to cabinet positions upon his inauguration, though without consulting the Conservative party directorate. The Conservatives rejected the positions, criticized the government for its refusal to dialogue, and entered into what it termed "reflexive opposition."

21. Recognizing the difficulty of seeking constitutional reform through the congress (where such reform required approval in committee and by each chamber by a two-thirds vote in two consecutive years), President Barco sought in 1988 to implement reform by means of a plebiscite. Opposition from elements of both traditional parties led to a bipartisan agreement to create a "Process of Institutional Readjustment." However, the legal implementation of this process was itself found to be unconstitutional by a surprisingly more activist judicial Council of State. Barco thus presented his constitutional reforms to the congress in 1988. They gained the first necessary approval in late 1988, in somewhat weakened fashion, but reflecting the absence of party discipline or coherence, they failed to gain passage the required second time in 1989 (see Bejarano 1990).

22. For a general analysis of the impact of drug trafficking on the Colombian state, political regime, and society, see Hartlyn (1993); see also Bagley (1988, 1989–90). For analyses of the extent and complicated nature of contemporary political violence and of human rights

violations in Colombia, see Americas Watch (1989) and Washington Office on Latin America (1989). A useful review of factors limiting effective presidential power in Colombia is Archer and Chernick (1988).

23. President Ospina proposed postponing presidential elections for four years and interim rule by a bipartisan four-man government council, with major organs of the state under equal control and with a two-thirds majority requirement for legislation. Yet the proposal was transmitted to the Liberals by Gómez, who personally opposed it, and official repression against Liberals continued as moderate Conservatives were being replaced by hardliners (see Wilde 1978, 51–58).

24. One Liberal lawyer who was a member of the Commission of Institutional Readjustment in 1957 did recommend a Swiss-style plural executive; the idea found little support, in part, as 2 Conservative leader of the time stated, because of the country's "Bolivarian tradition." See *Semana*, 23–30 Aug. 1957; interview by the author with R. Emiliani Román, summer 1982.

25. As a consequence of the horrendous violence in the country, virulent attacks by Gómez following his forceful ouster from power and conciliatory gestures by the Liberals, the church opted to become a "nonpartisan" force, strongly supporting the National Front agreement.

26. Betancur was ultimately left responsible for a military action that he did not fully control and that led to the death of dozens of individuals, including half the country's Supreme Court judges.

27. Two other presidential systems, Venezuela and Chile, had democratic transitions with important consociational elements. However, neither the transition of Venezuela in 1958 nor that of Chile in 1989 involved formal constitutional changes, and in Venezuela a full return to a model of competitive politics was achieved by 1968.

28. Alberto Lleras, the key Liberal negotiator of the National Front, had argued in 1946 (as presented in Whitaker 1950, 117) that the two-party system was "the best form of political organization" and worked well in Great Britain and the United States. However, it was unworkable in Colombia because that country's unitary, presidential system "did not contain either of the checks on power that enabled the two-party system to function successfully in the other two countries—in Britain, the check of cabinet responsibility to Parliament; in the United States, the check of the federal system, with its division of power between the central government and the states." Lleras's solution in 1945 and 1946, as in the 1950s, was coalition rule.

References

Abel, Christopher. 1974. "Conservative Party in Colombia, 1930–1953." Ph.D. diss., Oxford University.

Americas Watch. 1989. *The Killings in Colombia*. New York: Americas Watch.

Archer, Ronald P., and Marc W. Chernick. 1988. "El presidente frente a las instituciones nacionales: un 'semidios' paralizado." Manuscript, Universidad de los Andes, Bogotá.

Bagley, Bruce M. 1984. "National Front and Economic Development." In *Politics, Policies and Economic Development in Latin America*, edited by Robert Wesson. Stanford, Calif.: Hoover Institution Press.

———. 1988. "Colombia and the War on Drugs." *Foreign Affairs* 67, no. 1: 70–92.

———. 1989–90. "Dateline Drug Wars: Colombia: The Wrong Strategy." *Foreign Policy* no. 77 (Winter).

Bejarano, Ana María. 1990. "La paz en la administración Barco: de la rehabilitación social a la negociación política." *Análisis político* no. 9 (Jan.–Apr.): 7–29.

Blanksten, George I. 1958. "Constitutions and the Structure of Power." In *Government and Politics in Latin America,* edited by Harold E. Davis. New York: Ronald Press.

Cepeda Ulloa, Fernando, and Christopher Mitchell. 1980. "The Trend toward Technocracy." In *Politics of Compromise: Coalition Government in Colombia,* edited by Albert Berry, Ronald Hellman, and Mauricio Solaún. New Brunswick, N.J.: Transaction Books.

Chalmers, Douglas A., and Craig H. Robinson. 1982. "Why Power Contenders Choose Liberalization." *International Studies Quarterly* 26 (Mar.): 3–36.

Chernick, Marc W. 1988. "Negotiations and Armed Conflict: A Study of the Colombian Peace Process (1982–1987)." Paper presented to the 13th International Congress of the Latin American Studies Association.

Colombia, Departamento Administrativo Nacional de Estadísticas (DANE). 1971. *Estadísticas electorales, 1935–1970.* Bogotá: The department.

Davis, Harold E. 1958a. "The Political Experience of Latin America." In *Government and Politics in Latin America,* edited by Harold E. Davis. New York: Ronald Press.

———. 1958b. "The Presidency." In *Government and Politics in Latin America,* edited by Harold E. Davis. New York: Ronald Press.

Dix, Robert H. 1967. *Colombia: The Political Dimensions of Change.* New Haven: Yale UP.

———. 1977. "The Colombian Presidency: Continuities and Changes." In *Presidential Power in Latin American Politics,* edited by Thomas V. DiBacco. New York: Praeger.

Findley, Roger W., Fernando Cepeda Ulloa, and Nicolás Gamboa Morales. 1983. *Intervención presidencial en la economía y el estado de derecho en Colombia.* Bogotá: Universidad de los Andes, CIDER.

Fitzgibbon, Russell. 1950. "Pathology of Democracy in Latin America: A Political Scientist's Point of View." *American Political Science Review* 44 (Mar.): 118–28.

Gallón Giraldo, Gustavo. 1979. *Quince años de estado de sitio en Colombia: 1958–1978.* Bogotá: Editorial América Latina.

Hartlyn, Jonathan. 1984. "Military Governments and the Transition to Civilian Rule: The Colombian Experience of 1957–1958." *Journal of Interamerican Studies and World Affairs* 26 (May): 245–81.

———. 1988. *The Politics of Coalition Rule in Colombia.* Cambridge: Cambridge UP.

———. 1993. "Drug Trafficking and Democracy in Colombia in the 1980s." Barcelona: Working Papers of the Institut de Ciències Polítiques i Socials.

Huntington, Samuel P. 1968. *Political Order in Changing Societies.* New Haven: Yale UP.

Lambert, Jacques. 1967. *Latin America: Social Structure and Political Institutions.* Berkeley and Los Angeles: U California P.

Latorre Rueda, Mario. 1986. *Hechos y crítica política.* Bogotá: Universidad Nacional de Colombia.

Leal Buitrago, Franciso. 1984. *Estado y política en Colombia.* Bogotá: Siglo XXI.

Lijphart, Arend. 1984. *Democracies: Patterns of Majoritarian and Consensus Government in Twenty-one Countries.* New Haven: Yale UP.

Linz, Juan J. 1978. *Crisis, Breakdown and Reequilibration.* In *The Breakdown of Democratic Regimes,* edited by Juan J. Linz and Alfred Stepan. Baltimore: Johns Hopkins UP.

———. 1984. "Democracy: Presidential or Parliamentary. Does It Make a Difference?" Paper presented to the workshop on "Political Parties in the Southern Cone," the Wilson Center, Washington, D.C.

López Michelsen, Alfonso. 1963. *Colombia en la Hora Cero: Proceso y enjuiciamiento del Frente Nacional,* vols. 1, 2. Bogotá: Ediciones Tercer Mundo.

Losada, Rodrigo. 1976. *Las elecciones de mitaca en 1976: participación electoral y perspectiva histórica*. Bogotá: FEDESARROLLO.
———. 1979. "El significado político de las elecciones de 1978 en Colombia." In *Las elecciones de 1978 en Colombia*, edited by Rodrigo Losada and Georg Leibig. Bogotá: FEDESARROLLO.
McGreevey, William P. 1971. *An Economic History of Colombia, 1845–1930*. New York: Cambridge UP.
Mainwaring, Scott. 1990. "Presidentialism in Latin America." *Latin American Research Review* 25, no. 1: 157–79.
Oquist, Paul. 1980. *Violence, Conflict and Politics in Colombia*. New York: Academic Press.
Park, James Williams. 1985. *Rafael Núñez and the Politics of Colombian Regionalism, 1863–1886*. Baton Rouge: Louisiana State UP.
Ramírez Aljure, Jorge. 1986. *Liberalismo: ideología y clientelismo, 1957–1986*. Bogotá: n.p.
Reding, Andrew. 1987. "Nicaragua's New Constitution." *World Policy Journal* 4 (Spring): 257–94.
Riggs, Fred W. 1987. "The Survival of Presidentialism in America: Para-Constitutional Practices." Paper, Department of Political Science, University of Hawaii.
Skidmore, Thomas E., and Peter H. Smith. 1984. *Modern Latin America*. New York: Oxford UP.
Stokes, William S. 1945. "Parliamentary Government in Latin America." *American Political Science Review* 39 (June): 522–36.
Uribe Vargas, Diego. 1985. *Las Constituciones de Colombia. Segunda edición ampliada y actualizada*. 3 vols. Madrid: Ediciones Cultura Hispánica, Instituto de Cooperación Iberoamericana.
Valencia Villa, Hernando. 1987. "Vida, pasión y muerte del Tribunal Especial." *Análisis político* no. 2 (Sept.–Dec.): 92–97.
Valenzuela, Arturo. 1985a. "Hacia una democracia estable: La opción parlamentaria para Chile." *Revista de ciencia política* 7 (Dec.).
———. 1985b. "Origins and Characteristics of the Chilean Party System: A Proposal for a Parliamentary Form of Government." Washington, D.C.: Wilson Center, Latin American Program, working paper no. 164.
Valenzuela, Arturo, and Alexander Wilde. 1979. "Presidential Politics and the Decline of the Chilean Congress." In *Legislatures in Developing Countries*, edited by Joel Smith and Lloyd D. Musolf. Durham: Duke UP.
Vásquez Velásquez, Orlando E. 1985. *Elección popular de alcaldes: Itinerario de una reforma constitucional*. Medellín: Editorial Jurídica Universitaria.
Vázquez Carrizosa, Alfredo. 1979. *El poder presidencial en Colombia*. Bogotá: Enrique Dobry.
Vázquez Cobo Carrizosa, Camilo. n.d. *El Frente Nacional: Su origen y desarrollo*. Cali: n.p.
Vidal Perdomo, Jaime. 1970. *La reforma constitucional de 1968 y sus alcances jurídicos*. Bogotá: Editorial Presencia.
Washington Office on Latin America. 1989. *Colombia Besieged: Political Violence and State Responsibility*. Washington, D.C.: Washington Office on Latin America.
Whitaker, Arthur P. 1950. "Pathology of Democracy in Latin America: A Historian's Point of View." *American Political Science Review* 44 (Mar.): 101–18.
Wilde, Alexander W. 1978. "Conversations among Gentlemen: Oligarchical Democracy in Colombia." In *The Breakdown of Democratic Regimes: Latin America*, edited by Juan J. Linz and Alfred Stepan. Baltimore: Johns Hopkins UP.

10

CATHERINE M. CONAGHAN

Loose Parties, "Floating" Politicians, and Institutional Stress: Presidentialism in Ecuador, 1979–1988

The contemporary political history of Ecuador provides ample evidence for Juan Linz's argument concerning the hazards of presidentialism for democratic regimes in Latin America (see chapter 1). Since its most recent transition from military rule in 1979, the record of executive-legislative relations reads like a chronicle of the ills of presidential arrangements. Over the last decade, explosive conflicts between the two branches have resulted in teargassing of the congress, physical attacks on individual legislators, violence on the floor of the legislature, and actions that led to the kidnapping of President León Febres-Cordero by air force paratroopers in January 1987. At various junctures, the executive-legislative face-offs brought the new political regime to the edge of breakdown. While such a rupture has thus far been avoided (largely because the military has been unwilling to intervene), the chronic institutional stress in Ecuador's democracy has taken its toll. The public's regard for democracy has eroded in the face of the unseemly and sometimes bizarre interaction of presidents and legislators.

What are the sources of the recurrent executive-legislative stress in Ecuador? Much of the problem lies in the interface between presidential institutional arrangements and the party system. Ecuador's extremely loose multiparty system has made it difficult for presidents to marshal support for their policies within the congress. It also creates incentives for presidents to bypass or ignore the congress altogether in policy making. This tendency to govern without congressional cooperation has been reinforced by the exigencies of the economic and debt crisis in Latin America. In their efforts to deal with external actors, presidents and their coteries of policy-makers in the executive branch seek to insulate economic policy from the pressures exerted by parties, legislators, and interest groups. This estrangement between executive and legislative branches is not confined to Ecuador. Peru and Bolivia have struggled with similar dynamics since their respective transitions to civilian rule took place in the last decade.[1]

Yet as dismal as the history of presidentialism appears in Ecuador, parliamentarism cannot be easily prescribed as the institutional solution to the explosive relations among political elites. A parliamentary formula would, I believe, encounter serious difficulties, given the dynamics in Ecuador's party system, particularly those posed by the presence of diverse and unpredictable populist parties. Moreover, before prescribing parliamentarism, we need to address the question of exactly how such an arrangement would affect the economic policy-making capacity of countries like Ecuador that will be dealing with effects of the debt crisis for many years to come. As Juan Linz has so convincingly argued, regime stability hinges on the complex interplay of efficiency and efficacy in policy-making and legitimacy.[2] Would parliamentary arrangements enhance or erode the economic policy-making capacity of governments in the emergency situations in which they currently find themselves?

Before addressing some of these issues in greater detail, however, it is essential to examine the evolution of the current institutional structure and party system in Ecuador.

The Legacies of Oligarchical Politics

Ecuador's long experience with presidentialism began with the promulgation of its first constitution in 1830. New constitutions were framed in 1835, 1843, 1845, 1851, 1852, 1861, 1869, 1878, 1884, 1897, 1906, 1929, 1938, 1945, 1946, 1967, and 1978.[3] But despite this penchant for constitutional revision, presidentialism was always the organizing principle of Ecuadorean government; there was never a single interlude of parliamentary government. Instead, constitutional revisions oscillated between unicameralism and bicameralism, eradicating or creating the vice presidency, and declaring the dominance of the executive or the legislative branch. One of the most distinctive features of Ecuadorean constitutional history involved the institutionalization of corporatist representation in the legislature. The 1946 constitution created four national and eight regional senators who represented business interest groups, the armed forces, labor, education, and the press.

The presidential system in Ecuador did not yield a predictable rotation of executive power. There have been frequent interruptions in the normal presidential term in office. Such interruptions occurred via military interventions, the removal of the president by the legislature (with military backing), and the declaration of civilian dictatorships by presidents themselves. Data on presidential turnover is presented in table 10.1.

Direct popular election, even though installed by the constitution of 1846 as the vehicle for presidential selection, was not the most common means used to rotate

Table 10.1. Presidential Succession in Ecuador, 1931–1988

President	Means to Office and Term[a]	Disposition of Term
Luis Larrea Alba	N–D (08/31–10/31)	overthrown
Alfredo Baquerizo Moreno	N (10/31–08/32)	completed
Carlos Freile Larrea	N (08/32–09/32)	overthrown
Alberto Guerreo Martínez	N (09/32–12/32)	completed
Juan de Diós Martínez Mera	P (12/32–10/33)	impeached
Abelardo Montalvo	N (10/33–08/34)	completed
José María Velasco Ibarra	P (09/34–08/35)	resigned
Antonio Pons	N (08/35–09/35)	resigned
Frederico Páez	N–D (09/35–10/37)	resigned
Alberto Enríquez Gallo	N (10/37–10/38)	resigned
Manuel María Borreo	N (10/38–12/38)	completed
Aurelio Mosquera Narváez	C (12/38–11/39)	died
Carlos Arroyo del Río	N (11/39–12/39)	resigned
Andrés Córdova Nieto	N (12/39–08/40)	resigned
Julio E. Moreno	N (08/40–08/40)	resigned
Carlos Arroyo del Río	P (09/40–05/44)	overthrown
Provisional junta	N (05/44–05/44)	resigned
José María Velasco Ibarra	N (05/44–08/44)	
	C (08/44–03/46)	
	D (03/46–08/47)	overthrown
Carlos Macheno Cajas	N (08/47–09/47)	resigned
Mariano Suárez Veintimilla	N (09/47–09/47)	resigned
Carlos Julio Arosemena Tola	C (09/47–08/48)	completed
Galo Plaza Lasso	P (09/48–08/52)	completed
José María Velasco Ibarra	P (09/52–08/56)	completed
Camilo Ponce Enríquez	P (09/56–08/60)	completed
José María Velasco Ibarra	P (08/60–11/61)	overthrown
Carlos Julio Arosemena	N (11/61–07/63)	overthrown
Military junta	N (07/63–03/66)	resigned
Clemente Yerovi Indaburo	N (03/66–11/66)	completed
Otto Arosemena Gómez	C (11/66–08/68)	completed
José María Velasco Ibarra	P (09/68–06/70)	
	D (06/70–02/72)	overthrown
Military junta	N (02/72–01/76)	resigned
Military junta	N (01/76–08/79)	resigned
Jaime Roldós	P (08/79–05/81)	died
Osvaldo Hurtado	N (05/81–08/84)	completed
León Febres-Cordero	P (08/84–08/88)	completed

Source: adapted from Georg Maier, "Presidential Succession in Ecuador, 1830–1970," *Journal of Inter-American Studies and World Affairs* 13, nos. 3–4 (1971): 475–509.

a. *N* = assumption of power through nonelectoral means (can include succession by vice-president); *P* = assumption of power through popular election; *C* = assumption of power through constituent assembly; *D* = declaration of dictatorship after assumption of office.

executive office, especially in the period prior to 1948. Instead, individuals found their way to presidential office through a variety of routes—military seizures of power, informal intraelite negotiations, and formal constituent assemblies. Even when direct popular elections occurred, participation was severely circumscribed by literacy and registration requirements. In short, presidentialism was the facade for oligarchic politics practiced by contending groups among Ecuador's dominant classes. The extremely closed character of the political system was rooted in the country's sociostructural circumstances and dependent export economy. The combination of a labor-repressive hacienda system in the country's interior and an agricultural export enclave on the coast constricted urbanization, economic growth, and the class structure. As a result, middle- and lower-class groups remained relatively demobilized. The efficacy of traditional modes of social control and the relative cohesion among upper-class groups allowed for the persistence of an exclusionary style of politics in Ecuador well after it had been eliminated in many other Latin American countries.

The oligarchic structure of politics that persisted until the promulgation of the 1978 constitution had a profound effect on the evolution of the party system. Elite competition for office was organized initially in the nineteenth century around classic liberal (Partido Liberal Radical) and conservative (Partido Conservador Ecuatoriano) parties.[4] While Communist and Socialist parties were born in intellectual circles in the 1920s, their impact on elections was negligible, given the restrictions on the franchise. Ecuador's permutation of populism erupted in the 1930s under the leadership of José María Velasco Ibarra. *Velasquismo,* however, was devoid of the distributive/redistributive content of other Latin American populist movements, such as Peronism. Velasco Ibarra made antioligarchic appeals in a caudillo style while maintaining close ties with economic elites and traditional parties throughout his career. He gave birth to an extremely conservative and programmatically vacant type of populism in Ecuador, which has been replayed by a number of other politicians since his passing.[5]

The emergence of Velasquismo was followed by further fragmentation in the party system in the post–World War II period. Another populist party, the Concentración de Fuerzas Populares (CFP), was founded in 1946; it built its considerable electoral base in the city of Guayaquil.[6] The Liberal and Conservative parties were fractured by both personal rivalries and ideological fissions. As seen in table 10.2, a diverse multiparty system was crystalizing in Ecuador by the early 1970s. The system was composed of the traditional oligarchic parties, "personalist" and populist electoral vehicles, small left-wing groups, and new organizations of social democrats and Christian democrats. This fragmentation was the result of both old-fashioned leadership struggles and the appearance of a new generation of middle-class professionals who actively sought to modernize the party system. The use of a proportional representation formula in congressional elections reinforced the tendency toward party fragmentation.

Table 10.2. Parties in Ecuador, 1979–1983

Left	Center Left	Centrist/Populist	Right
Frente Amplio de Izquierda (FADI)	Izquierda Democrática (ID)	Partido Democráta (PD)	Partido Social Cristiano (PSC)
Movimiento Democrático Popular (MPD)	Democracia Popular (DP)	Frente Radical Alfarista (FRA)	Partido Liberal Radical (PLR)
Partido Socialista Ecuatoriano (PSE)		Pueblo, Cambio, Democracia (PCD)	Partido Conservador Ecuatoriano (PCE)
		Partido Roldosista Ecuatoriano (PRE)	Partido Nacionalista Revolucionario (PNR)
		Concentración de Fuerzas Populares (CFP)	Coalición Institucionalista Democráta (CID)
		Partido Velasquista (PV)	

Note: All parties that held at least one seat in the National Congress are included.

For our purposes, it is important to underscore the key features of the party system prior to the watershed military intervention of 1972. Under military rule after 1972, party life was essentially "frozen," though it reemerged in 1978 with many of its essential features intact. The centrifugal forces at work in the pre-1972 party system affected every dimension of political linkage—party-mass ties, party-activist relations, and interparty coalitions.

Party attachments in Ecuador, even among hard-core activists, tended to be loose and largely instrumental.[7] This was reflected in the proliferation of parties that served as personal electoral vehicles for political notables. It was also manifested in the tendency to bypass parties altogether and set up independent "fronts" to back particular candidates. This allowed politically ambitious individuals to attach themselves to what they hoped would be a winning candidate while avoiding any future stigma that could be attached to party membership.

With few solidary or purposive incentives to cushion intraparty struggles for power, elite conflicts led to "exit" and the creation of new organizational structures of an "independent" or openly partisan nature. The utilitarian calculus at work among elites was replayed in the relationships between the masses and parties. As the work of Amparo Menéndez-Carrión has skillfully demonstrated, the construction of extensive clientele networks was pivotal to electoral success.[8] Yet the centrality of clientelism made support for parties unstable and unpredictable; clientele networks quickly disintegrated if parties failed to "deliver the goods" and coalesced around more promising patrons. "Don't back no losers" was the operative rule for both masses and elites in Ecuador's predatory multiparty system.[9]

This game of musical chairs among political elites undermined the development of stable political coalitions. Parties cooperated in transitory electoral alliances that decomposed quickly after elections. Yet, the divisiveness of interparty relations was mitigated somewhat by the lack of a strong ideological polarization among parties and the parties' lack of interest in popular mobilization. Populist organizations like the CFP and the Federación Velasquista slid in and out of alliances with the traditional oligarchic parties.

Given the ephemeral character of parties and political *frentes*, societal groups sought refuge for their interests inside corporate organizations. Indeed, the presence of functional representatives in the congress testified to the importance of interest associations in Ecuadorean life. The most powerful elite groups were the regional chambers of industry, agriculture, and commerce.[10] These groups were sanctioned by the state and enjoyed a privileged status inside economic policy-making entities such as the Monetary Board. Thus, Ecuador developed a tradition of interest articulation that fell outside the confines of the party system. With the exception of the Communist party and the Christian Democratic party, which had links to the small trade union movement, parties did not develop organic ties to other types of organizations. In contrast to other party systems in Western Europe and Latin America, parties in Ecuador did not seal followers in a "total environment" in the workplace, community, and family.[11]

The detached and hyperelectoral character of parties contributed to the confrontational relations between the executive and legislative branches. Even a pro-government majority in the congress could easily erode under the pressures exerted by interest groups and electoral calculations. Congressional opposition was a standard feature in the interruption of presidential terms, and interest groups and the armed forces joined in the fray. In 1961, for example, the Velasquista majority crumbled. The congress's refusal to move on Velasco's legislative program created policy paralysis, which fueled popular discontent against the administration. The crisis was resolved by the overthrow of Velasco and the installation of Vice President Carlos Julio Arosemena.[12]

In Velasco's subsequent presidency (1968–72), congressional opposition preceded his declaration of a civilian dictatorship in 1970. In the midst of an economic downturn, the antigovernment congressional majority refused to act on Velasco's proposed tax reforms and expenditures cuts. This prompted Velasco to enact the measures by decree; the opposition, led by business interest groups, challenged the measures, and the Supreme Court overturned them. Velasco was incensed at this affront to executive power; after consulting the military, he dissolved the congress and declared a civilian dictatorship. Velasco's constitutional rupture laid the basis for a succession crisis that was subsequently resolved by the military intervention of 1972.[13]

In Ecuador, the interplay of presidentialism, a loose multiparty system, and oligarchic domination constricted democratization and produced frequent government turnovers through extralegal means. While the military intervention led by General Guillermo Rodríguez Lara in 1972 sought a break with this past, many of the same political dynamics resurfaced after the return to civilian rule in 1979.

Reformism, Democratization, and the 1978 Constitution

The bankruptcy of parties and institutions was a major factor underlying the military coup of 1972. The coup coincided with two important events: (1) the initiation of substantial oil exports and a major upsurge in state revenues, and (2) the presidential campaign that placed Assad Bucaram of the populist CFP as frontrunner. In his study of coup decisions in Ecuador, John S. Fitch argues that the military feared that civilian tutelage over oil revenues would bring massive misappropriations and waste of the new wealth.[14] This distrust triggered the coup that received support from business and middle-class groups.

The original coup coalition quickly disintegrated, however, when military and civilian technocrats seized the initiative and proclaimed the administration's commitment to progressive social change. While much less radical than the Peruvian military experiment under General Juan Velasco Alvarado, the Rodríguez Lara government set goals that included agrarian reform, increased regulation of business practices, and an improved standard of living for lower-class groups.

The experiment in military-led reformism in Ecuador was short-lived. Ferocious opposition to the reform measures was led by business interest groups. The role of such groups in this period was yet another display of their strength and tenacity in Ecuadorean political life. While the administration disallowed party activities, it did not ban interest group activity. With no restrictions on their operations, business groups were able to veto or subvert virtually all of the Rodríguez Lara reform proposals.[15] Ideological disagreements inside the military and its reticence in mobilizing lower-class support for the reforms further undermined the government's capacity to pursue the reforms.

General Guillermo Rodríguez Lara was forced from office by more conservative officers in January 1976. The new military triumvirate immediately announced its intent to sponsor a *retorno constitucional* (return to constitutionalism). They began with a series of "dialogues" in which parties and interest groups were permitted to put forth proposals on the new constitution and electoral arrangements.[16] Throughout the elongated transition, the military retained a high degree of control over the process.

The triumvirate created three civilian commissions to deal with issues in the transition. Two commissions were charged with preparing constitutions that were to be subject to a popular referendum in January 1978. One commission revamped the 1945 constitution, while the other prepared a completely new document. A third commission was charged with preparing a new law to regulate the operation of the party system.

The new constitution won the approval of 43 percent of the voters despite the campaign by business interest groups to jettison it. The constitution retained presidential arrangements, but it included important new departures from previous practices. By stripping away literacy requirements, the new constitution finally ensured universal suffrage. Functional representation was eliminated. The senate, a traditional bastion for dominant-class representatives, was swept away in favor of a unicameral legislature.

The president was, of course, endowed with substantial powers. The new constitution allowed the president to declare a "state of emergency" and suspend constitutional guarantees. The president was also at liberty to issue "emergency economic decrees." Presidential power was further enhanced by a new plebiscite option: presidents were given the power to subject issues to a public referendum at their discretion. As the following discussion of post-1979 politics shows, presidents made frequent use of the threat of a plebiscite and emergency economic decrees in their battles with the congress. Nonetheless, the president was somewhat weakened by his automatic "lame-duck" status. Not only were presidents not permitted to succeed themselves directly, but they were barred from ever holding the office again. No doubt the five presidencies of Velasco Ibarra loomed large in the minds of the constitution framers.

The congress retained many of its previous powers, including an important role in executive oversight. While the president was free to name his own ministers, the congress could summon ministers for *informes* and interpellations. In the event of a vote of censure, a minister was bound to resign. The congress held powers of appointment in important entities like the Supreme Court, Constitutional Tribunal, and Electoral Tribunal. The impeachment of the president, vice president, and other officers in the executive branch was also within the reach of the congress.

The new constitution required candidates for the presidency and congress to affiliate with a legally registered political party. The Tribunal Supremo Electoral (TSE) was charged with the task of party registration and supervision of elections. The idea underlying registration was that the Tribunal would act to check fragmentation by denying status to small parties that could not meet their affiliation requirements.[17] In practice, however, the disqualification of small parties was a political hot potato, and the TSE balked at abolishing them.

The newly devised election rules set forth two important provisions that, though not prescribed in the constitution, affected the tenor of executive-legislative relations: (1) the institution of a second-round run-off election in the event that no candidate receives a 50 percent of the vote in the first heat; (2) the same-day scheduling of congressional races and the first round of the presidential election. The use of the presidential run-off ensures against the election of a minority president and gives the incoming head of state a claim to a national mandate.

But the coincidence of the presidential first round with congressional elections makes it unlikely that a president will enjoy a clear-cut majority in Congress. In the 1980s, the unicameral congress was composed of seventy-one members; twelve were nationally elected deputies with four-year terms, while the remaining fifty-nine are provincial deputies elected for two-year terms from multimember constituencies. Voters cast ballots for party lists and have no opportunity to indicate

Table 10.3. Attributes of Executive and Legislative Branches according to 1978 Constitution

	President	Congress
Selection and structure	Direct popular election by majority in two-round system	Direct popular election to unicameral chamber; proportional representation formula used to select national and provincial deputies
	4-year term[a]	National deputies, 4-year term; provincial deputies, 2-year term
	No succession or reelection	Reelection permitted after sitting out one legislative period
	Party affiliation required	Party affiliation required
Powers	Appoints ministers and other offices in executive branch without congressional approval	Interpellation and censure of ministers and others; powers of impeachment with $2/3$ majority vote
	May declare state of emergency and suspend constitutional rights	
	May call plebiscite on issues of concern	
	May emit "emergency" economic decrees	
	Has total or partial veto over legislation	Can overturn president's veto by $2/3$ majority or reconsider legislation after period of 1 year
		Appoints members of Supreme Court, Constitutional and Electoral Tribunals
		May grant amnesty for political crimes

a. Changed from 5 years by amendment.

candidate preference. Both national and provincial deputies are elected through a proportional representation system, using the Hare quota (a largest-remainder calculation) to assign seats. This type of proportional representation is considered to favor smaller parties.[18] The key elements in the new institutional framework are summarized in table 10.3.

The 1978 constitution was a breakthrough in the democratization of Ecuador. The establishment of unrestricted suffrage and the removal of functional representation were important innovations in a political system plagued by elitism. Nonetheless, the problems inherent in dividing sovereignity between the executive and legislature remained. Both branches retained substantial powers, but the logic in Ecuador's peculiar multiparty system created few incentives for cooperation. Almost immediately after the inauguration of President Jaime Roldós in August 1979, the classic pattern of executive-legislative confrontation reemerged with a vengeance. The institutional stress deepened through the 1980s as officers of the executive branch struggled to maximize their autonomy, especially in the realm of economic policy making.

Pugna de Poderes: A Chronicle of Conflict, 1979–1988

Since 1979, spasmodic confrontations between the executive and legislative powers have occupied centerstage in Ecuadorean politics. These fights at various moments have brought the democratic system perilously close to a breakdown. Thus far, breakdown has been avoided by retreats on the part of the congress or the president. These retreats by politicians have included a denouement through *medidas coyunturales* (short-term political deals) and simple shelving of the issue at hand. "Muddling through" the bitter conflicts with transitory deals has become an entrenched *salida* (exit) in the face of irreconcilable tensions between the two branches. Before examining the logic and incentive structures underlying this behavior, let us briefly look at the critical events in the evolution of executive-legislative relations in the period 1979–88.

The first in the series of crisis-inducing struggles between the president and the congress began immediately with the inauguration of President Jaime Roldós on August 10, 1979. Roldós won the presidency as the candidate of the populist CFP; his running mate, Osvaldo Hurtado, was drawn from the Christian democratic Democracia Popular (DP). The Roldós-Hurtado ticket rolled up an impressive victory in the second-round run-off against the conservative candidate, Sixto Durán Ballén, of the Partido Social Cristiano (PSC). Roldós won 68 percent of the vote nationally, winning a majority in all but one province. The CFP did well in the earlier congressional race run in 1978, taking twenty-nine of the sixty-nine seats in the unicameral congress. With the fifteen seats won by the social democratic Izquierda Democrática (ID), Roldós should have been assured of congressional cooperation in his legislative program. Tables 10.4–10.6 present data on the presidential and congressional elections for the period under discussion in this section.

But the brittle clientelistic character of the CFP victory was soon in evidence. Throughout the campaign, Roldós consciously sought to distance himself from Assad Bucaram, the longtime standard bearer of the CFP. Bucaram's own presidential candidacy had been proscribed by a technicality written into new electoral laws by the military. Bucaram handpicked Roldós for the presidential nomination in the belief that he would be the dominant force in the Roldós administration. Bucaram supporters within the CFP promoted this belief throughout the campaign with sloganeering that proclaimed, "Roldós a la presidencia, Bucaram al poder" (Roldós to the presidency, Bucaram to power). Roldós, on the other hand, tried to distance himself from Bucaram during the campaign. He even created a new organization outside of the CFP apparatus called the *Fuerza del Cambio* (Force for Change—this was also used as a campaign slogan).[19]

As it became clear that the new administration's ministerial appointments were weighted heavily in favor of "independents" and Roldós "loyalists," Bucaram began his blistering personal attacks on Roldoós for passing up CFP stalwarts. A master of colorful expression, Bucaram referred to Roldós's cabinet appointments as

Table 10.4. Presidential Election Results, 1948–1988 (percentage of total valid vote by winners of presidential races 1948–1988)

Year	No. Candidates	Votes (%) for Winner
Single-round elections		
1948	4	41.07 (Galo Plaza)
1952	4	43.04 (Velasco Ibarra)
1956	4	29.03 (Camilo Ponce)
1960	4	48.71 (Velasco Ibarra)
1968	4	33.84 (Velasco Ibarra)
Two-round elections		
1978+	6	27.7 (Jaime Roldós)
1979*	2	68.5 (Jaime Roldós)
1984+	9	24.0 (Rodrigo Borja)
1984*	2	51.5 (León Febres-Cordero)
1988+	10	24.5 (Rodrigo Borja)
1988*	2	54.0 (Rodrigo Borja)

a. + indicates first round; * indicates second round.

chuchumecos —latecomers who had hopped on the winner's bandwagon.[20] With the election of Bucaram as president of the Congress, the struggle for control and clientelism within the CFP exploded into the *pugna de poderes*—a continual stand-off between the presidency and the congress. The split in the CFP tore the CFP congressional caucus into two factions, Roldosistas and Bucaramistas, of approximately equal numbers. Parties of the right were the immediate beneficiaries of the split; Bucaram sought alliances with deputies from the traditional Conservative and Liberal parties. With this hybrid alliance and control over the congressional agenda, Bucaram was able to throw the Roldós administration into a defensive posture by passing generous populist-style legislation that Roldós found necessary to veto.

The battle dragged on for close to a year and created an atmosphere of chronic public anxiety until Roldós's maneuvers chiseled away the oppositional coalition in the congress. In a bold move aimed at alarming the opposition, Roldós proposed a series of constitutional reforms to strengthen the powers of the executive; one of the provisions gave the president the right to dissolve the congress at least once during his term and call elections. Roldós threatened to use his powers to call a national plebiscite on the question if the congress rejected it. To underscore the popular support for his presidency, he made his announcement to a mass rally in the Plaza de San Francisco in Quito. At the same time, Roldós moved to create a new

Table 10.5. Congressional Seats Won by Parties in Elections

	1979	1984	1986[a]		1988
Right					
PSC	3	9	12 (+2) = 14		8
PLR	4	4	3		1
PCE	10	2	1		1
PNR	2	1	0		—
CID	3	—	0		—
VELAS	1	—	0		—
Subtotal	23	16	16	18	10
Populist					
CFP	29	7	6 (+1) = 7		6
FRA	—	6	3 (+1) = 4		2
PD	—	5	1 (+1) = 2		—
PRE	—	3	3 (+1) = 4		8
PCD	—	—	1 (+1) = 2		—
Subtotal	29	21	14	18	16
Center Left					
ID	15	24	14 (+3) = 17		29
DP	—	4	4 (+1) = 5		7
Subtotal	15	28	18	22	36
Left					
FADI	1	2	2 (+1) = 3		2
MPD	1	3	3 (+1) = 4		3
PSE	—	1	6		4
Subtotal	2	6	11	13	9
Total	69	71	59	71	71

Sources: 1979 figures from *El comercio,* 10 Aug. 1982; 1984 figures from *Revista Mensual de Noticias* no. 28, Apr. 1984, p. 22; 1986 figures from *Política y Sociedad* 3, no. 4 (July-Aug. 1986): 27; 1988 figures from Oscar Ayerve, *¿Quién gana la segunda vuelta?* (Quito: Taski, 1988), pp. 69, 74.

a. Midterm elections for 59 provincial deputies only. The 12 national deputies retained their seats. (Numbers of national deputies in parentheses.)

political party, Pueblo, Cambio y Democracia (PCD), to regroup his old supporters in the CFP with new pro-Roldós independents.

With these strokes, Roldós considerably upped the ante in his high-stakes power struggle with Bucaram. The specter of a plebiscite threatened to unleash a new dimension of popular participation and significantly increase Roldós's personal sway over the party system. The prospect of a loss in the plebiscite and new competition in the party system moved the Bucaram clique toward negotiations. Anxieties in both the legislative and executive branches regarding an electoral mobilization led to the creation of a Comisión de Notables composed of distinguished "nonparti-

Table 10.6. Percentage of National Vote by Party (Provincial/Congressional Elections)

	1978 Provincial Councillors	1979 Congress	1980 Provincial Councillors	1984 Congress	1986 Midterm Congress
Right					
PSC	3.6	8.6	2.4	11.5	12.6
PLR	18.1	8.0	7.6	6.0	8.4
PCE	12.0	7.9	5.6	3.5	1.3
PNR	3.4	7.5	3.3	2.2	1.8
CID	3.1	6.3	0.5	1.4	0.6
VELAS	6.6	2.6	3.0	0.9	—
Subtotal	46.8	40.9	22.4	25.5	24.9
Populist					
CFP	21.1	30.9	7.8	9.0	9.3
FRA	2.5	—	23.8	8.8	5.6
PD	—	—	—	8.0	4.8
PRE	—	—	—	5.1	5.1
PCD	—	—	—	2.7	2.7
Subtotal	23.6	30.9	31.6	33.6	27.5
Center Left					
ID	11.0	18.4	16.9	20.0	14.5
DP	—	—	19.9	7.3	9.5
Subtotal	11.0	18.4	36.8	27.3	24.0
Left					
FADI	6.0	3.1	4.1	5.1	6.1
MPD	—	4.8	5.1	6.5	7.4
PSE	4.5	1.9	—	1.8	4.5
Subtotal	10.5	9.8	9.2	13.4	18.0

Sources: The 1978, 1979, and 1980 figures are taken from FLACSO, *Elecciones en Ecuador* (Quito: Oveja Negra, n.d.). The 1984 and 1986 figures are from *Weekly Analysis* no. 22, 9 June 1986.

sans," such as former president Galo Plaza Lasso and Cardinal Pablo Muñoz, to me-diate the conflict. Management of the crisis by the commission defused an imme-diate confrontation through a plebiscite by prolonging discussions over the consti-tutional reforms; this allowed time for a recomposition of congressional alliances. With the memory of their poor electoral performance of 1979 still fresh and their congressional seats at stake, Conservative as well as Liberal deputies deserted the Bucaram coalition. The yearly election for the presidency of the congress brought a narrow defeat of Bucaram; he was replaced by Raúl Baca Carbo of the ID, who was backed by votes of the DP and Roldosistas.[21]

Economic policy and electoral ambitions fueled the subsequent encounters be-tween the presidency and the congress. A tragic plane crash in May 1981 ended the life

Table 10.7. Ministerial Turnover, 1979–1983

Ministry	No. Ministers	Average Stay in Office (months)
Public Administration	5	3.6
Welfare	6	4.9
Defense	5	5.9
Finance	5	9.2
Natural Resources	5	9.4
Health	5	10.1
Labor	5	10.9
Public Works	4	12.5
Foreign Relations	3	13.6
Agriculture	4	16.0
Industry	4	14.9
Government	4	14.9
Education	3	24.3
13 ministries	58	11.5

of President Jaime Roldós and brought Vice President Osvaldo Hurtado to the presidency. Hurtado had an even narrower base of support in the congress than Roldós. Moreover, the death of Roldós gave rise to further leadership struggles among coastal populists and produced another offshoot, the Partido Roldosista Ecuatoriano (PRE). Hurtado's small Christian democratic party (Democracia Popular) held only three congressional seats. Throughout his administration, Hurtado struggled to maintain a working legislative coalition through the allocation of ministerial appointments and appeals to the populist and center-left parties to band together to maintain democracy. Data on ministerial turnover in the Roldós-Hurtado governments is presented in table 10.7. But cooperation among center-left parties was unsteady. At several junctures, they joined ranks with the Right to oppose the new administration. Contrary to Hurtado's wishes, the congress elected Léon Roldós, brother of the deceased president, to take over the vice-presidential slot. As seen in table 10.8, center-left legislators frequently pressured Hurtado's ministers by forcing them to submit to congressional questioning and interpellations. On two occasions, the social democratic Izquierda Democrática voted alongside right-wing parties in the censure of two of Hurtado's ministers. (Data on ministerial interpellations can be found in table 10.9). The inconsistent behavior of the center-left parties in this period significantly heightened the capacity of right-wing deputies to use the congress as a forum for extremely disruptive (and threatening) attacks on the Hurtado government.

Catherine M. Conaghan

Table 10.8. Participation by Congressional Deputies in Ministerial Oversight, 1979–1983

Party	Frequency	%
Izquierda Democrática	11	17.5
Concentración de Fuerzas Populares	9	14.3
Social Cristiano	8	12.7
"Independents"	8	12.7
Coalición Institucionalista Democrática	7	11.1
Union Democrática Popular (FADI)	5	7.9
Partido Conservador	5	7.9
Partido Liberal	3	4.8
Movimiento Popular Democrático	3	4.8
Movimiento de Integración Nacional (ex-CFP)	3	4.8
Democracia Popular	1	1.6
Total	63	100.1a

Source: Nick D. Mills, Crisis, conflicto y consenso: Ecuador, 1979–84 (Quito: Corporación Editora Nacional, 1984), p. 80.
Note: Ministerial oversight processes are defined as requests for information and interpellations.
a. Rounding accounts for failure to obtain 100.

The ephemeral character of congressional alliances may not have been so crisis inducing if it were not for the considerable public dissatisfaction with Hurtado's economic policies and the personal enmity he inspired in dominant-class groups.[22] Coming to office in the first flush of the economic crisis, Hurtado faced mounting inflation, a renegotiation of the international debt and plummeting revenues from petroleum exports. His economic team recommended a stabilization program and the first package was applied in October 1982. Unhappiness in the private sector over monetary policy and Hurtado's antibusiness rhetoric coincided with popular-class frustration with stabilization. The result was a volatile combination of business and popular mobilization against the government. The Frente Unitario de Trabajadores (FUT) called for an indefinite national strike to protest the measures, and Hurtado responded by assuming emergency powers. Calls for the formation of a new interim government were made by sectors of the business community, especially the Chambers of Industry. Joining in the call for a termination of the Hurtado government was right-wing Congressman León Febres-Cordero, who would later win the 1984 presidential contest. Febres-Cordero suggested that Hurtado resign, that Vice President León Roldós be bypassed for succession, and that the president of the congress take over the government. In other words, one of the most visible leaders of the Right was proposing a clearly unconstitutional resolution of the crisis. But as in the previous case, the crisis dissipated as many relevant actors came to the conclusion that a pursuit of the conflict might lead to a rupture in the demo-

Table 10.9. Interpellations of Ministers by Congress, 1979–1988

Minister	Ministry	Date	Subject
C. Feraud	Government	05/80	Human rights violations
A. Mancero	Welfare	09/80	Women's pensions
R. Paz	Finance	09/80	Illegal reform of tariffs
*G. García	Education	08/81	Irregularities in job appointments
*C. Feraud[a]	Government	09/81	Irregularities in government purchases
M. Coellos	Health	10/81	Decree 211
C. Robalino	Finance	10/81	Decree 211
E. Ortega	Natural Resources	09/82	Electricity rate increases
O. Alcivar	Industry	09/82	Sugar price increase
J. Morillo	Finance	09/82	Sugar price increase
C. Vallejo	Agriculture	09/82	Sugar price increase
E. Ripalda	Public Works	08/83	Irregularities in road construction projects, telephone service
F. Swett	Finance	09/85	Irregular handling of banking case
J. Espinosa	Natural Resources	11/85	Gas price increase
*A. Dahik	Finance	09/86	Violation of constitution by Monetary Board
*J. Espinosa[b]	Natural Resources	08/87	Overpricing on petroleum contracts; electricity rate hikes
*L. Robles Plaza	Government	09/87	Human rights violations

Sources: Information for 1980–83 taken from Nick D. Mills, *Crisis, conflicto y consenso: Ecuador, 1979–1984* (Quito: Corporación Editora Nacional, 1984). Information for 1985–87 compiled from news accounts in issues of *Politica y sociedad.*
Note: *indicates that the interpellation ended in a vote of censure.
   a. Feraud resigned his post just prior to the vote of censure; therefore he was not officially removed as a result of the vote.
   b. Espinoza resigned his post for reasons of health prior to his interpellation.

cratic system. Trade union leaders and legislators moderated their opposition to the measures and proclaimed their commitment to maintaining the constitutional order.

Executive-legislative conflict reached a new high in the subsequent administration of President León Febres-Cordero, who was elected by a narrow margin in May 1984, defeating the social democratic candidate, Rodrigo Borja. The unexpected victory by the Right shocked the Center, the Left, and some of the populist parties into banding together in a congressional caucus, the *bloque progresista.* Holding a majority of seats, the *bloque* committed itself to opposing Febres-Cordero's neoliberal economic project and maintaining the democratic system.

Within days of the inauguration, the first crisis was already underway. The *bloque* opened the legislative season by exercising its powers of appointment to name new

Supreme Court justices. The president and progovernment parties in the congress denounced the "partisan" character of the appointments and challenged their constitutionality. What followed was an extended period of legislative paralysis that dragged through the first four months of the administration (August–December 1984).[23] Congressional activity came to a standstill after sessions were marred by tear-gas bombings, fisticuffs on the floor of the assembly, and walkouts by legislators on both sides. Meanwhile, Febres-Cordero had decided to physically bar the new appointees from their offices and banned publication of the appointments in the Registro Oficial, thus denying legal status to the congress's act.

The resolution of the dispute came after months of halting and acrimonious negotiations between the president of the congress and ID party leader, Raúl Baca Carbo, and President Febres-Cordero. Rather than arriving at any definitive resolution of the constitutional issue at stake, the two sides agreed to end the crisis via *la troncha* —a parceling out of the positions across the two sides. *Bloque* leaders regarded the deal as a political defeat, but believed it a necessary one. They feared that a continuation of the conflict would invite a shutdown of the congress by Febres-Cordero.[24]

Less than two months after the Supreme Court defeat, economic policy reignited the battle between the branches. The president rejected the congress's passage of a new law that substantially increased the minimum wage; he proposed a lower increase. Febres-Cordero challenged the procedures used by the congress to enact the hike and charged the body with constitutional violations. The president took his case to the adjudicating body, the Tribunal de Garantías Constitucionales (TGC). Despite a subsequent TGC ruling against the executive, Febres-Cordero ordered the publication of his own salary decree in the Registro Oficial. Once again, through his control over the government printing office, President Febres-Cordero was able to defy contending branches: neither the congress nor the TGC could force executive compliance. A resolution of the situation came in May 1985, when the TGC declared the president's behavior unconstitutional but allowed the salary law to remain on the books.

As in the case of the Supreme Court conflict, a crisis atmosphere prevailed during the struggle over the minimum wage. Harsh rhetorical attacks were launched by both sides, including references to the possibility of military intervention.[25] The conflict was exacerbated by class mobilization over the issue. Business interest groups heartily endorsed the president's modest salary increase. Popular-class organizations grouped in the Frente Unitario de Trabajadores (FUT) and the Frente Popular (FP) opposed Febres-Cordero's stabilization measures and favored the congressional wage hike. The *bloque progesista* in the congress openly endorsed the general strike called by unions to protest the neoliberal model. The government responded with a tough crackdown on strikers and demonstrators.

Febres-Cordero was able to play on the weakness and fragmentation in the party system to engineer a respite from confrontations with the legislature. His outright attacks on congressional authority were coupled with an intense personal lobby of deputies and overtures to two populist parties, the Concentración de Fuerzas Populares (CFP) and the Frente Radical Alfarista (FRA). Pressures on individual congressmen produced three early defections from the ranks of *bloque progresista* parties. Despite the erosion in its voting strength, the *bloque* was able to maintain a majority until the administration struck a deal with the CFP and FRA. This gave the government a docile majority in the congress from August 1985 through August 1986.

Midterm elections, however, reestablished a majority for the *bloque progresista* parties in 1986. The elections for provincial congressional deputies coincided with the first plebiscite called by a president. In order to rally support for constitutional changes and renew a mandate for his increasingly troubled presidency, Febres-Cordero called on voters to reject the law that obliged candidates to affiliate with a legally registered party in order to stand for election. He argued that the electoral law discriminated against "independents." With *bloque progresista* parties campaigning firmly for a "no" vote on the June plebiscite, the president went down to a major political defeat.[26] Sixty-nine percent of the voters rejected the change. Picking up new congressional seats, *bloque progresista* parties took control of forty of the seventy-one slots in the legislature.

The electoral victory of opposition parties set the stage for a renewal of institutional stress. In October 1986, the *bloque progresista* majority voted to extend political amnesty to two leading opponents of the administration, General Frank Vargas Pazzos and Abdala Bucaram. Bucaram, the populist mayor of Guayaquil and leader of the Partido Roldosista, had been forced to flee the country after his criticisms of the armed forces and Febres-Cordero were leaked to the press. General Frank Vargas Pazzos was the leader of two failed uprisings among air force personnel in March 1986 that brought attention to government corruption and irregularities in promotion policies.[27] Both Bucaram and Vargas were vociferous personal critics of Febres-Cordero.

The president's response to the congressional amnesty was simply to ignore it. His refusal to free Vargas generated frustration within the ranks of the air force that ultimately led to the kidnapping of Febres-Cordero in January 1987. Air force paratroopers seized the president and his entourage during a tour of the Taura base and threatened their lives if Vargas was not freed. After several hours in the hands of his captors, a humiliated Febres-Cordero agreed to free Vargas.

Just days after the Febres-Cordero kidnapping, the *bloque progresista* majority demonstrated its bitter attitude toward the president by passing a motion requesting his resignation. Opposition leaders in the congress argued that Febres-Cordero had provoked the incident by refusing to recognize the legality of the congressional amnesty. Although the *bloque* parties lacked the two-thirds majority for an impeachment vote, they passed a resignation request by a margin of thirty-eight to twenty-nine votes. Febres-Cordero scoffed at the congressional request as "immoral, unconstitutional, and lacking juridical force."[28]

The final confrontation of the Febres Cordero administration came in October 1987 over the interpellation of Minister of Government Luis Robles. The interpellation involved a long list of human rights violations committed by the administration and the police. Robles refused to respond to the charges, and the congress proceeded to vote his censure in absentia. Febres-Cordero nonetheless refused to remove Robles from office. Once again, the mobilization of societal actors around the issue intensified the executive-legislative confrontation. The police issued a communiqué condemning the censure. The president of the congress (Jorge Zavala of Izquierda Democrática) responded by threatening to impeach police officials. Trade unions in the FUT called a general strike to support the congress's ouster of Robles. Catholic church leaders criticized Febres-Cordero's flagrant violation of the constitution. Robles eventually resigned, but only after Febres-Cordero assumed "emergency powers" and cracked down harshly on FUT protestors.[29]

The president's reaction to the Robles censure surpassed even the high-handed tactics he used in 1986 in the interpellation of Minister of Finance Alberto Dahik. In September 1986, the *bloque progesista* coalition censured Dahik, one of the principal architects of the government's neoliberal economic model. Congress was teargassed by police in the course of the interpellation. While the administration went along with Dahik's resignation after the censure, it kept Dahik as an informal adviser on economic policy (complete with an office in the central bank).

From 1979 through 1988, Ecuador staggered through a succession of executive-legislative confrontations that created a near-permanent crisis atmosphere in the polity. Other societal and institutional actors frequently joined in the fray, adding to the drama and the disruption. What developed in this period was a high-risk game between the executive and legislative branches. Each accused the other of dark political motives and anticonstitutional behavior; each dared the other to back down or risk a breakdown in the democratic game. And at the edge of every precipice, one or the other did back down. The "logic" that drives this perilous game is complex and convoluted. It emanates in part from peculiarities in the party system. Another part derives from the compulsions of executive-centered economic policy making under conditions of extreme duress.

Loose Parties and "Floating" Politicians

The structural propensity toward presidential-legislative conflict was aggravated in Ecuador by the operation of a loose multiparty system, that is, a densely populated party system in which no party was able to capture more than 40 percent of the legislative seats in the congressional races of 1978, 1984, and 1986.[30] As noted earlier, it is a party system permeated by extreme linkage problems at the mass and elite levels. There are not just "floating" voters in these systems; there are "floating" politicians.[31] These linkage problems are not confined to the populist (CFP, PRE, FRA) and the old oligarchic parties (PC, PLR). They have also afflicted the more modern Marxist, social democratic, and Christian democratic parties (ID, DP), although perhaps to a lesser degree. Nonetheless, the highly instrumental character of elite attachments to parties makes for unpredictable behavior and volatility in executive-legislative relations.[32]

The weakness of the Ecuadorean party system has deep historical roots, and its complete analysis would take me well beyond the scope of this chapter. For my purposes, however, it is important to consider how electoral rules and an "antiparty" mentality among politicians have affected party development and contributed to the syndrome of institutional stress.

The law that currently governs the party system was formulated by a civilian commission as part of the transition process in 1978. The commission was led by Osvaldo Hurtado, the political sociologist who later became vice president and president. The new law was drawn up explicitly with the aim of rationalizing the party system. It required the licensing of parties by the Tribunal Supremo Electoral. Each party was required to pass a membership threshold and submit a party doctrine. Candidates for public office were, in turn, required to register with a legally inscribed party. In theory, these provisions were to check the tendency toward party proliferation by creating obstacles in the registration of "taxi" and personalist parties.

In practice, however, the results of the new party law were mixed. The outcome highlights the problems involved in rationalizing an already existing party system through juridical means. The new rules did not eliminate the fragmentation of parties and their organizational weakness. Instead, the law inspired new adaptations by individuals and parties already accustomed to operating within the logic of a weak party system. The provision requiring candidates to affiliate with a party essentially forced many of the politically ambitious into artificial associations with parties. It created a strata of leaders, in almost every party, who had little affective or ideological attachment to the organization. This lack of attachment laid the basis for what was called the *cambio de camisetas*—the desertion of legislators from their parties and their reaffiliation with other parties or assumption of "independent" status. This phenomenon was at play in the decomposition and restructuring of congressional alliances in the period 1979–88.

The problem of building and maintaining legislative alliances was aggravated by other factors in addition to the *cambio de camisetas*. The extreme multiparty system and proportional representation formula worked to ensure that no party could control a majority of seats in the legislature. Thus, alliance politics became central to both pro- and antigovernment forces in the legislature. But just as the relations of individual deputies to their parties are governed by instrumental and electoral calculations, the relations among parties are subject to the same dynamics.

Specifically, the party law undermines the prospects for preelectoral party alliances by disallowing the participation of multiparty "fronts" in elections. By law, candidates can be listed on the ballot under the insignia of only *one* legally inscribed party. Because only one party is credited on the ballot, the remaining parties in any electoral front are disadvantaged. Since the first round of the presidential election runs concurrently with congressional elections, parties are hesitant *not* to present their own presidential candidate fearing that a lack of "coattails" will hurt their congressional ticket. As a result, it is electorally rational for all parties to field separate presidential and congressional tickets, even if the ideological or programmatic differences among candidates are barely discernible to voters. Thus, due to electoral rules, alliance formation in the congress is a product of postelectoral horse-trading and short-term considerations. Parties are not bound by an electorally endorsed public commitment to cooperate. Cooperation among parties in the congress depends on a good deal of volunteerism and is constrained by parties' perception of its possible electoral effects. So, for example, Izquierda Democrática sometimes voted with rightist parties during the Hurtado government in order to establish an "oppositional" posture in preparation for the 1984 elections.

But volatility in the behavior of politicians cannot simply be explained as an "automatic" response by rational actors to certain types of electoral rules. The development of every party system depends, to a great degree, on the perceptions and values held by politicians themselves. What is striking in Ecuadorean political culture and style is the extent to which it has been permeated by an antiparty mentality—a predisposition that has been perpetuated by politicians themselves. One of the great early proponents of this position was the populist José María Velasco Ibarra, who dominated political life for thirty years with dictums like, "Give me a balcony and the people are mine." In the period since the 1979 transition, antiparty themes have been rearticulated by other politicians, most notably León Febres-Cordero. Indeed, his political career and his behavior in the presidency is emblematic of the lack of attachment of politicians to parties. Forced into affiliating with a political party in order to run for the congress in 1978, Febres-Cordero fell into the ranks of the rightist Social Christian party. Nonetheless, he always expressed a certain contempt for parties. In his 1984 bid for the presidency, he chose "Ecuador es mi partido" as one of his slogans. His own party (as well as others that supported his presidential bid) were completely marginalized in his administration. The plebiscite he proposed in 1986 was framed to do away with the party affiliation requirement for candidates to public office. Rather than using presidential resources to build up his own party, Febres-Cordero preferred to bypass parties altogether and create a clientelistic network through *unidades ejecutores*—commissions run through the office of the president to administer public works.[33] This bypassing of the Social Christian party was a cause of considerable frustration to long-time party activists.

Simply put, politicians of every stripe appear to be afflicted with a significant amount of distaste and disdain for the party system in which they operate. This has been an important theme in the numerous interviews that I have conducted with party leaders since 1984. They frequently acknowledge that personal ambitions underlie the tendencies toward party fragmentation and a lack of cooperative behavior. One congressman from the populist Partido Roldosista remarked that the problem was that of "too many parties—and each party prefers to maintain its own piece, its own particular space and leaders, and not to participate with others. . . . We could even talk about *huasipungo político* here."[34]

The devaluation of parties in the minds of politicians may be an important component to consider in understanding the whole tenor of executive-legislative relations. Because of this lack of commitment to party organization and programs, presidents are apt to see the congress more as a source of "irresponsibility" in policy making—as a site where personal ambitions and electoral considerations predominate over "rational" decision making. The denigration of party politics (and by extension, Congress) has been reinforced by the rise of exclusionary technocratic approaches to dealing with the current economic crisis.

Policy Making by Decree

By 1982, falling oil prices combined with the burdens of the international debt brought an end to a decade of petroleum-induced economic growth in Ecuador. Suddenly, the administration of austerity replaced the distribution of oil-generated surplus as the stuff of politics. The change in the policy environment had a dramatic effect on decision making, with important implications for interbranch relations. Decision making became tinged with a new economic fatalism. In the minds of presidents, a rational management of the crisis necessarily included a detachment from party politics, a bypassing of the congress, and a disregard for possible electoral retributions.

With the economic downturn of the eighties, "crisis management" by the executive predominated. Economic policy was defined, both by the Hurtado and Febres-Cordero administrations, as being outside the realm of interest group lobbying, party pressures, and legislative interference. Both administrations sought to insulate their economic teams from such "outside" influences. In both administrations, economic decision making became highly centralized in the hands of the president and three economic ministers.[35] In neither administration did the team include a party technocrat nor were the progovernment parties actively consulted in the formulation of policy. Hurtado described the decision-making processes that resulted in his economic stabilization program of 1982–83:

> We four (i.e., the heads of the Banco Central, Finance, Monetary Board and myself) exclusively ran economic policy. The cabinet ministries were consulted only on very specific problems. They were often informed only after we made decisions. . . . You can imagine what would happen if I would have subjected economic policy to debates within the party! No political party would have ever approved of the kind of economic policy I undertook. No party! . . . I made my appointments to the economic team on the basis of the fact that they were not Christian Democrats. I did not want economic policy in the hands of people who would

politicize it. Economic policy is so difficult, complex, and costly (in political terms) that I did not want an opposition to form to the policy because it was directed by party people. . . . I always thought that the future of my government and party rested on success in the conduct of economic policy and the confrontation of the economic crisis. That was my strategy. And within that strategy I was prepared to pay all the costs in the short term.[36]

Hurtado's description reveals some of the ambiguities in the relationships that develop between presidents and their parties within the context of an economic crisis. Hurtado sought to keep his party outside of policy making both because he saw it as incompetent (likely to "politicize" a technical matter) and because he sought to shield it from electoral retributions. Yet, while Hurtado was ready to "pay the cost," the costs for *him* would not be direct because Ecuador's presidents are constitutionally barred from ever seeking reelection.[37]

The marginalization of parties and the bypassing of the congress was even more evident in the subsequent administration of León Febres-Cordero. With initial economic stabilization measures already undertaken by Hurtado, Febres-Cordero sought to implement a neoliberal economic program. He enacted the core components of his neoliberal project by avoiding the opposition-controlled congress. Between 1984 and 1985, Febres-Cordero issued twenty-six "urgent" economic decrees. The measures included provisions to facilitate foreign investment, the reversal of the congress's minimum wage hike, and currency flotation.[38] As in the case of the Hurtado administration, the decisions were made by the president and his staff of "independent" technocrats and ministers.

At every step in the construction of the neoliberal project, the Febres-Cordero administration vigorously resisted the pressures emanating from the congress to change the course. This led to two highly charged conflicts that highlighted the impotency of the congress in matters of economic policy making—the 1985 confrontation over the minimum wage and the 1986 censure of Finance Minister Alberto Dahik. In both cases, the government was able to ignore the message sent by the congress. Interviews conducted with the members of the economic team indicate that the administration never considered changing its economic course, even after the Dahik censure.

Bypassing the congress, however, was not just a strategy to circumvent opposition. The impulse to make economic policy in this way was also rooted in the technocratic approach of the economic ministers who believed that the solution to the economic crisis involved the discovery and application of technically "correct" policies. In short, from the point of view of the economic team, pluralist politics (i.e., bargaining with parties and the congress) was irrelevant to the entire process. They deeply believed that economics was a science that *should* lie outside of the realm of politics.[39] Moreover, economic ministers tended to view congressmen as untrained and lacking in sufficient expertise to intervene competently into the policy-making process. Economics, in their view, was a realm that rightly belonged under the control of people schooled in the application of "correct" techniques. In an interview, Alberto Dahik flatly articulated this technocratic approach:

It is quite common in Latin American to use names. You are either a "Chicago boy," a "neoliberal," a "conservative." I think economic policy is either right or wrong. It's an actual thing. It's a positive thing. You either do things correctly or you do things incorrectly. If you have an excessive growth of the money supply, you will have inflation. And you don't have to be a "Chicago boy" or Keynesian to know that.[40]

In a similar vein, Central Bank President Carlos Julio Emanuel underscored the essentially technical character of economic policy making:

Let me bring this to your attention. Felipe González is a socialist and he has been very clear in saying one should not introduce ideology into economic policy because it's a technical thing. Of course there are political connotations to every measure we take. But we've got to think about how to solve the economic problem first before we think about ways of distributing. John Stuart Mill, way back in 1860, made one of the first fundamental discoveries: it is one thing to talk about the technical laws of production; it is another thing to consider how to distribute. There are basic laws that you cannot alter that have to do with technical issues of supply and demand, overvaluation of exchange rates, appropriateness of interest rates, and so forth.[41]

The price of this highly exclusionary and technocratic approach to economic policy making is high, both in terms of institutional stress and societal frustration. Since Congress is completely excluded from participation in the decision-making process, legislators have little incentive to assume anything but an oppositional stance (especially in reference to highly unpopular stabilization measures). With no effective access to policy making through the legislature or parties, social actors (popular sectors and trade unions) have no recourse but to take politics into the streets.[42] In both the Hurtado and Febres-Cordero governments, congressional support for popular mobilization against stabilization measures created highly explosive situations. The response of both presidents to the popular mobilizations was to assume "emergency powers" and crack down on the movements.

The Parliamentary Alternative? Some Speculations

The case of Ecuador aptly illustrates the syndrome of institutional stress that has characterized Latin American experiments in presidentialism. Juan Linz strenuously argues that parliamentary arrangements could put an end to the obstructive relations just described. While the theoretical arguments in favor of parliamentarism seem powerful, the implantation of these arrangements into the reality I just described would encounter serious difficulties. Parliamentarism could simply engender new, but nonetheless destabilizing, tendencies in the political system of Ecuador.

The peculiarities of Ecuador's loose multiparty system pose the most serious constraints on successful parliamentarism. As the tables on congressional elections show, the fragmentation of the vote across sixteen parties in the period 1978–88 ensured that no party held a majority in the legislature. Given this electoral reality, the constitution of a parliamentary government would have required the formation of a coalition across more than two parties, at least in the elections of 1979, 1984, and 1986. The most likely combination in this period would have included center-left, leftist, and populist parties.

Parliamentary arrangements, under these electoral conditions, would have thrust Ecuador's diverse populist parties into a pivotal role in the creation and maintenance of governing coalitions. Even with restrictions on votes of no confidence, the strategic position of populists could, I believe, create serious problems of governability. These problems could range from frequent dissolutions of the government to policy immobilism and a lack of coherence and cooperation inside government coalitions.

It is important to underscore that the populist parties under discussion (Partido Roldosista, Concentración de Fuerzas Populares, and Frente Radical Alfarista) operate with few ideological constraints. If past behavior is any indicator, these parties are capable of veering in and out of alliances with parties on the Left or Right. Such oscillations could entail the rapid dissolution of governments. Instability (actual or latent) in the executive branch due to the presence of populist parties in governing coalitions would significantly reduce the government's capacity to implement economic policy or negotiate with international creditors on debt issues. It is hard to imagine how governments could retain the support of populist parties in the application of stabilization programs, which are often the sine qua non of debt renegotiations. For example, it is difficult to believe that the Hurtado government could have weathered the storm of protest during the October stabilization of 1983 under parliamentary arrangements. The government would have fallen and stabilization would have been postponed, making Ecuador's debt rescheduling problematic if not impossible.

Keeping populists within the ranks of a government coalition could also entail deals that would significantly erode policy-making capacities. In exchange for their support, populists would no doubt demand control over clientele-maintaining entities within the state. This, of course, would have implications for any government's capacity to control public spending—and would create electoral advantages for the resource-dispensing populist parties.

Given the electoral trends in the legislative races over the last decade, rightist parties would be especially dependent on the "swing" vote of populists to form a governing coalition. The traditional animosity among rightist and center-left/leftist parties would probably preclude any other coalitional partner for the Right. Yet, the maintenance of rightist-populist coalitions would prove especially difficult when one considers the problems outlined above. Such coalitions could quickly dissolve in clashes over economic stabilization and neoliberalism.

Under parliamentary arrangements, the declining electoral performance of the Right and its ensuing dependence on the populist "swing" could ultimately translate into a permanent eclipse of the Right from executive power. If O'Donnell and Schmitter's ruminations about the conditions for a successful consolidation of democracy are correct, such a phenomenon could be as potentially destructive as presidential-congressional confrontations.[43] In a country like Ecuador, where the Right has traditionally held a "privileged position" in policy making, an electorally based "freezing out" of the Right from executive power could well lead it back to extrainstitutional forms of politics (i.e., coup baiting). Such behavior was clearly in evidence throughout the Hurtado administration.

Finally, it is clear that an institutional shift from presidentialism to parliamentarism would not remove the considerable threats to Ecuadorean democracy that emanate from societal forces. Even if a relatively stable parliamentary coalition could be maintained, the "mediation" problems that permeate the party system would not be solved. Parties remain detached from groups in civil society and have not been able to establish themselves as the interlocutors of social groups and classes. As a result, struggles over economic policy are still likely to spill out into the street, rather than become encapsulated and defused inside parliamentary institutions.

Other Alternatives? Suggestions from the South

This pessimistic assessment of a parliamentary experiment in Ecuador is based on the assumption that the basic features of the party system would remain intact. Certainly, this is an important assumption—and one that could be challenged. One could argue that Ecuador's party system is still in an initial "shaking out" stage after the transition from military rule. One might argue that the party system will, in time, settle down to produce a more manageable range of modern mass-based parties. The steady growth of the social democratic Izquierda Democrática and the waning of older personalist parties on the Right could be marshaled as evidence of the ongoing rationalization of the party system.

But there is also evidence to suggest that populist and other sorts of "flash" parties are not fading from the electoral scene.[44] As in many other countries in Latin America, populism has been rejuvenated by the failures of a variety of governments to deal with the economic crisis. While the CFP broke down as a result of the leadership struggles between Roldós and Bucaram in the early 1980s, populism was forcefully reconstructed in the 1988 election by Abdala Bucaram and his Partido Roldosista. Bucaram ran a campaign notable for its populist excesses. Although he lost his presidential bid to ID's Rodrigo Borja, Bucaram turned in a credible electoral performance by capturing 43 percent of the vote. Days after his loss, the Partido Roldosista proclaimed Bucaram its candidate for 1992.

Rather than bemoan the presence of populism, I think we have to accept it as a durable feature of many third-world polities. As Fernando Henrique Cardoso has acknowledged in the Brazilian case, "These are the parties we have, not those we want."[45] Any prescriptions for institutional change have to be assessed in light of the continuing presence of populism.

I have argued that populist parties would pose serious problems for the successful operation of a parliamentary system in Ecuador. Critics, of course, could counter that these parties can be just as destabilizing to presidential arrangements. I think both arguments are equally valid. Erratic parties of any sort can, under certain conditions, pose serious threats to almost any set of liberal democratic institutions we can imagine. The question is: Would parliamentarism somehow discipline these parties in ways presidentialism cannot? I remain skeptical that it could. While it cannot be denied that electoral systems and institutional arrangements create incentives and disincentives that affect the conduct of political parties, party behavior is not simply an automatic reflection of the formal "rules of the game." Populist parties in Latin America are part of a dense and complicated social reality. Their behavior, in part, must be seen as a response to the (often contradictory) demands emanating from their heterogeneous lower-class constituencies. So far, there is little evidence to suggest that the social bases of populism are disappearing in Latin America. On the contrary, one can argue that the economic crisis of the 1980s has increased social heterogeneity, which breeds populism (e.g., by expanding the informal sector and shrinking the trade union movement). A simple change in institutional structures will not cancel out the social reality that produces populism, nor is it evident why such an institutional change would necessarily move populist parties to become less volatile on policy issues or to disengage from the contentious distributive claims they press in the executive and legislative branches.

At the elite level, the idea of parliamentarism has never occupied a space in discussions of constitutional engineering in Ecuador. This probably stems from Ecuador's unbroken tradition of presidentialism since the nineteenth century. Even during the country's most recent institutional restructuring in the constitutional plebiscite of 1978, parliamentarism was not entertained as an option. There would be, I believe, little support among political elites for such a change, especially among parties of the Right, which would have the most to lose under such arrangements.

What can be done to the current institutional structure to allow for more constructive and creative relations between the executive and legislative branches? Perhaps the answer lies not in a parliamentary prescription but in an innovative suggestion proposed by one of Ecuador's own politicians, President Rodrigo Borja. In an interview in 1984, Borja suggested that a way out of executive-legislative impasse in Ecuador could lie in a division of legislative functions into two separate bodies. One body would be charged with the business of legislation, while the other would be charged with oversight function and "political vigilance" of the executive. Borja explained the reasoning behind his proposal:

In our legislatures, we can fall into emotional opposition, into political oversight, into interpellations, into impeachment, and not take care of the legislative goal that is essential and difficult. There is nothing more difficult in a country than legislating—to make laws that can forsee the variations in human behavior. There is nothing more difficult in the mind of man than to legislate. One can't legislate in the Latin American style with political problems, ideological discussions, conflict between parties, etc. . . . Under these circumstances, one can't legislate in tranquility, and that's why you have a legislative crisis. So the idea is to separate into one organ the ability to legislate and in another organ that is distinct and independent the exercise of control and vigilance over the executive. I think it's indispensable to reconcile democracy with efficacy. That's to say, make the democratic system an efficient system that gives rapid and certain responses to the problems of the collectivity.[46]

In short, Borja is arguing for more cooperative relations between the executive and legislature by concentrating the conflict-generating functions of the legislative branch into a separately elected body. Such an arrangement would allow for legislative oversight of the executive branch without undermining executive-legislative cooperation on policy-making functions.

Certainly, Borja's description is sketchy and one can envision a whole range of problems that could emanate from such a structure. Yet, Borja's proposal does parallel some of the recent arguments put forth by the Brazilian political theorist, Roberto Mangabeira Unger. Mangabeira Unger has argued in favor of multiplying the branches of government as a way of furthering democratization by extending and deepening the grasp of the electorate over government functions. Rather than looking at interbranch conflict as a constrictive and negative phenomenon, Unger argues that conflict among branches can be resolved by popular referendum—yet another vehicle for enlarging the scope of democracy.[47]

While these suggestions for institutional change initially may seem untenable or remote, they do challenge us as political scientists to expand our imagination regarding possible solutions to the institutional malaise affecting presidential systems in Latin America, and democracies everywhere. But as Mangabeira Unger's work reminds us, democracy is much more than just a set of bureaucratic structures subjected periodically to electoral competition. It is important that we not fall into the trap of thinking that the consolidation of democracy hinges on a technical question of "getting the rules right" (i.e., the political scientist's equivalent of an economist's "getting the prices right"). We also need to direct our attention to other issues—democratization in civil society, the nature of the repressive apparatus inside the democratic state, and the available routes to sustained economic growth and greater distributive justice. The future of democracy depends as much on our contemplation of these issues as it does on the choice between presidentialism and parliamentarism.

Notes

1. Catherine M. Conaghan, "Capitalists, Technocrats, and Politicians: Economic Policymaking and Democracy in the Central Andes," in *Issues in Democratic Consolidation: The New South American Democracies in Comparative Perspective,* edited by Scott Mainwaring, Guillermo O'Donnell, and J. Samuel Valenzuela (Notre Dame: U Notre Dame P, 1992), pp. 199–242.

2. For his discussion of the interaction of these variables and their relationship to the breakdown of democratic regimes, see the essay by Juan J. Linz, "Breakdown, Reequilibration," in *The Breakdown of Democratic Regimes,* edited by Juan J. Linz and Alfred C. Stepan (Baltimore: Johns Hopkins UP, 1978).

3. It should be noted that the 1938 constitution was never promulgated. A summary of the different features of these constitutions can be found in Hernán Salgado, *El congreso nacional del Ecuador 1986/88* (Quito: Instituto Latinoamericano de Ciencias Sociales, 1986), pp. 13–33.

4. Party development in the nineteenth century is discussed in Enrique Ayala, *Lucha política y origen de los partidos políticos en el Ecuador* (Quito: Corporación Editora Nacional, 1978).

5. The character of Velasquismo has been a subject of much debate in Ecuador. For a look at contending interpretations see Agustín Cueva, *El proceso de dominación política en el Ecuador* (Quito: Ediciones Solitierrra, 1973); Pablo Cuvi, *Velasco Ibarra: El último caudillo de la oligarquía* (Quito: Instituto de Investigaciones Económicas, Universidad Central del Ecuador, 1977); Rafael Quintero, *El mito del populismo en el Ecuador: Analisis de los fundamentos socio-económicos del surgimiento del "Velasquismo"* (Quito: FLACSO, 1980). For earlier treatments by North American scholars, see George Blanksten, *Constitutions and Caudillos* (Berkeley: U California P, 1951), pp. 42–51; Georg Maier, "The Impact of Velasquismo on the Ecuadorian Political System" (Ph.D. diss., Southern Illinois University, 1965). For an updated volume on Ecuadorean populism see Felipe Burbano de Lara and Carlos de la Torre Espinosa, eds., *El populismo en el Ecuador* (Quito: ILDIS , 1989).

6. While the CFP has proved to be an important political force in Ecuador, relatively little has been written about it. See John Martz, "Populist Leadership and the Party Caudillo: Ecuador and the CFP," *Studies in Comparative International Development* no. 3 (Fall 1983): 22–50.

7. Leon Epstein points to at least three types of incentives at work in explaining attachments to political parties: (1) utilitarian incentives—e.g., office holding, patronage; (2) solidary incentives—e.g., socializing; (3) purposive incentives—e.g., pursuit of specific goals or policies. See his *Political Parties in Western Democracies* (New York: Praeger, 1967), pp. 105–29. Alessandro Pizzorno has emphasized the importance of all three incentives in maintaining the stability of party systems. See his "Interests and Parties in Pluralism," in *Organizing Interests in Western Europe,* edited by Suzanne Berger (Cambridge: Cambridge UP, 1981), pp. 250–55. One exception to the pattern of instrumental attachment to parties in Ecuador may be the social democratic Izquierda Democrática, which has attempted to develop a party "myth." The "purity" and the mission of the ID is one of the recurrent images used by party leaders like Rodrigo Borja. See Edmundo Vera, *"Así nació la Izquierda Democrática"* (pamphlet, Quito, 1982).

8. Amparo Menéndez-Carrión, *La conquista del voto: De Velasco a Roldós* (Quito: Corporación Editora Nacional, 1986).

9. The phrase is taken from Milton Rakove, *Don't Make No Waves, Don't Back No Losers: An Insider's Analysis of the Daley Machine* (Bloomington: Indiana UP, 1975).

10. I have discussed the role of these organizations at great length in *Restructuring Domination: Industrialists and the State in Ecuador* (Pittsburgh: U Pittsburgh P, 1988).

11. For a discussion of the pervasiveness of party penetration within the context of an authoritarian regime in Latin America, see Paul Lewis, *Paraguay under Stroessner* (Chapel Hill: U North Carolina P, 1980). Lewis discusses the "total environment" created by the Colorado party, pp. 145–50.

12. This conflict is discussed at greater length in Peter Pyne, "Legislatures and Development: The Case of Ecuador 1960–61," *Comparative Political Studies* 9, no. 1 (1976): 69–92.

13. This period is discussed in John S. Fitch, *The Military Coup d'Etat as a Political Process: Ecuador 1948–1966* (Baltimore: Johns Hopkins UP, 1977), pp. 174–80.

14. Ibid., p. 181.

15. The politics of the period is discussed extensively in my *Restructuring Domination*.

16. Parts of the proposals put forth by groups and parties in the *diálogos* can be found in Luis Orleans Calle Vargas, *La constitución de 1978 y el proceso de reestructuración jurídica del estado 1976–1978* (Guayaquil: Universidad de Guayaquil, 1978).

17. Interview, Osvaldo Hurtado, Quito, 29 Mar. 1986.

18. Dick Leonard and Richard Natkiel, *World Atlas of Elections: Voting Patterns in 39 Democracies* (London: Hodder & Stoughton, 1987), pp. 2, 9, 42–43. The number of deputies was increased from sixty-nine to seventy-one in the 1984 congressional election. In the most recent round of elections in 1992, the total number of congressional seats was increased to seventy-seven.

19. Menéndez-Carrión, *La conquista del voto*, p. 407.

20. For a discussion of the popular political lexicon and the CFP's contribution, see the discussion in *Respuesta* 2 (Nov. 1987).

21. The clash is well treated in Nick D. Mills, *Crisis, conflicto y consenso: Ecuador 1979–1984* (Quito: Corporación Editora Nacional, 1984), pp. 35–51.

22. Howard Handelman, "Elite Groups under Military and Democratic Regimes: Ecuador, 1972–1984" (paper delivered at 12th Congress of the Latin American Studies Association, Albuquerque, N. M., Apr. 1985).

23. The progression of events in this period is laid out in "Cronología de la crisis política," *El comercio*, 16 Dec. 1984.

24. Interviews conducted by the author with *bloque* leaders in December 1984 revealed deep fears concerning possible use of the crisis by the executive to justify the declaration of a civilian dictatorship.

25. For example, Camilo Ponce (a deputy from the progovernment Social Christian party) referred to the behavior of the congress's president, Raúl Baca Carbo, as "dictatorial." He then called on the armed forces to "respect and comply respect for the Constitution" (*El comercio*, 9 Mar. 1985).

26. Febres Cordero's choice of the electoral law as the issue for the plebiscite allowed him to pursue his bitter personal conflict with former president, Osvaldo Hurtado. Hurtado was the author of the political party law and became the leader of the "no" campaign. For Hurtado's discussion of the plebiscite, see his *Victoria del no: Crónica de plebiscito* (Quito: Fundación Ecuatoriano de Estudios Sociales, 1986).

27. The events of March 1986 are discussed in Gonzalo Ortíz Crespo, *La hora del General* (Quito: Editorial el Conejo, 1986).

28. I have discussed the events surrounding the kidnapping in "Los Vargazos and the Crisis of Ecuadorean Democracy," *LASA Forum* (Spring 1987). For other accounts of the events surrounding the kidnapping, see John Maldonado, *Taura: Lo que no se ha dicho*

(Quito: Editorial el Conejo, 1988); Gonzalo Ortíz Crespo, *Operación Taura* (Quito: Editorial Plaza Grande, 1988); Fernando Artieda et al., *El secuestro del poder* (Quito: Editorial el Conejo, 1988).

29. The events surrounding the Robles interpellation are discussed in *Weekly Analysis of Ecuadorean Issues* no. 24 (29 Oct. 1987). For further discussion see Francisco Enríquez Bermeo, ed., *Febres Cordero y los derechos humanos: La interpelación al ministro Luis Robles Plaza* (Quito: Editorial el Conejo, 1988). For further discussion of human rights violations under the government, see Americas Watch and the Andean Commission of Jurists, *Human Rights in Ecuador* (New York: Americas Watch, 1988).

30. This definition of a loose multiparty system is taken from Ronald H. McDonald, *Party Systems and Elections in Latin America* (Chicago: Markham, 1971), pp. 23–92. It should be noted, however, that the social democratic Izquierda Democrática came close to breaking through the 40 percent threshold in the 1988 congressional election by taking twenty-nine of the seventy-one seats (exactly 40 percent). The ID performed poorly, however, in the 1990 midterm and 1992 congressional elections.

31. Much has been written on the "floating" voter (who is detached from party ties) in advanced industrial democracies. For an example of such a discussion, see Gallen Irwin and Karl Dittrich, "And the Walls Came Tumbling Down: Party Dealignment in the Netherlands," in *Electoral Change in Advanced Industrial Democracies: Realignment or Dealignment?* edited by Russell Dalton, Scott Flanagan, and Paul Beck (Princeton: Princeton UP, 1984), pp. 287–91.

32. For a collection of essays dealing with types of political linkages, see Kay Lawson, ed., *Political Parties and Linkage: A Comparative Perspective* (New Haven: Yale UP, 1980).

33. The official history of the administration's public works project can be found in Secretaria Nacional de Información Pública, *Pensamiento y obra: Gobierno constitucional del ingeniero León Febres Cordero Ribadeneyra* (Quito: SENDIP, 1988).

34. In Ecuador's traditional hacienda system, a *huasipungo* was a peasant's subsistence plot. The quotation is from an interview with Congressman Roberto Dunn, Partido Roldosista Ecuatoriano, Quito, 19 Dec. 1984.

35. This pattern, of course, was not confined to Ecuador. For references to a similar style of policy making in Brazil under José Sarney, see Maria do Carmo Campello de Souza, "The Brazilian 'New Republic': Under the 'Sword of Damocles'," in *Democratizing Brazil: Problems, Transitions and Consolidation,* edited by Alfred Stepan (New York: Oxford UP, 1989), p. 375.

36. Interview with Osvaldo Hurtado cited in n. 17.

37. Some Ecuadorean observers speculate that the long-standing intraparty rivalry between Osvaldo Hurtado and Julio César Trujillo (the 1984 DP presidential nominee) made Hurtado even less concerned about the electoral retribution that his party would suffer for sponsoring the stabilization package. Trujillo polled an embarrassing 3.7 percent of the vote in the first-round presidential election of 1984.

38. Febres-Cordero's use of emergency decrees is discussed by León Roldós Aguilera, *El abuso poder: Los decretos leyes económicos urgentes aprobados por el gobierno del Ing. León Febres Cordero* (Quito: El Conejo, 1986).

39. Simon Pachano's study of Congress indicates that in the period 1978–88, 52.5 percent of all deputies were lawyers; only 2.6 percent were economists. See *Los diputados: Una élite política* (Quito: Corporación Editora Nacional, 1991), p. 114.

40. Interview, Alberto Dahik, Quito, 5 Feb. 1987.

41. Interview, Carlos Julio Emanuel, Quito, 5 Feb. 1987.

42. For a general discussion of popular protest and stabilization programs, see John Walton, "Debt, Protest, and the State in Latin America," in *Power and Popular Protest: Latin American Social Movements,* edited by Susan Eckstein (Berkeley and Los Angeles: U California P, 1989), pp. 299–328.

43. O'Donnell and Schmitter have suggested that in the initial period following a transition electoral rules should be structured to "help" the Right in order to assure their representation and their loyalty to the new institutional arrangements. See Guillermo O'Donnell and Philippe C. Schmitter, *Transitions from Authoritarian Rule: Tentative Conclusions about Uncertain Democracies* (Baltimore: Johns Hopkins UP, 1986), pp. 61–64.

44. For a discussion of the continuing appeal of populist parties in Ecuador, see Jorge León, "Cambios estructurales y escena política en Ecuador 1978–88: Un ciclo político" (paper presented at 15th International Congress of the Latin American Studies Association, 4–6 Dec., 1989, Miami, Florida).

45. There may be many parallels between the developing party systems in Brazil and Ecuador. For a discussion of the peculiarities of parties in Brazil, see Fernando Henrique Cardoso, "Associated Dependent Development and Democratic Theory," in *Democratizing Brazil: Problems of Transition and Consolidation,* edited by Alfred C. Stepan (New York: Oxford UP, 1989), p. 322.

46. Interview, Rodrigo Borja, Quito, 6 Dec. 1984.

47. For his argument on these points, see Roberto Mangabeira Unger, *False Necessity: Anti-Necessitarian Social Theory in the Service of Radical Democracy* (New York: Cambridge UP, 1987), pp. 444–61. For a review of Unger's works, see Perry Anderson, "Roberto Unger and the Politics of Empowerment," *New Left Review* no. 173 (Jan.–Feb. 1989): 93–107.

11

CYNTHIA McCLINTOCK

Presidents, Messiahs, and Constitutional Breakdowns in Peru

As in most of Latin America, in Peru constitutional regimes have been presidential rather than parliamentary. Also like many other Latin American countries, Peru has suffered marked political instability since 1930. This chapter will explore the question: Has presidentialism been a significant factor in the breakdown of Peruvian constitutional regimes?

In their chapters for this volume, Juan Linz and Arturo Valenzuela hypothesize that a number of problems plague presidential regimes. Among these perils are: (1) the tendency of presidents, upon receiving what they may interpret—correctly or incorrectly—as an overwhelming mandate at the polls, to fashion themselves as messiahs of unlimited power; (2) the likelihood of intense conflict between the executive and the legislature, in part because of the implications of the phenomenon just mentioned and in part because of the weakening of the executive as political leaders prepare for the next election; (3) the rigidity of the electoral schedule, which does not allow for the ousting of a failed president or, in most Latin American countries, the immediate reelection of a successful one; and (4) the potential for political polarization in a dramatic, winner-take-all contest.

Other scholars have expressed concerns about presidentialism similar to those of Linz and Valenzuela. Especially among the Latin Americanists writing for this volume, the primary emphasis has been upon the frequency of executive-legislative conflict that culminates in deadlock (alternatively referred to as "stalemate" or "immobilism"). For the Venezuelan case, Michael Coppedge discerns "executive-legislative stalemate" under four different administrations, resulting in the shifting of power toward the presidency and away from the congress (chapter 12). A similar dynamic is observed in Colombia by Jonathan Hartlyn (chapter 9). In a review article on presidentialism in Latin America, the first item on Scott Mainwaring's proposed research agenda is the proclivity of presidentialism toward executive-legislative immobilism and the subsequent tendency of presidents to expand their powers (Mainwaring 1990, 171).

How are these concerns about presidentialism illuminated by the Peruvian case? Unfortunately, the period of democratic presidentialism in Peru has been short, perhaps too short for a valid test of these hypotheses. Between 1930 and 1980, Peru experienced approximately twenty years of constitutional government, but these governments could not be described as democratic in the full sense of the term (Cotler 1978a). As a result of intense conflict between the military and the reformist political party APRA (Alianza Popular Revolucionaria Americana), the party was barred from executive office at least until the 1960s, and this veto seriously distorted the operation of the political system.

Between 1980 and April 5, 1992, the regime was indisputably inclusive and formally democratic. But in the first two presidential elections, the triumphant party gained a stable majority in the legislature despite the country's multiparty system; accordingly, executive-legislative relations were smooth. During this period, the most severe problem of presidentialism was the tendency of presidents to fashion themselves as messiahs—a problem that was ultimately the key factor in the breakdown of democracy on April 5, 1992. President Fujimori's allegations to the contrary, Peru's executive had not been stalemated by the legislature, despite his party's minority status.

The next section of this chapter provides an overview of the two post-1930 constitutions and their implications for Peruvian politics. The discussion then examines the post-1930 breakdowns of constitutional government—in 1936, 1948, 1962, 1968, and 1992—and considers the role of presidentialism in these breakdowns. The final section looks at recommendations for constitutional revision, including parliamentarism as well as the suggestions most frequently made by Peruvian scholars of the constitution.

Constitutions and Politics in Peru: An Overview

Presidentialism has been a constant feature in Peru's twelve constitutions. The stipulations in all twelve correspond to Juan Linz's definition of presidentialism: "an executive with considerable constitutional powers—generally including full control of the composition of the cabinet and administration—is directly elected by the people for a fixed term and is independent of parliamentary votes of confidence" (Linz 1990, 52). The definition applies with the exceptions that the executive's control of the composition of the cabinet has not been total, and that in most of Peru's pre–twentieth-century constitutions the election of the president was indirect.

Not only does the principle of election of a president for a fixed term have a long history in Peruvian constitutions, but so does the prohibition against immediate reelection. This prohibition began in the constitutions of the 1820s and was only altered during the administration of President Augusto Leguía in 1920, expressly for his own "reelection." Leguía so manipulated the state electoral machinery that Peruvian constitution-makers' fears about immediate reelection were exacerbated (Chirinos Soto 1986, 218–19). Despite the prohibition against immediate reelection, incentives for loyalty to the president remain: a former president may run again after one intervening term, and under the 1979 constitution, a former president is automatically a senator for life. Indeed, since 1930, two of the four elected presidents, Manuel Prado and Fernando Belaúnde, were in fact reelected to the presidency, and the 1985–90 president, Alán García, is widely believed to want to run again.

There have been variations in the length of the president's term and in the rules for presidential election. Most of Peru's nineteenth-century constitutions stipulated indirect election of the president for a four-year term. The 1933 constitution—the only other twentieth-century constitution excepting the current document—provided for the direct election of the president for a five-year term. In 1939, the term was extended to six years. Noting the tendency of an administration to weaken over a six-year period (García Belaúnde 1986, 32; Rubio and Bernales 1981, 338), the 1979 constitution makers returned the term to five years.

Two of the most important innovations of the 1979 constitution concerned electoral procedures. First, suffrage became universal; illiterates and eighteen- to twenty-year-olds were allowed to vote for the first time. Second, the formula for accession to the presidency was modified. Specifically, under the 1933 constitution a candidate needed only a plurality of one-third of the ballots for accession to the presidency; in the case that no candidate secured one-third, one of the top three vote-getters was chosen president by the congress. In contrast, the 1979 constitution required an absolute majority of the ballots to win the presidency outright; in the case that no candidate won a majority, a runoff was held between the two front-runners.

The debate over the second-round procedure was the most explosive of the entire Constituent Assembly (Cotler 1986, 167; Handeman 1980, 14–15; Woy-Hazleton 1982, 42).[1] To a considerable degree, the debate reflected each party's perception of its own direct interests in the upcoming election. The Right felt most strongly about the need for a second round. Ultimately it prevailed, but only after intense bargaining: the Right won votes from the Left by agreeing to the Left's appeal to extend the franchise to illiterates, and it also mollified APRA by exempting the upcoming 1980 election from the second-round provision.

The primary argument of advocates of the second round was the point that Juan Linz has articulated: the contradiction between the strong claim to democratic legitimacy of a president and the possibility that, in fact, the president was elected by a minority, with only a few percentage points of the vote between him and other candidates (Linz 1990, 53; García Belaúnde 1986, 32–37). In particular, advocates of the second round were influenced by what they judged to be the success of the procedure in the French Fifth Republic; the tragedy of the democratic breakdown in Chile in 1973, which might have been avoided if a second round had been held; and the 1962 coup in Peru itself, to which the 1933 constitution's electoral formula was one of the most important contributing factors (see below).

What did Peru's presidentialism imply for its party system? No single effect can be clearly identified. Although the makers of the 1979 constitution assumed that the second-round provision would encourage the formation of strong party alliances with centripetal tendencies and perhaps even move Peru toward a two-party system (García Belaúnde 1986, 33–34; Rubio and Bernales 1981, 38–381), a two-party system did not emerge; indeed, the number of parties competing for the presidency was greater after the introduction of the second-round procedure than before.

Probably, Peru's proportional representation system mitigated against the bipolarizing proclivities of a presidential system with second-round balloting. Since 1963, seats in both houses of the legislature (the senate and the chamber of deputies) were allocated according to proportional representation by the d'Hondt formula (Reumpler 1986, 99). Prior to 1963, the party with the greatest vote in the jurisdiction received two-thirds of the seats, while the second- and third-place parties divided the remaining one-third (Reumpler 1986, 99).

Whatever the implications of Peru's constitutional provisions, the country has inclined toward a moderate multiparty system since 1930 (see tables 11.1 and 11.2). The norm has been three or four major parties, with relatively clear positions on the ideological spectrum (in other words, more similar to the Chilean than the Ecuadorean, Colombian, or Venezuelan pattern). Peru's minor parties have tended to be regional parties or vehicles of particular political personalities seeking to gain legislative seats or ministerial positions in their own right; they have not been clustered at ideological extremes.[2]

Despite the consistently presidential character of Peru's constitutional regimes, the question of the appropriate powers of the president relative to the congress has provoked debate since Peru's independence. Indeed, it was controversy on this question—rather than on centralism versus federalism or the relationship between church and state—that prompted the constitutional instability of the 1820s and 1830s (Werlich 1978, 67–68). During the period between 1823 and 1838, six constitutions—or half the total number to date—were drafted; key issues included emergency powers for the executive and the extent of indirectness of the vote (Werlich 1978, 85; Chirinos Soto 1986, 213).

Of Peru's twelve constitutions (1823, 1826, 1827, 1834, 1837, 1839, 1856, 1860, 1867, 1920, 1933, and 1979),[3] only three endured for long periods: those of 1860, 1933, and 1979. Of these three, that of 1860 was the most durable, remaining in force between 1860 and 1920, save for two brief interruptions (one during 1867). While the essence of all three was presidential, more parliamentary features were incorporated than in most Latin American constitutions. In particular, in all three an office of prime minister was established, and in the latter two the legislature wielded the right to censure the prime minister or his ministers (Reid 1987, 1–2; Hilliker 1971, 130; Chirinos Soto 1986, 236). In contrast to common parliamentary practice, however, the

Table 11.1. Peru's Major Parties and Their Electoral Tallies, 1978–1990

	Elections (% of valid vote)			
	1978 Constituent Assembly	1980 Presidential	1985 Presidential	1990 Presidential
Left				
IU (factionalized as FOCEP, UDP, PC, PSR)	29			
IU (FOCEP, PRT, UNIR, UDP, UI)		14		
IU			25	8
IS				5
Center				
APRA	35	27	53	23
AP		45	7	
Cambio 90				29
Right				
PPC	24	10		
CD			12	
FREDEMO				33

Source: Richard Webb and Graciela Fernandez Baca, *Perú en Números* 1991 (Lima: Cuánto, 1991), pp. 1028–30.

IU, Izquierda Unida; FOCEP, Frente Obrero Campesino y Popular; UDP, Unidad Democrática Popular; PC, Partido Comunista; PSR, Partido Socialista Revolucionario; PRT, Partido Revolucionario de los Trabajadores; UNIR, Union de Izquierda Revolucionaria; UI, Unidad de Izquierda; IS, Izquierda Socialista, party of Alfonso Barrantes; APRA, Alianza Popular Revolucionaria Americana; AP, Acción Popular; PPC, Partido Popular Cristiano; CD, Convergencia Democrática (coalition of PPC and rightist dissidents from APRA); FREDEMO, Frente Democrático (coalition of AP, PPC, and Mario Vargas Llosa's Movimiento Libertad).

prime minister was appointed by the president rather than the parliament, and the prime minister's power has varied according to the strength of his personality and his relationship with the president.

Of the three long-standing constitutions, legislative powers were greatest in the 1933 document. Especially as a result of the troubled executive-legislative relationship during President Fernando Belaúnde's first term (1963–68), the legislative powers in the 1933 constitution were judged excessive by the drafters of the 1979 model and were restricted, while executive power was enhanced. The increase in executive power was most dramatic on three scores: (1) the accountability of cabinet officials to the congress; (2) the economic policy-making powers granted to the executive; and (3) the permission to the legislature to delegate law making to the executive.

Under the 1933 constitution, the prime minister and his ministers were highly dependent upon the confidence of the congress (Rubio and Bernales 1981, 409–13; Chirinos Soto 1986, 242–58; Ruiz-Eldredge 1980, 286–90). Any single legislator

Table 11.2. Peru's Winning Parties and Their Strength in the Legislature, 1930–1990

Year	No. Candidates	Winner	Winner's Party	% of Vote	Legislative Majority?	Legislative Support Gained or Lost?
1931	4	Luis Sánchez Cerro	Unión Revolucionaria	51	Almost	Gained[a]
1939	2	Manuel Prado	No name	78	Yes	Gained[b]
1945	2	Jose Luis Bustamante y Rivero	Frente Democrático Nacional (a coalition with APRA)	67	APRA is dominant	No change
1956	3	Manuel Prado	Movimiento Democrático Pradista (with support of APRA but no coalition)	45	Yes[c]	Gained, via an alliance with APRA[c]
1963	4	Fernando Belaúnde Terry	Alianza Acción Popular–Democracia Cristiana	39	No	Gained in year before scheduled end of term
1980	15	Fernando Belaúnde Terry	Acción Popular	45	Almost	Gained; alliance with PPC lasts until Nov. 1984
1985	9	Alán García Perez	APRA	53	Yes	No change
1990[d]	9	Alberto Fujimori	Cambio 90	29	No	N.A.

Source: Unless otherwise indicated, the sources are Tuesta Soldevilla (1987) and, for 1990, El comercio, 17 May 1990, p. A6.
a. Werlich (1978, 196).
b. Chirinos (1984, 92), Werlich (1978, 221).
c. Pike (1986, 250), Werlich (1978, 257–58).
d. El comercio, 17 May 1990, p. A6.

from either of the two houses of congress could move an interpellation of a minister or prime minister, and the votes of only one-fifth of the legislators were required for the motion to be passed and the minister interrogated. A vote to censure the minister and compel his resignation could be taken immediately after the interrogation; it required for approval only a plurality of the legislators' ballots. The president had no power to dissolve either body of the congress.

The stipulations of the 1979 constitution made the censure and removal of a minister more difficult. Only the chamber of deputies, rather than both bodies of congress, had the right of interrogation and censure. At least 25 percent of the deputies had to move an interrogation, and at least one-third had to support it, for the motion to be passed and the minister interrogated. A three-day "cooling-off" period was then required prior to a vote censure, and an absolute majority of the deputies' votes was required for the censure and forced resignation of the minister. Also under most circumstances, the executive was granted a retaliatory power: if the chamber of deputies censured three cabinets, the president could dissolve it and call new elections.

Perhaps the most criticized of all the provisions in the 1979 constitution was article 211, clause 20: "Among the attributions and obligations of the President of the Republic are . . . to administer public finance; to manage public borrowing; and to promulgate extraordinary measures in economic and financial matters, when the national interest so requires and with the responsibility to make them known (dar cuenta) to the congress" (my translation). The stipulation was criticized because it was vague and, in part for this reason, enabled what constitutionalist scholars considered presidential abuse (Melo-Vega Castro 1989, 405–7; Eguiguren 1987, 433–34).[4] Both Presidents Belaúnde and García used the stipulation to issue economic decrees that were neither urgent nor extraordinary (see "Testing Hypotheses about the Peril of Presidentialism" below).

The 1979 constitution also restricted the congress's role in making the budget. The congress retained the right to discuss and vote on the budget but not to initiate expenditure (Bernales and Rubio 1988, 42). This change was a result of the perception that perpetual confrontations over the budget had obstructed effective economic policy making during the 1963–68 Belaúnde administration (Kuczynski 1977; Jaquette 1971).

Executive power over not only economic policy but any kind of policy was facilitated by another new provision in the 1979 constitution. Article 188 specified that "the congress may delegate to the executive power the authority to legislate, through legislative decrees, on the issues and for the period that the authoritative law specifies." Although this new provision was fully supported in the constituent assembly, the complacent Peruvian legislatures of the 1980s delegated authority to the executive much more regularly, for longer periods of time, and on a much greater array of issues, including even issues of a constitutional character, than had been anticipated by the drafters of the constitution (Bernales 1990, 138–45; Chirinos Soto 1986, 197).

While the 1979 constitution shifted powers from the legislature to the executive, it also provided a greater impetus to decentralization, which could potentially circumscribe the president's powers. Although regional entities had been proposed in previous constitutions, including the 1933 constitution, in practice these department-level bodies were either never established or quickly eliminated (Chirinos Soto 1986, 318–21; Barrenechea 1989, 8). For the first time, the 1979 constitution not only mandated regional governments but also stipulated that the senate should be elected from the regions.

The 1980–85 Belaúnde administration did little to advance regionalization, but the García government promoted it vigorously, and a federal system became operative in 1991 (Mendez 1989, 13; Schmidt 1989). Each of twelve regional governments was composed of differing numbers of members, roughly 40 percent of them elected by popular vote, 30 percent of them mayors of provinces, and 30 percent of them delegates from popular organizations (Barrenechea 1989, 7). The regional governments were to be quite powerful. They were to enjoy control over substantial financial resources and play a significant role in all phases of development planning; they were also to have the right to initiate legislation for their jurisdiction (Schmidt 1989, 13). The García government touted the regionalization program as its greatest achievement.

To a lesser degree, the 1979 constitution also circumscribed presidential power by enhancing the powers of municipal government. In 1963, in one of the most endorsed measures of his first administration, President Belaúnde restored the right of citizens to elect their municipal governments, which for almost fifty years previously had been appointed by the executive. Held once every three years in November, rather than once every five years in April like the presidential and congressional elections, the municipal elections are the only ones to provide midterm leadership opportunities to the political opposition as well as a barometer of citizens' political opinions. Although the municipalities are primarily responsible for day-to-day local problems (transportation, schools, recreation, and so forth) and historically have spent a mere 4 percent of the national public budget (Althaus et al. 1986, 21), the 1979 constitution expanded their role and provided potential new resources (Schmidt 1989, 6). In some municipalities—most saliently, municipalities in Lima that have been operated by the political Left, such as Villa El Salvador—popular organizations, which developed to work for satisfaction of basic human needs, have impeded the access of guerrilla groups to the community (Calderón Cockburn and Olivera Cárdenas 1989). The job of mayor of Lima is one of the most politically visible in Peru and has often been a stepping stone to presidential candidacy.

Testing Hypotheses about the Perils of Presidentialism: Breakdowns in Constitutional Governments in Peru, 1930–1968

Between 1930 and 1968, Peru suffered four breakdowns in its constitutional order: in 1936, 1948, 1962, and 1968. For each, this section tests Linz and Valenzuela's hypotheses about the dangers of presidentialism: exaggeration by the president of his mandate and power; paralyzing conflict between the executive and the legislature; the rigidity of the electoral schedule; and political polarization.

Overall, the analysis in this section finds limited support for these hypotheses during this period in Peru. The overwhelming scholarly consensus is that Peru's political problems between 1930 and 1968 were rooted not in constitutional forms but in the intense conflict between the oligarchy and the military, on the one hand, and the APRA party, on the other hand—a conflict in which all sides were willing to resort to violence to achieve their goals.[5] This conflict is not merely a necessary but also a sufficient explanation for the 1936 and 1948 breakdowns and a necessary but insufficient explanation for the 1962 and 1968 breakdowns. In the 1968 case, executive-legislative conflict was a factor in the constitutional rupture.

One of the most lucid characterizations of Peruvian politics during the 1930–68 period is that by Julio Cotler in the volume *The Breakdown of Democratic Regimes: Latin America:*

> Democracy [in Peru] developed in form but not in content. . . . Faced with increasing Aprista pressure, particularly after the crisis of the 1930s, the dominant groups found that they did not possess the means to meet demands for social reform. . . . It therefore became necessary to establish an alliance with the army and embark on a policy of violent repression. . . . Peru was enmeshed in a violent confrontation between APRA and the army. This confrontation was to define the political framework within which all subsequent events were to unfold. Throughout the period between 1930 and 1945, APRA sought to penetrate the military, endeavoring to undermine this pillar of the oligarchical order. This effort caused the military to redouble its opposition to APRA. (Cotler 1978a, 178, 183–84)

Founded in 1924 by Haya de la Torre, APRA was Peru's first reformist, mass political party, and it remains Peru's best institutionalized party. By the early 1930s, however, a political vicious circle was established in the dynamic of its relationship with the oligarchy and the military: Peru's oligarchy did not accept APRA as a legitimate political party; barred from executive political office, APRA's behavior was often intransigent and at times violent; and APRA's antidemocratic actions stiffened elites' resolve to repress the party. Elites' rejection of APRA was even incorporated into the 1933 constitution; article 53, outlawing "political parties of international organization," was used to repress APRA for decades.

The 1936 Constitutional Breakdown

The conflict between the Peruvian oligarchy and military, on the one hand, and the APRA party on the other became virulent in the aftermath of the 1931 election. In the election, Luis Sánchez Cerro, a dark-skinned army commander who had overthrown the dictator Augusto Leguía just a few months previously, defeated APRA's Haya de la Torre by 51 percent to 35 percent of the valid vote (Tuesta Soldevilla 1987, 299). While the election has been rigorously analyzed and endorsed as fair by historians, Haya de la Torre was incredulous; he did not think his defeat was possible (Pike 1986, 156–60; Stein 1980, 190–94).

The APRA party immediately charged fraud. While Haya's thoughts turned to seeking a pro-Aprista military coup, many APRA militants favored an Aprista-led revolution (Pike 1986, 160–64). The intemperate behavior of the Aprista members of the newly elected Constituent Assembly quickly alienated other parties, and within six weeks President Sánchez Cerro had built his original 44 percent plurality in the assembly into a working majority (Werlich 1978, 196). Sánchez Cerro then requested an emergency powers law, and upon its approval began to suppress APRA. Sánchez Cerro arrested hundreds of Aprista leaders, including its entire congressional representation.

All sides both suffered and perpetrated violence. In February 1932, a young Aprista made an unsuccessful attempt on the life of Sánchez Cerro. Then in July, Aprista activists rebelled in the city of Trujillo; about sixty army officers were killed in the struggle. When the army regained control of the city, it retaliated by rounding up and shooting between one thousand and five thousand suspected Apristas. Then in 1933, Sánchez Cerro was assassinated by an Aprista militant.

Although Linz and Valenzuela have hypothesized that formulas for succession upon the death of presidents are dangerously rigid, this was not the case in Peru in 1933. The 1933 constitution did not yet provide for a vice presidency; rather, in the event of vacancy in the presidential office, the congress was to elect a successor within three days (Werlich 1978, 201). Upon the assassination of Sánchez Cerro, the congress chose General Oscar Benavides as the new president. The congress was influenced by the general's effective performance as provisional president during a political crisis in 1914 and pragmatically disregarded the fact that, as an active member of the armed forces, Benavides was ineligible (Werlich 1978, 201).

At first, Benavides hoped to moderate the confrontation with APRA. He proclaimed a partial political amnesty. However, Benavides repeatedly postponed action on a key Aprista demand: special elections to fill the vacancies created in the legislature by the arrest of its Aprista members under Sánchez Cerro. APRA again plotted uprisings and the military again violated human rights. The Peruvian oligarchy's hostility toward APRA was reinforced when, in 1935, an Aprista assassinated the editor of the prominent newspaper, *El Comercio.*

In 1936, in this virulently polarized context, elections were due. Banned from direct participation, APRA threw its support to Luis Antonio Eguiguren, a respected leader from the Center Left. With the pro-Benavides and rightist groups divided among three candidacies, Eguiguren was winning a plurality of about 40 percent of the votes after two weeks of ballot counting (Werlich 1978, 210). Victory for an Aprista-backed candidate was unacceptable to Peru's elites, however, and the congress nullified the election. At Benavides's urging, the legislature agreed to extend his term for another three years, provide him dictatorial powers, and dissolve itself. In other words, Benavides staged his own coup.

The 1948 Constitutional Breakdown

The reason for the 1948 coup was the same as the 1936 constitutional rupture: the refusal of Peru's elites and military to allow APRA to exercise a significant share of political power. Relative to the 1930s, the positions of both Peruvian elites and the APRA party had mellowed, but not enough to enable the continuity of constitutional order.

The 1948 coup was made against the government of José Luis Bustamante y Rivero, a distinguished legal scholar without a political base of his own who had won the 1945 presidential election in a coalition with APRA, called the Frente Democrático Nacional (FDN). In contrast to 1936, not only was this Aprista-backed candidate allowed to assume the presidency. but the APRA party itself was allowed to compete for seats in the legislature (under a hastily improvised party label). Competing against only one rightist party in the 1945 election, the FDN won an overwhelming two-thirds of the vote, and APRA emerged as dominant in the legislature: it gained a small absolute majority in the senate and, on most occasions, sufficient votes from non-Aprista members of the FDN in the chamber of deputies to give it a majority there as well (Werlich 1978, 236).

The slight increase in elites' tolerance of APRA had various causes. First, at the end of World War II, the world political climate was prodemocratic. Also, during the war, the ideology of Haya and APRA moderated. Frightened by the Nazis and fascism, and impressed by Franklin D. Roosevelt, Haya and the party leadership shifted away from the Left in their positions about the United States, economics, and the legitimacy of violence as a strategy for gaining power (Cotler 1978b, 258–67; Werlich 1978, 242–43).

Also important was the success of the 1939–45 civilian administration of Manuel Prado in reducing political tensions, despite the fact that the election of Prado (the protégé of President Benavides) had been neither free nor fair. In office, Prado moved to return Peru to constitutional government. Congress reopened. Laws restricting political participation remained but were not strongly enforced. Prado also had the good fortune to be governing when Peru triumphed over Ecuador in a brief border war.

Despite Prado's success, the prohibition against his reelection did not become an issue. Rather, Peruvians were eager for a more complete democratic opening and apparently did not consider the diplomatic, but elitist, Prado the man for the job (Werlich 1978, 229–30). Ultimately, after considerable negotiation between Haya de la Torre and both former president Benavides and current president Prado, all sides agreed to back the presidential candidacy of Bustamante y Rivero. Competing only against the far-right Revolutionary Union, Bustamante y Rivero won the presidency in a landslide, and his coalition partner APRA dominated the congress, as mentioned above.

Within three years and a half years, however, the Bustamante y Rivero government fell to a rightist military coup.[6] Despite the artificial character of the alliance between Bustamante y Rivero and APRA, and the severe tensions between the president and the APRA-dominated congress, these difficulties were not at the root of the coup. Rather, the key problem was that APRA's behavior had not moderated enough to satisfy Peru's economic or military elites.

Although APRA's congressional leadership was not extremist in its ideological positions (not even proposing an agrarian reform or the vote for illiterates, for example), the party's rank and file remained militant. Union-organizing efforts were intensive, and street clashes between Aprista *bufalos* (the name used for Aprista thugs) and the party's enemies were frequent (Pike 1986, 225; Gilbert 1977, 120). Also, whatever APRA's ideological position in the legislature, its attitude was quarrelsome. Consider, for example, this characterization by Palmer (1980, 93): "APRA's majority . . . did almost everything imaginable to disrupt the orderly conduct of business." While such behavior was often understandable in the context of Bustamante's actions (the president named a prime minister who was not trusted by APRA without consulting the party, and his first cabinet included no Apristas), it was not reassuring to Peru's Right. The more intransigent APRA's behavior became, the further the oligarchy demanded that Bustamante distance himself from APRA, and then the more isolated, betrayed, and rebellious APRA felt, in another vicious circle.

Significantly, the spark that eventually ignited the military coup was the promulgation of a law upon which Bustamante and APRA agreed: the Sechura Contract, providing new exploration rights to the International Petroleum Company (IPC), a subsidiary of Standard Oil. Disingenuously, Peruvian elites attacked the contract through their newspapers, *El Comercio* and *La Prensa*. In early 1947, a *La Prensa* editor who had harshly condemned APRA, Francisco Graña, was assassinated. Most Peruvians presumed that Apristas were responsible, and an investigation eventually produced considerable evidence of Aprista guilt (Pike 1986, 227); Graña immediately became the Right's political martyr.

As the political crisis intensified, Bustamante tried to mediate. He forced the resignation of three Apristas in his cabinet at the time of Graña's assassination, thereby implying his belief in APRA's responsibility for the crime and also of course alienating the party from executive power. However, Bustamante did not accede to the Right's demand that he outlaw APRA once again. When the right-wing anti-Aprista parliamentary minority boycotted the legislative sessions of 1947 and 1948, the necessary quorum was lacking and all congressional activity halted. Although Bustamante continued to seek a political compromise that would restore legislative activity, both APRA and the Right began to plot against constitutional order.

APRA's plotting failed. Haya de la Torre sought support from Peru's military commanders for a pro-Aprista coup, but high-level promises of a coup attempt were never kept. Perceiving Haya de la Torre as too cautious, Aprista cadres in the lower ranks of the navy mutinied at Lima's port, Callao, in October 1948. Uncoordinated with the Aprista leadership, the protest was rapidly repressed. Not surprisingly (in effect, APRA was rebelling against its own government), Bustamante declared APRA illegal once again.

In yet another indication that the issue for Peru's Right was not Bustamante-APRA relations, but rather a political conjuncture that had allowed APRA an opening, the Right was not mollified by Bustamante's outlawing of APRA. It proceeded with its prior coup plots. After issuing a manifesto that accused Bustamante of being "soft on APRA," General Manuel Odría launched a successful coup (Werlich 1978, 245).

The 1962 Constitutional Breakdown

Just as General Benavides in 1936 acted against an electoral outcome he considered unacceptable, so did the Peruvian military veto the 1962 electoral result. The reasons behind the 1962 coup were more complex, however, and if any number of seemingly minor facts had been different, the coup might not have happened. In the event, however, primary blame for the coup is placed both on continuing anti-Aprismo within the military and pervasive doubt that any legitimate government could emerge from the electoral result.[7] As noted previously, the problematical 1962 electoral result was an important stimulus to the runoff provision in the 1979 constitution.

Although Manuel Prado was still president at the time of the 1962 coup, he was only a few weeks from completing what would have been his second full term. The coup was in no way against Prado, whose political skills were as evident as in his 1939–45 term. Once again, Prado had built political bridges, opening new political space to APRA without provoking the Right to extraconstitutional action.

The Prado administration was in many respects a model of successful presidentialism. First, the 1956 presidential campaign was not polarizing. Shortly before the election, a pact was made between Prado and APRA that APRA, which had suffered severe persecution under the eight-year dictatorship of Odría and was illegal at the time, would be returned its full political rights in exchange for its votes. In reaching this agreement, APRA allied with an oligarchical figure it knew and trusted rather than with the up-and-coming reformist, Fernando Belaúnde Terry; an APRA-Belaúnde alliance was logical from the perspective of ideology, but the Aprista leadership feared that Peru's oligarchy would not tolerate the triumph of such an alliance and harbored a long-term goal, victory in its own right in 1962.

In the legislature between 1956 and 1962, APRA wanted to demonstrate that it was no longer an obstreperous sect and that it could work with an oligarchical leader such as Prado—and it did so, ultimately gaining a prize it coveted, Prado's support in the 1962 election. For his part, Prado was honest, keeping his promises to APRA, and shrewd. For example, Prado avoided an outbidding contest for APRA votes with a conservative rival in the 1956 election and, when a rightist virulently attacked the administration, defused the situation by appointing him prime minister. Table 11.3

Table 11.3. Ministerial Stability in Peru, 1956–1990

Ministry	Number of Ministers				Increase in Last Half of Term over First Half?			
	Prado (1956–62)	Belaúnde (1963–68)	Belaúnde (1980–85)	García (1985–90)	Prado (1956–62)	Belaúnde (1963–69)[a]	Belaúnde (1980–85)	García (1985–90)
Economy & Finance	6	7	4	6	No	Yes	Yes	Yes
Interior[b]	4	9	5	5	No	No	Yes	Yes
War	2	4	4	3[c]	No	No	No	No
Agriculture	2	11	3	4	Yes	Yes	Yes	No
Education	10	8	5	4	No	No	Yes	No
Justice	7	12	6	6	No	Yes	Yes	Yes
Foreign Relations[b]	15	6	4	3				
Work & Social Welfare[b]	6	7	3	3	No	Yes	Yes	No
Transportation & Communication	5	6	4	6	No	No	No	Yes
Total	57	70	38	40	No	Yes	Yes	Yes
Average length of service (in months)	11.3	8.0	14.2	13.5				

Source: Tuesta Soldevilla (1987, 25–52) and his personal records for 1985–90.
a. The midway date in the term is set as February 1, 1966.
b. Because the source provides only the year, not the month, of the ministerial shift, slight errors in the calculation are possible.
c. The Ministry of War, the army's ministry, was formally grouped with the navy and air force ministries under a new Ministry of Defense in October 1987.

shows the ministerial stability of the Prado government, which was maintained throughout the six-year term.

Yet, as in 1945, another term for Prado was not an issue. From the perspective of the key political party, APRA, the entire premise of Prado's administration was the transition to APRA's legitimacy in 1962, and this principle would have been contradicted by a renewal of Prado's candidacy. Moreover, Prado was a banker, not a social reformist, at a time when, amid the Cuban revolution and Alliance for Progress, the need for social reform was becoming a maxim. In any case, Prado wanted to return to Paris (where he had spent much of his life).

In the 1962 election, the three candidates were Haya de la Torre (head of the Alianza Democrática, a coalition of APRA and Prado's party), Fernando Belaúnde of the Acción Popular, and (for the Right) the former dictator Odría. A major campaign issue was an alleged intent by APRA and Prado's party, given their incumbency, to commit fraud. Belaúnde charged that these parties were issuing fraudulent registration cards and that the progovernment National Election Jury had disqualified several small rightist parties but had qualified similarly small leftist parties that would draw votes away from Acción Popular. Both charges were investigated and found correct (Payne 1968, 41–43); Belaúnde urged the military to scrutinize the balloting carefully and announced that he would accept the electoral result only if it was verified by the military.

Unfortunately for the democratic process, the electoral result was extremely close (Tuesta Soldevilla 1987, 263). Haya beat Belaúnde by less than one percentage point, 32.9 percent to 32.1 percent, with Odría third at 28 percent. The four parties to Belaúnde's left polled about 6 percent. Worse yet, Haya's 32.9 percent was .4 percent below the one-third plurality necessary for his direct election, and the constitution required that the next president be chosen by the new congress.

Was the electoral result valid? About two weeks after the election, the military noted that it had acted to mitigate the possibilities for fraud but that irregularities had taken place in seven departments—all of which had given majorities to APRA. The military's charge may or may not have been accurate; if there had been fraud, it was not massive (APRA was to win a larger percentage of the vote in 1963 than it had in 1962). Yet the critical margin in the 1962 tally could not have been narrower.

In any case, the military relayed to Haya through President Prado the message that it would not accept an Aprista president. Accordingly, Haya began to bargain with Belaúnde, as an ideologically acceptable partner in a coalition. Although Haya's proposal was not unreasonable, Belaúnde rapidly rejected it and called for annulment of the elections (Bourricaud 1970, 302–5; Welrich 1978, 272; Payne 1968, 44–46; Jaquette 1971, 115–20). In the wake of his rejection by Belaúnde, Haya turned to Odría—APRA's archrival. The specter of a government led by the presidential candidate who had finished third, in an ideologically disparate coalition of two parties that had been enemies for decades, may have been the last straw for the military. The coup came within two days.[8]

The 1968 Constitution Breakdown

In the 1968 coup, the military's anti-Aprismo remained a factor, but the reasons behind it had changed considerably. Ironically, by this time the military perceived APRA not as dangerously leftist but as too cynically rightist. During the 1963–68 administration of Belaúnde, APRA allied with Odría's party to block various reform efforts by the executive and also generally to harass Belaúnde's cabinet officials. Accordingly, executive-legislative impasse was an important factor in the constitutional breakdown. However, the executive-legislative conflict was in some respects a symptom of the malady that worried the military, not the malady itself, which the military perceived to be the political opportunism and civic bankruptcy of *both* major parties, APRA and Acción Popular.[9]

For the 1963 election, in an apparent effort to assure the necessary one-third plurality, Acción Popular allied with the Democracia Cristiana. Both parties were ideologically diverse; as of 1963, neither was clearly to the right or the left of the other (Rojas Samanez 1986, 197–99; Werlich 1978, 279). The military government disqualified the three small further-left parties that had taken some votes from Belaúnde in the 1962 contest. Belaúnde emerged victorious with 39 percent of the vote over Haya de la Torre's 34 percent. Both Acción Popular's and APRA's tallies were greater in 1963 than they had been in 1962; only Odría's party suffered losses. However, APRA emerged with the most representatives in the legislature: 41 percent to 38 percent for the Alianza Acción Popular/Democracia Cristiana, with 18 percent for Odría's party (Cotler 1978b, 353).

As in the aftermath of the 1962 contest, the key question quickly became: what kind of political alliance could be forged to enable effective government? Again, the reformist ideology of both Acción Popular and APRA implied that they should become partners, but the short-term self-interest of the parties was against alliance. Acción Popular feared that an agreement with APRA would reduce the significant support that Acción Popular enjoyed from the military at the time, and the left factions within Acción Popular believed that APRA had become co-opted by the oligarchy. For its part, APRA perceived Acción Popular, the newer reformist party, as stealing its thunder; in its view, APRA had earned the right to go down in history as Peru's party of social reform.

In this context, APRA allied with Odría's party in the legislature. Neither Acción Popular nor APRA seemed to try very hard to modify this ideologically unnatural state of affairs until June of 1968. Then the two parties finally established an agreement that enabled more effective policy making. The development of the alliance at such a relatively late moment in the administration contradicts the Linz/Valenzuela hypothesis that party coalitions tend to break down rather than emerge as new elections loom. The key reasons for the parties' new interest in a coalition were APRA's calculation that working with Acción Popular would help to prevent a military coup (both in the present and in the wake of the 1969 election, which APRA appeared likely to win) and Acción Popular's calculation that working with APRA would enable Acción Popular's leaders to position themselves better after APRA's probable triumph. Acción Popular's decision was also facilitated by the fact that its sinking incumbent ship had been abandoned by the Democracia Cristiana in November 1967 and, for all practical purposes, by the large progressive wing of Acción Popular as well. These ruptures do support the Linz/Valenzuela hypothesis.

How detrimental to good government were the tensions between the executive and the legislature that prevailed during most of Belaúnde's term? Certainly, these tensions provoked serious ministerial instability between 1963 and 1968. During the five years and two months that Belaúnde governed in the 1960s, there were seventy different ministers at nine of the most salient ministries—almost twice as many as the thirty-eight different ministers at these ministries during the five years of his second term in the 1980s (see table 11.3). The legislature censured seven ministers, forcing their resignation, and three more ministers resigned directly out of fear that they would be censured (Power Manchego Muñoz 1989, 178). Yet there is no indication that any particularly effective minister was forced to resign (Kuczynski 1977, 282; Jaquette 1971, 175–77).

With respect to key issues, APRA's role was to push policies further away from those sought by the plotters of the 1968 coup. Yet the positions of APRA and the more conservative wing of Acción Popular—the sector led by President Belaúnde himself—were not that distant, especially in comparison with the distance between the policies favored by President Belaúnde and the coup-plotters.

Both President Belaúnde's conservative wing of Acción Popular and APRA favored an agrarian reform that respected agricultural efficiency and productivity and sought to change primarily the feudal labor conditions that still existed in much of the Peruvian highlands (Jaquette 1971, 131–38; Bourricaud 1967, 325–43; Hilliker 1971, 138–56). The most significant impact that APRA had on the agrarian reform bill was to assure that coastal sugar estates, where the party enjoyed its strongest political base, would not be affected. However, President Belaúnde did not pursue the agrarian reform vigorously in any case, and very few coastal haciendas of any type were affected (Werlich 1978, 285).

A second important issue was public finance. From 1964 to 1967, government deficits increased at the rate of 90 percent a year; inflation skyrocketed and, finally, in a rare step at the time, the currency was devalued (Jaquette 1971, 150; Kuczynski 1977, 75–218). The financial problem was a result of actions by both Acción Popular and APRA. For its part, Acción Popular greatly increased government spending, in particular for roads, housing, education, and irrigation projects. Nor did the APRA-led coalition in the legislature forfeit its own pet projects. Most important, however, the APRA-led coalition rejected Acción Popular's taxation bills. President Belaúnde, who was dubbed by one cartoonist at the time "the greatest economist since Marie Antoinette," did not vigorously pursue a solution to the fiscal crisis (Werlich 1978, 288; Kuczynski 1977, 282). Belatedly, after the partnership between

Acción Popular and APRA was formed in June 1968 and a more technocratically oriented cabinet was named, the crisis was actually resolved rather quickly (Werlich 1978, 289). The military coup plotters' impression was that neither party had put the national interest above partisan interest.

For the specific policy crisis precipitating the October 1968 coup, only the executive, and not executive-legislative relations, was responsible. The critical issue was whether President Belaúnde and his economic team were trying to cover up a favorable price for Peruvian crude oil to be granted to the International Petroleum Company (IPC), a subsidiary of Standard Oil. Conflict between IPC and Peru had been simmering for many years; Belaúnde had promised a speedy resolution in his inaugural address but had taken little action. In mid-1968, when internationally oriented technocrats entered Belaúnde's economic team, they saw a resolution to the IPC problem as important to Peru's international creditworthiness. The progressive group within Acción Popular, which was the largest constituency and which included the party's 1969 presidential candidate, was concerned. When a key Acción Popular negotiator denounced the government's agreement with IPC, the progressives repudiated Belaúnde. Even though it was never proven that Belaúnde's team had in fact tried to cover up an arrangement favorable to the company, the scandal left the president bereft of political support. The military coup came less than a month after the Acción Popular negotiator had attacked the government's agreement.[10]

Counterfactuals

Would parliamentarianism have helped to prevent the four military coups that Peru experienced after 1930? A judgment is difficult to make because the primary reasons for the coups were not clearly linked to the specifically hypothesized problems of the presidentialist system. Rather, the primary reason was the long-standing conflict between the APRA party, on the one hand, and the Peruvian oligarchy and military, on the other, which contorted the political behavior of virtually all the key actors and groups during this period. So, the question becomes whether parliamentarism could have ameliorated this conflict.

My judgment is: possibly. Sharing more explicitly in the responsibility for government would have pressured APRA to think less of its immediate partisan interests and, therefore, would have enhanced other actors' image of APRA.

Yet APRA's behavior in the legislature in periods when its power was significant—in particular its obstreperous conduct during the Bustamante era and its self-interested stance during Belaúnde's first term—suggests that APRA was distressingly far from a "parliamentarily fit" party. Nor, in 1962 and 1968, did Acción Popular act as a parliamentarily fit party, either. President Belaúnde preferred a coup in 1962 to collaboration with APRA, and between 1963 and 1968 his party was intensely divided over ideological issues.

Between 1933 and 1962, presidentialism may have had the advantage of producing certain leaders whose key role was to bridge the gulf between APRA, on the one hand, and the military and oligarchy, on the other. This responsibility was assumed by Presidents Benavides and Bustamante, both of whom failed at the task, and also by President Prado, who succeeded. In the context of the veto against an Aprista executive, the presidentialist system did compel an electoral alliance between these mediating leaders and APRA; if APRA's behavior was never parliamentarily fit during this period, it did indeed mellow—to such a degree that, ironically, by 1968 the military opposed the party for its perceived conservatism.

Testing Hypotheses about the Perils of Presidentialism: 1980–April 5, 1992

Until Alberto Fujimori's self-inflicted coup on April 5, 1992, Peru's constitutional regime had been stable. Perhaps surprisingly, given the intensity of guerrilla action in the country and its disastrous economic performance over the decade, Peru's democratic process had not come under a serious military threat during the entire 1980s decade (McClintock, 1989a). In contrast to other recently democratizing nations, such as Ecuador, Bolivia, and Argentina, there was neither a coup attempt nor a kidnapping of a president, nor even a military show of force that benefited the rebellious officers.

However, Peru's presidential system was increasingly flawed by one of the perils hypothesized by Linz and Valenzuela: the tendency of the president to assume the mantle of messiah. Increasingly during the decade, as presidential power grew, the political parties became ever more irrelevant and more "unfit." Ironically, then, the fact that Peru did not suffer from executive-legislative stalemate was an indication of a yet more serious imbalance in the relationship between the president and the political parties. As the president was the symbol of all political hope, he also became the target of all political frustration when citizens' high expectations were dashed. At this juncture, in the cases of Belaúnde and García, expectations were dashed, and the electoral schedule then appeared rigidly long. In the case of Fujimori, his arrogance was the key factor in the rupture of the constitutional regime.[11]

Presidential Campaigns and the Emergence of Political Messiahs

The 1980, 1985, and 1990 presidential campaigns were not polarizing. Rather, in each election a ground swell emerged about what issues were most important and about which leader could best handle them. Many Peruvians hoped to identify a "savior" for the nation. Especially in the cases of García and Fujimori, mandates at the polls may have exacerbated their proclivities to overestimate their own capacities and underestimate the abilities of others.

In 1980, Belaúnde of Acción Popular won as the gentlemanly candidate of democracy and statesmanship. The APRA party's longtime leader, Haya de la

Torre, had died only about a year previously, and its candidate, Armando Villanueva, was not an appealing choice; he was perceived as aggressive and in that respect too similar to the military, which citizens wanted to repudiate. The Marxist Left was divided; Peruvian voters have punished the Left whenever it has factionalized. Belaúnde won handily, with 45 percent of the valid vote to 27 percent for APRA and 14 percent for the leftist parties (see table 11.1).

In 1985, the ground swell for APRA's Alán García was even larger. An extremely articulate, brilliant politician, the youthful García resonated with Peruvian voters to a greater degree than any previous political leader. García had been Haya de la Torre's principal protégé, and under García's leadership APRA became Peru's first political party to survive the political passing of its founder. While García worked to soften the image of APRA as a sectarian party, he maintained the themes of spiritualist regeneration that had been salient under Haya (Pike 1986). García's message was for hope and change under an energetic, innovative leader.

The 1985 election was not at all polarizing. García won more than twice as many votes as the second-place candidate (see table 11.1), and his triumph had not been doubted by political analysts of any ideology for more than a year. The Left's Alfonso Barrantes finished second to García and had the right to a runoff (García had not quite won a majority of all the votes when null and blank ballots were counted); but, in part fearing that García would humiliate him in a second round, Barrantes withdrew his candidacy. The Center Right and the Right, represented by Acción Popular and the Convergencia Democrática (a coalition of the Partido Popular Cristiano and rightist dissidents from APRA), were in disarray after their unsuccessful administration.

For the 1990 election, political analysts feared polarization. The prediction was that, especially given the poor performance of the incumbent APRA government, the Aprista "political center" would be insignificant in the campaign, and the rightist Mario Vargas Llosa and the leftist Alfonso Barrantes would compete in a highly ideological and close contest that was unlikely to yield either candidate a majority in the legislature.

However, this prediction proved incorrect. As in 1980, the Left divided; Alfonso Barrantes split from the Izquierda Unida to form his own party, the Izquierda Socialista. As a result, the Left was demoralized. Given the discredit of the incumbent APRA government, for at least six months prior to the first round of the election it appeared that Vargas Llosa would win easily. But, Vargas Llosa's views were far to the right of the Peruvian electorate's, and the FREDEMO (Frente Democrático) campaign was badly flawed.

In the absence of viable candidates in the other major parties, the political unknown Alberto Fujimori emerged as a surprise second-place finisher in the first round of the election (see table 11.1). During his grass roots campaign, he achieved support as a self-made man, not a politician, who would be true to his campaign slogan, "Work, Honesty, and Technology;" as an opponent of Vargas Llosa's "shock" program; and as the one opposition candidate who could unify the Left and the Center Left in a second round. Although the second-round campaign between Vargas Llosa and Fujimori was vitriolic, the conflict dissipated immediately upon Fujimori's victory; Vargas Llosa left the country and Fujimori shifted to the right and sought political support from one of the parties in the FREDEMO coalition, Acción Popular. Fujimori won 62.5 percent of the second-round ballots to 37.5 percent for Vargas Llosa—about 67 percent more (Webb and Fernández Baca 1991, 1031).

Linz's concern (1990, 56–57) that runoff provisions offer undue influence to extremist parties was not evident in these elections. While scholarly assessments of what constitutes the "extreme" Left or "extreme" Right in Peru would vary, most analysts would probably agree that the "real" extremes have not been competing in the electoral arena; in other words, the extreme Left would be constituted by *Sendero Luminoso* (Shining Path) and the extreme Right by paramilitary groups such as the *Comando Rodrigo Franco*. The parties at both the Left and the Right in table 11.1 have done well in various electoral conjunctures and cannot be considered extremist.

Moreover, in 1980 the victorious party Acción Popular chose to ally with the more rightist Partido Popular Cristiano only after the election, and, as mentioned, in 1990 the foremost political star of the Left, Alfonso Barrantes, chose to break with the more leftist Izquierda Unida. In the view of most political analysts, Barrantes's decision doomed his 1990 presidential candidacy, but apparently the candidate consciously feared a repetition of the Allende tragedy and wanted to assure his independence from more leftist groups in case of his election.[12] The Right's presidential candidate in 1990, Mario Vargas Llosa of the Movimiento Libertad, was pushed toward the Center rather than the extremes by his coalition partners, the Partido Popular Cristiano and Acción Popular.

However, in part because Peru's electorates and candidates looked toward the political center rather than the extremes, and because the three electoral outcomes were interpreted as mandates, the three presidents tended to perceive themselves as supermen. All three were depicted in popular conversation and journalists' cartoons as would-be kings—and, in Fujimori's case, as a would-be emperor and would-be Augusto Pinochet. The trend during the period was toward exacerbation of the problem; while Belaúnde was a relatively passive president, García was an activist, and Fujimori is aggressive.

The campaigner Fernando Belaúnde was very different from President Belaúnde, and the hopes pinned upon the Acción Popular leader dissipated quickly. In the 1980 campaign, Belaúnde ran as a populist, making extravagant promises about the prospects for Peru's government; perhaps the most spectacular was his promise of "one million new jobs" (in a nation of about 17 million people at the time). While eloquent and as active as could be expected for a man in his late sixties at the time of the campaign, Belaúnde's profile receded upon his inauguration. In the popular imagination, Belaúnde remained powerful but aloof; he was portrayed in cartoons in the newsweekly *Caretas*, for example, as a king up in the clouds, looking down at the country. Belaúnde's campaign interest in jobs and in Peruvians' overall standard of living seemed to evaporate; as president, his focus (as in his earlier administration) was pet construction projects. Belaúnde's approval rating fell rapidly from almost 80 percent during his first six months to a mere 50 percent by the end of his first year. It was barely above 20 percent during the last three years of his term.[13]

Alán García raised hopes much higher and dashed them more completely. Indeed, in its annual survey of one thousand elite Peruvians, *Debate* (one of Peru's most prestigious newsmagazines) found that the second most praised achievement of García after his first year in office was "the return of hope."[14] García's extraordinary above–80 percent approval rating during his first year plummeted to below 20 percent during his final two years; this was even below the rating of his predecessor at the same point in his term.[15]

The power of President García was great.[16] In a pun on "APRA," his regime was called "Alanista." Others referred to it as a "constitutional dictatorship." Apparently García referred to his ministers as "secretaries"—a practice sometimes construed to mean that García perceived his ministers as his note takers. In its 1990 poll of elite Peruvians, *Debate* asked, "What were the worst defects of Alán García?" The three most common answers were "authoritarianism," "demagoguery," and "arrogance" (in that order).[17]

Ultimately, García's exclusionary policy making proved fatal to his government. The watershed decision of his administration (judged the worst error of his administration in the 1990 *Debate* poll, worse than his policy of international financial isolation) was his July 1987 attempt to nationalize ten commercial banks.[18] The takeover bid was a personal decision made by President García in consultation with only a handful of advisers and without significant input from his own party, not to mention other political groups. The nationalization attempt alienated the businessmen upon whom García's "heterodox" economic program depended and accordingly dealt the "heterodox" policy a fatal blow. It consumed most of the government's attention from July 1987 through the end of the year, distracting it at a crucial time in the administration, and also regalvanized Peru's political Right.

To an even greater degree than García, President Fujimori governed as a dictator—even prior to his assumption of dictatorial powers in April 1992. Whereas on most decisions García was constrained at least somewhat by his political party, Fujimori was not. Fujimori's "party," Cambio 90, was a loose amalgam of small-business groups and Peru's evangelical Protestant community that wielded little influence over Fujimori after his election. For example, in the *Debate* polls at one year into the presidents' terms, three of the four most powerful people of Peru after both Belaúnde and García were members of their political parties, but none of the four most powerful people after Fujimori was another Cambio 90 leader.[19] Almost all Fujimori's cabinet members were political independents appointed by Fujimori himself and indebted directly to the president, or to the president and international actors, for their power.[20]

Also, whereas Belaúnde's and García's public demeanor remained cordial, Fujimori's was aggressive. Not only did Fujimori alienate members of his own political party without apparent misgiving, but he confronted with gusto most of Peru's key political institutions. After only a few months in office, he attacked legislators as "professional demagogues," judges as "jackals," and the Catholic Church as "medieval and recalcitrant."[21] Peru's media were quick to criticize Fujimori's authoritarianism. In *Caretas*'s 1991 end-of-the-year issue, the first color photograph was of Fujimori in imperial garb with the comment, "During 1991, the year of the authoritarian itch, imperial insolence continued" (p. 41). The lead article for the January–February 1992 issue of *QueHacer* was entitled "The Difficulties of the Emperor" (p. 4).

In the view of the vast majority of political analysts, presidential megalomania was the primary reason for the president's rupturing of the constitutional order on April 5, 1992. Although most analysts agreed with President Fujimori about the serious problems in Peruvian democracy, and some even agreed that the coup could facilitate positive change for Peru, they did not perceive any direct, objective threat to Fujimori's power that would in some way have "required" a coup. As discussed in the next section, Fujimori was facing greater challenges from the legislature by late 1991 than previously, but political analysts believed that successful negotiation was possible; the problem was that Fujimori did not want to negotiate in the first place.[22] Said Fujimori, for example, in November 1991 as the legislature was beginning to challenge some of his initiatives: "Nothing, nobody can stop the government's program."[23]

The following are analysts' answers to the question, "What was the determining factor behind the coup?"

> Fujimori is what Weber would call an authoritarian personality. I know for certain that he never had any liking, nor respect, nor desire to govern the country democratically. From the beginning he tried to create the conditions that would permit the concentration of power.[24]

> Fujimori seeks the maximum possible direct personal power.[25]

> In contrast to other coups in which circumstances or historical context weigh the most, in this coup of April 5 what weighed more than specific circumstances was the will of a political actor.[26]

> This is the product of impatient men who refuse to work within a democratic process.[27]

> Alberto Fujimori, a clever, determined, impatient man, and president of Peru, thinks he knows better than the rest of his country's politicians put together.[28]

Executive Dominance over the Legislature

Presidents Belaúnde, García, and Fujimori enjoyed tremendous executive power. All three implemented policy without obstruction from the legislature.

President Belaúnde's Acción Popular allied with the more conservative Partido Popular Cristiano to achieve a majority in the legislature. Enduring until November

1984, this alliance facilitated a smooth relationship between the executive and the legislature. Replying to the question, "You did not feel that your hands were tied during your second term?" Belaúnde himself commented, "No, because during my second administration I had broad electoral support and a parliamentary majority. During my first term I did not."[29] The Belaúnde administration refined numerous dimensions of Peru's constitution, consolidated 1979 constitutional provisions and previous laws from the military regime, modified Peru's economic policy, and initiated various counterinsurgency measures (the use of the "emergency zone strategy").

During Belaúnde's term, 1,071 laws were passed (Bernales 1989, 162). Approximately 70 percent of them were presented by the executive, and 30 percent by the congress. Roughly 65 percent of the bills presented by the executive were ultimately approved, versus less than 10 percent of the bills presented by the legislature.[30] In addition, 336 "legislative decrees" were issued (under authority granted by article 188, which allows the legislature to delegate authority to the executive) and 667 "supreme decrees" (under authority granted by article 211, provision 20) (Eguiguren 1990, 181, 232). In other words, about one law or decree was approved each day of Belaúnde's term. The number of ministers interrogated was "minimal," and none was censured or removed (Bernales 1990, 169–70).

President García's APRA enjoyed an outright majority in both houses of the legislature. The APRA is a disciplined party, and there was no threat at any time by party members against the president; no APRA member resigned from the party, and no dissident faction formed. The number of laws and decrees approved was less than under Belaúnde, but this quantitative change reflected primarily the large task of administrative and legal restructuring that had confronted the first constitutional government after twelve years of military rule; qualitatively, García dominated the legislature at least as thoroughly as Belaúnde (Bernales 1990, 63). Among the three laws cited as "the most important" of the García administration were regionalization, which was formulated and promoted exclusively by the executive; bank nationalization, which was advanced by the executive although discussed and modified considerably in the legislature; and administrative simplification, which was formally presented under multiparty auspices but in fact had been designed exclusively by a research institution (Bernales 1990, 68–138).

During the first four years of García's term, 722 laws were passed; approximately half of them were presented by the executive, and half by the legislature (Bernales, 1990, 61). Roughly 75 percent of the bills initiated by the executive were ultimately approved, versus 10 percent of those initiated by the legislature (Bernales 1990, 61). In addition, during the first three years under García, 127 "legislative decrees" were issued and 662 "supreme decrees"—almost as many as during Belaúnde's entire term (Eguiguren 1990, 181, 232). As under Belaúnde, interrogations were few and censures nonexistent; in some cases, however, poor performances in interrogations by cabinet officials were followed by the officials' resignations (Power Manchego-Muñoz 1989, 173–75).

Table 11.4. Representation of Parties in the Legislature, 1990

	Senate	Chamber of deputies
FREDEMO	20	62
APRA	16	53
Cambio 90	14	32
IU	6	16
IS	3	4
Other	1	13
Total	60	180

Source: Richard Webb and Graciela Fernández Baca, *Perú en números 1991* (Lima: Cuanto, 1991), p. 1032.
Note: Some legislators (almost exclusively Cambio '90 legislators) left their party after 1990 to become independent.

In contrast to his predecessors, Fujimori's party did not enjoy a majority in the legislature. Cambio 90 held less than one-fourth of the seats in the two legislative houses (see table 11.4). Moreover, Cambio 90 was an amalgam of various distinct political groups, one of which—the evangelical Protestants—were rapidly disillusioned with Fujimori. Whereas originally Fujimori had been expected to seek support for his programs from APRA and the Left to build a majority coalition, his rightward political turn voided this option.

Yet, during his first eighteen months in office, Fujimori was as successful in implementing his programs as his predecessors had been. Using article 211, clause 20, and receiving legislative powers under article 188, Fujimori moved rapidly to reinsert Peru into the international financial community and liberalize the economy (Rubio 1992, 30). State expenditure was slashed, state revenue increased, tariff barriers cut, and foreign investment laws eased. With respect to counterinsurgency, Fujimori emphasized the establishment of civilian self-defense patrols *(rondas);* debated and in essence approved by the legislature, this policy was a major success, according to Fujimori himself.[31] With respect to the antidrug effort, in May 1991 Fujimori signed a crucial agreement with the United States that was much more to the right than where he had stood on the issue during his campaign, but he did not submit the agreement to the legislature for approval. Fujimori's bypassing of the legislature was criticized, but no effective effort was launched to compel legislative review of the agreement.[32]

Why could Fujimori dominate the legislature when his party was a distinct minority in it? In part because of constitutional provisions, in part because of the ten-year-old tradition of executive power under the 1979 constitution, and in part because political parties were weak and divided. APRA and its leader Alán García were discredited by their 1985–90 administration and were mired in charges of corruption—the primary concern of the legislature for much of 1991. The Left factionalized further. The FREDEMO alliance ended, and the parties that had joined together in the coalition reasserted their own platforms; gradually, many former FREDEMO members supported Fujimori's policies, especially his economic policies. However, as 1991 ended, tensions between the executive and the legislature increased. In November 1991, just as legislative power granted to Fujimori under article 188 was about to expire, Fujimori issued an avalanche of decree laws—some 126 of them (almost the same number as García had issued in three years)—on a host of important issues (upon many of which he had not been given authority to legislate). In a special session two months later, the legislature modified or repealed twenty-eight of them.[33] With respect to economic initiatives, the most important change introduced by the legislature was the exclusion of large mining companies from the group of state-owned companies that could be privatized.

However, the most intensely debated measures—and the vast majority of those that were modified or repealed—were about counterinsurgency.[34] Among the approximately fifteen new "national security" laws proposed by Fujimori were provisions that provoked Peru's leading newsweeklies to run front-page images of the president as Hitler and dressed half as a soldier and half as a civilian. Decrees would have obliged any person living in Peru to be drafted into the security forces and to surrender assets upon the request of the security forces, or face the charge of treason; banned the publication of any information deemed secret by the government, imposing sentences of five to ten years in prison for offenders; and required all public and private entities to hand over any information or documents requested by a national intelligence agency. All these provisions were rejected by the legislature; a bicameral congressional group was formed to examine and propose a new counterinsurgency package, which ultimately was widely endorsed.

The increasing acrimony between the executive and the legislature was apparent on other issues as well.[35] Disagreement over the 1992 budget was intense. To the consternation of the executive, the legislative approved an "agricultural emergency law" that declared the agricultural sector in a state of emergency, granted farmers a series of tax exemptions and protective tariffs, and precluded the demise of the Agrarian Bank. The chamber of deputies censured the minister of agriculture, Enrique Rossi Link; it was the first time that a minister had been asked to resign under the 1979 constitution. Smugly pointing out that the constitution did not stipulate a time frame for the minister's resignation, Fujimori kept him on. Fujimori threatened to dissolve the congress and call new elections if his ministers were censured. He insulted legislators, and they responded by suggesting that he might be impeached on grounds of moral incapacity.

Fujimori probably feared the emergence of greater opposition in the future. Exonerated from charges of illicit enrichment by the Supreme Court, García was returning as a protagonist on Peru's political scene, seeking to unify and galvanize opposition to Fujimori. Although it did not appear likely that García could actually achieve these goals, Fujimori may not have wanted to risk the possibility. The headline in one of Peru's major newspapers the day before the coup was: "The [economics] minister denounces sabotage against the economic program commanded by former president Alán García.[36]

While Peru's legislature was poised to be more vigorous in Fujimori's second twenty months than in his first twenty, overall there were no grounds for considering it obstructionist prior to April 5. Consider, for example, that whereas the legislature under Fujimori censured one minister in twenty months, the legislature during Belaúnde's first term had censured more than fifty ministers (Pease García 1992, 43). Although the legislature modified or repealed 22 percent of Fujimori's November avalanche of decree laws, it passed 78 percent of them. Overall, legislators remained eager to negotiate with Fujimori and his ministers on most issues—it was Fujimori whose actions at this time suggested to numerous analysts that he was actually trying to exacerbate tensions, precisely in order to justify his subsequent coup.[37]

The Political Weakening of the Executive and the Electoral Schedule

As Linz and Valenzuela hypothesize, the political weakening of the executive during the last half of the presidential term was a concern in Peru during this period. Having disappointed popular expectations, both Belaúnde and García suffered political weakening. For Fujimori, the exaggerated fear of political weakening was a factor in his decision to suspend the constitution. Although there was no major crisis as a result of Peru's electoral schedule (of course, no president died or resigned), by the midpoint in both Belaúnde's and García's administrations, their terms appeared excessively long.

Both Belaúnde and García were perceived as failures at least by the end of their third year in office; both leaders' approval ratings hovered around 20 percent in most polls by that time.[38] Public attention was focused on the next presidential election rather than on the incumbent government approximately two years before the event, or in other words with two-fifths of the incumbent's term remaining.

In the context of the weakening of the presidential administrations, political leaders distanced themselves from both presidents to try to assure their success in the next administration, just as Linz and Valenzuela hypothesize. The most salient examples are Manuel Ulloa, prime minister and minister of the economy from July 1980 through March 1983, and Luis Alva Castro, prime minister and minister of the economy from July 1985 through 1987. Both leaders feared that Peru's economic performance would deteriorate soon and that if they were to win the next presidential election, they should withdraw. Overall, as table 11.3 shows, in both the Belaúnde and García administrations ministerial turnover was higher in the last half of the term than in the first half.

However, the effect of leaders' distancing themselves from the president during the latter part of the terms was not highly deleterious. Manuel Ulloa was unpopular by the time of his departure, and Luis Alva Castro was not considered an outstanding economics adviser. There was no case of a minister whose departure was widely viewed as seriously damaging the executive.

Perhaps surprisingly, in the cases of the failed presidencies of Belaúnde and García, it is unlikely that parliamentarism (or at least parliamentarian rules without other concomitant changes) would have enabled the ousting of either leader prior to the end of his term. As mentioned previously, Belaúnde's Acción Popular allied with the Partido Popular Cristiano to enjoy a majority during most of Belaúnde's term, and Alan García's APRA held a majority throughout García's term. Despite the tarnishing of their images, both leaders were widely perceived as their parties' best chance to win the next election (after one intervening term). Neither Acción Popular nor APRA enjoyed a second leader who would have been an attractive replacement for Belaúnde or García. Mindful of the history of long political careers in Peru and frequent reelection of presidents, neither Acción Popular nor APRA legislators would have contemplated ousting their most charismatic leaders. While García's presidency was especially illegitimate toward the end of his administration, APRA remained an extremely disciplined party.

The problem of political weakening during the second half of a term could be alleviated not only by parliamentarism but also by other measures. I would endorse a term of four rather than five years, and I would also consider the possibility of establishing an independent, nonpartisan body that could decide whether to call for new elections under certain conditions. Overall, however, these changes were not favored by the Peruvian constitutional experts whom I interviewed (see Appendix). While some preferred a four-year term, the majority believed that five years were necessary to develop and implement presidential programs and for the parties to prepare their next campaign. Nor did these experts endorse the idea of establishing an independent body to call for new elections in the event of a political crisis; they doubted that any such entity could be truly independent, and they feared political machinations. The constitutional experts opted for "muddling through."

Linz and Valenzuela fear not only that the electoral schedule may extend a president's tenure beyond his welcome but that it may bar an effective president from a second term. In the Peruvian case, this question has been salient. When President García was extremely popular during his first two years in office, a constitutional amendment to allow a second term was discussed in political circles, but it was dropped as García's popularity fell. President Fujimori also advanced a reelection provision for Peru's new constitution. However, in my view and the view of most Peruvian constitutional experts, the possibility that an incumbent president will seek to manipulate the electoral machinery to his own advantage is too great, and the bar against reelection should remain, despite the concomitant rigidity in the electoral schedule.

Constitutional Reform? Parliamentary and Other Alternatives

Some of the hypothesized perils of presidentialism did not emerge under Peru's 1979 constitution. The most feared problem—stalemate between the executive and the legislature—did not happen. Political polarization, if it occurred at all, was not severe. However, these perils did not materialize in part because another of the hypothesized problem—the interpretation of the president as messiah—was severe. While popular mandates for each new president implied a weak legislature relative to the executive and limited polarization, they facilitated presidential arrogance. In the case of President García, the result of authoritarian policy making was primarily a calamitous economic policy; in the case of President Fujimori, the result was the demise of Peru's constitutional system.

What political reforms are most appropriate for Peru? The question, of course, is complex. Most analysts (but of course not President Fujimori) agree that personalism is excessive in Peruvian politics and that it is reinforced by a presidentialist system. But they do not agree about alternatives to the 1979 constitution. There is disagreement and uncertainty about whether or not the personalist, charismatic, directly elected president is the key legitimating principle of democracy, too deeply ingrained in Peruvian political culture to change within a generation.

Seeking insights about constitutional reform, during June and July of 1989 I interviewed eleven Peruvian experts on the constitution, among them at least one person linked to each major party of the era (see Appendix). I also reviewed the publications that proposed revisions of the constitution upon the tenth anniversary of its promulgation.[39] In 1992, in the wake of President Fujimori's coup, the discussion of constitutional reform became intense; by this date, in the context of Fujimori's extreme personalism and the continued erosion of Peru's political parties, proposals for reform were more radical than in the late 1980s (see Rubio 1992).

In the view of Peruvian experts, parliamentarism was not a viable alternative for the country at this time. There were two primary reasons: (1) a belief that, in a nation seriously threatened by an extremely shrewd and disciplined insurgency, the directly elected chief executive of presidentialism has greater legitimacy, and (2) a fear, similar to that expressed for Ecuador by Conaghan (chapter 10) and for various nations by Giovanni Sartori (chapter 3), that Peruvian parties are not "parliamentarily fit."

For many Peruvian constitutional experts, the direct election of the president is not only "an advantage" of presidentialism, as Linz (1990, 56) acknowledges but virtually the essence of democracy. Consider, for example, these statements:

> The popular vote for the election of the President . . . is the *sine qua non* of the presidentialist system and the basis for governmental authority. . . . Election by the Congress would weaken the figure of the President and divert from the people what they consider to be their principal form of political participation. (Rubio and Bernales 1981, 380)

> [An election should be] the crystallization of the yearnings of all the Peruvian people; [the second-round procedure] is one of the most democratic methods available. (*Resumen semanal*, 17–23 Feb. 1979, p. 2)

The principal virtue [of the constitution] is that . . . during ten years we have maintained a constitutional democracy that has permitted the people to elect its principal [national] and local authorities. (Bernales 1989, 165)

In the constitution of Peru, the principle of popular election of the president is sacred. (Chirinos Soto 1986, 216)

In the view of most Peruvian constitutional experts, a parliamentary system would not be highly legitimate. A prime minister is often selected as a compromise choice between ideologically distinct parties because of his capacity to make alliances among politicians, not because he meets the requirements that the people hold at the time for their chief executive. An election may be called suddenly to resolve a parliamentary impasse and would not necessarily entail the intensive elaboration of platforms and their submission to popular opinion that presidential campaigns require.

Presidentialism is deeply ingrained in Peruvian political culture. The fashioning of the president as messiah began not in the 1980s but in the 1920s and 1930s: APRA's Haya de la Torre in particular spoke in almost religious terms about "saving Peru" (Pike 1986). The process of an attentive citizenry reflecting upon campaign proposals, the building of a ground swell behind one candidate, the election of the "blessed" candidate amid extravagant hopes, and then a gradual popular disappointment and ultimate charges of betrayal and abandonment occurred several times prior to the 1980s (perhaps most clearly in the cases of Bustamante in the 1940s and Belaúnde in the 1960s). Note that even the leader of the Shining Path guerrillas is called not "Comrade Gonzalo" or "Compañero Gonzalo" but "Presidente Gonzalo."

A second crucial issue about parliamentarism is the weakness of Peruvian political parties. These parties are not judged "parliamentarily fit." Sartori (chapter 3) defines "parliamentarily fit" parties as those "that have been socialized (by historical trial, failure, and duration) into being relatively cohesive or disciplined, into behaving, in opposition, as a responsible opposition, and into playing, to some extent, a rule-guided fair game." In his comments at our conference, Sartori further described "parliamentarily fit" parties as "institutionalized national mass parties that are able to function with some discipline and are not purely spoils-oriented or collections of notables" (Coppedge 1989, 18). Conaghan (chapter 10) suggests that parties in some Latin American nations may not be responsible because they "remain detached from groups in civil society and have not been able to establish themselves as the interlocutors of social groups and classes."

As discussed above, Peru's parties were smaller in number, more disciplined, and more in contact with their constituencies than parties in Ecuador during the 1980s; but they were also smaller in number, more disciplined, and more in contact with their constituencies than they themselves were after 1990. Even prior to the Fujimori administration, however, Peru's constitutional experts worried that a parliamentary system would erode the ideological coherence and grass roots efforts of parties and would increase spoils-oriented activities among elites. Especially in the context of Peru's deep and prolonged economic crisis, immediate material gains are salient to Peru's politicians. Accordingly analysts worry that, even if votes of confidence were restricted to the "constructive" West German variety, parliamentarism would provide incentives to form ideologically disparate coalitions, which have been common in Peru even under presidentialism. Such coalitions would bring governments down but then quickly fall apart. The most cynical experts even feared that cabinet posts would be bought and sold.

At the same time that Peruvian analysts fear that Peru's parties are not parliamentarily fit, they are aware that "power is relational," as Mainwaring (1990, 171) puts it, and that accordingly presidentialism is a factor in the increasing debilitation of Peru's parties. Political experts perceive that the extraordinary prerogatives of Peru's executive are gradually marginalizing the nation's legislature and reducing parties to irrelevance. This concern became pronounced amid the failures of the conventional parties in the 1990 election and their inability to form a concerted opposition to Fujimori's programs despite his party's minority status.

However, Peru's analysts were divided about whether the most basic cause of the marginalization of the legislature is a political culture that favors executive power over legislative and is unlikely to change despite new constitutional principles, or is primarily a result of constitutional engineering, which could be modified.

Experts who believed that Peru's parties and legislature were unlikely ever to become parliamentarily fit pointed to a vicious cycle: low popular opinion of the legislature → low caliber of aspirants to parliamentary seats → low caliber of legislators → low opinion of the congress. To make their argument, experts cited the statistic that, of 220–odd investigative commissions named by the legislature between 1985 and 1990s, only 22 actually issued judgments.[40] Important laws that were in the jurisdiction of the legislature, such as the law of tenancy, languished there. The public opinion agency Apoyo interviews annually three hundred to four hundred elites from various professional sectors, asking them to evaluate key political leaders and institutions; while never ranking at the bottom of the list of twenty-odd institutions, the legislature consistently ranks below average.[41] Fernando Rospigliosi and Marcial Rubio suggest that low popular opinion of the parliament is a regionwide Latin American phenomenon with deep historical roots; whereas in Europe parliaments gained legitimacy as a result of their historical emergence in opposition to the monarchs, there was no similar tradition in Latin America.[42]

Even the scholars who doubted the capacity for significant change in the Peruvian legislature, however, agreed that executive power in the 1979 constitution should be reduced. A virtually unanimous recommendation was to revise article 212, clause 20 (granting the executive the right to make economic policy without approval or input from the legislature). Similarly, many experts desired conditions upon article 188, which allows the congress to delegate its powers to the executive. A third common recommendation was to give the prime minister a degree of autonomy and to provide that person, and possibly other ministers as well, more specific responsibilities.

Some scholars were more optimistic about the potential for parliamentarily fit politics in Peru and favored more far-reaching constitutional changes to strengthen parties. In time, as the discipline and coherence of parties improve, these scholars implied, a parliamentary system might be viable.

Among constitutional experts on the political Left, to strengthen political parties implied their democratization. One of the most important reforms advanced toward this end was regionalization (Bernales 1990, 324, 326). Implemented under García, this reform is discussed in the second section of this chapter. Other major recommendations for strengthening and democratizing parties were (1) midterm elections and (2) primaries in all political parties supervised by the National Elections Commission. Recommendations oriented to the professionalization of the legislature were (1) making the legislature unicameral; (2) establishing offices for coordination among the legislature, the executive, and the media; and (3) dismissing legislators who miss a certain number of sessions.

In the next few years, in the context of Fujimori's coup and the reform of the 1979 constitution, debate about constitutional alternatives might become more vigorous. Under the current circumstances, however, given Fujimori's capacity to shape the process for the election of a constituent assembly and to set the agenda for the assembly's debate, the prospects for the speedy implementation of a more appropriate constitution are bleak.

Appendix

List of Constitutional Experts Interviewed in Peru, June–July 1989

Political affiliation, if any, is given in parentheses.

Enrique Chirinos Soto (APRA, 1978–85; FREDEMO, 1989–90)*
Francisco Equiguren
Domingo García Belaúnde
Diego García Sayan†
Jorge Melos
Felipe Osterling (PPC)
Luis Pásara†
Roberto Ramirez del Villar (PPC)*
Fernando Rospigliosi
Marcial Rubio†
Fernando Tuesta Soldevilla

*Members of the Constituent Assembly that elaborated the 1979 constitution.
†Scholars who have directed research centers generally considered to be to the political Left or Center Left.

Notes

The time and insights of the Peruvian constitutional experts interviewed in June–July 1989 are much appreciated.

1. See also *Resumen semanal* no. 8, 17–23 Feb. 1979; nos. 22–26, 26 May–23 June 1979.

2. Several excellent works on Peru's constitutions comment on each provision. See especially Bernales and Rubio (1988), Chirinos Soto (1986), and Ruiz-Eldredge (1980).

3. For a complete list of constitutions and political statutes, see Tuesta Soldevilla (1987, 305).

4. Virtually every one of my interviewees (see Appendix) criticized this provision.

5. David Scott Palmer (1980) summarizes: "Probably the single most important factor in every coup since 1932 has been the military's antipathy to APRA." See also Cotler (1978), Gilbert (1977), Pike (1986), Bourricaud (1970), Stein (1980), Werlich (1978).

6. See especially Potocarrero (1983), Werlich (1978, 221–45), Gilbert (1977, 116–25), Pike (1986, 199–233), and Cotler (1978, 262–72).

7. For similar conclusions, see Payne (1968, 52–55, 81–82), Werlich (1978, 273), Hilliker (1971, 51), and Bouricaud (1967, 305–10).

8. On this period, see especially Payne (1968), Hilliker (1971, 58–56); Bourricaud (1967, 253–305), Chirinos Soto (1984, 176–79), Werlich (1978, 256–80), Jaquette (1971, 113–20).

9. Different scholars place varying degrees of blame on the distinct political actors. APRA's sabotage of Belaúnde's reforms is emphasized by Werlich (1978, 298–99) and by Cotler (1978b, 359, 365, 381, 382); the failure on the part of Belaúnde and Acción Popular to push hard for their promised reforms is stressed by Pike (1986, 258–60) and Jaquette (1971, 140–43). Even one of Belaúnde's own colleagues, Pedro-Pablo Kucynski (1977) criticizes Acción Popular as well as APRA, while making the conventional recommendation of the era for a stronger presidency.

10. Excellent scholarly works on this era include Cotler (1978b, 335–90), Kuczynski (1977), Werlich (1978, 280–99), and Jaquette (1971, 131–98).

11. For overviews of post-1980 national-level politics discussing issues of presidentialism versus parliamentarism, see Rubio (1990, 1992), Pásara (1992), Pease García (1988, 1992), Eguiguren (1992), and Bernales (1984, 1990).

12. See especially Bernales (1989), Bustamante Belaúnde (1989), and *La republica,* 6 July, 1989, p. 20.

13. Datum poll reported in *Caretas,* 2 Apr. 1990, p. 40E.

14. *Debate* 8, no. 39 (July 1986), pp. 30–31. Reduction of inflation was considered the number one achievement.

15. Datum poll reported in *Caretas,* 2 Apr. 1990, p. 40E.

16. Rubio (1990, 134–36) and Pease Garcia (1988, 95–101) provide useful discussions of the points in this paragraph.

17. *Debate* 12, no. 61 (Aug.–Oct. 1990): 29.

18. For the poll, see *Debate* 12, no. 61 (Aug.–Oct. 1990): 30. Thorp (1991, 136–37) provides an incisive discussion.

19. *Debate,* no. 15 (Aug. 1992): 32; *Debate* 8, no. 39 (July 1986): 20; *Debate* 13, no. 65 (July–Sept. 1991): 23.

20. *Latin American Regional Reports—Andean Group,* 7 Mar. 1991, p. 2, and *Latin American Weekly Report,* 21 Nov. 1991, p. 8.

21. *Caretas,* 22 Apr. 1991, p. 13; *Wall Street Journal,* 1 Apr. 1991, p. A8; *Washington Post,* 23 Mar. 1991, pp. A12–A14.

22. See my discussion in the next section. The point is made by former president Belaúnde in an interview in *Diario la República*, 29 Dec. 1991, p. 11; Pease García (1992, 5); and in seminars given by Eduardo Ferrero and Coletta Youngers in Washington, D.C., on April 14, 1992, and May 27, 1992, respectively. In *the Peru Report's* analysis, a key advisor is quoted as saying that Fujimori "could not stomach [the other] option which would be to invite the Chairman of the Senate along to the palace for a meal every time he wanted a law through Congress." *Peru Report 7*, no. 3 (May 1992): 3 in "Political and Economic Report."

23. Fujimori made the comment on nationwide television, on the prime time Sunday news program, "Panorama." See *Latin American Regional Reports—Andean Group*, 19 Dec. 1991, p. 3.

24. Enrique Bernales, interviewed in *Ideéle 4*, no. 37 (May 1992): 23. As a senator, Bernales had dealt extensively with Fujimori but was not considered a vehement opponent.

25. Rolando Ames in *Cuestión de estado*, publication of the Institute for Democracy and Socialism, Sept. 1992, p. 22.

26. Alberto Adrianzén M., cited in *QueHacer*, no. 76 (Mar.–Apr. 1992): 11.

27. Enrique Zileri, quoted in *New York Times*, 8 Apr. 1992, p. A8.

28. *The Economist*, 11 Apr. 1992, p. 41. For similar interpretations in English publications, see the *Latin American Weekly Report*, 16 Apr. 1992, p. 1; *New York Times*, 16 Apr. 1992, p. A3; *Washington Post*, 17 Apr. 1992, p. A29.

29. Boeker (1990, 169–70) interview with Belaúnde.

30. Bernales (1990, 61). Figures are approximate because they refer only to the first four years of Belaúnde's term.

31. On the discussion of counterinsurgency policy in general and the establishment of *rondas* in particular, see *Resumen semanal*, 31 Jan.–6 Feb. 1992, pp. 5–7; *Si*, 9 Mar. 1992, pp. 23–27; Lourdes Flores Nano's statement in *Ideéle*, May 1992, p. 7, and Fujimori's interview in which he is pleased about his advances on this front, *Andean Report*, Mar. 1992, p. 37.

32. *Expreso*, 26 May 1991, p. 4; *Resumen semanal*, 3–9 May 1991, p. 3; *Caretas*, 15 Apr. 1991, p. 25.

33. *Resumen semanal*, Jan. 31–Feb. 6, 1992, p. 1.

34. On the points in this paragraph, see *Ideéle*, no. 32–33 (Dec. 1991), pp. 4–14, no. 34 (Feb. 1992), pp. 5–9; *Latin American Regional Reports—Andean Group*, 19 Dec. 1991, p. 2; *Andean Newsletter*, no. 61 (10 Dec. 1991): 4–7; *Andean Report*, Dec. 1991, p. 193.

35. On the various points in this paragraph, see especially *Latin American Weekly Report* for 5, 12, 19 Dec. 1991, pp. 10, 4, 3 respectively.

36. *Expreso*, 4 Apr. 1992, p. 1. See also *Latin American Weekly Report*, 16 Apr. 1992, p. 1; *Peru Report*, 6, no. 3 (Apr. 1992), "Political and Economic Trend Report," p. 3.

37. For an admission of this plot by an anonymous coup plotter, see *Peru Report 6*, no. 3 (Apr. 1992), "Political and Economic Trend Report." One example is that Fujimori waited until the last minute to submit his 126 legislative decrees to the congress. Numerous analysts, including Pease García (1992) and Gustavo Gorriti (1993), believe this interpretation.

38. *Caretas*, 2 Apr. 1990, p. 40E.

39. See Bernales (1990), Bernales et al. (1989), the supplement to the newsweekly *Si*, "Los estrechos marcos de la constitución," 17 July 1989; op-eds by Enrique Chirinos Soto, *El comercio*, 3 July 1989; Enrique Bernales, *La republica*, 13 July 1989; Alberto Ruiz-Eldredge, *La republica*, 12 July 1989; and the editorial in *La republica*, 6 July 1989.

40. *La republica*, 8 July 1989, p. 20.

41. See *Debate*, no. 15 (1982): 44; *Debate 7*, no. 33 (July 1985): 56; *Debate 8*, no. 39 (July 1986): 32; *Debate 8*, no. 38 (May 1986): 28–29; *Debate 9*, no. 45 (July/Aug. 1987): 18; *Debate* 11, no. 56 (July/Aug. 1989): 28–29. See also Bernales (1990).

42. Fernando Rospigliosi made this point during our interview; Marcial Rubio mentioned it in "La constituyente: ¿Para que?" *Polemica*, no. 1 (1977): 30.

References

Althaus, Jaime de, Carlos Delgado, Eva Guerrero C., and Carmen Lopez. 1986. *Communidad, gobierno local y desarrollo provincial: El caso de Chancay.* Lima: Centro Peruano de Estudios para el Desarrollo Regional.

Barrenechea, Carlos L. 1989. "Regionalización: Entre la expectativa y la frustración." *Sur* 12, no. 120 (Apr.): 7–10.

Bernales, Enrique B. 1984. *El parliamento por dentro.* Lima: DESCO.

———. 1989. *La constitución diez años despues.* Lima: Fundación Freidrich Naumann.

———. 1990. *Parlamento y democracia.* Lima: Constitución y Sociedad.

Bernales, E. B., and M. C. Rubio. 1988. *Constitución fuentes e interpretación.* Lima: Mesa Redonda Editores.

Boeker, Paul H. 1990. *Lost Illusions: Latin America's Struggle for Democracy, as Recounted by Its Leaders.* New York: Markus Weiner.

Bourricaud, François P. 1967. *Power and Society in Contemporary Peru.* New York: Praeger.

Bustamante Belaúnde, Alberto. 1989. "La gloria de ser presidente." *Debate* 11, no. 56 (July-Aug.): 8–10.

Calderón Cockburn, Julio, and Luis Olivera Cárdenas. 1989. *Municipio y pobladores en la habilitación urbana.* Lima: DESCO.

Chirinos Soto, Enrique. 1986. *La nueva constitución al alcance de todos,* 4th ed. Lima: Editores importadores S. A.

Cotler, Julio. 1978a. "A Structural-Historical Approach to the Breakdown of Democratic Institutions: Peru." In *The Breakdown of Democratic Regimes,* edited by Juan J. Linz and Alfred Stepan. Baltimore: Johns Hopkins UP, pp. 178–205.

———. 1978b. *Clases, estado y nación en el Perú.* Lima: Instituto de Estudios Peruanos.

Eguiguren, Francisco P. 1987. *La constitución peruana de 1979 y sus problemas de aplicación.* Lima: Cultural Cuzco.

———. 1990. *Los retos de una democracia insuficiente.* Lima: Comisión Andina de Juristas y Fundación Friedrich Naumann.

García Belaúnde, Domingo. 1986. *Una democracia en transición: Las elecciones peruanas de 1985.* Lima: IIDH-CAPEL.

Gilbert, Dennis. 1977. "The Oligarchy and the Old Regime in Peru." Ph.D. diss., Cornell University, Latin America Studies.

Gorriti, Gustavo. 1993. "The Unshining Path." *New Republic,* 8 Feb.

Handelman, Howard. 1975. *Struggle in the Andes: Peasant Political Mobilization in Peru.* Austin: U Texas P.

Hilliker, Grant. 1971. *The Politics of Reform in Peru: The Aprista and Other Mass Parties of Latin America.* Baltimore: Johns Hopkins UP.

Jaquette, Jane S. 1971. *The Politics of Development in Peru.* Ithaca, N. Y.: Cornell University Latin America Studies Program Dissertation Series.

Kuczynski, Pedro-Pablo. 1977. *Peruvian Democratic under Economic Stress: An Account of the Belaúnde Administration, 1963–1968.* Princeton: Princeton UP.

Linz, Juan. 1990. "The Perils of Presidentialism." *Journal of Democracy* 1, no. 1 (1990): 51–70.

Mainwaring, Scott. 1990. "Presidentialism in Latin America." *Latin America Research Review* 25, no. 1: 157–79.

Melo-Vega Castro, Jorge, and Guillermo Fernández-Maldonado Castro. 1989. "Las Propuestas de Reforma Constitucional." In *La constitución diez años despues*, edited by Enrique B. Bernales. Lima: Fundación Friedrich Naumann, pp. 359–402.

Mendez, José Luis. 1989. "The Decentralization Process in Peru, 1985–1989." Paper presented at the Latin American Studies Association meeting, 24–27 Sept.

McClintock, Cynthia. 1989. "Peru: Precarious Regimes, Authoritarian and Democratic." In *Democracy in Developing Countries: Latin America*, edited by Larry Diamond, Juan Linz, and Seymour Martin Lipset. Boulder, Colo.: Lynne Rienner.

Palmer, David Scott. 1980. *Peru: The Authoritarian Tradition*. New York: Praeger.

Pásara, Luis. 1992. "Es el parlamento el lugar donde se construye la democracia? Los casos de Argentina y Perú comparados." Paper presented at the Latin American Studies Association meeting, 24–27 Sept.

Payne, Arnold. 1968. *The Peruvian Coup d'Etat of 1962: The Overthrow of Manuel Prado*. Washington, D.C.: Institute for the Comparative Study of Political Systems.

Pease García, Henry. 1988. *Democracia y precariedad bajo el populismo aprista*. Lima: DESCO.

———. 1992. "La democracia colapsada: Peru 1990–1992." Lima: IPADEL (mimeo.).

Pike, Frederick B. 1986. *The Politics of the Miraculous in Peru*. Lincoln: U Nebraska P.

Portocarrero M., Gonzalo. 1983. *De Bustamante a Odría: El fracaso del Frente Democrático Nacional 1945–1950*. Lima: Mosca Azul.

Power Manchego Muñoz, Jorge. 1989. "El modelo constitucional del regimen político peruano." *La constitución diez años despues*, edited by Enrique B. Bernales, pp. 167–82. Lima: Fundación Friedrich Naumann.

Reid, Michael. 1987. "The Flowering Seed: Notes on the Influence of the U.S. Constitution in Peru." Manuscript.

Reumpler, Henry. 1986. "Anti-Democratic Laws Governing the Military and the Opposition Parties in Argentina and Peru." M.A. thesis, Department of Government, Georgetown University.

Rojas Samanez, Alvaro. 1986. *Partidos políticos en el Perú*. Lima: Editorial F & A.

Rubio, Marcial C. 1990. "25 Años de estado peruano: Perspectiva social y constitucional." In *Estado y sociedad: Relaciones peligrosas*, edited by Juan Abugattás et al. Lima: DESCO.

———. 1992. *Constitución: Qué ponerle y qué quitartle*. Lima: DESCO.

Rubio, Marcial C., and Enrique Bernales B. 1981. *Perú: Constitución y sociedad política*. Lima: DESCO.

Ruiz-Eldredge, Alberto. 1980. *La constitución comentada: 1979*. Lima: n.p.

Schmidt, Gregory D. 1989. "Regional Governments in Peru: Transcendental Reform or Electoral Demagoguery?" Paper presented at the Latin American Studies Association meeting, Sept.

Stein, Steve. 1989. *Populism in Perú*. Madison: U Wisconsin P.

Thorp, Rosemary. 1991. *Economic Management and Economic Development in Peru and Colombia*. Pittsburgh: U Pittsburgh P.

Tuesta Soldevilla, Fernando. 1987. *Perú político en cifras*. Lima: Fundación Friedrich Ebert.

Werlich, David P. 1978. *Peru: A Short History*. Carbondale: Southern Illinois UP.

Webb, Richard, and Graciella Fernández Baca, *Perú en números 1990* (Lima: Cuanto, 1991), p. 1032.

Woy-Hazleton, Sandra. 1982. "The Return of Partisan Politics in Peru." In *Post-Revolutionary Peru: The Politics of Transformation*, edited by Stephen M. Gorman. Boulder, Colo.: Westview, pp. 33–72.

12

MICHAEL COPPEDGE

Venezuela: Democratic despite Presidentialism

Venezuelan history appears to contradict this volume's thesis that presidential democracies are prone to breakdown. Despite its presidential system, Venezuela has held seven consecutive fair and competitive elections from the inauguration of the regime in 1958 until the present. Four of these elections resulted in the transfer of executive power between the two largest parties, the center-left Acción Democrática and the center-right Copei (Christian Socialist party). These are characteristics of a well-institutionalized democratic regime, one that has lasted at least a generation and can be expected to survive until it faces some new and unsolvable crisis.

Venezuela's historical stability does not, however, invalidate the arguments against presidentialism. In fact, the Venezuelan presidential system manifests the same tendencies toward executive-legislative conflict and circumvention of the congress that have been observed in other Latin American countries. The fact that these problems have not brought about the breakdown of the regime during a thirty-four-year period must be credited to the country's unique advantages—uncommon leadership, unusually strong political parties, and extraordinary oil wealth.

Venezuelan Exceptionalism

The democratic regime that was launched in 1958 has survived the guerrilla insurgency of the sixties, the wave of authoritarian rule that swept the continent in the sixties and seventies, and, as of this writing (January 1993), the debt crisis of the eighties. This resilience qualifies Venezuela as the most successful democracy in contemporary Latin America, with the possible exception of Costa Rica. Its survival is quite remarkable in contrast to the experiences of other developing countries. What accounts for this stability?

Oil

The plausible connection between oil wealth and democracy has been noted many times by scholars, pundits, and armchair theorists. Simply put, oil is a lubricant that eases the social frictions that arise in a democracy. It lessens the need for hard choices. Under conditions of scarcity, politics tends to be a zero-sum game: one group gains only at the expense of another. But the larger the earnings from oil exports, the fewer losers there are. There is enough to go around.

This simple argument was best summarized for Venezuela by Terry Karl:

> In the short run, petrodollars financed an emergency plan that calmed the atmosphere during the transition to democracy. In the long run, petroleum provided the fiscal revenues upon which democratic administrations depended to maintain the ambiguous, and expensive, situation of fomenting the growth of a private sector while simultaneously granting favors to the middle and working classes. Concretely, each government granted extensive subsidies, contracts, and infrastructure to entrepreneurs while charging the lowest taxes on the continent and allowing some of the highest profits. At the same time, democratic governments could afford to support collective bargaining for the highest wages on the continent, price controls, huge food subsidies, and an agrarian reform.[1]

It is impossible to deny and easy to confirm that Venezuela has had an unusually large pie to share. As shown in table 12.1, Venezuela has ranked far ahead of any other Latin American country in terms of per capita gross domestic product since at least 1960. This sustained high level of economic prosperity cannot be ignored in any explanation of the stability of Venezuela's democratic regime. However, table 12.1 itself provides evidence that stable democracy does not depend on economic prosperity alone, for the second most prosperous country (by this measure) is Argentina, which is notorious for its failure to build a lasting democracy.

Furthermore, there are numerous ways to demonstrate that oil and democracy do *not* mix: (1) While Venezuela is wealthy, the unequal distribution of its wealth should intensify, rather than lessen, social conflict. (2) Venezuela's transition to democracy succeeded even though it took place during an economic slump, and the regime has survived more than a decade of economic stagnation or decline since 1979. (3) No other major oil exporter (including Saudi Arabia, Iran, Iraq, Kuwait, Indonesia, Nigeria, Mexico, Ecuador, among others) is known for its success with democracy. (4) The volatility of international oil prices has created extreme boom-and-bust cycles that may be more threatening to democratic government than moderate but steady growth, as in Colombia.

These arguments are rather crude, but so is the "obvious" argument that oil helps democracy. At this crude level of analysis, the only sustainable conclusion is that oil wealth helps a great deal in some ways but hurts in others; overall, it is not absolutely necessary for stable democracy, and it is certainly not sufficient.[2]

Table 12.1. Per Capita GDP for Latin American Countries (1988 dollars)

	1960	1970	1980	1988
Venezuela	**3879**	**4941**	**5225**	**4544**
Argentina	2384	3075	3359	2862
Uruguay	2352	2478	3221	2989
Mexico	1425	2022	2872	2588
Chile	1845	2236	2448	2518
Panama	1264	2017	2622	2229
Costa Rica	1435	1825	2394	2235
Brazil	1013	1372	2481	2449
Peru	1233	1554	1716	1503
Colombia	927	1157	1595	1739
Nicaragua	1055	1495	1147	819
Paraguay	779	931	1612	1557
Dominican Republic	823	987	1497	1509
El Salvador	832	1032	1125	955
Ecuador	771	904	1581	1477
Bolivia	634	818	983	724
Honduras	619	782	954	851
Haiti	331	292	386	319

Source: Inter-American Development Bank, *Economic and Social Progress in Latin America: 1989 Report* (Washington, D.C., 1989), p. 463. Countries are listed in order of their average rank for these four key years.

Political Learning by Wise Leaders

Democracy succeeded after 1958 largely because party leaders learned from the mistakes they had committed during Venezuela's first attempt at democracy, the 1945–48 Trienio.[3] All observers agree that Acción Democrática (AD) governed arrogantly during the Trienio, decreeing far-reaching reforms without consultation of the opposition and abusing its control of the government for partisan purposes.[4] The AD-led junta zealously (some say overzealously) prosecuted corrupt figures associated with the Medina government and thereby angered some conservatives. Despite some power sharing at the very top levels of government, such as the early appointment of Copei leader Rafael Caldera as attorney general, most hiring and firing in the bureaucracy was based on strictly partisan criteria, to AD's exclusive benefit, and the Labor Ministry used its resources to help AD solidify its control of the union movement.[5]

Most importantly, the junta and the Gallegos government embarked on a rapid expansion of public education and proposed various measures designed to assert state control over private schools, including their curricula, examination system, and teacher training. These measures antagonized the Catholic schools and the church in general, which then mobilized fierce opposition to the Trienio government. When Gallegos was overthrown in 1948, church officials publicly praised God for "divine" intervention, and the leaders of the two largest opposition parties offered their support to the new military government.[6]

AD's majoritarian governing style was clearly an obstacle to the consolidation of this first Venezuelan democratic regime. There is nothing undemocratic about majority rule in a consolidated democracy; indeed, democracy is often *defined* as majority rule. But AD erred in basing the legitimacy of its actions on democratic procedures when the legitimacy of the democratic procedures themselves was in dispute.[7] Democracy could not be consolidated until all important players agreed on the rules of the game, and these players would not consent to any rules that did not guarantee respect for their core interests.[8]

In effect, Venezuela suffered from a symptom of presidentialism—abusive majoritarian rule—before having a severe bout with the disease itself.[9] This experience turned out to be very useful ten years later, because the failure of the Trienio taught the leaders of AD and Copei to avoid majoritarian rule until a consensus on the rules of the game had been achieved. The experience of the Trienio helped immunize Venezuela from the harmful consequences of presidentialism.

When junior officers within the military finally overthrew the Pérez Jiménez dictatorship in 1958, AD leader Rómulo Betancourt and Copei leader Rafael Caldera led their parties toward the center of the political spectrum—AD to the right, and Copei to the left. Before 1958, the Venezuelan party system was polarized; by 1963, little ideological distance was left between the two main parties. To accomplish this rapprochement, Betancourt and Caldera negotiated a pact to ensure that the polarization of the Trienio would not occur again. They also provided assurances to the church, the military, and business leaders that their core interests would be respected.[10]

This pact, the Pact of Punto Fijo, contained three key provisions. First, the three presidential candidates in the 1958 election agreed that they would respect the results of the election and that the winner would form a government of National Unity, regardless of the election results. Congressional leadership posts and all appointive positions, including cabinet ministries and governorships, would be divided among the three signatory parties (AD, Copei, and the Democratic Republican Union, or URD). Second, all three candidates subscribed to a Common Minimum Program that would guide the policies of the first democratic government. And third, party leaders agreed to moderate their rhetoric and to restrain their militants from engaging in interparty violence so that political conflict would not get out of hand.

The terms of the pact were carried out quite well at first. Party leaders quickly condemned a couple of instances of violence at campaign rallies and prevented further outbreaks. Campaign rhetoric in 1958 was amazingly moderate, rarely venturing beyond expressions of support for unity and the Common Minimum Program. Rómulo Betancourt won the presidential contest by a wide margin, and formed a National Unity government even though his own party had won an absolute majority in both chambers. The terms of the Common Minimum Program were also respected. For example, Copei supported a very significant land reform program, and AD kept the issue of state supervision of private education off the agenda for the duration of the Betancourt government.

In time, some of the terms of the pact failed or were relaxed. Violence among the three signatory parties virtually disappeared, but it was replaced by a guerrilla war waged by the communists, who had been excluded from the pact, and defectors from AD and URD. Rhetoric became heated once more in the campaigns for the 1963 elections, and even more heated in 1968. URD withdrew from the National Unity coalition in 1960, and Betancourt's Adeco (AD party) successor, Raúl Leoni, formed a coalition without Copei in 1964. By 1968, Copei had won an election and was attempting to govern alone. But by that year, the democratic regime had been consolidated. Coup attempts from within the armed forces had ceased; the guerrilla war was over, and its combatants amnestied; and Acción Democrática had lost an election (by the narrowest of margins) and handed over power to an opposition party.

The agreements signed by political leaders in 1958 did more than just carry the country through the difficult transition years; their spirit of moderation and consensus became a part of the political culture of Venezuela. Even today, there is an informal "institutional pact" under which legislative positions (presidents and vice presidents of the two chambers, plus committee chairs and vice chairs) and certain key executive appointments are allocated among the largest parties. Party leaders strive to reach consensus on issues of transcendental national importance, such as defense, foreign policy, and petroleum policy. Party leaders also agree that no conflict should be allowed to escalate to the point where it could endanger the democratic regime.[11] These norms of political behavior have helped Venezuelan democracy through the potentially regime-threatening crises that are described below.

The importance of leadership in creating this state of affairs should not be minimized. The failure of the Trienio may have "taught" politicians to moderate conflict and seek consensus while democracy was being consolidated, but not all politicians were such good students of history as Betancourt and Caldera. The thinking of Caldera, Copei, and the Venezuelan church evolved considerably toward the center during the 1950s. Betancourt could have emerged in 1958 still cursing the Right for its earlier betrayal of a democratically elected government. In fact, many of his own party members were inclined to do just that. Signing a pact with the very people who had cheered the junta that had thrown AD out of power in 1948 and exiled, hunted, tortured, and murdered its members for ten years was not the obvious course of action. It was a controversial and courageous act that cost Betancourt the support of most of his party's youth movement.

Strong Parties

Still, it would be naive to believe that Venezuela is democratic today because two wise men willed its democracy into existence thirty years ago. Nothing they did would have had much impact if they had not had the support of strong political parties. By strong, I mean two things: (1) they practiced tight discipline, and (2) they penetrated most politically relevant organizations in society.

Venezuela's first large, mass-based political party was Acción Democrática. The political environment in which it was born shaped its organizational structure and disciplinary norms, which, because of AD's early success, were subsequently copied by all other significant parties. The founders of AD had spent most of their formative years either in exile or in the underground opposition to the Gómez, López Contreras, and later Pérez Jiménez dictatorships. These governments persecuted the opposition relentlessly, arresting party members, torturing them for information about their fellow members, and then sending them into exile or to unspeakably horrible prison camps. Organizational survival under these conditions required secrecy and blind obedience. Party members were grouped into clandestine cells of committed revolutionaries who communicated with other cells by code and sometimes did not even know their leaders' identities but obeyed their instructions nevertheless.

This extreme discipline was permanently enshrined in AD's statutes, which explicitly adopted the Leninist principle of democratic centralism as the rule governing relations between leading and subordinate party organs. The usefulness of such discipline was demonstrated to the nation during the 1945 coup against Medina, when AD militants risked their lives to seize police stations and armories around the country on the instructions of party leaders despite the fact that just two days earlier the national convention had ratified the leaders' qualified support for upcoming elections. When Copei and the URD began organizing during the Trienio, they drafted statutes that were clearly patterned on AD's.

The electoral law drafted by these three parties in 1946 helped extend this discipline to the legislative arena. Venezuelan voters had only a choice of parties, not of candidates. Under their absolutely closed-list scheme of proportional representation, voters stamped a single party *tarjeta*, consisting of a party's name, colors, and symbol and no candidates' names, in legislative elections. This single vote was used to allocate seats among parties in the national senate and chamber of deputies, the state legislative assemblies, and until 1979, the city councils.[12] Few voters even knew the candidates' names for these positions, and elected representatives did not necessarily feel much responsibility to their "constituents," for they owed their primary loyalty to the national party leaders who assigned them to a list and decided how high on it they would rank.

This electoral system (combined with the certainty of expulsion of anyone who vote against the party line) created nearly perfect party discipline in the Venezuelan congress. Discipline is so tight that congressional votes are almost never counted or recorded. Debate consists of one spokesman designated by his party standing to state (although often at great length) the party position on the legislation at hand. The actual vote is a foregone conclusion once the roll is called at the beginning of the day's session, because every legislator present votes a straight party line.

This exceptionally tight discipline became especially useful when it was combined with party penetration of other organizations. By cooptation, infiltration, or direct party sponsorship, virtually all organizations in civil society besides the church, the military, and business associations were subordinated to party control. Beginning in the early sixties, the officers of social organizations were chosen in elections conducted along party lines: each party put forward a slate of candidates for the vacant offices, and the organization's membership chose among them. This was the procedure that was followed in union elections, in peasant organizations, in the bar association, the medical association, societies of dentists, architects, accountants, economists, political scientists, public employees, teachers, professors, and other white-collar workers; and in student government, from the universities down to the junior high level (and sometimes below). Some say that even beauty contests were decided along party lines!

Party penetration of organizations played an important role in the establishment and consolidation of democracy in Venezuela. Control of organizations gave party leaders the ability to mobilize thousands of supporters on short notice to overthrow dictators in 1945 and 1958. It also gave them the ability to *restrain* supporters when democracy required restraint. The willingness of highly partisan labor leaders to hold back wage demands for political reasons during the Betancourt government, even to the point of accepting a 10 percent wage cut in 1961, was crucial in persuading business elites to support democracy.[13] Venezuela's comparatively low strike rate has continued to reassure the private sector since then.

Furthermore, the parties' ability to mobilize and restrain gave them authority to bargain effectively with military and business leaders during the pact making of the transition. They had the organization and numbers and discipline to make attractive promises and issue credible threats. And after the transition, control of organizations and, to some extent, the media gave party leaders a great deal of control over the political agenda—the power to decide what the issues were, how they were defined, and what got ignored.

It is important to remember that the three major factors that explain the stability of Venezuelan democracy are all rather unusual. In Latin America, no other country has enjoyed such wealth for such a long period of time. Few leaders have been as willing to put aside partisan and ideological differences for the sake of democracy as Betancourt and Caldera were, even after long periods of exile and repression. And while some other Latin American countries have similarly pragmatic parties, parties that are almost as well disciplined, equally unified, or highly penetrative, no other country has parties that possess all of these qualities in a competitive system.

Presidentialism during the Transition

Venezuela has had extraordinary advantages, but presidentialism is not one of them. In fact, if Venezuela had not had all of the advantages described above, presidentialism might have done away with democracy there. A good example of how presidentialism has interfered with democracy without undermining it completely comes from the transition period. Prior to the Pact of Punto Fijo, party leaders had agreed on four tactics to symbolize and manifest their unified commitment to democracy. Three of these have already been mentioned—the National Unity government, the moderation of political conflict, and the Common Minimum Program. A fourth tactic has received much less attention, however, because it was unsuccessful. This was the agreement to support a "unity candidate" for president.

Power sharing was an indispensable element in the pact making of the 1958 transition. Without an agreement to share power, the first government of the new democratic regime was likely to be overwhelmingly Adeco. The opposition needed guarantees that the new democracy would not be a repeat of the Trienio. Even Rómulo Betancourt agreed on that point. It was he, in fact, who suggested a National Unity government in discussions with Rafael Caldera and the URD's Jóvito Villalba in New York in January of 1958. Naturally, the leader of Copei was eager to cooperate. He knew his party had little chance of winning, so any cabinet posts it won in the bargain would be net gains. Furthermore, Caldera had become a true democrat during the Pérez Jiménez years and was anxious to shed Copei's image as the party of antidemocratic reaction. Participating in a government with AD would further this goal very nicely. Villalba believed he was in a stronger electoral position than Caldera, having been the legitimate winner of a 1952 election stolen by Pérez Jiménez, but he could not be sure of his chances because AD had been barred from the 1952 contest. Power sharing would guarantee his party some executive power and ensure that an AD-dominated government like the one Villalba had vigorously opposed during the Trienio would not return to power.

All three major party leaders therefore agreed on the need for power sharing. It was not clear, however, how to accomplish that goal in a presidential system, which necessarily concentrates a great deal of power in one person. Betancourt, Caldera, and Villalba agreed in January on the obvious formula: their three parties would nominate the same person, a "unity candidate," who would be chosen in roundtable negotiations among the three parties before the December 1958 election.

The search for the unity candidate dominated the attention of the parties and the media for most of the brief campaign and eventually failed. It created more disunity than unity, for two reasons. In the first place, the roundtable negotiations to choose the candidate created a situation in which the parties had to disagree publicly. First URD and then Copei suggested Dr. Martín Vegas as a possible unity candidate. AD rejected Vegas because of his lack of political experience and doubtful ability to deal with the military. Instead, AD suggested Admiral Wolfgang Larrazábal, the leader of the coup against Pérez Jiménez and the president of the provisional government, with the proviso that the three parties compose a consultative council to advise him on important matters. The URD then switched from Vegas to Larrazábal, but still disagreed with AD over the necessity of a consultative council.[14] Then URD accepted the idea of the council, but Copei rejected it, being opposed to a military president under any circumstances.[15] At one point, Betancourt desperately pushed for a three-man collegial executive, only to be rebuffed by the other parties.

The positions of the smaller parties complicated the picture even more. The Venezuelan Communist party, or PCV, supported the idea of a unity candidate, but was excluded from negotiations to select him, while the Venezuelan Socialist party rejected the whole idea of a unity candidate.[16] And the discussions were even more complex than I have been able to describe here. The important point is that for two full months of a six-month campaign, reports of these partisan disagreements and maneuvers were making front-page news every day, contradicting in practice the unity that was being claimed in principle.

In the second place, since so much time and energy had been invested in the search for a single candidate, responsibility for the failure of the search became a heated political issue. In September the URD, growing nervous as the elections approached with no candidate nominated, threw a wrench in the negotiations by independently nominating Admiral Larrazábal and inviting the other parties to endorse him as the unity candidate. Only the Communist party did. In the meantime, Copei nominated Caldera and AD nominated Betancourt, both on the condition that they would defer to a single candidate if one were found. So during October, the parties disputed whether their independent nominations violated the principle of unity, and if so, who violated it first.[17]

The Pact of Punto Fijo at the end of October was supposed to put an end to these disputes, but it didn't. The URD continued billing itself as the oxymoronic "Party of Unity," and the PCV stuck with the story that Larrazábal was the unity candidate.[18] The frictions generated by the task of looking for a unity candidate were wearing down the united front these parties all wanted to present for the first election.

The Pact of Punto Fijo takes on new meaning in the context of these negotiations. It was not the ideal expression of the spirit of unity, but a second-best compromise reached when the indivisibility of presidential power raised obstacles to the realization of that spirit. It was the failure to find the perfect candidate that made the pact necessary: when negotiations on the matter collapsed, there was general apprehension that unity was unattainable. The immediate purpose of the pact was to relieve that apprehension by legitimating the nomination of different candidates by each of the parties, provided that the other three aspects of unity were observed.

Presidents and the Congress

One of the most discussed problems with presidential systems is their tendency to foster conflict between the executive and the congress, resulting in stalemate and immobilism or attempts to circumvent the congress, which can lead to regime-threatening constitutional crises. Several scholars have suggested that the severity of these problems is a function of the type of party system a country possesses. For example, Scott Mainwaring and Catherine Conaghan argue that these problems are at their worst when the party system is fragmented and parties are undisciplined and fractionalized, as they are in Brazil and Ecuador.[19]

The chaos caused by parties at the disorganized extreme typified by Brazil and Ecuador is undeniable, but it would be a mistake to conclude that the solution lies at the opposite extreme, a dominant party system with highly disciplined parties. Mexico is not the ideal. A congress that blocks everything the president wants to do is undesirable, but so is a rubber stamp. If we are interested in democracy, we want some give and take between government and opposition in the congress. That give and take comes either from the lack of a governing-party majority, which forces the president to bargain with a coalition partner, or from imperfect party discipline, which forces the president to bargain with individual legislators. Parties in the congress can be so fragmented and so undisciplined that the government does not work; but if they are too monolithic and too disciplined, the system is undemocratic. The ideal is not at either extreme of fragmentation or discipline but at some happy medium.[20]

Venezuela's two large parties are near this happy medium with respect to fragmentation, but given their perfect discipline, the system has the potential to alternate between the worst aspects of both extremes. When the president's party lacks a majority in the congress, even by one vote, a handful of opposition party leaders can unite to block all of the executive's legislative program, and they can do it just as effectively as if the president had no supporters in the congress at all. Since presidents have no veto power, an opposition majority can even legislate over the president's head. And when the president's party does have a majority, even by one vote, the executive can act as though the opposition did not exist, because the support of his own party is virtually guaranteed.

Whether the Venezuelan congress actually realizes its potential to be either a rubber stamp or a stumbling block depends entirely on the will of the leaders of each party. Fortunately for democracy, the party leaders began the regime praising consensus and committed to mutual consultation on all important substantive issues. Even today, all major-party leaders agree that no conflict should be allowed to escalate to the point that it endangers the democratic regime. Nevertheless, this commitment to consensus and consultation has not prevented the parties from venturing close to the brink from time to time, in both majority and minority governments.

Majority Governments

The current democratic regime began with a four-party system, which became increasingly fragmented over the next two elections and then suddenly was transformed into a two-and-a-quarter party system in 1973. It has changed relatively little since then (table 12.2). Three presidents from AD—Rómulo Betancourt (1959–64), Carlos Andrés Pérez (1974–79), and Jaime Lusinchi (1984–89)—enjoyed AD majorities in both houses of the congress, although Betancourt lost his due to two divisions of AD during his term of office. Copei's loyalty to the National Unity coalition kept Betancourt at the head of a majority government for a few months longer, and President Leoni of AD also headed a coalition majority government for most of his term. The rest of the time, Venezuela has had minority governments.

The potential for abuse was present in each of the majority governments. For example, all three presidents who enjoyed AD majorities asked for, and received, special powers under section 8 of article 190 of the constitution to "dictate extraordinary measures in economic and financial matters when the public interest requires." However, not all of these governments seriously abused these powers.

The political climate of unity and consensus between AD and Copei prevented Betancourt's AD majority from becoming abusive. Betancourt was accused of dictatorial abuses by the opposition (the PCV—Venezuelan Communist party—and later the URD and the Movement of the Revolutionary Left, or MIR), and with some justification. During his first two years in office, he enjoyed considerable decree powers since the country remained under Pérez Jiménez's authoritarian 1953 constitution until the new democratic constitution went in effect in January of 1961. Five months after that, he obtained congressional authorization to rule by decree for a fixed period of time. And under both constitutions, Betancourt suspended certain constitutional guarantees for a little more than half of his five-year term. Permission for some open-air public meetings was denied, leftist newspapers were suppressed, homes and offices of suspected guerrillas were raided without warrants, and there were lengthy detentions without trial.[21]

While the governing parties (AD and Copei) ratified the suspension of guarantees in the congress over the strenuous protests of the other parties represented there, it would be unreasonable to interpret the government's actions as abusive majoritarianism, given the severe challenges to the state at the time: two major riots, several coup attempts, armed guerrilla insurgency, a nearly successful presidential assassination attempt, and urban terrorist bombings. It makes more sense to fault the URD for its demagogic (and politically counterproductive) opposition to the measures.

By the time AD won its next congressional majorities, however, there were no longer such good excuses for energetic exercise of presidential power. The presidency of Carlos Andrés Pérez (1974–79) provides an excellent illustration of the potential for a "tyranny of the majority" in a presidential system with a tightly disci-

Table 12.2. Percentages (and Numbers) of Seats in the Congress Won by Parties

President	AD	Copei	URD	MAS	Others
			Chamber of Deputies		
Betancourt (AD), 1959–64	57 (73)	15 (19)	26 (33)	—	3 (4)
Leoni (AD), 1964–69	37 (65)	23 (40)	16 (29)	—	24 (43)
Caldera (Copei), 1969–74	31 (66)	28 (59)	8 (18)	—	33 (71)
Pérez (AD), 1974–79	51 (102)	32 (64)	3 (5)	5 (9)	10 (20)
Herrera (Copei), 1979–84	44 (88)	42 (84)	2 (3)	6 (11)	7 (13)
Lusinchi (AD), 1984–89	57 (113)	30 (60)	2 (3)	5 (10)	7 (14)
Pérez (AD), 1989–	48 (98)	33 (67)	1 (2)	9 (19)[a]	9 (18)
			Senate[b]		
Betancourt (AD), 1959–64	63 (32)	12 (6)	21 (11)	—	4 (2)
Leoni (AD), 1964–69	49 (22)	18 (8)	16 (7)	—	18 (8)
Caldera (Copei), 1969–74	37 (19)	31 (16)	6 (3)	—	27 (14)
Pérez (AD), 1974–79	60 (28)	28 (13)	2 (1)	4 (2)	6 (3)
Herrera (Copei), 1979–84	48 (21)	48 (21)	0 (0)	5 (2)	0 (0)
Lusinchi (AD), 1984–89	64 (28)	32 (14)	0 (0)	5 (2)	0 (0)
Pérez (AD), 1989–	48 (22)	43 (20)	0 (0)	7 (3)[a]	2 (1)

Sources: Betancourt-Herrera governments—Consejo Supremo Electoral, La estadística evolutiva de los partidos políticos en Venezuela, 1958–1979; Lusinchi government—Consejo Supremo Electoral, Elecciones 1983; second Pérez government—El nacional, 7 Dec. 1988, D-1.

Figures reflect the initial distribution of seats among parties after the elections. Distributions in the Betancourt and Leoni governments changed greatly due to AD splits.
   a. MAS-MIR (Socialists and revolutionary leftists) electoral coalition.
   b. Excluding former presidents, who are senators for life.

plined majority party in power. Pérez assumed office at the beginning of the oil bonanza and had extremely ambitious plans for rapid development of the country. To put his plans into effect, he matched the flood of oil revenues with an avalanche of laws and decrees. In his first one hundred days in office, he issued an average of two new decrees, resolutions, or draft laws per day, and immediately became impatient with the slowness of the legislative process. In the second month of his term, he requested extraordinary powers to issue decrees on a wide and vaguely worded set of issues.[22]

As Terry Karl has noted, given the virtually automatic support of the AD majority, there would seem to be little need for decree powers, unless for some reason the president wished to free himself of accountability to his own party.[23] This was obviously one of Pérez's intentions, and his point of view is not hard to understand. He knew from fifteen years of relations between Venezuelan presidents and their perfectly disciplined parties that AD would eventually endorse just about any bill he proposed with few substantial objections. Seen in this light, the pro forma routine of consulting party leaders probably seemed like a luxury that the country could dispense with in a time of rapid economic change.

What is not so obvious is why party leaders would surrender their right to provide input on new legislation. They did hesitate; approval of the president's request took a little over a month, and in this time AD succeeded in limiting the special powers to twelve months and in requiring the president to submit decrees to specially created multiparty commissions for discussion (although their approval was not required prior to issuance). AD's eventual consent can only be understood as a by-product of the honeymoon Pérez enjoyed in his first year. He had just led his party to a massive victory; he had high approval ratings; his party, still buoyed by gratitude, trusted its leader and was in no mood to deny him what he wanted. But the same would be true *any* time a Venezuelan president wins a single-party majority: he takes the party's support for granted, and the party is only too eager to defer to his leadership. This is, I think, why all three AD majorities granted their respective presidents special powers.

All three of these presidents had the opportunity to abuse their party's trust, but Pérez was the only one who actually did it. The multiparty commissions were largely ignored; even AD leaders sometimes learned of decrees only after they had been published in the *Gaceta Oficial;* and the sheer volume of decrees went beyond any standard of responsible government—830 decrees and 51 new commissions in one year's time. Copei spokesman Eduardo Fernández complained: "I took an average: sixteen decrees a week. The Council of Ministers meets once a week. Each time that the Council of Ministers meets, it OKs sixteen decrees and creates a commission. . . . I think that this creates a situation of very profound confusion in the country."[24]

The third time AD won majority control of the congress, party leaders remembered how Pérez had abused his special powers. They put up firmer resistance when Lusinchi asked for similar powers in 1984 to deal with the debt crisis. This time, Copei and all of the other opposition parties except the minuscule URD voted against the enabling legislation, and the content of the decrees was strictly delineated in advance.[25] Lusinchi's use of his special powers was so circumspect that when they expired, the worst criticism Copei could muster was that they had been unnecessary to begin with, as proven by the fact that Lusinchi had done so little with them.[26] While Lusinchi did not abuse his AD majority, the fact that he received decree powers even when the need for them was questionable confirms the *potential* for an abusive rule by other presidents, and Pérez's example leaves no doubt.

Minority Governments

If presidents supported by a highly disciplined majority party have the potential to abuse their power, presidents at the head of minority governments have the opposite problem—too little power. Without a working majority in the legislature, a Venezuelan president faces tremendous obstacles to getting his legislative program approved. It is fruitless for him to try to win the cooperation of individual legislators because party discipline requires them to vote their party line. Of course, if the leaders of the opposition parties are in the mood to cooperate, an ad hoc working majority may be put together. But if they are not, there is a stalemate between the president and the congress.

Other scholarship on presidentialism has tended to focus on two possible outcomes to this situation of stalemate (see chapter 1). One is immobilism, a halt (more commonly, a slowdown) in the legislative process. The second is circumvention of the congress by the president, which has an unwelcome tendency to concentrate power in the executive branch while weakening the congress and may also provoke constitutional crises that can contribute to the breakdown of the democratic regime. In Venezuela, there is a third possible outcome: circumvention of the president by the congress, which also has the potential to provoke constitutional crises.

Circumvention of the president is possible because article 173 of the constitution deprives the president of any veto power. If the president disapproves of a bill that has been passed by a simple majority in the senate and the chamber of deputies, he may send it back to the congress for a second consideration. If the bill is passed again, even if it is only by a simple majority, it becomes law, regardless of the president's position (unless the Supreme Court decides that the law is unconstitutional). And any bill approved by a two-thirds majority becomes law without further reconsideration. The congress has the last word. The framers of the Venezuelan constitution probably intended for the repeated consideration to be a potent check on the congress's ability to legislate without presidential approval, but in practice, party discipline and the opposition parties' common interest in discrediting the government have made legislation by the opposition a reality on several occasions.

The final say of the Venezuelan congress does not prevent stalemate from developing into a constitutional crisis. One phase of stalemate ends when the congress passes legislation over the president's head, but another phase of stalemate begins when the congress waits for the president to execute the new law. And it is in this shifting of arenas that a stalemate becomes most dangerous. Stalemate engenders frustration in both branches at their inability to exercise their respective mandates; and that frustration tempts them to resort to extraconstitutional measures.

As of January 1993, minority governments had been in office in Venezuela nearly 52 percent of the time since the beginning of the democratic regime; if President Pérez completes his term without forming a coalition, minority governments will have been in office 57 percent of the time.[27] The country has not experienced a constitutional crisis severe enough to lead to a military coup, but it has had several opportunities and has weathered more than one crisis.

Legislation has definitely been hampered during these minority governments,

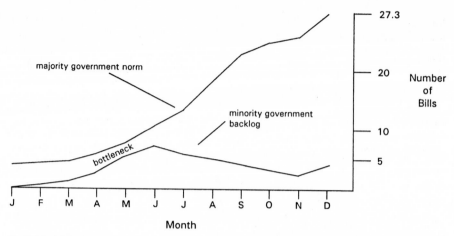

Fig. 12.1. Cumulative Number of Bills Passed in Majority and Minority Governments (Averages, 1959–1982). Data compiled from Congreso de la República, *25 años de legislación democrática* (Caracas: Ediciones del Congreso de la República, 1983.)

compared to the majority governments. In the aggregate, the difference in legislative performance is slight: minority governments approve an average of 23.9 laws per year, compared to 27.3 during majority governments.[28] But the more the data are broken down, the clearer the difference becomes. Figure 12.1 shows a significant delay in legislation approved in the course of each calendar year. The upper curve traces the cumulative number of laws approved during majority governments by month of the year averaged over the 1959–82 period; the lower curve traces the corresponding legislative backlog in minority governments, that is, the difference between the average number of laws approved by majority governments and the average number approved by minority governments, cumulated for each month. (The vertical distance between the two curves is therefore the average number of laws approved by minority governments.) Even a stalemated minority government manages to approve a certain fixed volume of legislation, probably composed mostly of the routine, unobjectionable legislation that occupies much of the attention of any legislature.[29] But it is a rather thin, and long, bottleneck: by June, the backlog of delayed legislation is more than half as large as the volume of legislation that would have been approved by the average majority government. The average minority government then legislates at an accelerated pace in the second half of the year, and reduces the backlog somewhat, but does not catch up completely by the year's end.

Furthermore, when the averages are set aside and the raw data are examined, legislative performance during minority governments shows several glaring failures. Majority governments tend to legislate relatively continuously; months in which no legislation is approved are few and scattered. But in minority governments, there are long gaps. There were two three-month stretches without legislation at the end of both the Betancourt and Leoni governments, three four-month gaps in the Caldera government, and two five-month gaps in the Herrera government. Overlapping the Pérez and Herrera governments, there was an eight-and-a-half-month period, from October 6, 1978, to July 27, 1979, during which no new laws were approved.

Still, we are looking only at the volume of legislation. A comparison of the content of legislation passed under majority and minority governments yields some interesting differences. Organic laws, reforms of politicoadministrative legislation, and ratification of measures concerning the primary sector (oil, mining, and agriculture) have been two to three times more likely to pass during majority governments, while reforms of social or cultural legislation and ratifications of social or cultural measures have been two to three times more likely to pass during minority governments.[30] Since this analysis is based on a small volume of legislation, these conclusions should be regarded as tentative. Still, they confirm the expected tendency for majority governments to decide on the more fundamental or controversial issues and to leave the less controversial issues to minority governments.

Stalemate during the Betancourt Government

An even better way to learn about the effects of stalemate is to examine the record of executive-legislative relations under minority governments. Rómulo Betancourt, the founder of AD, headed a National Unity government from 1959 to 1964. AD alone controlled majorities in both houses of congress, but with the addition of coalition partners Copei and the URD, Betancourt began his presidency with a working majority of 125 out of 129 seats in the chamber of deputies, and 49 out of 51 seats in the senate. However, by January 1962, AD had split twice and the URD had left the coalition. After that point, AD and Copei together retained their majority in the senate but controlled only 57 of the 129 seats in the chamber of deputies, leaving the Betancourt government vulnerable to stalemate during its last year and a half.

For the first two years, the spirit of unity that helped the transition to democracy succeed also prevented stalemate and constitutional crisis from occurring. Little legislation was initiated that had not been anticipated by the Common Minimum Program signed by the coalition parties before the election. In addition, the attention of the congress was distracted by its work as a constituent assembly until the new constitution went into effect in January 1961. Because the charter was so new, it anticipated all of the constitutional issues the Betancourt government faced.

These were anything but years of peace and harmony, however. The Betancourt government was threatened by the dissolution of its coalition, two splits in AD and one in the URD, three coup attempts, the leftist insurgency and urban terrorism, and intransigent opposition in the congress on nonconstitutional issues. After a particularly reprehensible terrorist act in September 1963, these threats to the regime united the parties loyal to the system to defend the constitutional order.[31] But during the twenty-one months between the second AD split and this rebirth of unity, the minority Betancourt government could not obtain approval of some of its most important initiatives. The budget for the National Agrarian Institute, for example, was cut severely in 1962 and 1963 by the opposition majority in the chamber of deputies, and these cuts slowed the pace of the agrarian reform.[32]

Stalemate during the Leoni Government

The next president from AD, Raúl Leoni (1964–69), also suffered a period of stalemate. Rather than continue the coalition with Copei, he began his government with a "broad base" coalition with the URD and the FND, while Copei adopted an "autonomous action" line of loyal opposition. The broad base did not last long, however: by the first quarter of 1968, both the Frente Nacional Democrático (FND) and the URD had withdrawn from the coalition, and AD had suffered a third split, its worst yet. The dissident AD faction formed a new party, the Movimiento Electoral del Pueblo (MEP), which led an obstructionist opposition majority in the chamber of deputies *and* the senate for the remaining fourteen months of Leoni's administration.

One consequence of this stalemate was a loss of executive leadership on oil policy. According to Franklin Tugwell, the Betancourt and Leoni governments had pursued a very effective policy of "assertive experimentation" before the MEP split. After the split, assertive experimentation gave way to a style of "cautious incrementalism with an eye to short-term considerations," which increased the bargaining power of the foreign oil companies vis-à-vis the state.[33]

This stalemate also led to the regime's first parliamentary crisis. In March 1968, the parties represented in the congress could not agree on one person to serve as president of the congress. Just before the vote was to be taken, outgoing acting president Luis Augusto Dubuc stepped out of the chamber to consult a colleague, and the next-in-charge officer, a man from Copei, took advantage of Dubuc's absence to call for an early vote, in which Copei's choice was elected.[34] AD at first refused to recognize the election result: for a while, Dubuc refused to turn over the presidency of the congress to his successor from Copei, and he and another senator petitioned the Supreme Court to annul the election. The crisis was defused only when President Leoni eventually recognized the new congressional officers.[35]

Stalemate during the Caldera Government

Rafael Caldera won the 1968 election with a plurality of 27.1 percent in a field of six candidates. His party, Copei, controlled only 31 and 28 percent of the seats in the senate and chamber of deputies, respectively. In spite of the abysmal weakness of his base of support, Caldera chose not to form a coalition government.[36] Stalemate was therefore practically guaranteed.

During the first year of the Caldera government, the stalemate was intractable: Led by AD, congressional opponents assailed the presidency at every opportunity: they removed the executive's right to appoint members of the judiciary (except on the Supreme Court) and placed it in the hands of a special panel dominated by opposition parties; they limited government borrowing to two-year periods; and they passed a law forcing all autonomous institutes and corporations with a majority of shares held by the government to appoint union representatives to their boards (AD's strength in the union movement surpassed that of Copei). AD tried briefly to persuade Congress to make Venezuela's state governors elective rather than appointed officials, and at one point seriously discussed the possibility of changing the constitution itself to a parliamentary system. Because of the standoff between the legislature and the executive, Venezuelan politics deteriorated into petty wrangling. Bitterness, fragmentation, and empty rhetoric became the rule, while the country drifted. Things got so bad that there were rumors of "restlessness" in the military. Even Fedecámaras [the peak business organization] attempted to reconcile the antagonists, inviting Copei and AD leaders to meet at its own headquarters (they declined).[37]

Caldera's congress was born paralyzed: for its first several weeks in March 1969, it did nothing but witness fruitless negotiations among the parties over the election of congressional officers. An odd winning slate was finally approved only with the support of the Civic Crusade, the electoral vehicle of former dictator Pérez Jiménez. This desparate tactical alliance gave the opposition ammunition against Copei for years.[38]

The conflict over judicial appointments a few months later was serious enough to provoke a constitutional crisis.[39] Before the Caldera government, all judges except Supreme Court justices were appointed jointly by the executive and the politicoadministrative body of the Supreme Court. In the latter half of 1969, the opposition majority in the congress passed a law that gave to the new National Judiciary Council the power to appoint twenty-five hundred to twenty-eight hundred judges. The majority of this council's members would be appointed by none other than the congress. Caldera challenged the law's constitutionality, and at the same time his minister of justice submitted a roster of nominations to the court for appointment. Both maneuvers were frustrated: the court upheld the law, eight to seven, and the politicoadministrative body, which was controlled by AD and URD sympathizers, refused to consider the justice minister's roster.

The controversy did not end here, however, because a new conflict arose *within* the opposition over nominations to the new National Judiciary Council. All of the opposition parties agreed on excluding Copei, but beyond that basic point there was little agreement. During the summer recess, AD led the delegated commission of the congress (which exercises certain congressional powers when the congress is not in session) to appoint two members to the council. The presidents of the senate and chamber of deputies, however, were not Adecos and called a special session of the congress to annul the appointments and name two different members to the council. AD and other parties boycotted the session, thereby preventing a quorum. Eventually a smaller party participated, the special session was held, and the council was appointed.

The judicial appointments crisis was the most severe manifestation of stalemate in 1969, but the same procedural plotting and intricate jockeying for partisan advantage was characteristic of the first year of the Caldera administration. President Caldera became convinced that some kind of legislative alliance was necessary. After lengthy negotiations, AD agreed to an informal alliance, called the Coincidencia, in which AD would support the government "on predefined 'areas of coincidence.'"[40] AD and Copei now controlled a majority in both houses.

The productive period of the Coincidencia lasted only a year and a half, and even then it meant only that AD would no longer obstruct its own legislative program: most of the significant legislation passed during this period originated in Acción Democrática, and AD retained its veto on legislation it opposed. For example, AD opposition led the congress to reject the finance minister's attempt to levy nine new taxes in order to balance the budget.[41] The Coincidencia did decrease controversy over foreign policy and prevent obstructionist delays in the election of congressional officers and the approval of the Budget Law and the Law of Universities. However, by no means can it be said that the Coincidencia made it possible for the Caldera administration to govern or function well. As Donald Herman observes, "The Adecos and Copeyanos apparently concluded that they would only keep the government's machinery functioning. . . . [The Copeyanos] likened AD's position to that of a doctor who gave his patient medicine to help him feel better but who did not cure him: the Adecos wanted to maintain the system, but they would do everything possible to minimize the effectiveness of Copei."[42] Stalemate was the fundamental reality of politics during the Caldera government. It underlay everything that happened.

Stalemate during the Herrera Government

When Copei candidate Luis Herrera Campíns won the presidential election of 1978, AD found itself once again in the opposition, and the president was once again without a working majority in the congress. President Herrera was even less tempted to form a coalition than Caldera had been, since his party controlled 43 percent of the seats in the combined houses of congress. But AD was just as determined to obstruct as it had been ten years previously, and it controlled 45 percent of the seats. The stage was set for another bout of stalemate.

In the first months of the Herrera administration, Acción Democrática applied the political equivalent of a full court press to the Copei legislative program. By August 1979, only two pieces of legislation had been approved in ten months. The frustrated Copei government then proposed to extend the spring session of the congress into August so that some very important bills could be approved.[43] Small third parties, weary of AD's obstructionism, were willing to support the extension, but AD prevented it for two days by boycotting the congress and thereby breaking quorum. On the third day, AD acceded to a voice vote on the extension but vigorously disputed the declaration by the Copeyano president of the congress that the extension then passed.

Based on these events, AD boycotted the congress for the next three weeks, and upon returning, it accused the governing party of "turning its back on duties that it has contracted before the constitutional system of the country" by having legislated without a quorum in the interim.[44] AD kept up this obstructionist line for the remainder of the Herrera government, with the result that two-thirds of all the legislation approved between 1979 and 1982 was approved on the last day of a session.[45]

Postscript and Prospects

Presidentialism has caused its usual mischief in Venezuela. In 1958, it hindered the achievement of unity in an important transitional election. In combination with minority governing parties in the Betancourt, Leoni, Caldera, and Herrera governments, it led to executive legislative stalemate. In combination with a majority party, it allowed President Pérez to circumvent the legislative process altogether. Most of the time, these situations have led to consequences no more serious than the concentration of power in the presidency and the erosion of power from an inefficient and unproductive congress. But more than once, the conflicts generated by presidentialism in the context of a strong party system—even a centrist, nearly two-party system—have carried Venezuelan politics to the outer limits of constitutionality.

At this writing (January 1993), Venezuela is undergoing its most severe constitutional crisis in thirty years, a crisis that is fundamentally the product of presidentialism. Now in his second government, President Pérez has very little political support. It is not just that his party lacks a majority in both houses of the congress; his problems are compounded by the fact that he has been isolated from his own party and from the voters since the very beginning of his administration. Many voters supported Pérez in the 1988 presidential election believing that he would bring back the state-led and oil-fueled prosperity of his first government, but within days of his inauguration, he initiated a draconian structural adjustment program that inflicted high short-term social costs. This surprise economic "package" left many Venezuelans—including activists in Pérez's own party—feeling personally betrayed by the president.

Pérez became even more isolated when riots and looting broke out in February and March 1989. Some citizens were appalled by the brutality with which the disturbance was repressed. Many more were appalled that the government did not respond immediately, and they transferred their gratitude to the active-duty defense minister, who reported the security forces' response on television.

In 1991–92, inflation was below 40 percent and the economy was growing rapidly, but polls showed most Venezuelans remaining pessimistic about their economic prospects. In the meantime revelations of corruption in the Lusinchi and Pérez governments abounded. The economic situation, the corruption scandals, and mushrooming crime rates in the wake of the riots all contributed to deepening public disillusionment with political parties. For example, when a 1988 poll asked respondents which party's ideas about governing the country were most like their own, 18 percent replied, "none of the above"; but when that same question was asked in September 1991, those replying "none of the above" had increased to 45 percent.[46] By November of 1991, 56 percent disapproved of Pérez's performance as president and only 35 percent approved; ratings of the government itself and of parties in general were even lower.[47]

When a coup against Pérez was attempted on February 4, 1992, the plotters encountered significant support, but probably from a minority of the population, as only about one-quarter of the respondents in the November poll believed a military solution might be possible. (Two-thirds opposed military intervention.) Nevertheless, it was a very serious uprising of more than one thousand army troops in four cities, more than seventy people were killed, and Pérez narrowly escaped assassination. The coup provoked a desperate search for drastic measures to prevent future coup attempts. Former President Caldera called for Pérez to resign, and he was seconded by the Movimiento al Socialismo (MAS) and prominent intellectual Arturo Uslar Pietri. In a parliamentary system, a call for resignation would have been entirely appropriate, but as a president elected to a fixed term, Pérez argued that resignation under pressure would amount to an unconstitutional "civilian coup." To complicate matters further, it was unclear who would replace Pérez if he were to resign because the office of his designated successor, the president of the senate, was vacant at the time due to a political deadlock in the senate.

Technically, it would have been possible to *force* the president to resign; however, in Venezuela's presidential system the procedures available for doing so are either so cumbersome or so threatening to the political leadership that it lacked the will to use them. Impeachment would have required charging Pérez with a serious criminal offense such as corruption. But since Venezuela's oil wealth had supplied most politicians with comfortable glass houses over the preceding thirty years, few were willing to cast the first stone. In theory, a constituent assembly would have had the authority to dismiss the president in the absence of criminal charges, but the constitution did not provide for such an assembly. In the time it would have taken to amend the constitution to permit a constituent assembly, for the assembly to deliberate, and for its decisions to be ratified in a referendum, Pérez probably could have finished his term. With the congress's sweeping constitutional powers and strong party discipline, it may have been possible to accelerate the process somewhat, but the leaders of AD and Copei were determined not to permit a constituent assembly because they feared its unlimited power to dismantle the system they had built for themselves. The congressional leadership instead toyed for several months, with a more limited set of constitutional amendments, but in September 1992 it decided not to act on even these reforms. In November the senate went so far as to pass a Copei resolution asking the president to submit to a referendum on finishing his term. The resolution was nonbinding, however, and when Pérez refused, the matter was dropped.

Days later, on November 27, 1992, officers from all three services staged a second coup attempt. Bystanders cheered as planes dropped bombs over the presidential palace. This attempt was defeated, too, after twelve hours of fighting and hundreds of deaths, but it is hard to imagine a more graphic symbol of the frustration caused by the fixed presidential term. In a parliamentary system, there are far easier ways to remove an unpopular leader from office.

The twentieth-century history of Latin America is replete with examples of politicians who, faced with similar crises, have remained intransigent, withdrawn their participation, appealed to the military to solve their problems, or in other ways unwisely sacrificed their long-term interest in preserving democracy on the altar of short-term political advantage. Venezuela's party leaders made those mistakes once but were wise enough to step back from the brink to save the regime from breakdown. Betancourt and Caldera agreed to share power; Leoni recognized the opposition leadership of the congress; Caldera negotiated the Coincidencia with AD; and AD ended its boycott of the congress during the Herrera administration with little more than verbal protests.

Latin American history is also replete with examples of leaders who tried to step back from the brink but looked on helplessly as their followers leaped or fell over the edge, often carrying democracy with them. Venezuela has avoided that fate so far because its unusually penetrative and well disciplined parties have given their leaders the ability to keep followers away from the edge. Oil wealth has helped prevent the economic disasters that have carried Venezuela's neighbors to the brink, but this does not mean that Venezuela has avoided regime crises; it only means that crises have been less frequent. Presidentialism has carried Venezuela to the brink more than once. Venezuelan democracy survived these close calls in the past because its leaders knew when to step back and were able to keep their followers behind them. If past patterns prevail, democracy should survive this crisis as well. However, now that parties are weaker and leaders seem to be taking greater risks, that outcome can no longer be taken for granted.

Notes

I am indebted to Scott Mainwaring, Matthew Shugart, Arend Lijphart, Steve Stedman, Juan Linz, and Cynthia McClintock for their comments, and to Pedro Pablo Permuy, Bobbie Mehr, and Rafael de la Dehesa for research assistance. This research was made possible by a Fulbright-Hays Grant for Doctoral Dissertation Research Abroad.

1. Terry Karl, "Petroleum and Political Pacts: The Transition to Democracy in Venezuela," in *Transitions from Authoritarian Rule: Latin America,* edited by Guillermo O'Donnell, Philippe C. Schmitter, and Laurence Whitehead (Baltimore: Johns Hopkins UP, 1986), p. 215.

2. Karl, "Petroleum and Political Pacts," has offered a series of more sophisticated arguments in favor of the oil connection for the Venezuelan case. First, she argues that oil-led development delayed the formation and organization of all social classes, which meant that only a small number of elites had to reach agreement in crucial political pacts. This assertion applies well to the economic elites, but by the time any relevant pacts were made, the key *political* elites were the heads of large, mass-based political parties; agreement was relatively easy at that point, not because social groups were underdeveloped but because they were exceptionally well organized. She also argues that (1) the Right was less intransigent because the oil companies had provided incentives for the oligarchy to transform itself from a class of landlords into a class of entrepreneurs; and (2) political parties were able to become well disciplined because other interest associations had not had a chance to develop, because of the enclave style of development characteristic of oil. These are both intriguing arguments that fit the facts of the Venezuelan case well, but I am not convinced that the causal connection is there. I suspect that a comparison with Ecuador, another late developer with an important oil sector (as well as a very conservative elite and a chaotic party system), would require placing greater explanatory weight on other factors originally identified by Daniel Levine—leadership, party discipline, and prior dictatorial repression, whose importance Karl also recognizes. See Levine, "Venezuela since 1958: The Consolidation of Democratic Politics," in *The Breakdown of Democratic Regimes,* edited by Juan Linz and Alfred Stepan (Baltimore: Johns Hopkins UP, 1978), pp. 82–109.

3. The Trienio began in October 1945, when junior officers backed by the young political party Acción Democrática (AD) overthrew General Medina Angarita and installed a civil-military "Revolutionary Junta," which promised a rapid transition to democracy. This junta, composed of four leaders of AD, two of the military conspirators, and one nonpartisan civilian, oversaw elections for a constituent assembly in October 1946 and congressional and direct presidential elections in December 1947. The presidential election was won by AD candidate Rómulo Gallegos, who was inaugurated on February 15, 1948. The Trienio ended on November 24, when Gallegos was overthrown after just nine months in office.

4. See John D. Martz, *Acción Democrática: Evolution of a Modern Political Party* (Princeton: Princeton UP, 1966); and Daniel Levine, *Conflict and Political Change in Venezuela* (Princeton: Princeton UP, 1973).

5. Glen L. Kolb, *Democracy and Dictatorship in Venezuela, 1945–1958* (Hamden, Conn.: Archon Books, 1974), pp. 23–24.

6. Levine, *Conflict and Political Change in Venezuela,* chaps. 3, 4; Kolb, *Democracy and Dictatorship in Venezuela,* p. 50.

7. Levine, *Conflict and Political Change in Venezuela.*

8. For an elaboration of this argument, see Terry Karl, "Imposing Consent? Electoralism vs. Democratization in El Salvador," in *Elections and Democratization in Latin America, 1980–1985,* edited by Paul W. Drake and Eduardo Silva (San Diego: U California, San Diego, 1986), pp. 9–36. For its application to the successful transition in Venezuela, see Karl, "Petroleum and Political Pacts."

9. In view of Lijphart's observation of the majoritarian bias of presidential governments, and of Linz's argument that a majoritarian style is risky during transitions to democracy, it is tempting to blame the majoritarian style of the Trienio on presidentialism. However, presi-

dentialism should not be blamed in this case because Acción Democrática was so much larger than the other parties at the time that it would have behaved just as arrogantly in a parliamentary system. AD won Trienio elections with 70 to 79 percent of the vote and controlled majorities of between 75 and 86 percent of the seats in legislative bodies. It is hardly surprising, therefore, that most Adecos felt that they had a mandate to govern during those years and did not take the nascent opposition very seriously. Given the size and strength of the party and the weakness of any organized opposition, the AD governments would have behaved in a majoritarian fashion whether the regime had been presidential or parliamentary. Governments in far weaker positions do so today in parliamentary Great Britain and Spain.

10. The story of the transition can be found in several accounts of the early years of the regime, among which are Martz, *Acción Democrática*, and Robert J. Alexander, *The Venezuelan Democratic Revolution* (New Brunswick, N.J.: Rutgers UP, 1964). Levine emphasized the importance of isolating conflicts and moderating leadership in *Conflict and Political Change in Venezuela*, which is briefly synthesized in his "Venezuela since 1958," and more thoughtfully developed in his "Venezuela: The Nature, Source, and Prospects of Democracy," in *Democracy in Developing Countries: Latin America*, edited by Larry Diamond, Juan J. Linz, and Seymour Martin Lipset (Boulder, Colo.: Lynne Rienner, 1989), pp. 247–89. Karl's interpretation in "Petroleum and Political Pacts" is compatible with Levine's two earlier works but places the transition in the context of oil-led development and emphasizes the class content of pact making during the transition.

11. In a 1985 survey of AD party leaders, two-thirds believed that "avoiding open political conflict that could endanger the democratic system" was a good reason for having a pact with Copei. Michael Coppedge, "Strong Parties and Lame Ducks: A Study of the Quality and Stability of Venezuelan Democracy" (Ph.D. diss., Yale University, 1988), p. 369.

12. Three dramatic reforms of the electoral system were adopted in 1988 and 1989. First, the position of mayor was created at the municipal level. (Previously, municipal executive officials were the presidents of city councils, elected indirectly by the councils.) Second, state governors became directly elected rather than appointed by the president. The first elections under these new provisions were held in December 1989. Third, starting in 1993 legislators will be elected by a system similar to the West German system: half in single-member districts, and half by party ballots by proportional representation, perhaps with some freedom to reorder and choose among individual candidates. I expect party discipline to become looser under these reforms.

13. Karl, "Petroleum and Political Pacts," pp. 210–15.

14. Velázquez, "Aspectos de la evolución política de Venezuela en el último medio siglo," in *Venezuela moderna: Medio siglo de historia, 1926–1976*, edited by Ramón J. Velázquez, Arístides Calvani, Carlos Rafael Silva, and Juan Liscano (Caracas: Fundación Eugenio Mendoza, 1976), pp. 173–75.

15. *El universal*, 16 Oct., 1958.

16. *El universal*, 6 Oct., 1958.

17. See *El universal*, 23 Oct., 1958.

18. *El universal*, 13 Nov., 1958.

19. Scott Mainwaring, "Institutional Dilemmas of Multiparty Presidential Democracy: The Case of Brazil" (paper prepared for the 15th International Congress of the Latin American Studies Association, Miami, 3–6 Dec. 1989); and Catherine M. Conaghan, chap. 10 herein.

20. One also hopes that, whatever the degree of fragmentation and discipline, bargaining between government and opposition is based as much as possible on the content of leg-

islation rather than on vote buying or personal favors. One of the worst attributes of Brazilian "democracy" is that the party system is so unwieldy that vote buying (subtle or not) and personal favors are often the *only* way a president can put a majority together.

21. Alexander, *Venezuelan Democratic Revolution*, pp. 127–30.

22. Terry Karl, "The Political Economy of Petrodollars" (Ph.D. diss., Stanford University, 1982), pp. 208–13.

23. Ibid., pp. 219–20.

24. Quoted in ibid., p. 231.

25. *Ley Habilitante: Ley orgánica que autoriza al Presidente de la República para adoptar medidas económicas o financieras requeridas por el interés público, Gaceta oficial,* no. 33,005, 22 June 1984 (Caracas: Distribuidora Capitolio, 1984); Margarita López Maya, Luis Gómez Calcaño, and Thaís Maingón, *De Punto Fijo al pacto social: Desarrollo y hegemonía en Venezuela (1958–1985)* (Caracas: Fondo Editorial Acta Científica Venezolana, 1989), p. 97.

26. Interviews with Eduardo Fernández and Leonardo Ferrer, *El nacional,* 23 June 1985.

27. Minority governments are defined here as those in which the president's party, together with the other parties with cabinet representation, controls less than half of the seats in the chamber of deputies.

28. The data cited in this paragraph were compiled from Congreso de la República, *25 Años de legislación democrática* (Caracas: Congreso de la República, 1983.) The dates referred to are the dates of publication in the *Gaceta oficial,* but the president must promulgate laws within ten days of legislative sanction unless he returns them for further consideration, so the dates are approximately correct. Notice that the Venezuelan congress is remarkably unproductive; the average number of laws approved by the legislatures of other countries is much higher. The U.S. Congress averages 500–600; the British Parliament, 100; the French Parlement, 110; and the Spanish Cortes and the Colombian congress, 70 each. Comparisons from Arnoldo José Gabaldón and Luis Enrique Oberto (Comisión Bicameral de la Reforma Parlamentaria), *La reforma parlamentaria: Necesidad y alternativas de modernización de la acción legislativa* (Caracas: Congreso de la República, 1985), 1:14n.

29. For a descriptive survey of the nature of Italian legislation, see Giuseppe DiPalma, *Surviving without Governing: The Italian Parties in Parliament* (Berkeley: U California P, 1977), chap. 2.

30. These conclusions are based on an unpublished analysis by Pedro Pablo Permuy, who classified all Venezuelan legislation from June 1959 to December 1982 by type of law (organic, ratification, regular, reform) and subject matter (industry, finance, agriculture, labor, politicoadministrative, social, or cultural). The basic data came from Congreso de la República, *25 Años de legislación democrática.*

31. John D. Martz, *The Venezuelan Elections of December 1, 1963. Part I: An Analysis* (Washington, D.C.: Institute for the Comparative Study of Political Systems, 1964), p. 29.

32. Alexander, *Venezuelan Democratic Revolution,* p. 182.

33. Franklin Tugwell, *The Politics of Oil in Venezuela* (Stanford: Stanford UP, 1975), p. 157.

34. In order to win the vote, Copei had persuaded the elderly former dictator López Contreras to show up in the senate chamber and reactivate his status as senator for life.

35. Velázquez, "Aspectos de la evolución política de Venezuela," pp. 285–86.

36. It may be that Caldera would have preferred to form a coalition but simply could not do so, given the limited choice of partners.

37. Tugwell, *Politics of Oil in Venezuela,* p. 103.

38. Velázquez, "Aspectos de la evolución política de Venezuela," pp. 295–96.

39. My account of this controversy is based on ibid., pp. 307–9.

40. Tugwell, *Politics of Oil in Venezuela*, p. 104. Tugwell says that the importance of this pact was pressed upon AD by the party's old guard—Betancourt, Leoni, and Barrios—presumably in the interest of preserving the democratic regime.

41. Donald L. Herman, *Christian Democracy in Venezuela* (Chapel Hill: U North Carolina P, 1980), pp. 145–46.

42. Ibid., p. 116.

43. My account of this crisis is my interpretation of the events referred to in a partisan document: Acción Democrática, *Documentos sobre la crisis parlamentaria de agosto de 1979* (Caracas: Partido Acción Democrática, 1979), esp. pp. 13–19.

44. AD, *Documentos sobre la crisis Parlamentaria*, pp. 18–19.

45. Calculated from information in Congreso de la República, *25 Años de legislación democrática*.

46. "La inseguridad es el problema que más preocupa a los venezolanos," *El universal*, 1 Oct. 1991, pp. 1–18.

47. Alba Sánchez, "Poll Respondents Reject CAP, Support Caldera," translation of article in *El nacional*, 26 Jan. 1992, p. D-2, in *Foreign Broadcast Information Service—Latin America Report* 92–037 (25 Feb. 1992), pp. 25–27.

Notes on Contributors

Catherine M. Conaghan is associate professor of political studies at Queen's University in Kingston, Ontario. She is author of *Restructuring Domination: Industrialists and the State in Ecuador* and co-author with James Malloy of *Unsettling Statecraft: Democracy and Neoliberalism in the Central Andes* (1994). Her current research focuses on the public sphere and political change in Peru.

Michael Coppedge is assistant professor at the Paul H. Nitze School of Advanced International Studies (SAIS) of the Johns Hopkins University. He is the author of *Strong Parties and Lame Ducks: Presidential Partyarchy and Factionalism in Venezuela* (1994).

Charles Gillespie was assistant professor of political science at the University of Wisconsin, Madison, before his untimely death in 1991. He earned his Ph.D. degree from Yale University and was widely considered the preeminent scholar on Uruguayan politics. In addition to many articles dealing with transitions to democracy and with Latin American and Uruguayan politics, he authored *Negotiating Democracy: Politicians and Generals in Uruguay* and co-authored and co-edited *Uruguay y la Democracia* (3 volumes).

Luis Eduardo González teaches at the Universidad de la República, Montevideo, Uruguay. He is also director and founding partner of CIFRA/González, Raga, & Asociados, a Uruguayan consulting firm. He has published several articles on political parties and redemocratization and is the author of *Political Structures and Democracy in Uruguay*.

Jonathan Hartlyn is associate professor of political science at the University of North Carolina at Chapel Hill. His publications include *Latin American Political Economy*, co-edited with Samuel A. Morley; *The Politics of Coalition Rule in Colombia; The United States and Latin America in the 1990s: Beyond the Cold War*, co-edited with Lars Schoultz and Augusto Varas; and "The Dominican Republic: Contemporary Problems and Challenges," in *Democracy in the Caribbean*, edited by Jorge Domínguez, Robert Pastor, and DeLisle Worrell. He is also co-author with Arturo Valenzuela of "Democracy in Latin America since 1930," forthcoming in *Latin America since 1930: Economy, Society and Politics*, volume 6 of *The Cambridge History of Latin America*, edited by Leslie Bethel.

Bolívar Lamounier is co-founder and senior researcher of the *Instituto de Estudos Economic os, Sociais e Politicos de São Paulo* (IDESP) and professor of political science at the Catholic University of São Paulo. Among the many works he has authored, edited, or co-edited in Portuguese are *Parties and Elections in Brazil* (with Fernando Henrique Cardoso), *Parties and Democratic Consolidation in Brazil* (with Raquel Meneguello), *How Democracies Are Reborn* (with Alain Rouquie and Jorge Schwarzer), and *Presidentialism or Parliamentarism: Prospectives on Brazil's Institutional Reorganization* (with Dieter Nohlen). He has been a member of the Brazilian Presidential Commission for Constitutional Studies and several other Brazilian commissions and international scholarly panels and of the Academic Council of the Woodrow Wilson International Center.

Juan J. Linz is Sterling Professor of Political and Social Science at Yale University. He holds degrees in law, political science, and sociology and has contributed to books on authoritarianism, fascism, political parties, nationalism, religion, and politics. He is the author of *Crisis, Breakdown, and Reequilibration*, volume 1 of a four-volume work, *The Breakdown of Democratic Regimes*, which he co-edited with Alfred Stepan, and of "Totalitarian and Authoritarian Regimes" in *Macropolitical Theory*, volume 3 of the *Handbook of Political Science*, edited by Fred L. Greenstein and Nelson W. Polsby. He is co-author and editor, with Larry Diamond and S. M. Lipset, of *Democracy in Developing Countries*. He has written extensively on the transition to democracy in Spain and is co-authoring with Alfred Stepan a book titled *Problems of Democratic Transition and Consolidation: Southern Europe, South America, and Eastern Europe*. In 1987 he was awarded the Premio Príncipe de Asturias de Ciencias Sociales, and he holds honorary degrees from the Universidad Autónoma de Madrid, Georgetown, Granada, and Marburg.

Cynthia McClintock is professor of political science at George Washington University. Her published works include *Peasant Cooperatives and Political Change in Peru, The Peruvian Experiment Reconsidered* (co-edited with Abraham Lowenthal), and numerous articles on agrarian reform, peasant rebellion, and political change in Peru. She is currently engaged in comparative research on revolution and redemocratization in Peru and El Salvador. In April 1994 she became president of the Latin American Studies Association.

Arturo Valenzuela is professor of government and director, Center for Latin American Studies, Georgetown University. His research interests include the origins, consolidation, and breakdown of democratic regimes, authoritarianism, political parties, and the nature and functioning of democratic regimes. He is the author of *Political Brokers in Chile: Local Government in a Centralized Polity, The Breakdown of Democratic Regimes: Chile*, and with Pamela Constable, *A Nation of Enemies: Chile under Pinochet*. He is co-author or co-editor of *Chile: Politics and Society* and *Military Rule in Chile* (with J. Samuel Valenzuela), *La Opción Parlamentaria para América Latina* (with Juan J. Linz and Arend Lijphart), and *The Failure of Presidential Democracy* (with Juan J. Linz). He has been a visiting scholar at Oxford University, the University of Chile, the Catholic University of Chile, the University of Florence, and the University of Sussex. Prior to joining the Georgetown faculty, he was a professor of political science and director of the Council on Latin American Studies at Duke University.

Index

351

Library of Congress Cataloging-in-Publication Data

The Failure of presidential democracy / edited by Juan J. Linz and Arturo Valenzuela.
   p.   cm.
   Issued also in a 1 v. hardbound ed.
   Includes bibliographical references and index.
   Contents: v. 1. Comparative perspectives — v. 2. The Case of Latin America.
   ISBN 0-8018-4640-4 (pbk. : v. 1 : acid-free paper). — ISBN 0-8018-4784-2
(pbk. : v. 2 : acid-free paper)
   1. Presidents.   2. Cabinet system.   3. Democracy.   4. Representative government and repre-
sentation.   5. Latin America—Politics and government—Case studies.   6. Presidents—Latin
America—Case studies.   I. Linz, Juan J. (Juan José), 1926–   .   II. Valenzuela, Arturo, 1944–   .
JF255.F35   1994
321.8'042—dc20

                                                                       93-27222

4990049

Printed in the United States
3586

9 780801 847844